Language Teacher Identity

Language Teacher Identity

Confronting Ideologies of Language, Race, and Ethnicity

Edited by Sílvia Melo-Pfeifer and Vander Tavares

WILEY Blackwell

This edition first published 2024
© 2024 John Wiley & Sons Ltd

All rights reserved. No part of this publication may be reproduced, stored in a retrieval system, or transmitted, in any form or by any means, electronic, mechanical, photocopying, recording or otherwise, except as permitted by law. Advice on how to obtain permission to reuse material from this title is available at http://www.wiley.com/go/permissions.

The right of Sílvia Melo-Pfeifer and Vander Tavares to be identified as the authors of the editorial material in this work has been asserted in accordance with law.

Registered Offices
John Wiley & Sons, Inc., 111 River Street, Hoboken, NJ 07030, USA
John Wiley & Sons Ltd, The Atrium, Southern Gate, Chichester, West Sussex, PO19 8SQ, UK

For details of our global editorial offices, customer services, and more information about Wiley products visit us at www.wiley.com.

Wiley also publishes its books in a variety of electronic formats and by print-on-demand. Some content that appears in standard print versions of this book may not be available in other formats.

Trademarks: Wiley and the Wiley logo are trademarks or registered trademarks of John Wiley & Sons, Inc. and/or its affiliates in the United States and other countries and may not be used without written permission. All other trademarks are the property of their respective owners. John Wiley & Sons, Inc. is not associated with any product or vendor mentioned in this book.

Limit of Liability/Disclaimer of Warranty
While the publisher and authors have used their best efforts in preparing this work, they make no representations or warranties with respect to the accuracy or completeness of the contents of this work and specifically disclaim all warranties, including without limitation any implied warranties of merchantability or fitness for a particular purpose. No warranty may be created or extended by sales representatives, written sales materials or promotional statements for this work. This work is sold with the understanding that the publisher is not engaged in rendering professional services. The advice and strategies contained herein may not be suitable for your situation. You should consult with a specialist where appropriate. The fact that an organization, website, or product is referred to in this work as a citation and/or potential source of further information does not mean that the publisher and authors endorse the information or services the organization, website, or product may provide or recommendations it may make. Further, readers should be aware that websites listed in this work may have changed or disappeared between when this work was written and when it is read. Neither the publisher nor authors shall be liable for any loss of profit or any other commercial damages, including but not limited to special, incidental, consequential, or other damages.

Library of Congress Cataloging-in-Publication Data Applied for:
Paperback ISBN: 9781394154531

Cover Design: Wiley
Cover Image: Courtesy of "Cidadão Angustifólio"
© 2011 Alexandre Zampier

Set in 9.5/12.5pt STIXTwoText by Straive, Pondicherry, India

SKY10066495_020724

Contents

About the Authors   *xii*
Foreword: Filling the Gaps in Language Teacher Education: A Prologue   *xviii*
Ofelia García

1   **Language Teacher Identity and Education in the Crossfire of Evolving Raciolinguistic and Monolingual Ideologies**   *1*
Sílvia Melo-Pfeifer and Vander Tavares
1.1   Introduction: How and Why Did We Get Here?   *1*
1.2   Addressing the Key Concepts of This Volume   *4*
1.3   The Volume in a Nutshell   *9*
1.4   Conclusion   *16*
         References   *18*

Part 1   Experiences of Identity Construction of Plurilingual Language Teachers   *21*

2   **Future Teachers of Two Languages in Germany: Self-reported Professional Knowledge and Teaching Anxieties**   *23*
Sílvia Melo-Pfeifer and Vander Tavares
2.1   Introduction: Moving Beyond the Dichotomy of Native/Non-native Foreign Language Teachers in the Study of Professional Knowledge and Teaching Anxiety   *23*
2.2   Teachers of Two Languages and Foreign Language (Teaching) Anxiety: Crisscrossing Two Research Fields   *25*
2.2.1   Teachers of Two Languages: Why Do They Matter?   *25*
2.2.2   Foreign Language (Teaching) Anxiety   *27*

vi | *Contents*

2.3	The Empirical Study	*29*
2.3.1	Context and Participants	*29*
2.3.2	Data Collection Instrument	*31*
2.3.3	Data Analysis	*31*
2.4	Findings	*32*
2.4.1	Representations of Teachers' Knowledge	*32*
2.4.1.1	Quantitative Analysis	*32*
2.4.1.2	Qualitative Analysis	*34*
2.4.2	Representations of Teachers' Emotions: A Focus on Language Anxiety	*37*
2.4.2.1	Quantitative Analysis	*37*
2.4.2.2	Qualitative Analysis	*38*
2.5	Discussion of the Results, Unanswered Questions, and Further Research Perspectives	*39*
2.6	Implications for Teacher Education Programs	*41*
	References	*42*

3   **Exploring Identities and Emotions of a Teacher of Multiple Languages: An Arts-based Narrative Inquiry Using Clay Work**   *45*
Eric K. Ku

3.1	Introduction	*45*
3.2	Identities and Emotions in Teaching Multiple Languages	*46*
3.3	Clay Work as Arts-based Narrative Inquiry	*47*
3.4	Methodology	*48*
3.4.1	Data Collection	*48*
3.4.2	Data Analysis	*49*
3.5	Park's Narratives	*50*
3.5.1	Learning Japanese and English	*50*
3.5.2	Teaching Korean and English	*53*
3.6	Discussion	*58*
3.6.1	Multiple Identities and Emotions as a TML	*58*
3.6.2	Race and Ethnicity in Teaching Multiple Languages	*59*
3.7	Reflections on Using Clay Work	*60*
	References	*61*

4   **Emotional Geographies of Teaching Two Languages: Power, Agency, and Identity**   *63*
Vander Tavares

4.1	L2 Teachers' Experiences: Beyond Ideologies	*64*
4.2	Understanding Teaching Through Emotional Geographies	*65*

4.3	Research Design: Autoethnography	*68*
4.3.1	Data Collection and Analysis	*69*
4.4	Findings in Stories	*71*
4.4.1	Teaching Portuguese as an Additional Language	*71*
4.4.2	Teaching English as a Second Language	*73*
4.5	Discussion and Conclusion	*75*
	References	*78*

5 Teaching Languages in the Linguistic Marketplace: Exploring the Impact of Policies and Ideologies on My Teacher Identity Development *82*
Jonas Yassin Iversen

5.1	Introduction	*82*
5.2	Language Teaching in Norway	*83*
5.3	The Linguistic Marketplace	*85*
5.4	A Poststructuralist Perspective on Teacher Identity	*87*
5.5	Autoethnography	*89*
5.6	Teaching a Language of Convenience: Destabilizing Identity	*90*
5.7	Teaching a Language of Necessity: Disintegrating Identity	*92*
5.8	Teaching a Language of High Prestige: Regaining Agency	*93*
5.9	Teacher Identity in the Linguistic Marketplace	*95*
5.10	Practical Implications for Language Teacher Education	*96*
	References	*97*

Part 2 Emergent and Critical Perspectives on Language Teacher Education Programs *103*

6 Cultivating the Critical: Professional Development as Ideological Development for Teachers of Racialized Bi/Multilingual Students *105*
Kate Seltzer

6.1	Introduction	*105*
6.2	A Critical Translingual Approach to PD: Theoretical Framings	*106*
6.3	Project Design and Methods	*108*
6.3.1	Project Overview	*108*
6.3.2	Participants	*109*
6.3.3	Data Collection and Analysis	*110*

viii | *Contents*

6.3.4	Researcher Positionality	*111*
6.4	Findings	*112*
6.4.1	"I Don't Want to Contribute to the Problems That I Feel Are Just, Like, Inherent in Our System"	*112*
6.4.2	"Who Educates the Educators?"	*114*
6.4.3	"I Have to Think and Really, Concretely, Make Sure That It Happens"	*115*
6.5	Discussion and Implications for Language Teacher Education	*117*
6.6	Conclusion	*119*
	References	*120*

7 "The Words Flowed Like a River": Taking Up Translanguaging in a Teacher Education Program *123*

Cecilia M. Espinosa, Melissa L. García, and Alison Lehner-Quam

7.1	Introduction	*123*
7.2	Methodology	*125*
7.2.1	The Setting	*126*
7.3	Translanguaging and Translanguaging in Teacher Education	*127*
7.4	Capitalizing on Our Languaging Practices: Cecilia's Story of Her Pedagogical Practices	*129*
7.5	Serving the Campus Community Through Multilingual Library Services and Collections: Alison's Story of Her Pedagogical Practice	131
7.6	Child Development Reflections: Melissa's Story of Her Pedagogical Practice	*134*
7.7	Implications and Conclusion	*136*
	References	*138*

8 Linguistic Journeys: Interrogating Linguistic Ideologies in a Teacher Preparation Setting *142*

Ivana Espinet

8.1	Introduction	*142*
8.2	Developing Teachers' Stances and Leadership	*143*
8.3	Pre-service Teachers at a Community College	*145*
8.3.1	Starting Points: Examining Our Language Practices	*147*
8.3.2	Widening the Lenses: Understanding District and School Language Policies	*150*
8.3.3	Learning from Experienced Teachers	*152*
8.4	Conclusion	*154*
	References	*155*

Contents | ix

Part 3 Confronting Ideologies of Ethnicity, Language, and Accent *159*

9 Racialization of the Japanese Language in the Narratives of Brazilian Undergraduate Students *161*
Fabiana Cristina Ramos Patrocínio and Paula Garcia de Freitas
9.1 Introduction *161*
9.2 Methods and objectives *163*
9.3 The Racialization of the Japanese Language *164*
9.3.1 Perception of Non-descendants as Japanese Students *164*
9.3.2 The Perception of Descendants as Japanese Learners *168*
9.3.3 A Parallel Between the Effects of Racialization Among Descendants and Non-descendants *170*
9.4 Discussion *174*
9.5 Conclusion *176*
References *178*

10 Ethnic Accent Bullying, EFL Teaching and Learning in Mongolia *180*
Bolormaa Shinjee and Sender Dovchin
10.1 Introduction *180*
10.2 Ethnic Accent Bullying *184*
10.3 Research Methodology *186*
10.3.1 Data Collection and Analysis *187*
10.4 Overt Ethnic Accent Bullying *188*
10.5 Covert Ethnic Accent Bullying *190*
10.6 Conclusion *192*
References *194*

Part 4 Disrupting Raciolinguistic Ideologies *199*

11 Englishes as a Site of Colonial Conflict: Nuances in Teacher Enactment of a Transraciolinguistic Approach *201*
Patriann Smith, Crystal Dail Rose, and Tala M. Karkar-Esperat
11.1 Immigrant Multilingual Teachers Crossing Transnational Boundaries *204*
11.1.1 Teacher Beliefs About English for Teaching Language and Literacy *204*
11.1.2 Tensions Between Teacher Beliefs and Practice Based on Context *205*

x | *Contents*

11.1.3 Teacher Enactment of Ideologies About English in Teaching *206*
11.1.4 Former "Foreign-Born" Literacy Teachers in the United States *207*
11.2 Raciolinguicizing World/Global Englishes in a "Post-colonial" Transnational World *208*
11.3 Methods *210*
11.3.1 Participants *210*
11.3.2 Data Sources, Collection, Procedures *211*
11.3.3 Analysis *211*
11.4 Findings *212*
11.4.1 Colonially Inherited Raciolinguistic Ideologies *212*
11.4.1.1 Preference for Standardized English in the Home Country *212*
11.4.1.2 Emphasis on Basic Language Skills *214*
11.4.2 Sources for Inadvertently Subscribing to Raciolinguistic Ideologies *215*
11.4.3 Transraciolinguistics in World Englishes as Part of a "Postcolonial" Era *217*
11.5 Conclusion *220*
References *222*

12 The Raciolinguistic Enregisterment and Aestheticization of ELT Labor *226*
Vijay A. Ramjattan
12.1 Introduction *226*
12.2 Aestheticizing and Racializing Labor *228*
12.3 The Consequences of Raciolinguistically Enregistered Aesthetic Labor in ELT *229*
12.3.1 Employment Discrimination *229*
12.3.2 Lower Wages *232*
12.3.3 Just Whiteness for Sale *233*
12.3.4 Erasure of Expertise and Compensatory Identity Work *235*
12.4 Concluding Thoughts *237*
References *239*

13 Issues of Legitimization, Authority, and Acceptance: Pakistani English Language Teachers and Their Confrontation of Raciolinguistic Ideologies in ELT/TESOL Classrooms *242*
Kashif Raza
13.1 Introduction *242*
13.2 The Anecdotal Narrative and Raciolinguistic Ideologies *244*
13.3 English as a Lingua Franca-Aware Teaching and Learning *246*

Contents | **xi**

13.4 Two-way Multilingual Turn in TESOL *248*
13.5 Research on English Language Teaching in the Gulf *252*
13.6 Conclusion and Implications for Confronting Raciolinguistic Ideologies *253*
References *254*

14 Language Student-Teachers of a Racialized Background: The Transracial Construction of the Competent Language Teacher *258*
Sílvia Melo-Pfeifer
14.1 Introduction *258*
14.2 Empirical study *261*
14.2.1 Participants and methodology of the larger study *261*
14.2.2 The Comparative Case Study: Student-teachers 2 and 5 *263*
14.3 Findings *265*
14.3.1 Student 2: "Oh Man, You Can See It So Clearly!?" *265*
14.3.2 Student 5: "It Could Have Been That I Am Cuban or Something" *268*
14.4 Discussion *271*
14.4.1 The Interplay of Raciolinguistic and Language Teaching Ideologies: Passing or Posing as a Native-speaker Teacher? *271*
14.4.2 The Transracial Construction of the Competent Language Teacher *274*
14.5 Conclusion *276*
References *277*

Postface *281*
Rahat Zaidi
Index *285*

About the Authors

Sender Dovchin is a Senior Research Fellow and the Discipline Lead of Applied Linguistics and Languages Group at the School of Education, Curtin University, Australia. She is a Discovery Early Career Research Fellow by the Australian Research Council. She has authored numerous books and articles in international peer-reviewed journals focusing on linguistic racism, translanguaging, and global Englishes.

Ivana Espinet is an Assistant Professor at Kingsborough Community College. She holds a PhD in Urban Education from the CUNY Graduate Center and an MA in Instructional Technology and Education from Teachers College, Columbia University. She is a former project director for CUNY New York State Initiative on Emergent Bilinguals. She is interested in the use of multimodal and collaborative methodologies to learn about emergent bilinguals in school and in out-of-school programs.

Cecilia M. Espinosa, PhD, is an Associate Professor in the Department of Early Childhood and Childhood at Lehman College/CUNY. Cecilia co-authored the book *Rooted in Strength: Using Translanguaging to Grow Multilingual Readers and Writers* (with Ascenzi-Moreno).

Ofelia García is a Professor Emerita in the PhD programs in Urban Education & Latin American, Iberian, and Latino Cultures at The Graduate Center, City University of New York. She has published extensively and has been elected to membership in the American Academy of Arts and Sciences and the National Academy of Education.

Melissa L. García teaches at the City University of New York (CUNY)— Lehman College. Her research interests examine children's literature with emphasis on the Caribbean region, multilingual learners, and the global

About the Authors | **xiii**

context. She earned a doctoral degree in Caribbean literature from the University of Puerto Rico, Rio Piedras. She has taught in kindergarten through college classrooms. She currently works with both pre- and in-service teachers. Her most recent project is a two-volume anthology on Caribbean children's literature with the University of Mississippi Press.

Paula Garcia de Freitas has a PhD in Linguistics from the Federal University of Santa Catarina, holds a Master's degree in Languages (Italian Language and Literature) from the University of São Paulo, and a Bachelor's Degree in Languages—Portuguese and Italian—from the University of São Paulo. She is a Professor of Italian in the Languages Course at the Federal University of Paraná, collaborating with the Postgraduate course of this same university in Applied Linguistics and Language Teacher Training. Leader of the Research Group *Núcleo de Estudos em Língua Italiana em Contexto Brasileiro* (NELIB/CNPq), she is also active in the following areas: teaching methodology, Italian language, language teaching, language learning, and Italian culture, (language) teacher training, task-based teaching, and learning, analysis, reflection, and production of didactic material.

Jonas Yassin Iversen is an Associate Professor of Education at Inland Norway University of Applied Sciences. His research focuses on multilingualism in education, including multilingual teaching strategies for newly arrived migrant students, preservice teachers' experiences with multilingualism in teacher education, and minority language instruction inside and outside of mainstream education.

Tala M. Karkar-Esperat serves as an Assistant Professor in the Department of Curriculum and Instruction at Eastern New Mexico University. Her research is focused on multiliteracies, new literacies, preservice teachers' literacies, literacy coaching, international students' online literacies, and pedagogical literacy practices. She has studied teachers' pedagogical content knowledge of multiliteracies and traditional literacies in the classroom and developed the pedagogical content knowledge of multiliteracies survey to guide pre-service teacher preparation for teaching literacy in contemporary classrooms. She wishes to improve the scholarship surrounding preservice teachers' use of new literacies and multiliteracies. Her recent publication is titled *Compassionate Love: Improving International Student Online Learning Through New Literacies* and is published in *International Journal of Qualitative Studies in Education*.

Eric K. Ku is a Specially Appointed Associate Professor at Hokkaido University, Japan. His research interests span across both language teaching/

learning and sociolinguistics, specifically language teacher identities, multilingualism, linguistic landscapes, and visual and arts-based methods of qualitative research. He is the author of the newly published monograph *Teachers of Multiple Languages: Identities, Beliefs and Emotions*. He has also published in academic journals, such as *Critical Discourse Studies* and *English Teaching & Learning*, as well as chapters in various edited volumes. He currently serves on the Editorial Advisory Board of *TESOL Journal*.

Alison Lehner-Quam is an Assistant Professor at Lehman College, City University of New York. She teaches information literacy sessions, develops and maintains children's and education book collections, and provides individual research support for education students. Her areas of research include explorations into information literacy experiences of teacher education students as well as inquiry into the impact of culturally and linguistically relevant children's book experiences on children and education students. She has served as chair of the Instruction for Educators Committee (ACRL EBSS) and also serves on the Maxine Greene Institute Board and the New York City School Library System Library Council.

Sílvia Melo-Pfeifer is a Full Professor of Romance Language Teacher Education (University of Hamburg, Germany). Her main research interests relate to pluralistic and arts-based approaches to language learning and teaching, in teacher education and in research. She has co-edited *Visualising Multilingual Lives* (2019) and *The Changing Face of the "native speaker": Perspectives from Multilingualism and Globalization* (2021), among other titles, and some issues of international journals, including *International Journal of Bilingual Education and Bilingualism* (on multilingual interaction, in 2018), *European Journal of Higher Education* (on expatriate teachers in Higher Education, in 2019), and *Language and Intercultural Communication* (on Arts in Language Education, in 2020).

Fabiana Cristina Ramos Patrocínio has a degree in Languages Portuguese-Japanese from São Paulo State University, with a specialization in teaching methodology. She worked as a Japanese language teacher at public schools in the states of São Paulo and Paraná and is a former substitute professor at the Department of Modern Foreign Languages of the Federal University of Paraná. She was a scholar of the Japanese government for linguistic and cultural studies in Japan by both the Japan Foundation and the Japanese government. She is interested in language studies within Critical Applied Linguistics, focusing on language as a social practice, critical literacy, culture and identity, and decolonial studies.

Vijay A. Ramjattan is an Academic English instructor at the University of Toronto. His research interests pertain to the intersection of language and race with respect to (language teaching) labor. His interdisciplinary peer-reviewed work has appeared in such journals as *Equality, Diversity and Inclusion*, *Race Ethnicity and Education*, *Intercultural Education*, *Journal of Industrial Relations*, *Applied Linguistics Review*, and *Teaching in Higher Education*. He received his PhD in Adult Education and Community Development from the University of Toronto and is a member of the Language, Culture, and Justice Hub at Brandeis University.

Kashif Raza is a PhD student at the University of Calgary, specializing in Leadership, Policy, and Governance. He has previously taught in Pakistan, the United States, and Qatar. His research interests include policy development, educational leadership, TESOL/applied linguistics, ESP law, translation, and political economy. He is the co-editor of *Policy Development in TESOL and Multilingualism: Past, Present and the Way Forward*.

Crystal Dail Rose graduated with a PhD in Curriculum and Instruction with a focus on Language, Diversity, and Literacy Studies from Texas Tech University in 2020, and worked on planning, piloting, and building a year-long residency with the Tarleton State University US PREP Leadership Team, while serving in various capacities as Site Coordinator, Assistant Professor, Research Lead, Curriculum Redesigner, and edTPA Regional Coordinator. She is passionate about her work supporting preservice teachers as they teach in a year-long residency in partner districts. Her research interests lie in practice-based teaching, coaching, observation, and assessment as a way to challenge preservice teachers to engage multicultural, multilingual learners and to be day one ready to serve all students.

Kate Seltzer is an Assistant Professor of Bilingual and ESL Education at Rowan University whose overarching goal is to help schools and teachers build on students' rich language practices while also disrupting their own ideologies about these students and their ways of using language. A former high school English Language Arts teacher in New York City, Dr. Seltzer currently teaches pre- and in-service teachers of bilingual students. She is co-author of the book, *The Translanguaging Classroom: Leveraging Student Bilingualism for Learning* as well as several book chapters and articles in journals such as *English Education*, *Research in the Teaching of English*, and *TESOL Quarterly*.

Bolormaa Shinjee is currently a PhD candidate at the School of Education, Curtin University, Australia. Previously, she worked as a Senior Lecturer at xvi | *About the Authors*

the National University of Mongolia and an English teacher in Japan. She obtained her Master's degree in TESOL from Flinders University, Adelaide, Australia. Her main research interests include linguistic racism, language policy, and translanguaging.

Patriann Smith is an Associate Professor of Literacy Studies in the Department of Language, Literacy, Ed.D., Exceptional Education & Physical Education at the University of South Florida. Her research interests include Black immigrant literacies; Black immigrant Englishes; standardized and non-standardized English ideologies; transcultural teacher education; international literacy assessment; and cross-cultural, cross-racial, and cross-linguistic literacy practices. Her recent publications include "Characterizing competing tensions in Black immigrant literacies: Beyond partial representations of *success*" in the *Reading Research Quarterly*, "How does a Black person speak English? Beyond American language norms" in the *American Educational Research Journal*, and "A transraciolinguistic approach for literacy classrooms" in *The Reading Teacher*. She is co-author with Dr. Arlette Willis and Dr. Gwendolyn McMillon of the book *Affirming Black Students Lives and Literacies: Bearing Witness* (2022) published by Teacher College Press and author of the forthcoming book *Black Immigrant Literacies: Intersections of Race, Language, and Culture in the Classroom* (2023) to be published by Teachers College Press.

Vander Tavares is a Postdoctoral Researcher in education at Inland Norway University of Applied Sciences, Norway (Norwegian: Høgskolen i Innlandet) and holds a PhD from York University, Canada. His research interests include language teacher identity development, critical second language education, internationalization of higher education, and identity in multilingual/multicultural contexts. In 2021, he was the recipient of the *Equity, Diversity and Inclusion (EDI) Award* by the Canadian Bureau for International Education (CBIE) for having demonstrated "significant contributions via behavior, research, initiatives or community engagement that fosters equity, diversity and inclusion through international education." He is the author of *International Students in Higher Education: Language, Identity, and Experience from a Holistic Perspective* (Rowman & Littlefield), editor of *Social Justice, Decoloniality, and Southern Epistemologies within Language Education: Theories, Knowledges, and Practices on TESOL from Brazil* (Routledge).

Rahat Zaidi is a Professor and Chair of Language and Literacy in the Werklund School of Education at the University of Calgary. Her research expertise focuses on multilingual literacies that clarify intersectional understandings across sociophobia, diversity, immigration, and pluralism. Through her research, she advances social justice and equity, transculturalism, and identity positioning in immigrant and transcultural contexts, all of which are particularly relevant and pertinent to the intertwining social, cultural, and political contexts in which society functions today.

Foreword

Filling the Gaps in Language Teacher Education: A Prologue
Ofelia García

Urban Education & Latin American, Iberian, and Latino Cultures Program, The Graduate Center, City University of New York, USA

In the last decade, dominant ideologies about language and language education have been questioned. Critical scholars have shown how the idea that "native speakers" have only one named language is false. The language education field has, for the most part, moved past a monolingual/monoglossic ideology, making more room for the complexity of language practices and of speakers. However, the focus and more inclusive views on students and their languaging have not impacted much the ideologies surrounding language teachers and their preparation. By foregrounding the experiences of language teachers of more than one language, as well as racialized language teachers, this volume by Sílvia Melo-Pfeifer and Vander Tavares clearly shows how the language taught continues to be closely linked to one nation, one culture, one people, one dominant racial group, leaving teachers of multiple languages and identities behind.

Much research has focused on the learning context of the classroom and students, but little has focused on the main actor in the classroom—the language teacher and the ways they are impacted by sociopolitical ideologies about language. The multilingualism of learners, and multilingualism as a goal, is often recognized, but rarely are the multilingual/multiracial/multiethnic identities of language teachers acknowledged or valued. In fact, the paradigm of a "good" language teacher continues to be that of a "monolingual" "native speaker" of the "target language." We continue to prefer to have one teacher teach one language, and we assign these teachers one language identity even when they are plurilingual. This volume brings into view this contradiction. It reminds us of the capacities of plurilingual and racialized language teachers whether they are teaching one language, two, or more. And at the same time, the contributions in this book often highlight these teachers' anxieties about their own complex identities and languaging. Some chapters describe the ways in which these teachers are "othered" because they do not "fit" the traditional mold of what a "foreign" language teacher should be.

In many ways, and despite the advances in the applied linguistic and sociolinguistic fields, we have not broken free from the monolingual "othered" ideology in foreign language education. The language taught is made to be for "foreign" lands and cultures, taught preferably by someone who learned the language in that "foreign" land. For example, in the United States, Spanish-speaking teachers in the Southwest were not allowed to be teachers of Spanish until 1965. Instead, teachers of Spanish were required to be those who learned "Castilian Spanish" in Spain and studied the literary texts of Cervantes and others. The Spanish of racialized Mexican American teachers was considered a "jargon," unsuitable for literary pursuits and specially so to teach White Americans. It wasn't until the second half of the 20th century that it was possible to even hire US Latinx teachers to teach Spanish (García & Alonso, 2021).

Although language teachers are supposed to advance the bilingualism of students, they are caught in bilingualism as an ideology (Heller, 2007), an ideologically constructed understanding as simply L1 + L2 produced by a monolingual who has learned the two languages sequentially and separately. That is, in most of the world, bilingualism is understood as simply what monolinguals acquire, not based on the complexity of local and Indigenous language practices. Thus, even teachers hired to be bilingual teachers most often cannot perform their duties as bilingual individuals.

Today, bilingual programs in the United States readily hire bilingual Latinx teachers from racialized groups. But for the most part, they are not allowed to behave as bilinguals themselves. That is, they often teach what is called "the Spanish side" of the instruction, leaving the "English side" to an English monolingual speaker. It is often said that to teach a language one has to behave monolingually. This is rampant in the scholarly literature, even when thinking of family language policy. One parent, one language is the common advice. The same for teachers. One teacher, one language is what works, creating the conditions for monolingual immersion and for subjectivities of inferiority among teachers who are themselves bilingual.

The common notion that speakers should always behave monolingually is what causes the insecurity, fear, and burnout among teachers whose multiple identities and complex language practices are not in any way valued. The concept of plurilingualism, which has opened up spaces in our understanding of complex multilingual practices, has also done little to challenge the ideologies about who language teachers should be. The European Union has adopted plurilingualism as a value, but language teachers continue to be expected to perform monolingually according to standards that have emerged from the way that White-dominant monolingual teachers "do" language. Thus, the teachers' plurilingualism is seldom acknowledged.

Even though the concept of translanguaging has also advanced our thinking about the value of local language practices in the development of bi/multilingualism, it is taken up more easily when the teacher herself has met monolingual standards and can be trusted to teach the named language according to external standards. That is, plurilingual teachers' translanguaging lesson designs are seldom valued for leveraging the language practices of the local community. Instead, they are judged to be the result of the bilingual teachers' "jargon," their confusion, their mixing of languages, and their code-switching. These chapters make clear that unless teacher education programs raise the teachers' critical consciousness of the bilingual ideologies that are operating, White monolingual teachers of one language will continue to be more valued than others, despite the fact that these "other" teachers are able to connect to the local communities of linguistic and cultural practices more easily. Teachers who have been socialized into language through translanguaging practices can better understand the "academic" value of translanguaging, as well as how to use it to engage students in learning what is considered an additional language. Because these teachers often share histories of oppression and racialization with many of the students they teach, they are also able to enact care, cariño, and trust in ways that transform the students' potential for learning.

Overall, these chapters make evident what the editors call "the pervasiveness of native-speakerism, the monolingual mindset, the White listener-observer norms, and blatant (linguistic) racism" (Introduction). It makes us notice the teachers and their lack of preparation to behave in ways that leverage the community's translanguaging practices. It warns us that these monoglossic ideologies of bilingualism are actually doing us harm. By focusing on what Vijay Ramjattan (in this volume) calls "the esthetic qualities of teachers," that is, their race, gender, and ways of speaking a monolingual standard, we are missing out. Speaking about English language teaching, Ramjattan warns of the "deskilling of the ELT profession," since these teacher qualities are considered better "credentials" than actual teaching experience.

This last statement is the most important. What is real in language education? Is it to ensure that students acquire another language and become truly plurilingual? Or is that language education inculcates the values of monolingualism and Whiteness, resisting and forgetting processes of colonization and nation-building that continue to operate today? It is this latter proposition that has operated in the education of language teachers in the past and that continues to work today.

Melo-Pfeifer and Tavares' volume is important because it brings to our consciousness how we are wasting an important resource, the resource of people, of teachers who have themselves experienced linguistic and social discrimination. These teachers can help students learn another language without othering, doing so with and alongside local communities, and ensuring their inclusion. It is time that we question our ideologies of who the "good" teachers of languages are and delink languages from the concepts with which they have operated—spoken homogeneously by one people, a symbol of one nation without social class, gender, racial, or linguistic differences. Only when we recognize the messiness of the language education enterprise would we be able to acknowledge the great asset of teachers whose identity is not wrapped up in one language, one culture, one nation, but who push these boundaries, as they have for centuries, and as they continue to do today.

References

García, O., & Alonso, L. (2021). Reconstituting U.S. Spanish language education: U.S. Latinx occupying classrooms. *Journal of Spanish Language Teaching, 8*(2), 114–128. https://doi.org/10.1080/23247797.2021.2016230.

Heller, M. (2007). Bilingualism as ideology and practice. In M. Heller (Ed.), *Bilingualism: A Social Approach* (pp. 1–22). Palgrave Macmillan.

1

Language Teacher Identity and Education in the Crossfire of Evolving Raciolinguistic and Monolingual Ideologies

Sílvia Melo-Pfeifer[1] and Vander Tavares[2]

[1] *Department of Languages and Aesthetic Disciplines Education, Faculty of Education, University of Hamburg, Germany*
[2] *Department of Teacher Education and Pedagogy, Faculty of Education, Inland Norway, University of Applied Sciences, Norway*

1.1 Introduction: How and Why Did We Get Here?

It is always difficult to explain how a volume is born or what moved the editors toward an editorial project around a specific theme. We would like to start this introduction by explaining the genesis of the present publication, which began at a time when in-person activities were still significantly impacted by the global pandemic. Sílvia and Vander had never met in person before they decided to work together. And still up to this day, they have only met virtually. They had heard about each other's work, they have a friend in common (who is also a common co-author, Inês Cardoso), and they knew something about each other: that they both speak Portuguese and taught or were teaching (in) languages that do not happen to be their first languages.

Sílvia is Portuguese, and completed her entire education, from primary to higher education, including her PhD, in Portugal, where she studied to become a French and Portuguese language teacher. Her parents are the so-called retornados from Angola, a country where they had lived in for more than 15 years before it regained its independence. During her PhD, she met "the one" in Spanish classes in Spain and moved to Germany some years later (in 2016), a country whose official language she never dreamed of learning before. She then became a full professor at a German university,

---

Language Teacher Identity: Confronting Ideologies of Language, Race, and Ethnicity,
First Edition. Edited by Sílvia Melo-Pfeifer and Vander Tavares.
© 2024 John Wiley & Sons Ltd. Published 2024 by John Wiley & Sons Ltd.

being involved in French and Spanish language teacher education programs. She is a happy mother of two multilingual children, who are happy to know and speak the language of their "mãe maluca." She, as a Portuguese speaker, usually teaches French and Spanish teacher candidates mostly in German or through translanguaging using German and one of the other two languages according to the audience. When she met Vander, she used to tell him how difficult and sometimes frustrating it was to adjust to another language and academic culture. She laughed about the "linguistic" incidents she caused (and still causes) during her teaching in German. Of course, humor and playfulness are great ways to get to know ourselves, express our fears and frustrations, and expose our emotional precarity (Dovchin, 2022).

Vander is Canadian–Brazilian with schooling experiences in both Canada and Brazil. Following his graduation from the PhD program in linguistics and applied linguistics at York University in Toronto, he moved to Norway, initially to take up a position of postdoctoral researcher to develop and conduct a research project on language teacher education and identity development. As part of the preparation for his upcoming position of associate professor at the same institution, he has been learning Norwegian as an additional language. Like Sílvia, Vander has also learned French and Spanish, but it has been the journey of now learning Norwegian—for a different purpose (work), under different life circumstances (as an adult immigrant worker), within a prescribed time frame of two years, and in a new country—which has been the most challenging for him, both linguistically and emotionally. Indeed, in conversations with Sílvia, Vander shared his feelings of frustration, anxiety, and also embarrassment considering his numerous linguistic and social faux-pas in Norwegian. In conversation about these experiences, Vander and Sílvia became even more aware about how ideologies of language manifest themselves in each other's contexts (Norway and Germany) and how they navigate them while being the *other*.

So, when the two of us met online, it was academic love at first sight! We engaged in conversations that helped us better understand our own academic multilingual lives, and dig deep(er) into our memories to understand our fears, anxieties, coping strategies, and more or less humorous ways of dealing with all of the above. In that meeting, we also discovered that we were both teachers (or teacher educators) of two languages, expatriates, and invested in learning the language of the countries that are now included in our repertoire of home: German and Norwegian. While this narrative is being constructed about our origins and languages, we should acknowledge that, as time went by, we started crisscrossing our narratives with others putting forward issues related to race, ethnicity, nationality, and accent.

1.1 Introduction: How and Why Did We Get Here? | 3

And we discovered ourselves being multilingual expatriate White academics, both based in the so-called Global North.

When Rachel Greenberg, the commissioning editor, reached out to Sílvia with an invitation to propose a volume to Wiley Blackwell, the book was sort of already instilled in our minds! We invited those authors we knew personally (or whom we received advice about through colleagues) who have worked to address different aspects of multilingual identities of language teachers, raciolinguistic ideologies, and teachers' agency in disrupting raciolinguistic ideologies. The first title we proposed for the book was *Foreign Language Teacher Identity: Confronting Ideologies of Language, Race, and Ethnicity*.

We did not think about the name of the book too much until January 2023, when Ofelia García agreed to write the Foreword. Her first question was as simple as it was disruptive: "Do you really want to call it *foreign* languages?" (email exchange). She was challenging us to become more "accurate" and "inclusive" (her words), exactly as we wanted to be from the very beginning, but we needed the cognitive scaffolding to really become. It was not just that some chapters were not directly connected to the so-called foreign language education: it was about misrepresenting the speakers and the relationship they establish with their languages. It was misrepresenting the teaching practices of teacher educators and practitioners represented in the volume, and equally important, it was an act of othering toward a research field that so intimately connects to others. "Foreign" was dividing, unequally, teachers (and their students), languages, contexts, and practices where flexibility, complexity, and fluidity have been the norm, but hardly recognized as such.

Following our biographical accounts, the spontaneous meeting of the two editors, and the encounters with experts we had along the way, this volume has emerged to address language teacher identity and professional development at the intersection of ideologies of language, race, and ethnicity—concepts which we will address in the next section. In this sense, our research says as much about us as it does about the object being researched. The same can be said of this project, though not only in relation to the two editors but also and together with all contributing authors.

Language Teacher Identity: Confronting Ideologies of Language, Race, and Ethnicity covers issues and gaps in connection with the latest developments in research about language teacher education, particularly around language teacher identity. The field of language (teacher) education has been struggling with issues related to monolingualism and native-speakerism (Holliday, 2015; Slavkov et al., 2022), perceptions of what counts as competence and authenticity in the classroom, and the accommodation of diversity in school systems. So, while the multilingual turn in (language) education has been announced (May, 2014), the pervasiveness of monolingual constructs prevails, through which the language teacher being characterized as native speaker still holds currency over terms that reflect the world's reality, such as the multicompetent speaker (Cook, 1992; see also Ortega, 2014, for a critique).

In the broader field of teacher education, the "place" of teachers with a transnational background has been acknowledged and their professional paths have received growing attention (Bräu et al., 2014; Georgi et al., 2011; Lengyel and Rosen, 2015; Rosen and Lengyel, 2023). However, in the field of language teacher education, in general, the study of those issues is still to be developed, with particular emphasis on *linguistically, ethnically, and racially minoritized* teachers. Additionally, despite the recognition that language teachers draw on their multilingual repertoires to teach and construct their professional identities, a significant gap remains in relation to exploring the experiences of *teachers who teach two or more languages*. In other words, our knowledge of language teacher experiences has relied primarily on associating one teacher with one language in the context of instruction and identity development, despite the boundary-breaking complexities within experiences of identity construction for language teachers acknowledged in recent research. This volume contributes to bridging some of these gaps with investigations that critically discuss ideologies of race, ethnicity, language/accent, (im)migration, and their impact on language teacher identity, aiming at empowering minority and minoritized language teachers from the earlier years of their careers onward.

1.2 Addressing the Key Concepts of This Volume

When defining the scope of this volume, the first compositum we needed to disentangle was "language teacher identity," once we had agreed to remove the qualifier "foreign." "Language teacher identity" is made of three complex concepts, each adding a new intricate layer of interpretation to the other(s) and leading to a transformation of each and all of them simultaneously: "language," "teacher," and "identity." Each of these terms is complex per se: what is a language? What can be defined as a language? What makes a teacher? What constitutes our identity? Or, in partially combined duets, what is language identity? What makes a language teacher?

At a glance, recent discussions inspired by postcolonial and decolonial theories (Makoni and Pennycook, 2006) and others focused on translanguaging (García and Li Wei, 2013) have exposed the need to rethink the

1.2 Addressing the Key Concepts of This Volume 5

founding concept of "language" itself: one that has been embedded in Eurocentric and colonial nation-building ideologies that tend to associate one set of grammar features—that spoken by the majority—exclusively to one country and to one people. Such construction of languages is therefore more political than it is linguistic as it fuels and reproduces (mono)normative ideologies at the expense of linguistic diversity, especially that which is reflective of minoritized speakers. In studies based on translanguaging within bilingual education, the argument put forward against named languages rests on the fact that such labels misrepresent the real, multilayered, and multisemiotic repertoires of bilingual (and often minoritized) individuals. In this context, the languages of bilinguals are not only categorized hierarchically but also viewed as two distinct (monolingual) meaning-making systems that follow strict social conventions of language use.

Taking this issue into account, our conception of language is that of a social practice of its users (Ortega, 2014), rather than a decontextualized set of pre-given rules (phonological, morphological, and so on). If we think of pedagogical approaches, chapters included in Macedo (2019) have already vastly illustrated how colonial languages are still mistaught, underlying the need to decolonize the (language) curriculum, by which we mean resisting epistemic monoculture and hegemonic language ideologies that delegitimize the multilingual speaker and their language use in everyday social practices. One way of resisting such ideologies is through translanguaging in the classroom, as a way to co-construct meaning and legitimize students' and teachers' repertoires (reminder: teachers are multilingual too!), and by including translanguaging in language teacher education programs (Prada, 2019). The chapters by Seltzer, Espinosa and colleagues, and Espinet all depart from such a perspective and demonstrate, both critically and creatively, what translanguaging in (language) teacher education programs can look like, being transformative for both teachers and their (future) students alike.

As for "teacher," the discussion is just apparently simple. Is being a teacher a career, a profession, a métier, a passion? What makes the specificity of a teacher as a "professional" in comparison to other professionals? Teachers are said to be responsible for educating the future generations, but this assertion should be taken carefully because they are not the only agents at play within the school system. They can enact linguistic and educational policies, but also resist them (independently of their scope and their expected outcomes). As Menken and García (2020) recalled, teachers, regardless of being teachers of languages or other school subjects, are agentive actors that can turn out to be policymakers in the classroom and the school at large. Nevertheless, teachers are also victims of worsening working conditions, both material and social; are deprived of voices in some teaching contexts; and/or have to cope with increasing mental health issues, such as burnout, insecurity, and fear.

And then we arrive at the third concept of the formula: identity. Poststructuralist perspectives reject identity as stable, fixed, and unidimensional, characterized by a single character trait (Ayres-Bennett and Fisher, 2022). Reducing identity to underscore a language, a nationality, or a religion, as Maalouf (1998) warned, is the shortcut to extremist positions. Now that we have foregrounded what identity is not, it is then possible to assert that identity is multifaceted, negotiated, co-constructed, and reconstructed in social (inter)action, which considers the aims and needs of the individual as well as the features of the surrounding social context. This is the position espoused in this introduction. This explains why one might choose to make salient (and even assert) a facet of what they understand to be their identity on one occasion, but enact other facets more prominently on another. Some characteristics involved in the enactment of one's identity might be denied, claimed, or auto- and hetero-assigned at different points in time and space. Identity, Block and Corona (2016) claimed, is an assemblage of units such as age, gender, sex, sexual orientation, ethnicity, race, and a constellation of affiliations, such as religious, linguistic, familial, or professional affiliation. Identity is intersectional, meaning that each characteristic enriches, alters, and adds to the dynamics between the others.

In line with the complexity we have delineated in relation to the three concepts aforementioned, the identity of a language teacher is not stable or determined by the fact that he or she teaches a (specific) language, as some literature have us believe by describing the identity of ESL, French, or Portuguese teachers. It is fluid (Neokleous and Krulatz, 2020) and influenced by sociological aspects such as gender, age, class, race, ethnic origin(s), accent, among others. And it is also influenced, and sometimes determined, by one's linguistic profile, including the language(s) one teaches, the languages learned previously, and which beliefs one holds regarding language education: the reasons why they believe that learning a specific language is (or is not) useful for a specific target audience in a particular sociolinguistic context. On a more macro, historical, and geopolitical level, the identity of a language teacher is also determined by their position in the local society and the value this society attributes to (being) a teacher, in general, and to a *language* teacher, more specifically.

This volume focuses on two groups who remain underrepresented in the literature and consequently deserve more recognition, because of the hyperdiversity of our societies at the very least: teachers of two or more languages and racialized language teachers. While these two categories are not mutually exclusive (as it would be the case of racialized teachers of two languages), we will shortly provide a separate account of the two groups, in order to magnify what makes them distinct per se. The first theme, on teachers of two or more languages, covers special constructs that are prominent in the default "language teacher" literature (meaning the teacher of a specific language), but analyzes them with a multilingual focus. Language teacher knowledge, teacher anxiety, and teacher emotions, for example, are topics already covered in the literature (De Costa, 2015). The novelty of this volume is that such issues are addressed not only side by side, but also in hybridity, and through a multilingual lens: teachers of two or more languages, typically when these languages are not the teachers' L1, face some of the same prejudices and obstacles which teachers of one language do (e.g. does the teacher speak "well" and "correctly" in both languages, could he or she be a native speaker—based on not only the accent but also their look and behavior—if so, in which language? And why should this matter?).

Yet, teaching two or more languages brings those issues to a more complicated, intersectional place: are those emotional experiences comparable in (teaching) each language? Are those feelings dealt with equally and why (not)? What kind(s) of self-perception does a teacher of two or more languages develop? What sociological aspects emerge more predominantly in each language identity? How do issues of power manifest in relation to teaching each language? How do language ideologies differently influence each teaching context? The chapters by Melo-Pfeifer and Tavares, Tavares, Iversen, and Ku exploit issues related to experiences of identity construction when teaching multiple languages and of being confronted with linguistic ideologies through/and discourses about professional competence that clash with one's own beliefs, self-perception, life experiences, and teaching qualifications. These critical moments of self-reflection, which offer potential for personal and professional development, are difficult to navigate as language teachers work to prioritize curriculum mandates, students' learning and expectations, their own well-being, and their relationships with colleagues and, sometimes, parents: relationships that may even be in conflict.

The second theme covers issues related to teachers' racialized identities, which are perceived as either conforming to or transgressing social and cultural expectations tied to a specific language as a result of prevailing raciolinguistic ideologies. We understand raciolinguistic ideologies as those intersecting and mutually naturalizing linguistic and racial categories (Rosa, 2019; Rosa and Flores, 2020). In the field of language and teacher education, they refer to how racialized teachers' language practices (and professional competence) come to be perceived as a deviation from the "standard" or, on the other hand but by the same token, as legitimate. In the chapters included in this volume, the racialization of pre-service and in-service language teachers is not limited to Indigenous populations or immediately connected to colonialism. Here, racialization also permeates the experiences of pre-service teachers of Japanese in Brazil who are considered illegitimate, and actually in some cases denied admission into a Japanese language program, due to the lack of an Asian phenotype. Conversely, racialization also enables in-service teachers of Spanish in Germany to be able to "pass" for a native speaker of Spanish because of their perceived skin color and complexion that approximate the teacher to an imagined native speaker. Therefore, the connection between race and language (Alim et al., 2020) becomes salient to understand the identity construction of language teachers (and researchers, such as in Ortega, 2021, and some chapters in the present book).

In this volume, chapters also illustrate the ways in which raciolinguistic ideologies intersect with language and language teaching ideologies (Ortega, 2021). Their combined presence only further demonstrates the pervasiveness of native-speakerism, the monolingual mindset, the White listener–observer norms, and blatant (linguistic) racism. The chapters by Patrocínio and de Freitas; by Smith, Rose, and Karkar-Esperat; and by Melo-Pfeifer bring to light some of the struggles language teachers may encounter simply because they do not look like an imagined native speaker of the target language, echoing Rosa's argument on race and language (Rosa, 2019). Particularly in the study by Melo-Pfeifer, we are able to understand that moments of struggle are also moments of agency in which teachers sometimes manage to manipulate dominant ideologies in their favor, yet without openly challenging them.

Transversal to the chapters on the racialized bodies of language teachers is another raciolinguistic ideology: passing for a native speaker. It has been claimed that the ideology of the native speaker is a zombie or walking-dead concept with malignant power (Slavkov et al., 2022; see particularly the introduction). Indeed, the pervasive effects of native-speakerism are very real: Melo-Pfeifer analyzes how pre-service teachers consider their ability to pass or not pass for a native speaker as a threshold of professional competence, while Raza, as a self-identifying non-native teacher, addresses linguistic racism and prejudices in his teaching practices as a way to disrupt prejudice.

The combination of the issues covered in this volume illustrates the complexity of language teacher identity and the impossibility of studying it more comprehensively unless we, on the one hand, interrogate the ideologies and mainstream perspectives governing the understanding of each concept in isolation (i.e. language, teacher, identity) and unless we, on the other hand, also address the interconnectedness of raciolinguistic and dominant language (education) ideologies.

1.3 The Volume in a Nutshell

This volume is thematically organized around four areas that individually deal with specific issues in connection with language teacher identity. While this thematic organization might be at odds with the very principle of addressing the intersectionality of language teacher identity, it helps to unfold the different layers of the construct "language teacher identity," such as teachers' own multilingualism, their multilingual pedagogies that challenge the notion of "language," and their strategies to cope with and disrupt their racialization and the racialization of their métier. Taken separately, each section offers a specific lens to underscore the uniqueness of a specific characteristic of language teachers' identities. Taken together, in a posteriori interpretation, they expose the complexity of identity construction for teachers of one or more languages, through a superposition of all identity layers, offering a kaleidoscopic vision of what it might look like to be a (racialized) teacher of two or more languages.

The first thematic area examines identity-related experiences of teachers of two (or more) languages; the second foregrounds the enactment of multilingual pedagogies, translanguaging, and their transformative potential in terms of identity construction; the third explores the impact of ideologies of ethnicity, language, and accent on both identity construction and pedagogical practices of teachers; and the final focuses on the ways in which teachers employ agency to disrupt raciolinguistic ideologies.

Part 1 is titled *Experiences of Identity Construction of Multilingual Language Teachers* and encompasses four chapters about experiences related to language identity construction of teachers of two or more languages. By focusing on this particular population, the chapters underscore different struggles and positionalities of teachers of two languages. They offer methodologically differentiated and in-depth accounts of what it means to be confronted with monolingual and market-based ideologies and expectations, leading to distress and anxiety, emotional setbacks, and emotional labor.

The first chapter in this part, by Sílvia Melo-Pfeifer and Vander Tavares, is titled *Future Teachers of Two Languages in Germany: Self-reported Professional Knowledge and Teaching Anxieties*. Melo-Pfeifer and Tavares aim to understand how these individuals (re)present themselves as future teachers of two languages in Germany by combining written and visual productions made by the student teachers themselves. In this chapter, Melo-Pfeifer and Tavares analyze and compare the self-created profiles of the student teachers as future teachers of two languages (either two modern languages or one modern language and German as the language of schooling). Combining content and multimodal analysis over the data, the authors map out the differences within and across the student teachers' representations of disciplinary and pedagogical knowledge, and the emotions attached to their work, namely, teaching anxiety, according to their language teaching profiles. The authors draw out implications for language teacher education programs based on the analysis.

The second chapter in this part, by Eric K. Ku, is titled *Exploring Identities and Emotions of a Teacher of Multiple Languages: An Arts-based Narrative Inquiry Using Clay Work*. Ku works with a South Korean scholar at a university in Japan who has taught Korean and English language courses as well as conducted content courses using Japanese and English as the media of instruction. The author employs semi-structured interviews and uses a clay work session to explore the identity and emotional dynamics involved at the intersection of teaching multiple languages and using multiple languages as the medium of instruction. Data analysis is conducted through thematic analysis of interview and clay work data with a particular focus on the use of conceptual metaphors. Ku demonstrates that teaching multiple languages involves identity/emotional work that is constantly changing, multifaceted, and possibly in conflict and fragmented. Ku concludes by discussing the findings in relation to language teacher education and reflecting on the methodological applications of clay work in language teaching research.

The next chapter, by Vander Tavares, is titled *Emotional Geographies of Teaching Two Languages: Power, Agency, and Identity*. In this chapter, Tavares argues that the experiences of L2 teachers who teach two or more languages have received less attention in the scholarly literature due to the monolingual foundation of language education (research). Following an auto-ethnographic approach (resorting to memory and teaching journals) and the concept of "emotional geographies" (Hargreaves, 2001), Tavares (re)interprets and discusses his own experiences as a teacher of two languages in Canada: English (mostly as an additional language) and Portuguese (predominantly as a heritage language). He problematizes and deconstructs three language ideologies (monolingualism, native-speakerism, and linguistic purism) that emotionally impacted his sense of self as an L2 teacher and his interactions with his students. Tavares illustrates that when his professional expertise and role as a teacher were questioned or rejected, by either students or even the students' parents, moral and professional distance toward students emerged as a result.

The first part is concluded with Jonas Yassin Iversen's chapter, titled *Teaching Languages in the Linguistic Marketplace: Exploring the Impact of Policies and Ideologies on My Teacher Identity Development*. Iversen explores his experience as a teacher of English, Norwegian, and Spanish in Norway, teaching in the "linguistic marketplace," where languages are commodified and valued according to demand. Iversen reflects on the complex interplay of different language ideologies in each of these teaching contexts as follows: teaching English as a language of "high prestige" to newly arrived migrant students to Norway; teaching Norwegian as a language of "necessity" to (the same) newly arrived students, who wish to transfer into Norwegian-language-based mainstream education for social mobility; and teaching Spanish as a language of "convenience" in a lower secondary context. Following an auto-ethnographic approach, Iversen reveals the impact that such configurations had on his own teacher identity development as he attempted to implement multilingual teaching approaches within the three teaching settings. The author concludes by calling on teacher education programs to better prepare future language teachers to understand, work with, and navigate language policies that impact the professional identity of language teachers.

Part 2 is titled *Emergent and Critical Perspectives on Language Teacher Education Programs* and includes three contributions whose investigations are situated in the context of initial teacher education. Although they focus on the American context, their findings can inspire researchers and practitioners all over the world, as the authors reflect on struggles that are common to other geographic and sociolinguistic settings, such as the need to adopt linguistically and culturally responsive teaching practices across the board. The three contributions have translanguaging pedagogies in common, which were developed powerfully in the United States after its emergence in the Welsh context and are currently being reconfigured and problematized to better fit other contexts, going beyond the emergent bilingual school population in the United States.

In *Cultivating the Critical: Professional Development as Ideological Development for Teachers of Racialized Bi/multilingual Students*, Kate Seltzer describes a year-long professional development (PD) project that invited three teachers of English to engage with critical theories of language, namely translanguaging, and to unpack how those theories disrupt deficit-oriented perceptions of and approaches to teaching racialized bi/multilingual students. Seltzer outlines the PD series and explores what surfaced when teachers were given the opportunity to grapple with ideologies that inform deficit-informed perceptions and approaches. Findings show that when given the space and time to do so, teachers articulated critical shifts in their thinking and connected those shifts to more expansive pedagogical possibilities for their students. Seltzer's project has meaningful implications for language teacher education, particularly for those teachers who identify as White, monolingual English speakers teaching racialized bi/multilingual students.

The chapter *The Words Flowed Like a River: Taking Up Translanguaging in a Teacher Education Program* by Cecilia M. Espinosa, Melissa García, and Alison Lehner-Quam, presents narratives of the ways the three of them—two teacher educators and an education librarian—actively advocated for translanguaging in education programs. Espinosa, García, and Lehner-Quam propose a perspective of strength and possibility that normalizes their students' bi/multilingualism and views it as an asset and resource. The authors describe the ways in which they have begun to integrate translanguaging and an awareness of raciolinguistic perspectives into their practices and reflect on how these were transformative for both college student teachers and teachers alike. In their own words, the authors make recommendations for (language) teacher education based on their experiences as, the "three stories illustrate that change can begin with individual agency and faculty coming together to re-imagine what it means to take a perspective of strength towards the languaging practises our teacher candidates bring with them."

In *Linguistic Journeys: Interrogating Linguistic Ideologies in a Teacher Preparation Setting*, Ivana Espinet demonstrates that teacher education programs have the capacity to re-imagine how students learn and participate in their classrooms. Espinet engages with the following questions: How do teacher educators prepare teachers to work with emergent bilinguals in ways that not only build on their strengths but also learn to create learning spaces where students can more fully participate because their sociocultural and linguistic strengths are leveraged? How do prospective teachers develop theoretical and pedagogical understandings as they learn to craft a curriculum where students engage deeply as readers and composers of texts in the different content areas and across content areas? Espinet works with teacher candidates who are not only diverse, but also bilingual backgrounds. Yet, most of them grew up in spaces where the norm was the rigid separation of languages. These were spaces where the teacher candidates were told that to be successful, they had to speak solely in English. What happens when they are invited to leverage on their languaging repertoire as they learn to leverage on their students' linguistic repertoire? As the bilingual teacher candidates take up translanguaging, how do their teaching voices develop?

Espinet's chapter describes the journey of bilingual teacher candidates attending a university in a large urban setting where they come across transformative encounters.

Part 3 is titled *Confronting Ideologies of Ethnicity, Language, and Accent* and focuses on the impact of ideologies on experiences of language teacher identity construction and on the educational experiences of language learners of a minoritized background. The two powerful accounts of the mechanisms leading to the racialization of student teachers foreground evidence of the role of (hetero-perceived) phenotype and accent, among other aspects, in the assignment and/or development of language teachers' identity.

The first chapter, by Fabiana Patrocínio and Paula Garcia de Freitas, is titled *Racialization of the Japanese Language in the Narratives of Brazilian Undergraduate Students*. Patrocínio and de Freitas discuss how Japanese language undergraduates at a Brazilian public university perceive and represent Japanese language teaching in their narratives and reflections about their own experiences in the context of Japanese language teaching-learning. Issues related to belonging and legitimacy, the influence of being (or not) of Japanese descent (with a supposed visual identification), and manifestations of the "impostor syndrome" are identified in the narratives of Japanese language students. These themes raise a discussion about the effects of such issues on learners' perceptions of themselves as learners and as future teachers within Japanese language education. Through the analysis of students' narratives, the authors underscore linguistic ideologies that reinforce the image of a culture, a language, and idealized speakers that tend to propose standards to follow, perpetuate homogeneous discourses, generate hierarchies, and establish unequal power relations. Drawing a dialogue between decolonial studies and raciolinguistic ideologies, Patrocínio and de Freitas problematize how linguistic ideologies present in students' narratives relate to the teaching-learning processes and how they affect their perception of linguistic and speaker authenticity.

The second chapter of this section is titled *Ethnic Accent Bullying, EFL Teaching and Learning in Mongolia* by Bolormaa Shinjee and Sender Dovchin. This chapter investigates English as a Foreign Language (EFL) teachers' attitude toward varied English accents of their EFL students with rural or ethnic minority backgrounds and increases awareness of "ethnic accent bullying" in EFL teaching settings in Mongolia. Since the establishment of democracy in 1990, the English language has emerged as the most favored international language in Mongolian schools. However, there is a growing difference in students' English language competencies, particularly speaking skills and pronunciation, due to their varied socio-economic, geographical, and ethnic backgrounds in tertiary institutions where they are required to pass IELTS with a 6.5 score or equivalent skills. The students from remote areas or of ethnic minority backgrounds tend to experience "ethnic accent bullying" in the forms of "laughing" and "joking" toward their "ethnic English accents" due to not only their "ethnic minority backgrounds" but also their lack of access to "standard" English communicative settings. Shinjee and Dovchin highlight how discriminatory attitudes occur both intentionally or unintentionally, not only by students' EFL peers but also by EFL instructors. The authors argue that there is a need for university EFL teachers to increase their awareness of "ethnic accent bullying" among regional and ethnic minority students and to minimize those prejudicial behaviors in the EFL classrooms.

Part 4 of the volume is titled *Disrupting Raciolinguistic Ideologies* and includes four chapters dealing with language teachers' agency to deal with and even benefit from their racialized identities. The chapters included in this section show how racialized language teachers cope with and even manipulate the racialization of their bodies made by the White listener–observer. Against the entitlement of the White listener–observer to define what should be a legitimate and authentic language teacher body (as a proxy of legitimate and authentic linguistic and pedagogical practices), the authors reflect on language teachers' strategies that go beyond coping with this problem and include the use of raciolinguistic ideologies as an object of analysis to improve their teaching practices, learning outcomes, and career prospects.

The first chapter is titled *Englishes as a Site of Colonial Conflict: Nuances in Teacher Enactment of a Transraciolinguistic Approach* by Patriann Smith, Crystal Rose, and Tala Karkar-Esperat. The authors explore the role of raciolinguistic ideology as steeped in (post)colonialism in language teachers' identity. They focus on the impact and the power of racialization based on (post)colonization as a function of institutional norms, on the use of language by former literacy teachers, as well as on their ways of navigating postcolonial ideologies as English teacher educators. Through this study, the authors invite literacy and language teachers and educators to address raciolinguistic ideologies and their associated institutional norms, which reinforce such ideologies through Englishes central to literacy and language instruction in US schools.

Vijay A. Ramjattan, in his chapter titled *The Raciolinguistic Enregisterment and Estheticization of ELT Labor*, argues that due to the colonial spread of the English language around the world, embodied Whiteness and "nativeness" in English are deeply intertwined. Ramjattan claims that, through the process of raciolinguistic enregisterment where people come to "look like languages" (Rosa, 2019), native English speakers are often imagined to be

White. In this chapter, Ramjattan explores the consequences of this racialized aesthetic labor. First, it contributes to less employment opportunities and material rewards for racially minoritized teachers, who are positioned as never sounding right for ELT (even when they do conform to hegemonic conceptions of sounding right). Moreover, it furthers the deskilling of the ELT profession by making the aesthetic qualities of teachers better "credentials" than actual teaching experience, training, and so on. Ramjattan concludes the chapter by outlining possible tactics to disrupt conceptions of the White native speaker of English as the ideal worker in ELT.

In *Issues of Legitimization, Authority, and Acceptance: Pakistani English Language Teachers and Their Confrontation of Raciolinguistic Ideologies in ELT/TESOL Classrooms*, Kashif Raza reflects on his own positionality as a so-called non-native teacher of English and on a program designed to counter student teachers' own raciolinguistic ideologies and prejudices about non-native teachers. Raza unpacks raciolinguistic ideologies toward Pakistani English language teachers and the manifestations of these ideologies in English language classrooms in non-Anglophone contexts. The author reflects on the added value of designing instruction moments that call language teachers to rethink language classrooms from a two-way multilingual angle where English works as a resource, language education goes beyond English language learning, and learners' and language teachers' linguistic repertoires are utilized for multilingual pedagogical approaches.

This volume is concluded with a chapter by Sílvia Melo-Pfeifer, titled *Language Student-Teachers of a Racialized Background: The Transracial Construction of the Competent Language Teacher*. Melo-Pfeifer analyses biographical, problem-centered interviews, reconstructing the experiences of two student teachers of Spanish belonging to visible and audible minorities in Germany. Melo-Pfeifer focuses on how they cope with the fear of being underestimated as speakers and teachers in the field of language education. Melo-Pfeifer engages in the reconstruction of the student teachers' everyday racialized experiences, which are not limited to their multilingualism but extend to their names, appearance, clothing, and ability (or not) to abide by (or even transgress) the supposed non-marked White listener and speaker norms (associated with the native speaker). The chapter focuses on self-reported instances of transracial and multilingual performances (following Alim, 2016) during their professionalizing path to demonstrate that student teachers' transracial experiences result from the interconnection of raciolinguistic and foreign language teaching ideologies.

Together, these chapters not only reconstruct the lived experiences of teachers of two languages and racialized language teachers—two underrepresented groups within the research literature—but also offer critical insights, important recommendations, and new directions for language teacher education (research). The authors challenge us to look at language teachers beyond the sole perspective of a particular language taught and incite us to take an intersectional view of the teacher that considers much more than only their multilingual profile, but also their multicultural humanity in which faces, bodies, voices, and emotions cannot be disregarded. The contributions to this volume allow us to examine, under a magnifying glass, the pervasiveness and perversity of raciolinguistic and monolingual ideologies in language education, which have the power not only to harm and discriminate against students (as it has been already vastly treated in the literature) but also to disparage and discourage language educators. Therefore, language equity and social justice in (language) education must be seen as issues equally related to (language) teachers and to the broader school population.

1.4 Conclusion

This volume systematically addresses issues originating from the intersection of ideologies of race, ethnicity, and language in the contexts of language teacher identity and education. While there is literature dealing with similar issues, they tend to focus on teachers and teacher education programs mostly *of* and *in* English. Most of the research literature has also focused on language learners, particularly of English as an additional language. This volume considers such issues in language teacher preparation programs, as many teacher educators have been concerned with teachers' experiences in the classroom. Therefore, we believe that our volume fills a timely gap in the scholarly literature, bringing together, from a holistic perspective, intersectional ideologies of race, ethnicity, language, and language pedagogies, and how they manifest simultaneously in language(s) education as well as language teacher identity experiences. Some intersecting elements of language teacher identity construction are not considered in the present volume due to its intentional thematic focus. Aspects of language teacher identity such as social class, religious affiliation, physical characteristics, and sexual orientation could be included in a subsequent volume with the aim of further diversifying and complexifying the professional portraits outlined in this volume. It would be of utmost relevance to crisscross the findings discussed in this volume with other hegemonic ideologies such as ableism and heteronormativity in order to continue to "peel (additional layers of) the onion," which we metaphorize to understand the identity of

1.4 Conclusion | **17**

the language teacher. Such research should aim to help us understand how the different layers interrelate and gain more or less visibility and importance in a teacher's life.

Additionally, the existing literature tends to focus on the teaching and learning of English as well as on teachers of English. In our volume, we include a diverse range of languages, such as English, French, German, Japanese, Norwegian, Portuguese, and Spanish, though English ended up occupying an important position in many of the chapters. There remains the need and space, in a future volume, for the inclusion of teachers of other languages, such as Arabic, Chinese, or Russian, given the number of speakers and learners these languages have. Although this is an important direction for future volumes to consider, we demonstrate, through the complexity and diversity of chapters here included, that this volume does critically engage with the study of the interception of monolingual and raciolinguistic ideologies in language teacher identity construction. This is due to the fact that the linguistic ideologies confronted in this volume are not specific to a given language, but are rather transversal in contemporary language and teacher education. Rather than allocating specific ideologies to the teaching and learning of particular and single languages in a one-to-one mapping, the present volume shows that language ideologies such as native-speakerism or the racialization of language teachers' bodies are widespread across different languages. Therefore, the field's critical engagement with these ideologies cannot be thematically exhausted only in the teaching and learning of the languages covered by this volume.

The research presented in this volume reflects a range of linguistic and cultural contexts and, in this sense, may be viewed as an attempt to disrupt the continuity and the impact of ideologies on language, such as monolingualism and native-speakerism, and race on the experiences of professional identity development of language teachers around the world. As such, the chapters in this volume offer important implications for language teacher education programs from a variety of pedagogical, political, and linguistic perspectives. As co-editors, we hope that the book will contribute to empowering language teachers as they navigate conflicting mandates, ideologies, needs, and perceptions of who they are, of what and how they (should) teach, and how they (should) sound and look like. Finally, this volume also has a strong emphasis on the position, criticality, and positionality of authors, visible in a great number of chapters that embraced auto-ethnography as an in-depth strategy to engage with their lived experiences, on par with the growing trend that the field has called for and gradually seen (Adams et al., 2014; Canagarajah, 2012; Ortega, 2021).

References

Adams, T. E., Jones, S. H., & Ellis, C. 2014. *Autoethnography*. Oxford University Press.

Alim, H. S. (2016). Introducing raciolinguistics: racing language and languaging race in hyperracial times. In H. S. Alim, J. R. Rickford, & A. F. Ball (Eds.), *Raciolinguistics: How Language Shapes Our Ideas About Race* (pp. 1–32). Oxford University Press.

Alim, H., Reyes, A., & Kroskrity, P. (Eds.) (2020). *The Oxford Handbook of Language and Race*. Oxford.

Ayres-Bennett, W., & Fisher, L. (2022). Towards interdisciplinarity in multilingual identity research. In W. Ayres-Bennett & L. Fisher (Eds.), *Multilingualism and Identity. Interdisciplinary Perspectives* (pp. 1–18). Cambridge University Press.

Block, D., & Corona, V. (2016). Intersectionality in language and identity research. In S. Preece (Ed.), *The Routledge Handbook of Language and Identity* (pp. 507–522). Routledge.

Bräu, K., Georgi, V., Karakaşoğlu, Y., & Rotter, C. (2014). *Lehrerinnen und Lehrer mit migrationshintergrund*. Waxmann

Canagarajah, S. (2012). Teacher development in a global profession: an autoethnography. *TESOL Quarterly, 42*(2), 258–257,

Cook, V. (1992). Evidence for multi-competence. *Language Learning, 44*(4), 557–591.

De Costa, P. I. (2015). Reenvisioning language anxiety in the globalized classroom through a social imaginary lens. *Language Learning, 65*(3), 504–532. https://doi.org/10.1111/lang.12121.

Dovchin, S. (2022). *Translingual Discrimination*. Cambridge University Press.

García, O., & Li Wei. (2013). *Translanguaging: Language, Bilingualism and Education*. Palgrave Pivot.

Georgi, V., Ackermann, L., & Karakas, N. (2011). *Vielfalt im lehrerzimmer. Selbstverständnis und schulische integration von lehrenden mit Migrationshintergrund in deutschland*. Waxmann.

Hargreaves, A. (2001). Emotional geographies of teaching. *Teachers College Record, 103*(6), 1056–1080.

Holliday, A. (2015). Native speakerism: taking the concept forward and achieving cultural belief. In A. Swan, P. Aboshiha, & A. Holliday (Eds.), *(En) Countering Native speakerism: Global Perspectives* (pp. 11–25). Palgrave Macmillan. https://doi.org/10.1057/9781137463500.

Lengyel, D., & Rosen, L. (2015). Minority teachers in different educational contexts: Introduction. *Tertium Comparationis, 21*(2), 153–160.

Maalouf, A. (1998). *Les Identités meurtrières*. Grasset.

Macedo, D. (Ed.) (2019). *Decolonizing Foreign Language Education: The Misteaching of English and Other Colonial Languages*. Routledge.

Makoni, S., & Pennycook, A. (Eds.) (2006). *Disinventing and Reconstituting Languages*. Multilingual Matters.

May, S. (Ed.) (2014). *The Multilingual Turn: Implications for SLA, TESOL and Bilingual Education*. Routledge.

Menken, K., & García, O. (Eds.) (2020). *Negotiating Language Policies in Schools. Educators as Policymakers*. Routledge.

Neokleous, G., & Krulatz, A. (2020). Intercepting and fluid identities. From reflexive teacher educators to reflective teachers. In B. Yazan & K. Lindahl (Eds.), *Language Teacher Identity in TESOL. Teacher Education and Practice as Identity Work* (pp. 231–249). Routledge.

Ortega, L. (2014). Ways forward for a bi/multilingual turn in SLA. In S. May (Ed.), *The Multilingual Turn* (pp. 32–53). London: Routledge.

Ortega, Y. (2021). 'I wanted to be white': understanding power asymmetries of whiteness and racialisation. *Whiteness and Education, 6*(2), 147–162.

Prada, J. (2019). Exploring the role of translanguaging in linguistic ideological and attitudinal reconfigurations in the Spanish classroom for heritage speakers. *Classroom Discourse, 10*(3–4), 306–322.

Rosa, J. (2019). *Looking Like a Language, Sounding Like a Race. Raciolinguistic Ideologies and the Learning of Latinidad*. Oxford University Press.

Rosa, J., & Flores, N. (2020). Reimagining race and language: from raciolinguistic ideologies to a raciolinguistic perspective. In H. Alim, A. Reyes, & P. V. Kroskrity (Eds.), *The Oxford Handbook of Language and Race* (pp. 90–107). Oxford University Press.

Rosen, L., & Lengyel, D. (2023). Research on minority teachers in Germany. Developments, focal points and current trends from the perspective of intercultural education. In M. Gutman, W. Jayusi, M. Beck, & Z. Bekerman (Eds.), *To be a Minority Teacher in a Foreign Culture*. Springer.

Slavkov, N., Melo-Pfeifer, S., & Kerschhofer-Puhalo, N. (Eds.) (2022). *The Changing Face of the "Native Speaker". Perspectives from Multilingualism and Globalization*. De Gruyter.

Part 1

Experiences of Identity Construction of Plurilingual Language Teachers

2

Future Teachers of Two Languages in Germany: Self-reported Professional Knowledge and Teaching Anxieties

Sílvia Melo-Pfeifer[1] and Vander Tavares[2]

[1] *Department of Languages and Aesthetic Disciplines Education, Faculty of Education, University of Hamburg, Germany*
[2] *Department of Teacher Education and Pedagogy, Faculty of Education, Inland Norway, University of Applied Sciences, Norway*

2.1 Introduction: Moving Beyond the Dichotomy of Native/Non-native Foreign Language Teachers in the Study of Professional Knowledge and Teaching Anxiety

As society becomes increasingly more multilingual, teachers of two languages gain more prominence in research connected to (the so-called foreign/second[a]) language education. A key sociolinguistic feature of these teachers is their ability to teach (in) two languages, thereby meeting the needs of diverse groups of students simultaneously. In order to meet such aims, however, teachers of two languages need adequate and contextualized training that can prepare them to teach effectively in such contexts. Nevertheless, research concerned with teachers' sense of preparedness for the foreign/second (L2) teaching profession has been largely based on studies of teachers of one language. Moreover, the same research has been overwhelmingly characterized by studies focusing on English as a second language (ESL). In this chapter, we explore the self-representations of future

---

a Despite the call to abandon the adjective "foreign" to refer to languages, the authors maintain it here to guide the reader on discussing teachers of two so-called foreign languages or one foreign language and the language of schooling. In any case, we consider both profiles to be "teachers of two languages," despite the different curricular status of the two languages.

Language Teacher Identity: Confronting Ideologies of Language, Race, and Ethnicity,
First Edition. Edited by Sílvia Melo-Pfeifer and Vander Tavares.
© 2024 John Wiley & Sons Ltd. Published 2024 by John Wiley & Sons Ltd.

teachers of two languages in relation to their perceived professional knowledge and teaching anxieties through drawings and responses to a questionnaire. We examine two groups of future teachers of two languages based in Germany: one who will be teaching German and a foreign language (FL) and one who will be teaching two foreign languages (FLs).

Three knowledge domains are commonly recognized as being part of teachers' professional competencies and knowledge (Baumert and Kunter, 2013): subject-specific knowledge, subject-specific didactic knowledge, and general pedagogical–psychological knowledge. The first concerns the mastery of subject content (such as FLs or mathematics); the second relates to the methodologies of and knowledge about teaching and learning processes with regard to specific subjects (e.g. pluralistic approaches to languages and cultures); and the third relates to knowledge about learning motivations, evaluation processes, or to how to manage classroom activities. Teachers of two FLs potentially display characteristics that differ from other teachers: they have to display linguistic, pragmatic, and intercultural knowledge about two different languages (with the same status or not), display knowledge about how to teach specific linguistic features of those languages alongside common issues attached to the teaching and learning of (foreign) languages, and make proof of pedagogical skills specific to teachers of languages.

If we think specifically about teachers of two FLs, we might infer that it is at the level of mastery of subject content that they probably most distinguish from teachers with other profiles. These may include teachers from just one FL, teachers from the so-called mother tongue and a FL, or combining one FL and another subject. Teachers of two FLs are called to display high levels of knowledge in the two languages (which is usually perceived in terms of near-nativeness) while being characterized by their "double non-nativeness" or even "double deficit" (which might be a case of self- or hetero-perception). Because speaking and teaching a FL are typically expected to be connected with a high degree of expertise, teachers of two FLs could be expected to feel more anxious about their subject knowledge than teachers who just teach one FL.

Researching the professional knowledge and anxiety of teachers of two languages thus poses questions that go beyond the dichotomy of native/non-native in the study of teachers' professional development. While native teachers might (or might not) themselves be plurilingual, teachers of two FLs are definitively plurilingual, having learned the two languages themselves as students or as heritage language speakers. This means that teachers of two FLs were apprentices of observation (Lortie, 1975) for those languages, having observed, experienced, and interiorized practices of teaching and learning each of those languages (probably) separately and across their life span as students. This theory explains that "student teachers arrive for their training courses having spent thousands of hours as schoolchildren observing and evaluating professionals in action" (Borg, 2004, p. 274). Teachers of two FLs are thus different in terms of exposure to FL teaching practices, which might be mediated by different language ideologies and didactic methodologies. Consequently, they would have spent much more time observing FL teachers, which might (or not) give them a great sense of self-confidence, because of their much more extensive "time on observation," following the famous "time on task" hypothesis. They might thus feel more skilled in terms of pedagogic knowledge and more identified with the FL teacher education profession. Going beyond the dichotomy of native/non-native in this contribution, we ask the following research questions:

1) How do two different profiles of teachers of two languages (mother tongue and FL/two FLs) differ in terms of self-perceived subject-specific knowledge, subject-specific didactic knowledge, and general pedagogical–psychological knowledge?
2) How do these two groups express and differ in terms of teaching anxiety?
3) What relationship can be established in terms of self-perceived professional knowledge and teaching anxiety for teachers of two languages?

We begin this chapter by arguing for the importance of research on teachers of two languages. We proceed to review and discuss past research on FL teaching anxiety, identifying three types of anxiety experienced by teachers and three domains of knowledge that constitute the professional competencies and knowledge of teachers. Subsequently, we present the methodological construction of the study and the findings, divided into two themes, each being analyzed both quantitatively and qualitatively: knowledge and emotions. The contribution is concluded with new research questions and implications for teacher education programs.

2.2 Teachers of Two Languages and Foreign Language (Teaching) Anxiety: Crisscrossing Two Research Fields

2.2.1 Teachers of Two Languages: Why Do They Matter?

Bilingualism has been a fundamental topic of research in applied linguistics and (foreign/second) language education. The majority of early research on bilingualism, however, has been oriented by perspectives of psycholinguistics.

2 Future Teachers of Two Languages in Germany

When viewed from the "social turn" (e.g. Ortega, 2011), the experiences of teachers teaching two languages constitute a more recent area of inquiry within these fields. The growing attention toward this area can be linked to at least two key phenomena. On the one hand, transnationalism has informed large-scale sociolinguistic societal changes, which continue to have direct implications for all levels of education. In the United States, K-12 classrooms are increasingly multilingual in terms of the student population, with students of a bilingual background occupying a central place (Reyes and Kleyn, 2010). On the other hand, the prevailing monolingual bias in second and FL education (Cook, 1997) has been confronted by evolving multilingual and plurilingual frameworks that recognize and celebrate linguistic diversity in the individual, which remained largely obscured in the past (Block, 2013).

The increased recognition of linguistic plurality, at both the societal and individual level, places new challenges and opportunities for teacher education. Concerns related to preparing teachers to be able to plan, teach, and assess (in) two languages while promoting equity for all students remain at the forefront (Reyes and Kleyn, 2010). Indeed, although the use of two languages by teachers in the classroom is not uncommon, especially in postcolonial contexts, teachers need pedagogical training that is not only adequate but also contextual to the social realities in which their teaching takes place. When speaking about the African context, Clegg and Afitska (2011) argued that at the core of teacher education should be a pedagogy that "prepares teachers to use the wide range of strategies which they need in order to support their learners working in two languages" (p. 74). More often than not, the two languages which teachers and students are working with within schools are interlaced in a matrix of unequal power relations (García, 2013). This sociolinguistic reality makes it essential that language teachers receive a kind of training attuned to equity and diversity in order not to perpetuate inequalities in and through their teaching.

Palviainen et al. (2020) found that teachers teaching in two languages tend to employ a "flexible" kind of bilingual teaching. Flexible bilingualism (García, 2009) involves teachers combining the two languages, while bilingualism based on strict separation, as the name suggests, means that the two languages do not come into contact since each language is used for an exclusive purpose. For example, a teacher might teach Spanish in the morning, but English in the afternoon. However, in their study, Palviainen et al. (2020) underscored that teachers teaching from a flexible bilingualism stance developed such practices over time and through personal experience, instead of learning about them in their teaching programs. The teachers' own beliefs played an important role in the approach they employed in their practice. Although the authors worked with teachers of different sets of two languages (Finnish-Swedish, Russian-Finnish, and Arabic-Hebrew), they found that all teachers aimed to develop bilingualism in the students as something natural, while paying attention to situated matters of diversity and equity between the two languages. Overall, the findings reinforce the growing need for training focusing on two languages in teacher education.

Recent research has also considered the identity-related experiences of teachers teaching two languages in two different sociolinguistic settings. Tavares (2022) illustrated how language teacher identities are developed and enacted contextually through interactions with multiple stakeholders, including students, parents, and even teaching materials. The author also demonstrated the ways in which language ideologies such as monolingualism and linguistic purism can interfere with the process of teacher identity construction within a particular sociolinguistic context. Tavares (2022) highlighted the role of emotions, such as feelings of anxiety, doubt, and frustration within the process of negotiating identity, especially when the legitimacy of his identity was questioned by students on the basis of different varieties spoken by him and the students, which were also interlaced unevenly in ideological power. Feelings of anxiety and insecurity can emerge particularly in response to the "clash" between teacher and student when one variety is more "prestigious" than the others or when the same language is understood through the native/non-native dichotomy.

2.2.2 Foreign Language (Teaching) Anxiety

As with any subject teaching, teaching a FL is an emotional experience that involves the whole individual. In this section, we examine specifically the sense of preparedness and imagined professional knowledge of future teachers of two languages. Therefore, we center on FL teaching anxiety, which is anxiety understood in relation to teaching the target language in the classroom. Horwitz et al. (1986) defined anxiety in connection to language *learning* as "a distinct complex of self-perceptions, beliefs, and behaviors related to classroom language learning arising from the uniqueness of the language learning experience" (p. 128). Indeed, while anxiety has been researched extensively in applied linguistics at least since the 1980s, it has been contextualized mainly around language learning and language production (Dewaele, 2017), which includes three stages: input, processing and interpreting the language, and output (MacIntyre and Gardner, 1994).

Despite being a prominent topic of research in applied linguistics, anxiety can be difficult to research. Quantitative research methods have been the mainstream for this topic; however, studies have produced contradictory results at times given the complex and dynamic nature of anxiety as a construct (Dewaele, 2017), while simultaneously reflecting predominantly situations connected to oral communication (Horwitz, 2001). FL anxiety may be language-specific because it might correlate to FL achievement and (perceived) proficiency in the target language. In the same way, it might be gender-specific and related to teaching-specific languages. Early research indicated that female students feel more embarrassed by their mistakes in the L2 in public speech situations (Coleman, 1996).

From another angle, students' anxiety is related to perceived teacher support (Palacios, 1998). It is important to note that most of this research has had English as the language of study, for both students and teachers. For the latter group, studies on anxiety have typically compared native and non-native teachers of English (Fraschini and Park, 2021; Martínez Agudo, 2017; Liu and Wu, 2021, on Chinese Teachers of English; Suzuki and Roger, 2014, on Japanese teachers of English).

When considering teachers, teaching anxiety may be viewed as a sign of insecurity and uncertainty about what to do in teaching scenarios. It can be classified into three types (Çubukçu and Dönmez, 2011, based on Fuller, 1969): self-centered, task-centered, and student-centered. Each of these types of anxiety can be understood in the form of a question. The self-centered type, for example, as "do I have the skills to teach a subject?" As for the task-centered type, "do I have the skills to develop tasks and activities?" And finally, student-centered anxiety as "do I have the skills to teach all the students?" Or "how will students react to my teaching/to the subject?" When it comes specifically to teaching a FL, this anxiety may originate from teachers' conceptualization of their roles as teachers, which has to do with the cultural pressure to conform to an idealized L1-teacher identity (Fraschini and Park, 2021; Suzuki and Roger, 2014).

Anxiety can originate from teachers' perceptions of students' needs and expectations (Suzuki and Roger, 2014). Such perceptions are "located" in students who might fall behind, who might threaten the status of the teacher, and in exam-related expectations (Suzuki and Roger, 2014). When anxiety is "located" in the self, rather than others, it may be related to concerns over accuracy in the FL (Suzuki and Roger, 2014) and the perceived lack of proficiency in the FL (Gregersen et al., 2014; Suzuki and Roger, 2014). Still on the self as the focus of research, Fraschini and Park (2021) have offered important insight into anxiety tied to FL teaching. The authors explained that anxiety is influenced by (perceived or real) unequal power relations between native and non-native speakers, the perceived inability to answer questions "on the spot," lack of preparation, and interaction with colleagues, learners, and parents. Since FL teaching is a precarious field, anxiety is also related to job (in)security, in addition to uncertainty and unpredictability felt in the classroom (Fraschini and Park, 2021).

Dewaele (2017) reported that the more languages one knows, the less anxious multilinguals feel. This suggests that multilingualism plays an important role in how teachers and students might experience anxiety. However, in the English language classroom, multilingual non-native teachers still feel more anxious than their native speaker teacher counterparts. Regardless of the teacher's linguistic profile, research demonstrates that teachers tend to feel anxious in relation to how to appropriately integrate students' multilingual repertoires into pedagogy when teaching in multilingual contexts. Melo-Pfeifer (2021), in a study with German future teachers of French or Spanish, found that student teachers of a migrant background felt more student-centered anxiety. In the same study, she also found out that mother-tongue speakers of Spanish reported feeling more self-centered anxiety than mother-tongue speakers of French.

This review of the literature on teachers of two FLs and the experience of language anxiety in language teaching shows that, at least in theoretical terms, dual language teachers may suffer more from anxiety. This may be due to the fact that the ghost of the "native speaker" is doubled. However, this potential greater propensity to suffer from language anxiety could possibly be counterbalanced by a greater teaching repertoire and more professional knowledge, acquired through cumulative training. This study focuses precisely on this interface.

2.3   The Empirical Study

This chapter presents a study of an exploratory nature, first and foremost due to the lack of studies that could inform the one in focus in terms of theoretical and methodological perspectives. Our aim is therefore to generate new research questions that can be addressed in future research in line with the purpose of exploratory studies.

2.3.1   Context and Participants

The University of Hamburg is the biggest university in North Germany. Data from 2015 stressed that among its 42,000 students, 12% have a migrant background (Präsidium der Universität Hamburg, 2015). Hamburg itself is a vibrant city with a very diverse population, with around 30% of citizens with a migrant background. At the primary school, according to data from 2020, 50% of all pupils had a migrant background (first, second, and third generations). Among the most visible communities are Turkish, Polish, Russian, Afghan, Iranian, Portuguese, Ghanaian, Serbian, Italian, and Greek (data from early 2014).

2 Future Teachers of Two Languages in Germany

Data were collected in four summer semesters in Hamburg (Germany) among pre-service teachers of (at least) French and Spanish, during the first meeting of the seminar on "Spanish & French didactics," in the third year of the bachelor program (in the EU, countries adhering to the "Bologna agreement," student teachers have to go through 3 years Bachelor and 2 years Master). In total, 218 students participated in the data collection and they consented to have their questionnaires analyzed. Because, in Germany, teacher education paths allow students to combine languages with other subjects (for example, French and Chemistry or Spanish with Sport and Religion), in the data collected we have all sorts of subject combinations.

For the purpose of this study, we focus on pre-service teachers of two languages. We divided the profiles around two cohorts: teachers of two FLs (39 students out of 218, making 18% of the total) and teachers of German (the majority language and language of schooling) and a FL (in our case, French or Spanish). This second cohort makes 29 student teachers (13% of the total).

To get a clearer picture, we analyzed the percentage of the number of students with and without a migrant background. From the total corpus (218 participants), 32 have a migrant background (14,5%). In the two cohorts named above, 23 out of 39 student teachers of two FLs have a migrant background (59%) and 9 out of 29 student teachers of German and a FL have a migrant background (31%). This makes the difference in the two cohorts already apparent: student teachers of two FLs tend, more than the other cohort, to have a migrant background.

Within the combinations of the two FLs, Spanish-English is the most common: 20 out of 39. Other combinations include French and English (9), French and Spanish (8), and French and Russian (2). In the second cohort, 20 students combine Spanish and German and 9 combine French and German. In a more detailed analysis, we could come to 80% of students in the cohort Spanish-English and 35% of students in the cohort Spanish-German with a migrant background. This would mean that the combination Spanish-English is mostly frequented by students who are or were newcomers to Germany. In almost 50% of French-English student teachers, we can observe the same tendency.

Considering the average of university students at the university with a migrant background presented above (12%), this makes the number of student teachers of two languages greatly exceed it: 59% for teachers of two FLs and 31% for teachers combining German and one FL have a migrant background. And if we compare the number of teachers with a migrant background in the country, all school subjects combined, which amounted to 10.7% in 2016 (Klovert, 2018), the difference is even more significant.

2.3.2 Data Collection Instrument

We developed a questionnaire to characterize the linguistic profile of future teachers of Spanish and French at the Master's level at the University of Hamburg. The aim was to identify the representations of various language cultures of the participants and to analyze their profiles as future teachers exploring, for example, their fears, images of the ideal teacher, and representations of the future teaching profession. This questionnaire was used for the first time in 2013, at another German university, subsequently improved in terms of language and formatting, and then reused annually with each new student group. Recently, to study "professional heritage" among student teachers, a question on the profession of the parents was added in 2019.

The questionnaire was divided into three parts. The first part related to the identification and sociolinguistic profile of students, with questions about subject combinations, origin, and language competences. In this section, students were asked to provide a pseudonym for anonymizing their questionnaires. The second part elicited representations about languages and cultures, with "free association exercises" about different languages (Romance languages, curricular FL, languages of origin, and German). The third part elicited representations about the profession of FL teacher with two different exercises: completing sentences and drawing a teacher and a student ("What do a language teacher and a student look like?," following the research with visual methods according to Kalaja and Melo-Pfeifer, 2019). Prior to the drawing tasks, which constituted what Valencia et al. (2020) call "multimodal identity texts," the students were presented with four incomplete sentences to complete: "A FL teacher is ...," "FL teachers are afraid of ...," "A FL teacher loves ...," and "a FL teacher needs ...," tapping into students' representations about teacher knowledge, emotions, and anxieties. The choice of the research method of drawing can be justified as follows: First, beliefs cannot always be explicitly explained or captured in words; second, drawing allows the combination of verbal and non-verbal elements, which together can create new interpretations about the teaching profession.

2.3.3 Data Analysis

For the analysis of the answers to the open-ended questions, we opted for quantitative and qualitative content analysis (Burwitz-Melzer and Steininger, 2016). We first conducted a frequency analysis of deductive (theory-based) categories. Subsequently, we conducted an interpretative deepening of the data by analyzing exemplary answers or phenomena in detail, including some of the visual representations as well.

2 *Future Teachers of Two Languages in Germany*

Table 2.1 Categories for analysis of teachers' knowledge and personality.

	Definition	Example
Expertise	"(Subject-matter) Content Knowledge"	Grammar skills, good pronunciation, cultural experience in the target language country
General pedagogical and subject didactical knowledge	"Pedagogical content knowledge" and "general pedagogical knowledge" or "interdisciplinary [knowledge] for the production and optimisation of teaching-learning situations" (Ortenburger, 2016, p. 561)	Diversity of teaching methods
Personality traits	"The dimensions of extraversion, neuroticism, openness to experience, agreeableness and conscientiousness" (Czerwenka and Nölle, 2014, p. 475)	Motivation, patience, creativity, enthusiasm, anxiety

Source: Adapted from Czerwenka and Nölle (2014) and Ortenburger (2016, p. 561; used in Melo-Pfeifer, 2019).

For the analysis of the open-questions related to FL teacher identity, we categorized student teachers' answers focusing on the dimensions of the following teachers' knowledge and personality traits (see Table 2.1).

Considering the aspects presented in the state of the art, we focused more closely on language and teaching anxiety, as shown in categories in Table 2.2.

2.4 Findings

2.4.1 Representations of Teachers' Knowledge

In this section, we first present a quantitative analysis of our data around the three categories of teachers' knowledge presented in the methodology, followed by a more detailed presentation of students' specific answers, which might help to uncover commonalities and differences between both groups.

2.4.1.1 Quantitative Analysis

The quantitative analysis of pre-service teachers' answers in the two cohorts does not show pronounced differences between them (see Table 2.3). Analyzing their answers to "A Foreign Language teacher is ..." and "A Foreign Language teacher needs ..." makes it clear that, at this stage of

2.4 Findings | **33**

Table 2.2 Categories for analysis of teaching anxiety (Fuller, 1969).

Teaching anxiety	Definition (based on Fuller, 1969)	Examples from the corpus (English translation)
Self-centered anxiety	Anxiety about whether they can do their task successfully or not and what others will think of them; usually related to teachers' content knowledge	Pupils who are better than him; Wrong pronunciation, not speaking authentically; Missing vocabulary; Making mistakes in front of his pupils
Task-centered anxiety	Anxiety about being an effective teacher (materials, methods, etc.); usually connected to teachers' pedagogical know-how	Incorrect assessment
Student-centered anxiety	Anxiety about and search for how to cover each student's mental, emotional, and social requirements; usually related to students' personality and cognitive issues	High achievement gap between the pupils; Ignorance of the pupil's language of origin; Pupil as native speakers

Table 2.3 Comparative quantitative analysis of student teachers' perceptions about FL teachers' competencies.

	Teachers of two FLs		Teachers of German and a FL	
	A FL teacher is...	A FL teacher needs...	A FL teacher is...	A FL teacher needs...
Oriented toward expertise in the language(s)	16.6	26%	18%	24%
Oriented toward general pedagogical and subject didactical knowledge	16.6%	14%	**26%**	12%
Recognizable through personality traits	**66.6%**	**60%**	**55%**	**63.5%**

their initial teacher education, they favor personality traits above subject-matter content knowledge and pedagogical and didactic knowledge.

There is a clear correspondence between their definition of a FL teacher and the listing of their needs. The personality and expertise of a teacher presented in the definitions correspond to certain developmental tasks and features the student needs to acquire in order to become a teacher. So, for example, when a student teacher defines a FL teacher as usually someone not speaking the language as a native speaker but still has to show "authority in that language," the student associates the need to "acquire a high level of proficiency in the foreign language" (answers from teachers of two FLs). Interestingly, the most salient difference, from our perspective, is the more relevance attached to pedagogical and methodological knowledge displayed by future teachers of just one FL, which could be a sign of a higher value attached to this dimension, potentially originating from task-centered anxiety. We concluded this analysis by stating that, in terms of professional development, both cohorts seem to share the same representations of what being a teacher of a FL is and what their needs are. They seem to have developed the same expectations about their profession and share a common professional vision as members of an imagined community. In the next section, we will analyze this data through student teachers' voices.

2.4.1.2 Qualitative Analysis

In both groups, the students emphasize linguistic expertise, referring to it in terms of "mastery": "solid command of the language," "an advanced level of linguistic skills" or "someone who has near-native competence in a language" (students with 2 FLs) or "good knowledge of the language" and "confident in his/her language of instruction" (students with one FL). If we analyze the lexical choices, though, it seems that teachers of two FLs seem more specific about the idea of achieving a native-like competence level: while the first students speak of a solid and high command of the language, good knowledge, as a student of one FL puts it, seems less normative. The same could be said about the contrast between attaining a near-native competence or having confidence in the language. In both groups, the command of grammar is mentioned, but the "large vocabulary" is just mentioned by a student with one FL. Another finding in these examples is that being a native is not connected to formal learning environments, while the teacher of just one FL seems to see the target language as attached to the schooling system ("language of instruction").

Aspects related to "language awareness" are just mentioned by a pre-service teacher of two FLs. Both groups also refer to knowledge of the target culture(s), explaining that a teacher of a FL should be "culturally competent" (student with two FLs) and "have a lot of knowledge about the language of the country" (a teacher of one FL).

In terms of pedagogical and subject knowledge, both groups highlight the capacity to assist students in their learning process, placing "good teaching methods" (an example from a student with two FLs) and the "quantity of material or the diversification of methodologies" (student with one FL) at the core of their definitions. Questions related to "experience and preparedness" to become a teacher are just mentioned by one teacher of two FLs, which could be related to more time on observation spent by this group.

Finally, in terms of personality traits, both groups refer to aspects such as "interesting," "dedicated," "communicative," "creative," "extroverted," "open," "with loads of motivation," "patience," and "empathy."

The drawings produced by the student teachers also show these commonalities. Table 2.4, without being extensive or representative of both cohorts, presents the most common tendencies in terms of visual representation of teacher professional knowledge: the teacher leading specific grammatical teaching and learning moments, a teacher-centered approach to the classroom, corroborated by the blackboard and textbooks as predominant

Table 2.4 Visualizations of professional knowledge.

	Teachers of two FLs	Teachers of German and a FL
Oriented toward expertise in the language(s)		
	(French and Spanish)	(Spanish and German)

(*continued*)

Table 2.4 (Continued)

	Teachers of two FLs	Teachers of German and a FL
Oriented toward general pedagogical and subject didactical knowledge	 (Spanish and English)	 (Spanish and German)
Recognizable through personality traits	 (English and French)	 (Spanish and German)

methodologies depicted, and the representation of the teacher as a happy person with positive attitudes toward the act of teaching.

In terms of specific subject knowledge, both groups depict predominantly moments of explicit grammar (or lexical teaching) teaching. General pedagogical and subject didactical knowledge are, at this phase of their professional path, almost reduced to the selection of teaching materials and to the diversity of those materials. The picture by the student of Spanish and English here reproduced intends to show the balanced use of media, grammar, and group work ("Balance, Kombination aus Medien, Grammatik, Gruppenarbeit"), with a TV in the background, representing a rather traditional media use in the classroom. Personality traits depicted are common to those mentioned in the open answers: mostly motivated and patient, but also, extended in the drawings, versatile ("vielseitig"), fluent ("fließend"), differentiated ("differenziert"), and cool guy ("cooler Typ").

While the similitudes prevail in the analysis, we could ask ourselves to what extent the differences might be relevant. While we cannot say that these answers are representative of the two groups, they might open pathways for further research.

2.4.2 Representations of Teachers' Emotions: A Focus on Language Anxiety

In this section, we analyze the answers to the question about teachers' fears, which can be related to potential anxieties felt by pre-service teachers. While proposing what a FL teacher is afraid of, as asked, the students might be establishing an indirect connection to their own insecurities, through personal identification and projection.

2.4.2.1 Quantitative Analysis

The quantitative analysis of pre-service teachers' answers about teaching anxieties shows more differences than the analysis of their perceptions of required professional knowledge (see Table 2.5). In all three categories, tendencies might be described that could open up further research perspectives.

The most visible difference is how teachers of just one FL seem to display a more pronounced self-centered anxiety, which we saw in the theoretical section as attached to teachers' content knowledge, i.e. their knowledge of the target language they are teaching.

Additionally, while teachers of two FLs spent more time observing teachers as apprentices, they reported more anxiety related to both tasks and students. These anxieties are more related to pedagogical issues (lack

Table 2.5 Teaching anxiety as defined by the two cohorts.

Teaching anxiety	Teachers of two FLs (%)	Teachers of German and a FL (%)
Self-centered anxiety	46	62
Task-centered anxiety	18	11
Student-centered anxiety	36	27

of pedagogical and specific didactic knowledge), meaning that despite (or perhaps because) more contact with classroom dynamics in the FL, they might get more anxious about their profession.

2.4.2.2 Qualitative Analysis

Self-centered anxiety is the kind of teaching anxiety that mostly affects both cohorts, visible in terms of FL anxiety discursive manifestations. A common concern, by student teachers in both groups, is a perceived lack of competence in the target language(s), such as forgetting words or pronouncing words incorrectly: "not speaking the language perfectly" (a student of two FLs) and "not knowing something and making mistakes" (a teacher of one FL). This insecurity is worse if "native speakers" of the target language are present in the classroom, as they are perceived as being more competent than the teacher himself/herself. Future teachers of two FLs report that a teacher fears "native speakers in the class" and "pupils who speak their language of instruction better than they do." A future teacher of German and one FL reports the same fear but limits the problem to fluency: "students who speak the language more fluently than he [the teacher] does." Being perceived as someone with an accent is also thematized by both groups as a sign of lack of proficiency and expertise in the target language(s): they frequently just finish the sentence "a foreign language teacher is afraid of ..." with the word "accent." Following student teachers' answers, self-centered anxiety might be due to two factors: fear of exposure as "impostor" by the native speaker and comparison of competences by and with the native speaker.

Task-centered anxiety is, at this point of teacher development, the least present in students' answers, but is more frequently mentioned by future teachers of two FLs. Both groups lack classroom practice, meaning that they are not aware of issues related to being or becoming an effective FL teacher and developing teachers' pedagogical know-how. Despite the rarity of items connected to this category, student teachers of two FLs reveal that they are anxious about "conveying difficult grammar structures well," "teaching incorrectly," "evaluating students," and "teaching the wrong pronunciation of a word." Student teachers of one FL reveal fear of "difficult questions about grammar" and "silence in the classroom." In both cohorts, the fear of not knowing how to answer students' questions related specifically to grammar and vocabulary is very present.

In terms of student-centered anxiety, two sources of anxiety could be uncovered in student teachers' answers in both groups: the fact that students might lack motivation to learn the target language and, related to self-centered anxiety, the fact that they might be native speakers of the language.

This anxiety is expressed in quite dramatic terms: "fear of native speakers in the class correcting him [the teacher] and thus questioning their professionalism" (a student of two FLs) and "fear of native speakers who make fun of the teacher with the classmates behind their back" (a student of one FL). Other reported sources of student-centered anxiety are "students who don't pay attention and do not follow teachers' instructions" (a student of two FLs) and "lack of motivation" (a student of one FL).

Following these answers, it seems plausible to assume that self-centered anxiety might be connected to the other two anxieties: student teachers fear or feel uncomfortable with the idea that native speakers can expose the teacher as an "impostor," lacking linguistic knowledge (example), with consequences for classroom management. Two connections between different teaching anxieties can be formulated: first, the fear of losing the expert face (self-centered anxiety) and therefore the control over the class (student-centered anxiety), potentially leading to what they see as the reversal of typical classroom hierarchies; second, the fear of uncertainty related to the management of classroom interaction (task-centered anxiety), by not being able to answer unexpected questions related to grammar and vocabulary (self-centered anxiety).

2.5 Discussion of the Results, Unanswered Questions, and Further Research Perspectives

We begin this section by reflecting upon the first research question: "How do two different profiles of teachers of two languages (mother tongue and FL/two FLs) differ in terms of self-perceived subject-specific knowledge, subject-specific didactic knowledge, and general pedagogical–psychological knowledge?" Our explorative study shows that representations of future teachers of two FLs and teachers of mother tongue and one FL are similar at this initial point of their teacher education paths. Both are pronouncedly vocal about teachers possessing specific personality traits (such as motivation and patience), which we might think are not specific to teachers of FL, but reveal perceived expectations related to teaching and being a teacher.

Addressing the second research question, "How do these two groups express and differ in terms of teaching anxiety?," while our review of the literature could make us advance that teachers of two FLs might feel more anxious about their linguistic competencies because of what we labeled double "non-nativeness," the quantitative analysis seems to go in the opposite direction. Even if we could advance an explanation to this fact in particular, it would be plausible to think that teachers of two FLs might have developed a more flexible perspective of what the command of a FL encompasses. Additionally, teachers of one FL and the mother tongue (German) might be "contaminated" by ideologies of nativeness and normativity, thus making them feel more anxious. We could thus hypothesize that the different status of the two languages (two FLs or a mother tongue and a FL) might lead to different outcomes in terms of anxiety. In any case, in both groups, answers show a very strong orientation toward correction, norm, and comparison to native speaker competences. This is an issue that our explorative study could uncover, but further research is needed.

In terms of the more expressive task-centered and student-centered anxieties by teachers of two FLs, we could claim that this group, because of more exposure to classroom practices, might have developed a more "realistic" view of the knowledge necessary to become a FL teacher than the other cohort would have. As we observed, at the same point in their career development, teachers of one FL are more strongly oriented toward the mastery of the target FL.

The third research question asked: "What relationship can be established in terms of self-perceived professional knowledge and teaching anxiety for teachers of two languages?" We could observe that, in both cohorts, subject-specific knowledge and pedagogical and didactic knowledge were just superficially present in their answers. Nevertheless, while student teachers of two FLs tend to be more exigent when describing FL teachers' command of the target language(s), student teachers of one FL show more anxiety connected to a possible lack of expertise (self-centered anxiety). This apparent contradiction should be exploited in further studies, specially designed to understand the interconnection between these elements.

An issue that was not exploited in this study was how our results might interrelate with two dichotomies present in the literature: native/non-native student teachers and students with or without a migrant background. Sure, these two dichotomies would also need to be crisscrossed, as having a migrant background may mean being a native speaker of the target languages Spanish, English, or French in the German context, or choosing two FLs (for example, having a Portuguese background and learning Spanish and English). We identified that the combination of two FLs (one being English) was predominant among student teachers with a migrant background (see the description of the participants). This interplay of dimensions of FL teachers' identities supports the need to see teachers' identities from an intersectional perspective, going beyond gender, ethnic background, and the native/non-native divides.

We do not claim that the results of our exploratory study are representative of the two profiles of FL teachers under consideration. In fact, for a better explanation or even refutation of our results, further empirical research is needed. More specifically, more quantitative and qualitative studies are necessary, resorting to different methodologies, including arts-based approaches (Leavy, 2015), which might allow a freer representation of mental states and feelings, such as anxiety.

2.6 Implications for Teacher Education Programs

The present chapter has shown the complexity of pre-service FL professional identity development in the making for teachers of two languages. It shows the multiplicity of aspects that can play a role in teachers' professional identity development and makes a point suggesting that there is much more to research than the more traditional dichotomy of native/non-native teachers. This dichotomy, while still heuristically productive, might intersect with other aspects of future teachers' identities that would be important to account for, namely the status of the languages they are about to become teachers of.

We considered two categories of teachers of two languages: two FLs and the combination of teaching the majority language and one FL. This comparison, even if not conclusive because of the exploratory nature of the empirical study, is relevant to illustrate the relevance of analyzing and comparing different teachers' profiles, as they are connected to different needs and subjective perceptions of their professional knowledge, needs, and anxieties.

In this specific contribution, we argue that student teachers' perspectives within initial FL teacher education are situated alongside questions of teaching anxiety. We thus consider, with Williams et al. (2015), that explicitly discussing (FL) teaching anxiety with student teachers should get them "to consider the roots of their anxiety and what they can do to overcome it" (p. 89). By using reported (FL) teaching anxieties to support professional development from the very beginning, teacher trainers would be focusing on agency and empowerment strategies to alleviate feelings of anxiety through the development of coping strategies such as accepting that uncertainty and unpredictability are part of the teaching profession and not a negative outcome. Moreover, teacher trainers should emphasize that teaching a FL is far more than focusing on "language performance," but encompasses sensitivity toward the students and the context. Teaching a FL is not just about oneself, but as much about others.

References

Baumert, J., & Kunter, M. (2013). The COACTIV model of teachers' professional competence. In M. Kunter, J. Baumert, W. Blum, U. Klusmann, S. Krauss, & M. Neubrand (Eds.), *Cognitive Activation in the Mathematics Classroom and Professional Competence of Teachers* (pp. 25–48). Springer.

Block, D. (2013). Moving beyond "lingualism": multilingual embodiment and multimodality in SLA. In S. May (Ed.), *The Multilingual Turn* (pp. 54–77). Routledge.

Borg, M. (2004). The apprenticeship of observation. *ELT Journal, 58*(3), 274–276.

Burwitz-Melzer, E., & Steininger, I. (2016). Inhaltsanalyse. In D. Caspari, F. Klippel, M. Legutke, & K. Schramm (Eds.), *Forschungsmethoden in der Fremdsprachendidaktik* (pp. 256–268). Narr Verlag.

Clegg, J., & Afitska, O. (2011). Teaching and learning in two languages in African classrooms. *Comparative Education, 47*(1), 61–77.

Coleman, J. (1996). *Studying Languages: A Survey of British and European Students*. London: CILT.

Cook, V. (1997). Monolingual bias in second language acquisition research. *Revista Canaria de Estudios Ingleses, 34*(1), 35–50.

Çubukçu, Z., & Dönmez, A. (2011). The examination of the professional anxiety levels of teacher candidates. *Eğitimde Kuram ve Uygulama, 7*(1), 3–25.

Czerwenka, K., & Nölle, K. (2014). Forschung zur ersten Phase der Lehrerbildung. In E. Terhart, H. Bennewitz, & M. Rothland (Eds.), *Handbuch der Forschung zum Lehrerberuf* (pp. 468–488). Waxmann.

Dewaele, J.-M. (2017). Psychological dimensions and foreign language anxiety. In S. Loewen & M. Sato (Eds.), *The Routledge Handbook of Instructed Second Language Acquisition*. London: Routledge (433–450).

Fraschini, N., & Park, H. (2021). Anxiety in language teachers: exploring the variety of perceptions with Q methodology. *Foreign Language Annals, 2021,* 1–24. https://doi.org/10.1111/flan.12527.

Fuller, F. (1969). Concerns of teachers; a developmental conceptualization. *American Educational Research Journal, 6,* 207–226.

García, O. (2009). *Bilingual Education in the 21st Century*. Wiley Blackwell.

García, O. (2013). From Diglossia to Transglossia: bilingual and multilingual classrooms in the 21st century. In C. Abello-Contesse, P. M. Chandler, M. D. López-Jiménez, & R. Chacón-Beltrán (Eds.), *Bilingual and Multilingual Education in the 21st Century: Building on Experience* (pp. 155–175). Multilingual Matters.

Gregersen, T., Macintyre, P. D., & Meza, M. D. (2014). The motion of emotion: idiodynamic case studies of learners' foreign language anxiety. *Modern Language Journal, 98*, 574–588.

Horwitz, E. (2001). Language anxiety and achievement. *Annual Review of Applied Linguistics, 21*, 112–126.

Horwitz, E., Horwitz, M., & Cope, J. (1986). Foreign language classroom anxiety. *The Modern Language Journal, 70*(2), 125–132.

Kalaja, P., & Melo-Pfeifer, S. (Eds.) (2019). *Visualising Multilingual Lives More Than Words*. Multilingual Matters.

Klovert, H. (2018). *Lehrer mit Migrationshintergrund Wichtig. Oder überbewertet?* Spiegel on-line. https://www.spiegel.de/lebenundlernen/schule/lehrer-mit-migrationshintergrund-berichtenaus-ihrem-alltag-a-1195142.html

Leavy, P. (2015). *Method Meets Art*. The Guilford Press.

Liu, M., & Wu, B. (2021). *Teaching Anxiety and Foreign Language Anxiety Among Chinese College English Teachers*. SAGE Open, April–June. https://doi.org/10.1177/215824402110165

Lortie, D. (1975). *Schoolteacher: A Sociological Study*. London: University of Chicago Press.

MacIntyre, P., & Gardner, R. (1994). The subtle effects of language anxiety on cognitive processing in the second language. *Language Learning, 44*, 283–305.

Martínez Agudo, J. (Ed.) (2017). *Native and Non-native Teachers in English Language Classrooms. Professional Challenges and Teacher Education*. Berlin: De Gruyter.

Melo-Pfeifer, S. (2019). "Ich werde Fremdsprachen lehren, also (wer) bin ich?" – Berufsbezogene Überzeugungen künftiger Fremdsprachenlehrerinnen und -lehrer für Französisch und Spanisch in der ersten Phase der Lehrerausbildung (Bachelor). *Zeitschrift für Romanische Sprachen und ihre Didaktik, 13*(2), 9–33.

Melo-Pfeifer, S. (2021). Who's afraid of the big bad plurilingual wolf? Teaching anxiety among foreign language student-teachers with and without a migrant background. *Oral Presentation at the 19th World AILA congress, August 15th to August 20th (Gröningen)*.

Ortega, L. (2011). SLA after the social turn: where cognitivism and its alternatives stand. In D. Atkinson (Ed.), *Alternative Approaches to Second Language Acquisition* (pp. 167–180). Routledge.

Ortenburger, A. (2016). Lehrer und Lehrerinnen. In M. Dick, W. Marotzi, & H. Mieg (Eds.), *Handbuch Professionsentwicklung* (pp. 559–565). UTB.

Palacios, L. M. (1998). *Foreign Language Anxiety and Classroom Environment: Study of Spanish University Students*. Unpublished doctoral dissertation. University of Texas, Austin.

Palviainen, Å., Protassova, E., Mård-Miettinen, K., & Schwartz, M. (2020). Two languages in the air: a cross-cultural comparison of preschool teachers' reflections on their flexible bilingual practices. *International Journal of Bilingual Education and Bilingualism, 16*(6), 614–630.

Präsidium der Universität Hamburg (2015). *Jahresbericht 2014. März 2015.* https://www.uni-hamburg.de/uhh/fakten/jahresberichte/jb-2014.pdf.

Reyes, S. A., & Kleyn, T. (2010). *Teaching in Two Languages: A Guide for K–12 Bilingual Educators.* Corwin Press.

Suzuki, H., & Roger, P. (2014). Foreign language anxiety in teachers. *JALT Journal, 36*(2), 175–200.

Tavares, V. (2022). Teaching two languages: navigating dual identity experiences. *Pedagogies: An International Journal,* 1–22. https://doi.org/10.1080/1554480X.2022.2065996

Valencia, M., Herath, S., & Gagné, A. (2020). Unpacking professional identity. The use of multimodal identity texts and duoethnographies in language teacher education. In B. Yazan & K. Lindahl (Eds.), *Language Teacher Education and TESOL.* London: Routledge (101–121).

Williams, M., Mercer, S., & Ryan, S. (2015). *Exploring Psychology in Language Learning and Teaching.* Oxford: Oxford University Press.

3

Exploring Identities and Emotions of a Teacher of Multiple Languages: An Arts-based Narrative Inquiry Using Clay Work

Eric K. Ku

Research Faculty of Media and Communication, Hokkaido University, Japan

3.1 Introduction

To be a teacher of multiple languages (TML), one must learn not only to manage multiple linguistic systems and pedagogical approaches but also to navigate the complex web of identities and emotions that come with each of the languages taught. Thus, teaching multiple languages involves negotiating various identities and emotions that are constantly changing, multifaceted, and possibly, in conflict and fragmented. Furthermore, TMLs' experiences of teaching different languages may differ depending on a range of factors, such as native speaker (NS) or non-native speaker (NNS) identities, language proficiency levels, and motivations to teach each language. Race and ethnicity can also be a significant factor that impacts TML's different experiences when teaching different languages. For example, a TML may prefer to teach one language over another if the teaching of a certain language has a stronger connection with their racial or ethnic identity, or vice versa.

Through arts-based narrative inquiry, this study explores the identities and emotions of a single TML participant, Park (pseudonym), including how ideologies of racial and ethnic identity impact the way he frames his language teaching experiences. At the time the study was conducted, Park was a tenure-track professor of business at a university in Japan. I originally met Park as a colleague and through initial conversations became aware of and interested in his background as a TML.

Language Teacher Identity: Confronting Ideologies of Language, Race, and Ethnicity,
First Edition. Edited by Sílvia Melo-Pfeifer and Vander Tavares.
© 2024 John Wiley & Sons Ltd. Published 2024 by John Wiley & Sons Ltd.

3.2 Identities and Emotions in Teaching Multiple Languages

The term "TMLs" refers to language teachers who have had the experience of teaching more than one language (Ku, 2023). TMLs are often overlooked in educational workplaces and research because of the monolingual tendency for language teachers to be seen only based on the language they are currently teaching. A language teacher may have past or current experiences in teaching other languages but that is often not recognized. In fact, prior to the term "TML," there had not yet been an established term that could be used in research or in teaching contexts to refer to teachers who have taught multiple languages. Thus, not only has there been a lack of TML research but also the studies that do examine TMLs are scattered and difficult to find, resulting in a lack of a continued dialogue among scholars studying TMLs (Ku, 2023).

Ku (2023) provides a comprehensive literature review of existing TML studies in applied linguistics research, and one of the common themes is exploring TMLs' language teacher identities, such as experiencing teaching as both NS and NNS teachers. For example, some studies explore TMLs who began as NS teachers and then shifted to teaching as NNS teachers (Fan and de Jong, 2019; Kim and Smith, 2019; Kramsch and Zhang, 2018; Mutlu and Ortaçtepe, 2016). This transition can involve experiencing the negative impact of native-speakerism and feeling like an imposter as a new NNS teacher, thus resulting in emotions such as anxiety, frustration, and incompetence. Other studies have examined TMLs who transitioned the other way around, from being a NNS to a NS teacher (Aslan, 2015; Kim and Smith, 2019; Li and Lai, 2022; Mutlu and Ortaçtepe, 2016; Tavares, 2022). Such a transition also involves complex emotions, such as a newfound confidence as a NS teacher and sadness upon realizing the differential treatment NS teachers receive.

In addition to addressing issues around NS and NNS teacher identities, TML studies have also looked at the ways race, ethnicity, and culture manifest differently when teaching different languages, and how that impacts teachers' identities and emotions. For example, Ku (2023) explored a particular language teacher, Ann, from Taiwan who had taught English in Taiwan, and Mandarin Chinese in India and the United States. Ann had language teacher education degrees, training, and experience in both languages, but as someone who identifies as ethnically Chinese, she still felt a deeper connection in teaching Mandarin Chinese as a cultural insider, whereas teaching English simply felt like teaching a school subject (see also Kim and Smith, 2019; Luo and Gao, 2017; Mutlu and Ortaçtepe, 2016;

Tavares, 2022). Emotions, such as feeling a closer cultural, racial, or ethnic connection to one of the languages a TML teaches over the other, have a reciprocal relationship with teacher identity, shaping while also being shaped by their teacher identities involving or going beyond culture, race, and ethnicity.

3.3   Clay Work as Arts-based Narrative Inquiry

This study will use clay work as part of an arts-based narrative inquiry. A narrative inquiry is "an approach to the study of human lives conceived as a way of honoring lived experience as a source of important knowledge and understanding" (Clandinin, 2016, p. 17). Thus, an arts-based narrative inquiry uses art as a medium in any step of the process of conducting a narrative inquiry (Kim, 2016, p. 138). This exploratory study uses "clay work," which involves participants molding clay by hand in response to a prompt.

One of the benefits of using art in research is that art can "tap into what would otherwise be inaccessible [and], make connections and interconnections that are otherwise out of reach" (Leavy, 2020, p. 31). Research on clay work in education, psychology, and social work has shown that what makes clay unique is its ability to be easily manipulated in form and texture directly in participants' hands, providing an alternative, somatic-based language to express oneself and develop new understandings (Bar-On, 2007; Buchanan, 2016; Sholt and Gavron, 2006). Furthermore, clay work is particularly suitable for exploring emotions because emotions are deeply connected to touch and clay offers a tactile way to connect with emotions and cognition (Dickson-Swift et al., 2009). While many forms of arts-based research have been used in applied linguistics or language teaching research (see Kalaja and Pitkänen-Huhta, 2020), clay work has not yet been used in any language teacher studies.

For this study, I decided to use clay work with Park for two reasons: (i) clay's ability to serve as an alternative way of expressing oneself and (ii) the difficulty Park had in talking about his prior teaching experiences. In my initial conversations with Park, he expressed some difficult feelings toward language teaching, such as shame, guilt, and feeling like an imposter. I also noticed some embodied reactions from Park as we were talking about language teaching, such as hand-wringing, closing his eyes, and grasping his head with his hands. It seemed like talking about past teaching experiences was emotionally difficult and using clay as an alternative, embodied medium might have helped him express his emotions and experiences.

3.4 Methodology

3.4.1 Data Collection

This arts-based narrative inquiry consisted of a semi-structured interview and a clay work session. We first spent about one hour for the semi-structured interview and then about 25 min for the clay work session. I prepared an interview guide with six topics I wanted to address: his educational background, moving to Japan, his career as an academic, language learning experiences (Korean, English, Japanese), language teaching experiences (Korean, English), and future career plans. The topics helped guide the interview while also giving the participant enough space to voice whatever thoughts or stories came to mind. The semi-structured interview was audio-recorded with Park's informed consent.

After the semi-structured interview, we started the clay work session:

1) Part 1: Warm-up
    i) Prompt 1: A simple topic that asks the participant to make something *concrete* and personal (i.e. "Use clay to make a model of the house you lived in in your childhood.").
    ii) Prompt 2: A simple topic that asks the participant to make something *abstract* and personal (i.e. "Use clay to show how you felt when you first moved to Japan.").
2) Part 2: Target activity

    i) Prompt 1: Language teaching experiences (past and present) (i.e. "Use clay to show what your experience was like teaching Korean" and "Use clay to show what your experience was like when you first started teaching English.").
    ii) Prompt 2: Current experiences in academia (i.e. "Use clay to show any current experiences you have had in academia recently.").
    iii) Prompt 3: Future career goals (i.e. "Use clay to show your career goals for the future.").

These prompts were inspired by the "DrawingOut" workshops (DrawingOut, 2022), designed by Gameiro et al. (2018). DrawingOut is "a group workshop designed to help people express their experience of invisible diseases" through metaphor-based drawing activities (DrawingOut, 2022). Though DrawingOut was designed to be used to discuss sensitive health topics such as depression or infertility, the structure of the workshops provides a model for how an arts-based research method can be used with participants who have little to no experience with the arts-based technique itself.

In the clay work session, I adapted the scaffolded structure of the DrawingOut exercises by starting out with two simple "warm-up" prompts. These allowed the participant to get used to handling clay and using clay to respond to a prompt. The first warm-up prompt is more "concrete" (i.e. making a model of a house) and the second is more "abstract" (i.e. showing how you feel). The warm-up prompts were followed by the "target activity," which asks the participant to use clay to express their TML experiences. The prompts were chronological, asking the participant to first think about their experiences in the past, then the present, and then the future. The clay work session was video-recorded with Park's informed consent.

Park had no formal experience using clay other than when playing with his young child. I reassured Park that no artistic expertise was needed and that there were no right or wrong ways to handle the clay. I also encouraged him to have fun with the activity as much as possible.

For the clay work session, I chose to use packaged "paper clay," which can be easily purchased in dollar stores (i.e. in Japan, 100-yen stores), stationery shops, craft supplies stores, and online shops. I chose paper clay because it is affordable, easily found, and easily moldable by hand without any tools or machinery. Furthermore, unlike other common hand-moldable, clay-like materials, such as playdough, paper clay naturally dries into a solid form without needing to be fired or baked. However, one of the drawbacks of paper clay is that it can be quite messy, leaving a lot of clay residue on your hands and work surfaces. Thus, playdough may be a better option.

3.4.2 Data Analysis

Analyzing clay work and semi-structured interviews required a multi-modal analysis that examined meaning-making in both visual and spoken mediums. In other words, the clay work and interviews were treated holistically as interconnected means of expression (rather than as isolated data), each co-constructing meaning of and for the other (Ibrahim, 2022; Riessman, 2008). Melo-Pfeifer and Chik (2022, p. 506) have called this a "multimodal translanguaging," in which a combination of data composed of various semiotic resources is considered, rather than only focusing on verbal data. The primary method of data analysis was thematic analysis, which involved reading through the interview transcripts multiple times with photographs of the clay work laid out side-by-side for instant comparison, coding both the interviews and clay work for patterns, and categorizing the patterns under thematic headings (Barkhuizen et al., 2014; Riessman, 2008). With clay work, I focused on analyzing the metaphors

3.5 Park's Narratives

The following are narratives of Park's experiences as a multilingual language learner and a TML. Interspersed within Park's narratives will be some analytical explanations on the use of two recurring metaphors: English as "chaos" and "artificial," and Japanese and Korean as "harmony" and "natural."

3.5.1 Learning Japanese and English

Park began learning Japanese informally in junior high school in South Korea. He was interested in Japanese popular culture, namely anime and manga, and one of his junior high school teachers approached him with the opportunity to informally take Japanese lessons after school. Park described this arrangement as "not usual" and "a unique case." In high school, Park began taking formal Japanese classes to fulfill the foreign language requirement. Park estimated that roughly more than half of his high school classmates also chose Japanese. In addition, Park had started learning English from the first grade. For Park, learning English and Japanese were two completely different experiences:

Excerpt 3.1

After [starting to learn Japanese in junior high school], I realized that Korean language and Japanese language are similar to each other, so much so that I just, I felt some special feeling which I cannot feel when I study English. Because for us, for me, English is like some subject to study, just not a language for me. I just realized that studying Japanese is like studying a language for me, so from that time, I really gave up studying English and just concentrated on study Japanese from that time. So I think almost all the people in Korea who can speak Japanese usually cannot speak English. They separated from studying English and they chose Japanese instead. There are lots of people like that. Including me.

3.5 *Park's Narratives* | 51

Park explained that, in his opinion, the way in which Japanese and Korean are similar is both grammatical and cognitive, influencing the role Japanese plays in his life. This is why he made the distinction between learning Japanese as learning a language and learning English as learning a subject:

Thus, for Park, English was an alien entity, both linguistically and cultur-

---

Excerpt 3.2

Word order of Japanese and Korean language are the same with each other, so if we are using real time, true time, to study Japanese, we can use it in our conversations. It's really easy to apply it in our conversations. For English, we have to make whole sentences before we talk. We have to make a sentence in our head and then we speak. So it's really burdensome for us. But when it comes to Japanese, we can say with thinking because word order is the same [as Korean]. So it's not that hard for us. It's easy for applying to conversation I think. That's why I felt it's like a language, not some subject or something.

---

ally disconnected from other parts of his life. Starting from Park's childhood, English had only ever been a "subject" that needed to be studied with little connection to Korean. Furthermore, English had little relevance to the Japanese pop culture he was interested in as a child.

After high school, Park attended college in South Korea, majoring in accounting, and later moved abroad to Japan to complete his master's and doctorate degrees in accounting. Park knew that he wanted to leave South Korea for his graduate studies and at first, he considered the United States. However, he realized that his English was not proficient enough and studying in the United States would be too expensive. Therefore, since he already knew Japanese and Japanese graduate school tuition was more affordable, he decided to do his graduate studies in Japan.

Graduate studies in Japan required him to learn academic Japanese, but that was not too difficult for Park. In fact, Park remarked that he "didn't have many problems" when learning to write academic papers in Japanese. After his graduate studies, Park obtained a tenure-track faculty position as an assistant professor at a university in Japan. At the time of the interview, he had been at the university for about six years, and during this time, using Japanese for his academic duties (i.e. teaching, research, administrative work, advising) had not been a problem.

52 | 3 *Exploring Identities and Emotions of a Teacher of Multiple Languages*

However, more recently, the need to learn English has resurfaced in his life:

Excerpt 3.3

I just started to write a paper in English recently. I wanted to write more papers in English and writing is not that big problem, because I can use services like Editage. But when it comes to presentation, I can report, but I cannot talk with them, like some question and answer session, like my listening is not that good, and my speaking is not that good, so I felt a big problem with this.

Park's experiences in learning Japanese and English as foreign languages both began during his childhood in South Korea and were key factors in his ability to study, live, and work abroad in Japan and progress in his academic career. Over the years, Park has felt a change in the way he thinks and communicates, particularly in Korean and Japanese. He described the experience of using a "mixed language" that he attributes more generally to how Korean people living in Japan have adapted to being bilingual:

Excerpt 3.4

For Korean people in Japan, when we have a conversation, in Japan, we are using Korean and Japanese, mixed Korean and Japanese. It's really easy for us because word order is the same. So, sometimes we cannot… in our daily life we using Japanese more, when we are having conversation with family or friend we are using Korean, so we are using both of them, but those two languages have same word order so it's really easy for mixing. So, sometimes when we have to use only Korean or Japanese, we need time to think about the word or vocabulary, sometimes, but if we can use mixed language, we don't need time for that kind of vocabulary. So the easiest way to have a conversation, mixed language. So I think it's an interesting thing. When I went to Korea, I had to use Korean only, then I sometimes I need to think of Korean word before I say it, so I realized that mixed language is most convenient for me. Some of my friends agree with that.

While Park never felt an affinity toward learning English, he immediately felt a "special feeling" when learning Japanese because it was linguistically more similar to Korean and culturally relevant to his interests in Japanese pop culture (Excerpt 3.1). This special feeling not only led to a long-term interest in learning Japanese and studying and working in Japan but also a feeling that Japanese could more easily be used alongside or mixed with Korean (Excerpt 3.2). Thus, Park was able to integrate Japanese into his linguistic repertoire and language learner identities more easily than he did with English. In fact, Park had an embodied experience of going back to South Korea and realizing that he had difficulty teasing apart his use of Korean and Japanese (Excerpt 3.4). Thus, for Park, Japanese is framed as a foreign language that is in harmony with and feels like a natural part of his personal and professional identities.

3.5.2 Teaching Korean and English

Park's first experience with language teaching (and any teaching in general) was in teaching Korean during the first year of his Master's degree program in Japan, immediately after graduating from college in South Korea. This was also his first year living in Japan. Park attributes his motivation to teach Korean to one of his friends who is of Korean heritage but had lived all her life in Japan:

Excerpt 3.5

A friend was Korean Japanese. Confused about her identity because she was Korean but born in Japan. Can speak Japanese but not Korean. Appearance was Japanese even though she was Korean. She was a foreigner for her whole life in Japan. Went to Korea to find her identity, Korea was her mother country. Even in Korea, she was a foreigner because her appearance was Japanese and she can't speak Korean. So she was really confused about her identity and she talked about that with me so I just thought I want to teach Korean to Korean Japanese who cannot speak Korean but want to speak Korean.

In his first year in Japan, Park found a volunteer teaching position at a non-governmental organization in Tokyo teaching Korean to people of Korean Japanese heritage once a week. Park taught there for one year. The students were taking his class to better understand Korean culture

54 | 3 Exploring Identities and Emotions of a Teacher of Multiple Languages

and their identity. Park described their motivation to learn Korean in this way:

Excerpt 3.6

They just want to know their own mother country. They just want to know more about their mother country, that's all. They didn't study Korean for some score or something, they just wanted to know their own country more.

The students' motivation to learn Korean impacted Park's experience of teaching Korean. Because the students were generally not focused on scores or testing while taking his class, Park felt that they were able to go beyond simply learning Korean:

Excerpt 3.7

It was a good cultural exchange with them. Including language, I exchanged a lot of things with them. What they experienced in Japan for their whole life, and what they were concerned about with their identity. For the languages, education, because they didn't study Korean just for some test, they just really want to know about their mother language, so it's a real different motivation from the people who want to study Korean for the score. It was really . . . I think, a pure motivation I think, we can exchange a lot of things including language or culture or life or something.

In fact, during the clay work session, when asked to show his experience of teaching Korean using clay, Park created a star (see Figure 3.1a). He described teaching Korean as "twinkling" because "every moment in the class was really interesting and really meaningful."

In addition to the students' "pure" motivation to learn Korean, another factor that made teaching Korean a positive experience was that it was a voluntary position, something he had "always wanted to do before coming to Japan" and "not something mandated by anyone." Furthermore, the fact that he was an unpaid, volunteer teacher actually freed him from feeling pressure or fear of making mistakes as a new teacher with no prior teaching experience.

Park decided to stop teaching Korean after one year because he was too busy. As a second-year MA student, he needed more time to write papers and write his thesis. After he completed his MA degree, he enrolled in a

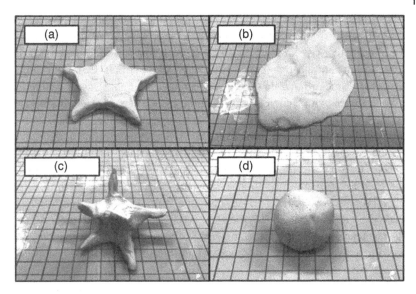

Figure 3.1 (a) "Star," (b) "Flat," (c) "Explosion," and (d) "Ball."

doctorate program in accounting and no longer felt like he had enough time to do volunteer teaching.

Six years later, after completing his doctorate degree, Park obtained a tenure-track teaching position at a university in Japan, where he began teaching English for the first time. Prior to this, Park had never received any English teaching training nor had he even considered the idea of teaching English:

> **Excerpt 3.8**
>
> Actually, teaching language is not what I want. It's duty for me here, but actually I didn't think I would be teaching language in the university. I never thought of that when I was in graduate school. Furthermore, the language I'm teaching is English. I never thought of that.

Thus, Park felt completely unprepared during his first year. However, teaching freshmen university English classes was one of the responsibilities of his new job position. He described the way he felt when he first started teaching English:

> **Excerpt 3.9**
>
> It was really hard for me to make some materials. I just felt guilty because I never taught English, never taught it to people, and I never studied for education and I think my English is not that good to teach someone but it was my duty so I didn't have any choice to just teach it.

To prepare for his English classes, he spent a lot of time studying how to teach English from various websites, YouTube videos, and library books. During the first year of teaching English, Park only slept about two to four hours a day in order to prepare for his classes. Sometimes, Park slept in his arm chair for fear that if he slept in his bed, he would not wake up when his alarm rang. When asked to depict his initial experiences of teaching English in the clay work session, Park molded the clay into a flattened slab, representing the exhaustion he had experienced (see Figure 3.1b). Eventually, Park created a curriculum based on using news articles on cultural topics, such as festivals or cultural customs. His goal was to design a curriculum in which students were using English as a tool to learn more about the world, rather than solely focusing on studying English.

Other ways Park coped with the sudden responsibility of teaching English was to teach the class using Japanese as the medium of instruction and making a disclaimer about his background to his students at the beginning of each semester:

Excerpt 3.10

At the first class, I told my students that my major is not linguistics or English, so I think I cannot teach you English very deeply, but let's use English to learn something else, or some culture or something. So I said I cannot teach you English that much, but let's use English to learn another thing. So they understood what I was saying and they agreed with it so that's why I could keep teaching English so far.

Park's students seemed to respond well to the disclaimer. In fact, after his first year of teaching, Park received an "Excellence in Teaching" award two years in a row from his university, based on end-of-the-semester student evaluations. Park humbly explained that he did not think the award was necessarily a result of the quality of his teaching:

Excerpt 3.11

I was surprised and I think I know the reason because I memorized all the students name in my class and I called them by name. So that's why they thought of me in a good way, because I remember all their names, so they felt like they needed to concentrate on the class more I think. Because if I don't know the name of the student, if they don't concentrate, I don't know who he is, but now I know all of them, so it's a motivation for them to concentrate in class. So, I think it's the reason, I think. I think it's not about the language education things, I think. I made a good relationship with them. That's all. Not about the teaching.

At the time of the interview, six years into teaching English at the same institution, Park was using the same curriculum he had created during his first year of teaching, albeit with some minor updates each year. In reusing the same curriculum each year, Park has mostly "gotten used to teaching English," and more importantly, "I can sleep as much as I want." Park has also continued to use Japanese to teach his English classes and give the same disclaimer as part of his "routine" during the first day of each semester. He expressed that overall, teaching English "is not that big of a problem anymore."

When looking back on his first year of teaching English, Park recalls the feeling of not being able to ask for help or confide in any of the colleagues at his university. He explained that because he was expected to be an English teacher, he thought it would have been "a little weird" if he had asked someone about teaching English. Instead, he "pretended to be an expert for everyone here." The only person he remembered talking to about his difficulties in teaching English was a Swedish friend from a different institution who had majored in English education.

In the six years that he has been teaching at the university in Japan, Park was never given a chance to teach what he actually wanted to teach: Korean or accounting. Park had asked other colleagues if they thought it would be possible for him to teach Korean instead of English, and they thought it would not be possible, given that there were already fewer English teachers than necessary. Furthermore, instead of teaching accounting, he had only taught statistics and research methodology courses for graduate students.

In the clay work session, when asked to depict his current experience as a teacher, Park created a ball of spikes, which he described as an "explosion" (see Figure 3.1c). For Park, the explosion represents the immense stress of juggling multiple roles: English teacher, graduate student supervisor, researcher, husband, and father. In fact, Park was looking forward to 2024 when he will be allowed to take a sabbatical and he hopes life can "calm down" for him.

In contrast to the explosion, when asked to depict hopes and dreams for his future, Park created a smooth ball (see Figure 3.1d). To him, the ball represents the hope for "a perfectly balanced life," an ideal future where he could have enough time to do research, teach classes, and spend time with his family. Park predicts that he will likely continue to have to teach English classes in the near future, though he would love to have the opportunity to teach Korean.

Throughout Park's narratives of teaching Korean and English, Park employs opposing metaphors, with teaching Korean as "harmony" and "natural" and teaching English as "chaos" and "artificial." These metaphorical attitudes toward his language teaching experiences also impacted Park's language teacher identities. Teaching English introduced immense chaos into Park's life, including feeling exhausted from lesson planning (Excerpt 3.9) and isolated from the fear of asking for help from his colleagues. These forms of chaos led him to distance himself from his English teacher identity in various ways. First, Park expressed that teaching English was a "duty" imposed by Park's employer (Excerpt 3.8), a job he had never thought he would be doing (Excerpt 3.8). Second, Park used a disclaimer about his NNS English skills during the first day of his English classes in order to highlight that he did not have the academic qualifications of a "good" English teacher (Excerpt 3.10), effectively distancing himself from traditional expectations of an English teacher and aligning himself with his students as a fellow English learner instead. In keeping his English teacher identity at an arm's length, Park was treating his English teacher self as an artificial "other" detached from his other identities. This was also apparent when Park discredited the "Excellence in Teaching" awards he had received for his first two years of teaching English by insisting that the awards were simply a result of the rapport he had built with students rather than from the quality of his English teaching (Excerpt 3.11).

In contrast, his experiences of teaching Korean were completely different, even though Park began teaching both languages without any formal training. While teaching English was a painful, difficult, and lonely task, teaching Korean was motivating, fulfilling, and community-oriented. Teaching Korean was something that Park was interested in doing, even as a volunteer. Furthermore, teaching Korean involved building relationships with the Korean Japanese community (Excerpt 3.7). Indeed, Park's motivation to teach Korean mirrored the "pure motivation" his Korean students had. Park also adopted the identity of a cultural guide for his students who "just wanted to know their own country more" (Excerpt 3.6). It is no surprise that Park remembers his time teaching Korean as a happy and fulfilling experience, or has he described it in the clay work session: "twinkling" (Figure 3.1a).

3.6 Discussion

3.6.1 Multiple Identities and Emotions as a TML

As language teacher research has shown, becoming a language teacher involves negotiating multiple identities and emotions (Kayi-Aydar, 2015a; Yazan, 2018). For Park, navigating such identities and emotions was further complicated by teaching multiple languages. Transitioning from teaching one language to another not only involves engaging in a different language, pedagogical approaches, and curricula but also possibly engaging in new identities and emotions connected to the new language taught (Ku, 2023). Li and Lai (2022) have described the career transition from teaching one language to another as an opportunity "to construct different meanings for their professional identities, which entailed continuities and discontinuities across first and second-career settings" (p. 11). The discontinuities between Park's transition from teaching Korean to teaching English were apparent in how he described his identities and emotions for each role: from cultural and linguistic expert to imposter, community to isolation, passion to anxiety, respectively. This is in line with findings from previous TML studies that have also shown that part of teaching multiple languages is figuring out how to navigate the discontinuities of nonlinear career trajectories (Fan and de Jong, 2019; Kim and Smith, 2019; Ku, 2023; Mutlu and Ortaçtepe, 2016).

In addition to being a TML, Park was also an "accidental teacher" (Yoshihara, 2018) in that he had never planned on being a language teacher. Therefore, Park's "accidental" career path did not follow a linear path, resulting in teacher identities and emotions that were nonlinear and multifaceted, sometimes even conflicting and a site of inner struggle (Chang, 2018; Kayi-Aydar, 2015b). For Park, teaching Korean was an unexpected opportunity he had stumbled upon and teaching English was a required duty, both of which he has no preparation or professional development in. The major shifts in Park's identities and emotions as he transitioned from teaching Korean to English reflect how previous studies have shown teacher identities and emotions to be nonlinear, dynamic, and inconsistent, constantly adapting to the needs and conditions of changing teaching contexts (Kayi-Aydar, 2015a; Ku, 2020; Yazan, 2018; Yoshihara, 2018).

3.6.2 Race and Ethnicity in Teaching Multiple Languages

While Park did not explicitly mention "race" or "ethnicity" when talking about his experiences as a TML, he did discuss the significance of the cultural and ethnic backgrounds of the Korean Japanese students taking his Korean class. Park explained that one of the factors motivating him to teach Korean was his interest in the experiences of Korean Japanese people and in helping them learn about the Korean language and culture. Furthermore, although he was not Korean Japanese himself, Park was a Korean person who had moved to Japan for his education and career. Thus, Park may have empathized with his students' challenges in navigating the same two cultures and languages. In contrast, with English teaching, Park lacked a sense of cultural expertise and connection with an ethnic community. Previous TML studies have also shown that experiencing strong cultural or ethnic connections when teaching one language over another plays a significant role in language teachers' processes of negotiating and developing TML identities (Kim and Smith, 2019; Ku, 2023; Mutlu and Ortaçtepe, 2016; Tavares, 2022).

In addition, Park expressed conflicting ideologies regarding ethnicity, culture, and language. On the one hand, Park recognized and experienced the diverse and fluid boundaries of ethnicity, culture, and language in his own mixed use of Japanese and Korean as well as the bicultural, bilingual backgrounds of his Korean Japanese students. And yet, Park also expressed monocultural and nationalistic ideologies around language and ethnicity toward himself and his Korean Japanese students. Namely, he seemed certain that, deep down, they were essentially "Korean" and that their "mother country" was Korea. Park repeated this belief several times, which seemed to help him position himself in alignment with his Korean Japanese students. Even when asked whether Park's mixed use of Japanese and Korean might parallel his ethnic identity as a Korean person living long-term in Japan, Park rejected that idea, insisting that he was definitely still Korean. While Park viewed his language use as fluid and dynamic, he approached his and his students' racial and ethnic identity from a binary and singular perspective.

3.7 Reflections on Using Clay Work

From my experience, using clay work with semi-structured interviews from a narrative inquiry approach was an insightful way for the participant to express themselves. While Park was certainly able to verbalize all of his language learning and teaching experiences, his clay work applied different physical states from the material world (e.g. lying flat, explosion) to represent his embodied, emotional experiences of language learning and teaching, re-interpreting thoughts and emotions into a visual form (Bar-On, 2007; Buchanan, 2016). Interestingly, none of the physical states Park conveyed through clay work (e.g. twinkling like a star, a flattened slab) were mentioned during the semi-structured interviews that took place prior to the clay work session. In other words, the clay work session did provide the participant with an alternative medium of expression, and through clay work, the participant did convey his experiences in a novel way in "dialogue" with (Bar-On, 2007) his verbal responses from the semi-structured interviews. I encourage scholars interested in arts-based methods of research to apply clay work in exploring their own areas of inquiry, especially with research that interrogates participant perspectives.

References

Aslan, E. (2015). When the native is also a non-native: "Retrodicting" the complexity of language teacher cognition. *Canadian Modern Language Review, 71*(3), 244–269.

Bar-On, T. (2007). A meeting with clay: individual narratives, self-reflection, and action. *Psychology of Aesthetics, Creativity, and the Arts, 1*(4), 225.

Barkhuizen, G., Benson, P., & Chik, A. (2014). *Narrative inquiry in language teaching and learning research.* Routledge.

Brandão, A. C. L. (2021). First experiences of teaching EFL in metaphors. *Teaching and Teacher Education, 97*, 103214.

Buchanan, F. (2016). Touching on emotions: using clay work in a context of relational empowerment to investigate sensitive issues. In (ed. L. Bryant). *Critical and Creative Research Methodologies in Social Work* (pp. 189–203). Routledge.

Chang, Y. J. (2018). Certified but not qualified? EFL pre-service teachers in liminality. *Journal of Language, Identity & Education, 17*(1), 48–62. https://doi.org/10.1080/15348458.2017.1401929.

Clandinin, D. J. (2016). *Engaging in Narrative Inquiry.* Routledge.

Dickson-Swift, V., James, E. L., Kippen, S., & Liamputtong, P. (2009). Researching sensitive topics: qualitative research as emotion work. *Qualitative Research, 9*(1), 61–79.

DrawingOut. (2022). *DrawingOut.* https://www.drawingout.uk/.

Fan, F., & de Jong, E. J. (2019). Exploring professional identities of nonnative-English-speaking teachers in the United States: a narrative case study. *TESOL Journal, 10*(4), e495.

Gameiro, S., Bliesemann de Guevara, B., El Refaie, E., & Payson, A. (2018). DrawingOut—an innovative drawing workshop method to support the generation and dissemination of research findings. *PLoS One 13*(9), e0203197.

Ibrahim, N. C. (2022). Visual and artefactual approaches in engaging teachers with multilingualism: creating DLCs in pre-service teacher education. *Languages, 7*(2), 152.

Kalaja, P., & Pitkänen-Huhta, A. (2020). Raising awareness of multilingualism as lived—in the context of teaching English as a foreign language. *Language and Intercultural Communication, 20*(4), 340–355.

Kayi-Aydar, H. (2015a). Multiple identities, negotiations, and agency across time and space: a narrative inquiry of a foreign language teacher candidate. *Critical Inquiry in Language Studies, 12*(2), 137–160.

Kayi-Aydar, H. (2015b). Teacher agency, positioning, and English language learners: voices of pre-service classroom teachers. *Teaching and Teacher Education, 45*, 94–103.

Kim, J. -H. (2016). *Understanding Narrative Inquiry: The Crafting and Analysis of Stories as Research*. SAGE Publications.

Kim J., & Smith, H. Y. (2019). Beyond nativeness versus nonnativeness in the construction of teacher identity in the context of Korean as a foreign language. *The Sociolinguistic Journal of Korea, 27*(2), 25–50.

Kramsch, C., & Zhang, L. (2018). *The Multilingual Instructor*. [E-book version]. Oxford University Press. https://global.oup.com/academic/product/the-multilingual-instructor-9780194217378?lang=en&cc=au.

Ku, E. K. (2020). Dear Eric: an autoethnodrama of exploring professional legitimacy as a transnational EFL instructor. In B. Yazan, S. Canagarajah, & R. Jain (Eds.), *Autoethnographies in ELT: Transnational Identities, Pedagogies, and Practices* (pp. 88–106). Routledge.

Ku, E. K. (2023). *Teachers of Multiple Languages: Identities, Beliefs and Emotions*. Multilingual Matters.

Leavy, P. (2020). *Method Meets Art: Arts-based Research Practice*. Guilford Publications.

Li, Z., & Lai, C. (2022). Identity in ESL-CSL career transition: a narrative study of three second-career teachers. *Journal of Language, Identity & Education*, 1–15.

Luo, H., & Gao, P. (2017). A study of Chinese fulbright TAs in the U.S.: implications for second language teacher education. *Journal of the National Council of Less Commonly Taught Languages, 22*, 67–102.

Melo-Pfeifer, S., & Chik, A. (2022). Multimodal linguistic biographies of prospective foreign language teachers in Germany: reconstructing beliefs about languages and multilingual language learning in initial teacher education. *International Journal of Multilingualism, 19*(4), 499–522.

Mutlu, S., & Ortaçtepe, D. (2016). The identity (re)construction of nonnative English teachers stepping into native Turkish teachers' shoes. *Language and Intercultural Communication, 16*(4), 552–569.

Riessman, C. K. (2008). *Narrative Methods for the Human Sciences*. Sage Publications.

Sholt, M., & Gavron, T. (2006). Therapeutic qualities of clay-work in art therapy and psychotherapy: a review. *Art Therapy, 23*(2), 66–72.

Tavares, V. (2022). Teaching two languages: navigating dual identity experiences. *Pedagogies: An International Journal*, 1–22.

Yazan, B. (2018). A conceptual framework to understand language teacher identities. *Journal of Second Language Teacher Education, 1*(1), 21–48.

Yoshihara, R. (2018). Accidental teachers: the journeys of six Japanese women from the corporate workplace into English language teaching. *Journal of Language, Identity & Education, 17*(6), 357–370.

4

Emotional Geographies of Teaching Two Languages: Power, Agency, and Identity

Vander Tavares

Department of Teacher Education and Pedagogy, Faculty of Education, Inland Norway, University of Applied Sciences, Norway

Additional language (L2) education research and practice have struggled to diminish the epistemological and pedagogical influence of monolingualism and native-speakerism in the field. Perspectives anchored in multilingualism and plurilingualism have gained prominence in the last two decades as they seek to move away from such prevailing ideologies. Multilingual and plurilingual pedagogies tend to position teachers' and students' linguistic repertoires as assets for teaching and learning by recognizing, among other aspects, the inextricability of language and identity as well as the synergetic linguistic interaction contextualizing language use in everyday life (Melo-Pfeifer and Schmidt, 2012; Tavares, 2022). Plurilingual pedagogies, in particular, focus on a "holistic view of a speaker's plurilingual competence" (Prasad, 2020, p. 903), in which linguistic and cultural knowledges are integrated, regardless of "proficiency levels within and across languages" (Chen et al., 2022, p. 2). Chen et al. (2022) explained that plurilingualism "validates the long existing social phenomenon of flexible language use as documented in many parts of the world" and makes space in the traditional (English) language classroom to fuse the "social realities [of learners] and language teaching and learning" (p. 2).

Despite the progress made toward plurality and diversity, the experiences of L2 teachers who teach two or more languages have received less attention in the scholarly literature. Exploring the experiences of plurilingual L2 teachers of two languages is important as it can offer insight into how these teachers construct their identities and navigate multiple teaching contexts

---

Language Teacher Identity: Confronting Ideologies of Language, Race, and Ethnicity, First Edition. Edited by Sílvia Melo-Pfeifer and Vander Tavares.
© 2024 John Wiley & Sons Ltd. Published 2024 by John Wiley & Sons Ltd.

where different social, cultural, and political forces are at play. In this chapter, I draw on the conceptual framework of emotional geographies (Hargreaves, 2001) to make sense of and discuss my experiences as a teacher of two languages in Canada: English and Portuguese. Through an autoethnographic approach, I examine the ways in which language ideologies—monolingualism, native-speakerism, and linguistic purism—within each teaching context impacted my sense of self as an L2 teacher and my interactions with the students. The reflections I present foreground the complexity of the L2 teaching profession in relation to questions of power, agency, and identity. This chapter contributes to a better understanding of how L2 teachers emotionally navigate their experiences of teaching two languages. Prior to describing my experiences, I present an overview of research concerning L2 teachers' identity-related experiences.

4.1 L2 Teachers' Experiences: Beyond Ideologies

The socio-political configuration of the context in which L2 teachers work will influence the extent to which language ideologies are sustained and permeate into the teaching profession. Woolard (1998) defined language ideologies as "representations, whether explicit or implicit, that construe the intersection of language and human beings in a social world" (p. 3). As an ideology, monolingualism, for instance, creates a fixed association between one person-language-place (Krulatz et al., 2018), which results in a conflict for those whose identity is defined by plurality and international movement. Native-speakerism positions the native speaker as the most superior linguistic and cultural representative of a particular language (Holliday, 2015). In a similar vein, linguistic purism preserves the belief that a language should remain "pure," when it comes to the "interference" of linguistic content "originating in dialects, sociolects and styles of the same language" (Thomas, 1991, p. 12), leading to policies, discourses, and attitudes that inferiorize or erase linguistic diversity.

Such ideologies have a direct impact on the work and identity of L2 teachers of a transnational and/or translingual background. Notions of "authenticity" and "legitimacy" have been constructed in such a way that marginalizes L2 teachers who learned the language of instruction as an additional language, who are commonly categorized as "non-native" speakers. Yet, the same notions are not tied only to language. Teachers of a racialized background generally encounter challenges that are based on race, ethnicity, and accent, which have nothing to do with the actual competence or qualification of language teachers (Kubota and Fujimoto, 2013). Conversely, social and educational spaces informed by policies and practices that attempt to recognize, promote, and build on cultural and linguistic diversity potentially offer the same teachers better conditions wherein their transnational/translingual identities and pedagogies can be enacted. This sociocultural setup is more supportive for these teachers when we understand that pedagogy and identity cannot be separated from each other (Tavares, 2022).

Gallardo (2019) explained that L2 teachers of a transnational background construct their identities selectively and agentively. She argued that transnational "teachers' sense of self is not fixed by a particular culture or language" (p. 38), as a monolingual/monocultural orientation would prescribe, but rather by a combination of choices made to reflect one's pluralized identity. The same sense of self is true for L2 learners of a plurilingual background, whose daily lives are characterized by hybridity and negotiation. Yanaprasart and Melo-Pfeifer (2021) examined the experiences of non-native, plurilingual L2 teachers working in Geneva and found that "teachers' competences are not evaluated [by students] in terms of being a native or non-native teacher, but instead of as being able to speak one, two or more languages" (p. 201). In this sense, L2 learners may draw on their own lived experiences of plurality to redefine their professional expectations for and stereotypical images of L2 teachers, language learning, and proficiency.

4.2 Understanding Teaching Through Emotional Geographies

Hargreaves (2001) held that "teaching and learning are not only concerned with knowledge, cognition, and skill. They are also *emotional practices*" (p. 1056, italics in original). Whether intentionally or not, teaching emotionally affects both teacher and student as it unfolds within emotional experiences, such as excitement, boredom, or frustration. Even the language used to qualify the performance and behavior of teachers and students is cemented in emotion: a "passionate" teacher and a "resilient" student are some common examples. The colonial and authoritative nature of teaching has contributed to the social distance between teachers and students: teachers are viewed as the ones who know and talk, while students learn and listen. Hargreaves (2001) defined emotional geographies as "the spatial and experiential patterns of closeness and/or distance in human interactions and relationships that help create, configure and color the feelings and emotions we experience about ourselves, our world and each other" (p. 1061).

Emotional geographies in teaching are contextual, simultaneously subjective and objective. This means that closeness and distance are culturally influenced. Relationality and emotionality between teachers and students, parents, and colleagues take on cultural frames that determine one's experience and expression of emotional geographies (Hargreaves, 2001). Furthermore, emotional geographies are both psychological and physical: they transpire within real close/distant physical proximities, but such physical experience is accompanied by the *feeling* of social and emotional proximity one experiences toward another. Put differently, a teacher can be physically distant from a student, but still feel close in terms of emotional and social bonds, or vice versa (Finlayson et al., 2021; Tavares, 2021). Lastly, there is always a certain degree of agency in how teachers do their teaching: it is not just a product of a particular environment, though it is still situated in it. As such, the investment which teachers make into closeness/distance is influenced by the surrounding circumstances, but materialized through the agency of teachers themselves.

Hargreaves (2001) identified five emotional geographies of teaching that are related to *distance*. These are sociocultural, moral, professional, political, and physical distances. This chapter is concerned primarily with distance, rather than closeness, between myself and the students. Thus, it considers the five distances aforementioned, which are explained as follows. The sociocultural distance relates to the experiential and sociological difference that exists between the teacher, the student, and the student's parents, as they belong to different social communities (Dodman et al., 2022). For instance, socioeconomic status, age, location of school/home for both teachers and students, professional background of teachers and parents, and race/ethnicity emerge as some of the factors that can potentially sustain sociocultural distance. The difference between each actor leads to knowledge and experience gaps between them. Consequently, teachers, students, and parents tend to rely on stereotypes and assumptions about one another to fill in the gaps (Tavares, 2020). In so doing, however, the actors only extend the distance between them.

Moral distance "can occur when teachers feel their purposes are being threatened or have been lost" (Hargreaves, 2001, p. 1067). Rather than praise, support, and acknowledgment, teachers are drawn apart by students' and parents' suspicion, questioning, and disapproval in relation to their performance, pedagogy, qualification, expertise, and ensuing decisions. Indeed, students' and parents' confrontation toward pedagogical decisions can affect teachers' sense of professional and personal identity, and a teacher's subsequent interactions with students (Tavares, 2022). However, teachers also learn from constructive, critical feedback. As for professional distance, it is enforced by the complexities and images of teaching as a profession, which continue to evolve today. For example, the devalorization of teaching, increased neoliberalism and bureaucratization, and continuous surveillance of performance impact how teachers teach by modifying the expectations of students and parents upon the teacher. Conflicts arising between teachers, students, and parents in relation to teaching expertise and best teaching practices play a role in maintaining professional distance.

The physical aspect of teaching is also central to how teachers, students, and parents relate to one another. Hargreaves (2001) explained that "emotional understanding and the establishment of emotional bonds . . . require proximity and some measure of intensity, frequency, and continuity in interaction" (p. 1070). On this view, the less teachers meet to interact with students and parents in person, the more distance they tend to experience. Yet, it is not just the physical distance between individuals in an interaction, but also the ways the interaction is physically configured. The setting in which the physical interaction takes place and who stands/sits and talks/listens are interactional components that affect relationship building (Smidekova et al., 2020). Finally, teaching is intwined in politics. This refers to the power relations which teachers navigate in relationship with others and respond to through a variety of emotions. Traditionally, teachers hold more power than students on the basis of how unevenly teacher and student positions have been configured: teachers know everything, and students absorb information (Tavares, 2023a). The same power differential exists between teachers and principals, teachers and parents, and between colleagues. The lack or availability of support from a colleague in an interaction inserted in uneven power relations, as an example, can determine the ways teachers feel at a given moment and increase the distance between them.

Teaching is an emotionally complex experience that changes based on contextual and interpersonal aspects. Put differently, the nature of teaching is not only dynamic but also often unpredictable when it comes to how teachers might feel. Yet, not all emotions experienced are considered appropriate for teachers to express relative to how teachers are expected to behave in order to be considered "good teachers." Teachers engage in emotional work to meet such behavioral expectations, which "means that individuals can either seek to align one's inner feelings to a socially mandated emotional display or *perform* the emotion devoid of authentic feelings" (Finlayson et al., 2021, p. 84, italics in original). In either case, teachers may experience conflict to their sense of self—to their identity. Confronting such expectations within a sociocultural system contextualized by uneven power relations can incur a number of risks for teachers, though there are also rewards. Emotional geographies as a conceptual framework illuminate our understanding of the sources and impacts of distance/closeness on the professional and personal lives of teachers (Hargreaves, 2001).

4.3 Research Design: Autoethnography

Autoethnography continues to gain prominence in L2 education research as the field attempts to address issues of epistemological marginalization. The shift toward social justice requires that diverse voices are heard and critical approaches are used in both research and practice. Autoethnography has been particularly useful in recent years to highlight the challenges faced by language teachers of a transnational and translingual background (e.g. Sánchez-Martín, 2020; Zacharias, 2019) in a field strongly shaped and influenced by ideologies of native-speakerism and monolingualism. Autoethnography works by centering on the self (auto) in order to understand cultural processes and experiences (ethno) through analytical writing (graphy) (Ellis et al., 2011). The focus on the self means that autoethnography embraces subjectivity and emotionality. Put differently, the approach refuses notions of objectivity in research that are based on the supposed ability of researchers to remove themselves from the research.

Since autoethnography includes memory as a source of data, selectivity becomes a central feature of autoethnographic research. Meaningful past experiences are selected by the researcher for they function as sites of analysis (Denzin, 1989). The process of remembering is contextualized by observations and emotions lived through in the past. In addition to memory, other sources of data may include artifacts produced by the researcher prior to the analysis of data, such as notes, interviews, and photographs, which can also be co-constructed between participants. Because the self is centrally embedded in the production, collection, and analysis of data, autoethnographic research relies on reflexivity. Tending to reflexivity entails being aware of one's own position in the world and involvement in the research (Palaganas et al., 2017). Awareness of one's values, beliefs, and goals is important as these subjective aspects influence the ways through which we look back to past experiences with knowledges and practices that change over time.

In interpreting my experiences, I rely on knowledge gained from academic study and lived experiences that are connected to transnationalism and plurilingualism. Yazan et al. (2020) drew attention to the conceptual and experiential "baggage" researchers bring into autoethnography as "they hold the authorial power to recount and analyze their *own* stories in their *own* voice" (Yazan et al., 2020, p. 4, italics in original). This means that any reflection, interpretation, and discussion is interlaced in not only subjectivity but also agency, both of which come into play in terms of how a story is understood and told by the researcher. My academic study is situated in interdisciplinary and critical perspectives on L2 education, which has accompanied my professional experience as a teacher of both English and Portuguese as an L2 as well as my personal experience as a transnational individual to Canada from Brazil. Reflexivity enables the researcher to identify and make their interpretative lenses clear.

4.3.1 Data Collection and Analysis

For this inquiry, I have considered two sources of data: memory and teacher journals. The latter contained notes I wrote in response to observations, self-reflections, and reminders to myself. I wrote notes at my desk, in the classroom, based on observations of students working individually or in groups: the dynamics in play, the questions they raised, the level and kind of engagement they performed (e.g. silence, whispering, debating), and the emotions they expressed (or not) while working on a particular task (e.g. boredom, enthusiasm, excitement). I wrote notes from self-reflections and in the form of reminders typically after a class at my desk or during the commute home. I jotted down notes about how I would approach the teaching of a lesson differently next time, or basically what worked and what did not. Reminders, on the other hand, were related to deadlines, housekeeping items, announcements, and communication with students. In the end, I considered four teacher journals I had used in teaching two courses, English and Portuguese, totaling about 100 pages of content. Working through this content helped me remember, contextualize, and understand how I made sense of my past experiences (Zacharias, 2019).

Indeed, because autoethnography tends to be about past experiences, personal memory occupies a fundamental place in how data is collected. Researchers engage in different activities to access recollections of past experiences. Thinking, reflecting, writing, and dialoguing with a colleague are some of the ways in which data is accessed (Chang, 2008). I made a list of key events I could recall so as to define part of my experiential repertoire in teaching the two languages. I expanded on each event by writing out notes next to them in relation to what happened, why, how, who was involved, and the ways I responded to these events, both emotionally and pedagogically. The analysis of this content, along with the content in the teacher journal, followed a thematic analysis. I manually assigned codes to each sentence, title, or word, while also drawing arrows toward or circling content that spoke to me. To conclude the analysis, I transferred all content to a new list, organized by broader categories (Gbrich, 2007), so I could start reconstructing my experiences. The two languages served as "umbrellas" under which I organized my experiences.

This inquiry reflects my experience of teaching a Portuguese as an L2 course to beginners at a college in a large Canadian city. Though I have taught this course several times, I focus on only one iteration in this autoethnography, which took place within the last 10 years. Twelve adult students were attending the course, most of whom could be considered heritage speakers of Portuguese, whose parents or grandparents had immigrated to Canada from Portugal. Although the course was designed for beginners, these students had diverse forms of previous contact with the language at home, where cultural values and images were also transmitted. Students of a non-heritage background included Canadian-born and international students. The course could be taken as a standalone credit course, which was often the case for students in relationships with Portuguese-speaking nationals, or as a course whose credits would count toward a student's full degree. We met for three hours weekly for a period of four months.

Portuguese is an international language with official status in countries and territories located in South America, Europe, Africa, and Asia. However, the official varieties occupy noticeably different positions within the linguistic hierarchy of Portuguese. The varieties of Portuguese spoken in mainland Portugal remain at the top for a number of political reasons, including colonial power over the former colonies and its association with Europe. Varieties from the Azores are often regarded inferiorly as "rural" or "broken" (Cardoso et al., 2022; Silva, 2015). The largest number of speakers of Portuguese is found in Brazil. Yet, similar to other post-colonial contexts, language (variety) intersects powerfully with ethnicity and race in the country. As such, the "Brazilian variety" is not only reflective of the Brazilian speaker of upper socioeconomic status but also evocative of inferiorizing remarks when race and ethnicity are considered and then juxtaposed with Portuguese from Portugal (Oliveira, 2016). Outside conversations within the Lusophone context, the existence of African varieties is largely forgotten.

The teaching of English took place more frequently given the nature of the course. I taught English daily for about 5 hours each day at a private language school to adult students, aged normally between 18 and 35, who came to Canada to study the language for both professional and academic development. A typical class consisted of 10–15 students from various linguistic, racial, ethnic, and socioeconomic backgrounds. Moreover, I taught the four skills (i.e. reading, writing, listening, speaking) at different levels, which means I had four classes to teach every day to four different groups of students. These were day-time classes, while Portuguese was an evening course. Most instructors at the language school were transnational, plurilingual teachers as well. Thus, the students had contact with diverse varieties of English, which was also their overall experience outside the school, as the school was located in a large, multicultural city in Canada.

4.4 Findings in Stories

4.4.1 Teaching Portuguese as an Additional Language

Portuguese has been interlaced in two historical processes that have impacted its cultural development. First, Portuguese, as with many European languages, was a language of colonization. Second, Portuguese has become a language of recent diasporic movements, including in Canada. Although "Portuguese" is often framed as a single language—as in "I speak Portuguese"—it is socially contextualized broadly through different national varieties. Two varieties have received the most attention: the ones spoken in Portugal and Brazil. In the classroom, this divergence was also evident. On the first day of class, a student of Portuguese heritage raised her hand after I had introduced myself and shared some housekeeping announcements. She asked whether I would be teaching the Portuguese or Brazilian variety. I referenced the Brazilian variety, but while pointing to the textbook, I explained that both varieties were going to be presented whenever an important grammatical difference emerged. This question evoked several others, originating from what appeared to be very personal places for the students. In the next several minutes, we went back and forth in discussing, and to some degree, problematizing, linguistic and cultural differences between the two varieties (Tavares, 2022).

My responses were formulated through a preoccupation to maintain cordial and professional bonds. Put differently, I worked on producing an answer that would avoid creating any distance between me and the students right on the first day. At the same time that I was aware of the tensions arising from the hierarchical differences ascribed to the two varieties in the students' comments, I prioritized student learning by saying that the differences should not be (viewed as) a problem. The students' comments within this conversation framed their parents' way of speaking Portuguese as the point of departure for their beliefs and opinions. Aiming to pause this discussion for the time-being, I decided on a break. Shortly after, a student left her desk and approached me to communicate her decision to leave the course. Surprised, I asked her why. She responded that she was interested in learning the Mozambican variety of Portuguese due to her upcoming trip to Mozambique. I attempted to hold her interest in the course by explaining that the course could still be beneficial for her in many ways, including in providing a grammatical foundation for the language. Her decision, however, was conclusive, as she put on her backpack, reinforced her desire to learn that specific variety, and finally, left the room.

Maintaining my sense of authenticity was an emotional challenge, not only in that particular moment but also through the next several days. I felt disappointed, frustrated, and worried that the student could not believe in me, as a language teacher, and by extension, my knowledge and pedagogy, when I proposed that she could still learn something from me/my course. It was as if I, as a speaker of a variety other than the Mozambican, could not offer *any* relevant knowledge to that student, who seemed to espouse a monolingual, native-speakerist preference (Krulatz et al., 2018) for learning Portuguese. This was also a matter of identity, for identity is enacted/denied in micro-interactions. With the departure of that student, the preference for the Portuguese variety gained momentum. Fewer than a handful of students had stated the desire to learn the Brazilian variety. Additionally, students in this latter group were more indifferent to the differences in the language. Such a position resulted from their more recent and superficial exposure to the language, especially since their contact with the language was not mediated through previous generations.

Within this context, I began to view the class as two groups of students, with different sets of expectations upon me. One group was very much invested in how and what variety was taught—these were the students of Portuguese heritage. The other group was considerably less interested in the linguistic differences. I felt as though the stakes were always higher with the first group, which led me to (over)think the planning and delivery of the course. In the several classes that followed the introductory class, I sensed that I had control over the dynamic of the course: I always felt (over)prepared, including by anticipating what kinds of questions students might have in relation to the content in focus in any particular class. After marking and returning the first test to students, however, an unexpected situation emerged. A student brought her test back the next class with comments made by her mother, who was a native speaker of Portuguese, in the margins. The student came over to my desk and questioned my assessment. The student explained that, according to her mother, the responses she provided on the test should have been marked as correct. I carefully explained why they were wrong, which was not a matter of variety. Still, the student embodied disbelief and dissatisfaction once I refused to change my assessment, and therefore, her grade.

The tension resulting from that interaction caused a certain distance between me and that student for the rest of the term. On a certain level, I knew she remained unhappy with the outcome and resistant to my decision. My conversations with her after that day were always enwrapped in caution. Despite my attempts, the distance between us widened in another lesson whose topic was the cuisine of Portuguese-speaking countries. A page of the textbook included a photograph of *churrasco*, the Brazilian-style barbecue where thick cuts of meat are grilled in swords. However, as a vegetarian, I did not "promote" the dish in the classroom as my beliefs about animal welfare were more individually important to me than a collective, cultural practice. The same student made an unserious remark about whether I should be teaching the course at all. In her eyes, I could not be an authentic teacher and speaker of Portuguese if I did not proudly embrace that food-related cultural practice. Though I did not give it too much thought once the class was over, I realized that a static, and perhaps stereotyped, cultural identity was still expected of myself.

One of the lessons in the final month of the course revolved around the immigration of Portuguese-speaking peoples. I identified this lesson as an opportunity to initiate discussions and reflections about transnationalism, plurality, and diversity. As part of the teaching, I asked students to reflect on the history of movements of their own families. For me, approaching this lesson in such a manner was an act of agency, for I hoped to evoke in the students similar engagements with plurilingual and translingual identities that I had. Kayi-Aydar et al. (2019) affirmed that teacher agency is also "located in dialogic relationships with institutions, learners and other key stakeholders" (p. 1). I specifically asked students to think about aspects of their lives that could possibly reflect affiliation to more than one culture. One student raised her hand and responded that she was born in Canada to Portuguese parents, and though she spoke Portuguese, she "spoke it with an accent." Another student, who immigrated to Canada from Eastern Europe and married a Portuguese national, explained that she loved it that in her home, "everything was a combination of languages and cultures." I concluded the lesson by connecting the students' experiences to mine as an attempt to approximate us. In retrospect, I believe this activity had a productive outcome.

4.4.2 Teaching English as a Second Language

At the English as a Second Language (ESL) school, my teaching experience was considerably different when it came to students' images, expectations, and experiences with the English language. Many of the students lived with host families who also spoke English as an additional language. Administrative and teaching staff at the school were not only plurilingual but some also transnational to Canada. This sociocultural context was, in my view, essential for how positively the students perceived their teachers. The archetypal native speaker of English was almost mythical in the midst of such linguistic diversity, both within and outside the classroom. In fact, the students reported interacting daily with others who spoke English as an additional language outside the classroom in their service encounters at places such as a bank, restaurant, subway station, or shopping mall. Unlike in the Portuguese course, these students did not hold "heritage" ties to English.

The reasons behind some of the distance I experienced were thus unrelated to linguistic or cultural divergence. Rather, the logistical configuration of teaching played an important part in sustaining distance. Every day, teachers rotated around different classes. For a semester, for instance, I would teach four different groups of students at different levels of proficiency. The classes with each individual group were for one of the basic skills. As such, I only spent close to an hour a day with the same class. Teaching was also designed in a way that prioritized methods conducive to that particular skill—listening, reading, and writing classes required less oral participation from students. The last class of the day focused on the development of speaking skills and involved conversational peer interaction around a range of themes. Despite the design, I felt as though the length of time the students studied at the school was the greatest barrier to connecting with them.

The courses at the school were organized around month-long curricula. In other words, a course began on the first day of a month and ended on the last. Based on this organization, students could study for as short as one month and receive a certificate relative to that time. While I met the students every day, it was challenging to feel close to those students who would come for only one month, which was often the case with students from South America who came during their holiday month. Students from Asia tended to stay much longer: around six months. Naturally, the more consistent and prolonged amount of time spent with these students afforded me the chance to get to know them better. Getting to know the students on a more personal level was difficult in general since the school had a set curriculum that all teachers were expected to follow. For a student to move on to the next month's course, they depended entirely on passing the tests associated with the month they were in, which resulted in great pressure for all involved.

The month-long course arrangement influenced the expectations of some of the students in relation to language proficiency. Many of the students expected me, as their teacher, to help them develop "full fluency" in English in one month. Though they would not reference sounding like a "native speaker," they still voiced a strong desire to finish the course with a kind of fluency that was impossible to actually develop in thirty days. There were instances when a student and I would experience emotional distance because of our clashes in this regard. I recall an episode when a student complained to me that he was improving linguistically in all of the other teachers' courses, but not mine. I felt as though my professional ability and teacher identity were questioned again, although at a deeper level, I would choose to not give this tension too much attention. Yet, since I could not change that student's way of thinking, our mutual distrust meant that I always experienced a certain distance from him, despite being close to and in the same space with him every day.

I found much support in the other nearly two dozen teachers teaching daily at the ESL school, who had similar experiences to mine. Discussing these challenges and experiences with colleagues not only brought us closer but also served to validate some of the choices I would make as a teacher in how to respond to a particular situation or student. The ESL teachers were evaluated through formal observations by the school management and through student feedback, which affected the extent to which I would feel comfortable to embody some emotions and behaviors toward the students, despite the support received from colleagues. Feedback from both management and students was considered final and included in each teacher's file. Therefore, the stakes were high, but also because a student could begin their studies on the first day of the month and write an evaluation of me by the last, differently from students studying for a longer sojourn, with whom I would then have the opportunity to build better relationships. This led me to often engage in what Finlayson et al. (2021) called a performance of emotions: one meant to adhere my teacher emotions to the socially and professionally accepted.

4.5 Discussion and Conclusion

While the emotional experiences of L2 teachers continue to be examined extensively in the literature, such knowledge overwhelmingly reflects the experiences of teachers of one language. This chapter focused on my experiences as a teacher of two languages from a perspective of emotional geographies, which I now bring into context for analysis. L2 education is directly influenced by the sociopolitical environment of where it takes place (Tavares, 2023b; Yanaprasart and Melo-Pfeifer, 2021), in addition to factors stemming from global, broader processes. I have described the sociopolitical environment of my teaching primarily in its connection to sustaining/challenging language ideologies. Since English and Portuguese hold considerably different places in the Canadian sociolinguistic landscape (Cardoso and Tavares, 2020), a teacher teaching these two languages would encounter and navigate distinct experiences within each teaching context. In the Portuguese course, most students tended to be heritage learners and therefore engaged with the language predominantly in more ideological ways, especially when compared to how the students at the ESL school approached the teaching of English.

Emotional geographies help contextualize why teachers feel the way they do in interactions and relationships with others (Hargreaves, 2001). In such interpersonal engagements, patterns of emotional distance and closeness gain shape within different kinds of geographies. In teaching both languages, I experienced moral and professional distance toward students when my professional expertise and role as a teacher were questioned or rejected by the students, or as in one case, by a student's parent. As a result, feelings of worry, anxiety, and frustration led me to overact and reconsider my identity as an individual and a teacher. This distance I experienced demonstrates that the (language) teaching profession still faces systematic issues of inferiorization (e.g. Gu and Day, 2013; Gutiérrez, 2000). For instance, the belief that teachers do not know *enough* in their pedagogical choices or the expectation that teachers are responsible for students' linguistic development caused me not only distance toward students but also identity conflict. However, identity conflict is not the result of only *being a teacher*, but being a teacher with a particular social identity, which I explain below.

A considerable sociological distance prevailed between me and some of the students in the Portuguese course. This had to do with the linguistic, cultural, social, and political differences—both real and imagined—between the varieties we spoke (Brazilian and Portuguese) and sought out (Mozambican, by one student). Additionally, there was a sociological difference in being either a local or transnational individual. Within the construction of the local, being (or not) a heritage speaker of Portuguese also came into play. I understood this sociological distance to be the product of language ideologies. A monolingual perspective framed me as inadequate to teach (from) one variety to those who spoke another. For one student, the impact was such that she left the course. Linguistic purism also assigns hierarchical value to different varieties: these will vary from purest to least pure (see Melo-Pfeifer, 2016). Varieties that emerged through colonization, such as the Brazilian and Mozambican, are often viewed inferiorly (Silva, 2012). These ideologies also make their way into the language classroom through a variety of mechanisms and reproduce hierarchical relationships that cause distance between teachers and students.

Conversely, the social context of the ESL school was more conducive to a multilingual, multicultural experience. An expectation to sound like a particular speaker was never explicitly in place for me, though it likely still existed for some students. Therefore, the sociological gap enforced by dichotomies such as local/transnational, native/nonnative, and monolingual/plurilingual was not a factor that could have compromised the sense of closeness the students and I developed with one another. However, on some occasions, I still felt socially distant from students, despite being in direct contact with them consistently (daily and for at least one hour) and physically (same classroom). Such a distance was mediated logistically and the product of the need to fulfill curricular mandates, follow tight schedules, also and especially meet the expectations of administrators in their promise to students of quick linguistic development, though potentially at the cost of teacher–student relationships. Thus, as a teacher of two languages, emotional geographies helped me identify which patterns contributed to my experiences of distance in each teaching context.

Teaching two languages was an emotionally challenging experience circumscribed by ideologies and expectations that resulted in feelings of distance. Yet, teachers are never merely a product of the sociocultural environment, stripped of emotion, power, or agency. Agency, in particular, is contextually enacted in relation to calculating risk or reward. In both contexts, I found myself performing an emotion in order to meet the expectations of students and administrators. Although such performance is not unique to L2 teaching, but rather to the teaching profession in general, it is a form of agency that embodies the teacher's identity and combines the processes of feeling, thinking, and decision-making, even if the outcome is not the one initially hoped-for. The study of emotions in L2 teacher education enables teachers and teacher candidates to critically examine their own practice in relation to their relationships with others and their social positioning in contexts defined by power relations. Emotional geographies are one conceptual means by which such critical examination and self-reflection can occur. In juxtaposing the experiences of teaching two languages, emotional geographies help reveal common and divergent patterns.

Teacher education programs have been called upon to promote better and (more) critical opportunities for prospective teachers to reflect on their practice. This chapter contributes to strengthening the importance of systematic self-study that focuses on emotions as a site of professional development and identity construction for language teachers. For teachers of two languages more exclusively, certain types of interactions with students might be a source of enjoyment in one context, but of tension in another. Emphasis on language ideologies as something that manifests differently across teaching contexts is important for teachers of two languages to be able to identify the complex ways in which their professional identities might be threatened or accepted by students' attitudes to language (pedagogy) in interaction with them. Lastly, this chapter reveals some of the possible intricacies of teaching two languages when one is specifically a heritage language. Teacher education programs should therefore also equip prospective teachers to understand the additional layers of working with heritage language learners, precisely so when the variety of the heritage community differs from that which the teacher speaks.

References

Cardoso, I., & Tavares, V. (Eds.). (2020). *Teaching and Learning Portuguese in Canada: Multidisciplinary Contributions to SLA Research and Practice.* Boa Vista Press.

Cardoso, I., Tavares, V., & Graça, L. (2022). Língua portuguesa no Canadá: Das dinâmicas comunitárias às experiências identitárias. In F. C. del Olmo, S. Melo-Pfeifer, & S. Souza (Eds.), *Português Língua não materna: Contextos, estatutos e práticas de ensino numa visão crítica* (pp. 53–75). University of Porto Press.

Chang, H. (2008). *Autoethnography as Method.* Walnut Creek, CA: Left Coast Press.

Chen, L., Karas, M., Shalizar, M., & Piccardo, E. (2022). From "promising controversies" to negotiated practices: a research synthesis of plurilingual pedagogy in global contexts. *TESL Canada Journal, 38*(2), 1–35.

Denzin, N. K. (1989). *Interpretative Biography.* Thousand Oaks, CA: Sage.

Dodman, M. J., Cardoso, I., & Tavares, V. (2022). Communicating and understanding the other through experiential education: Portuguese language and culture in Toronto. In F. Carra-Salsberg, M. Figueredo, & M. Jeon (Eds.), *Curriculum Design and Praxis in Language Teaching: A Globally Informed Approach* (pp. 131–143). Toronto, Canada: University of Toronto Press.

Ellis, C., Adams, T. E., & Bochner, A. P. (2011). Autoethnography: an overview. *Historical Social Research/Historische Sozialforschung*, 273–290.

Finlayson, E., Whiting, E., & Cutri, R. M. (2021). 'Will this build me or break me?': the embodied emotional work of a teacher candidate. *Studying Teacher Education, 17*(1), 82–99.

Gallardo, M. (2019). Transcultural voices: exploring notions of identity in transnational language teachers' personal narratives. In M. Gallardo (Ed.), *Negotiating Identity in Modern Foreign Language Teaching* (pp. 17–43). Palgrave Macmillan, Cham.

Gbrich, C. (2007). *Qualitative Data Analysis: An Introduction.* Thousand Oaks, CA: Sage.

Gu, Q., & Day, C. (2013). Challenges to teacher resilience: conditions count. *British Educational Research Journal, 39*(1), 22–44.

Gutiérrez, K. (2000). Teaching and learning in the 21st century. *English Education, 32*(4), 290–298.

Hargreaves, A. (2001). Emotional geographies of teaching. *Teachers College Record, 103*(6), 1056–1080.

Holliday, A. (2015). Native-speakerism: taking the concept forward and achieving cultural belief. In A. Holliday, P. Aboshiha & A. Swan (Eds.), *(En)Countering Native-Speakerism: Global Perspectives* (pp. 11–25). Palgrave MacMillan.

Kayi-Aydar, H., Gao, X. A., Miller, E. R., Varghese, M., & Vitanova, G. (Eds.). (2019). *Theorizing and Analyzing Language Teacher Agency.* Multilingual Matters.

Krulatz, A., Steen-Olsen, T., & Torgersen, E. (2018). Towards critical cultural and linguistic awareness in language classrooms in Norway: fostering respect for diversity through identity texts. *Language Teaching Research, 22,* 552–569.

Kubota, R., & Fujimoto, D. (2013). Racialized native speakers: voices of Japanese American English language professionals. In S. A. Houghton, & D. J. Rivers (Eds.), *Native-Speakerism in Japan* (pp. 196–206). London, UK: Multilingual Matters.

Melo-Pfeifer, S. (2016). Public understanding of linguistic planning and national speakers' linguistic rights: a case study on the orthographic reform debate in Portugal. *Language in Society, 45*(3), 423–443.

Melo-Pfeifer, S., & Schmidt, A. (2012). Linking "heritage language" education and plurilingual repertoires development: evidences from drawings of Portuguese pupils in Germany. *L1–Educational Studies in Language and Literature, 12,* 1–30.

Oliveira, L. A. (2016). Desconstruindo três mitos persistentes sobre a língua portuguesa. *Porto das Letras, 2*(1), 22–36.

Palaganas, E. C., Sanchez, M. C., Molintas, M. P., & Caricativo, R. D. (2017). Reflexivity in qualitative research: a journey of learning. *The Qualitative Report, 22*(2), 426–438. https://doi.org/10.46743/2160-3715/2017.2552.

Prasad, G. (2020). 'How does it look and feel to be plurilingual?': analysing children's representations of plurilingualism through collage. *International Journal of Bilingual Education and Bilingualism, 23*(8), 902–924.

Sánchez-Martín, C. (2020). Critical autoethnography in TESOL teacher education: a translingual and cultural historical activity theory perspective for transnational spaces. In O. Z. Barnawi, & A. Ahmed (Eds.), *TESOL Teacher Education in a Transnational World: Turning Challenges into Innovative Prospects* (pp. 105–118). New York, NY: Routledge.

Silva, E. (2012). Making and masking difference: multiculturalism and sociolinguistic tensions in Toronto's Portuguese-Canadian market. *Portuguese Studies Review, 20*(2), 59–78.

Silva, E. (2015). Humor (re)positioning ethnolinguistic ideologies: "You tink is funny?". *Language in Society, 44*(2), 187–212.

Smidekova, Z., Janik, M., Minarikova, E., & Holmqvist, K. (2020). Teachers' gaze over space and time in a real-world classroom. *Journal of Eye Movement Research, 13*(4), 1–20.

Tavares, V. (2020). Challenging cultural stereotypes in the pluricentric Portuguese as a foreign language classroom. In I. Cardoso, & V. Tavares (Eds.), *Teaching and Learning Portuguese in Canada: Multidisciplinary Contributions to SLA Research and Practice* (pp. 164–186). Roosevelt, NJ: Boa Vista Press.

Tavares, V. (2021). *International Students in Higher Education: Language, Identity, and Experience from a Holistic Perspective*. Lanham, MD: Rowman & Littlefield.

Tavares, V. (2022). Teaching two languages: navigating dual identity experiences. *Pedagogies: An International Journal 18*(3), 497–518. https://doi.org/10.1080/1554480X.2022.2065996.

Tavares, V. (2023a). A century of Paulo Freire: problem-solving education, conscientização, dialogue and TESL from a Freirean perspective. In V. Tavares (Ed.), *Social Justice, Decoloniality, and Southern Epistemologies Within Language Education: Theories, Knowledges, and Practices on TESOL from Brazil*. New York, NY: Routledge.

Tavares, V. (Ed.). (2023b). *Social Justice, Decoloniality, and Southern Epistemologies Within Language Education: Theories, Knowledges, and Practices on TESOL from Brazil*. New York, NY: Routledge.

Thomas, G. (1991). *Linguistic Purism*. Longman.

Woolard, K. (1998). Introduction: language ideology as a field of inquiry. In B. Schieffelin, K. Woolard, & P. Kroskrity (Eds.), *Language Ideologies* (pp. 3–47). Oxford University.

Yanaprasart, P., & Melo-Pfeifer, S. (2021). Students' perceptions of plurilingual nonnative teachers in higher education: an added or a mudded value? In J. Pinto, & N. Alexandre (Eds.), *Multilingualism and Third Language Acquisition: Learning and Teaching Trends* (pp. 185–206). Language Science Press. https://doi.org/10.5281/zenodo.4449784.

Yazan, B., Canagarajah, S., & Jain, R. (2020). *Autoethnographies in ELT: Transnational Identities, Pedagogies, and Practices*. New York, NY: Routledge.

Zacharias, N. T. (2019). The ghost of native speakerism: the case of teacher classroom introductions in transnational contexts. *TESOL Journal, 10*(4) e499. https://doi.org/10.1002/tesj.499.

5

Teaching Languages in the Linguistic Marketplace: Exploring the Impact of Policies and Ideologies on My Teacher Identity Development

Jonas Yassin Iversen

Faculty of Education, Inland Norway University of Applied Sciences, Norway

5.1 Introduction

Though language teachers' identities have been extensively researched (Kayi-Aydar, 2019; Swearingen, 2019; Yuan, 2019), limited research has been conducted on teachers teaching more than one language (for some exceptions, see Ku, 2023; Tavares, 2022; also Melo-Pfeifer & Tavares, 2024). The present chapter contributes to this literature with an autoethnographic presentation of my experience as a teacher of English, Norwegian, and Spanish in Norway, teaching in the "linguistic marketplace," where languages are commodified and valued according to demand (Block and Cameron, 2002; Blommaert, 2010; Bourdieu, 1991). The guiding question for this paper is how different language ideologies within each teaching context impacted my overall language teacher identity development, as I attempted to implement multilingual teaching approaches within the three teaching settings.

I was born and raised in Norway and grew up speaking Norwegian at home. I am currently a teacher educator, having previously completed a teacher education program through which I became qualified to teach English, Norwegian, and Spanish. As part of my formal Spanish language training, I studied Spanish as a one-year study abroad and later completed a master's degree in English and modern language teaching. My studies introduced me to multilingual approaches to language teaching and learning, and what I was reading convinced me that all forms of language learning

---

Language Teacher Identity: Confronting Ideologies of Language, Race, and Ethnicity,
First Edition. Edited by Sílvia Melo-Pfeifer and Vander Tavares.
© 2024 John Wiley & Sons Ltd. Published 2024 by John Wiley & Sons Ltd.

should be built on students' linguistic resources (e.g. Cenoz, 2009; Cummins, 2000; García, 2009) and that language learning can promote cross-cultural awareness and critical understanding (Byram, 2008; Kramsch, 1993). During my master's studies, I taught Spanish as a second modern language at a lower secondary school. When I graduated, I was hired to teach English and Norwegian to newly arrived students [i.e. students who had recently moved to Norway and were in the process of acquiring Norwegian (and for some students, English) for the first time in order to continue their education in Norway].

The experience of teaching different languages in different contexts opened my eyes to the commodification of languages in the linguistic marketplace (Block and Cameron, 2002; Blommaert, 2010; Bourdieu, 1991). Through my teaching practice, I encountered English as a language of "high prestige" to newly arrived migrant and refugee students in Norway. I also experienced Norwegian as a language of "necessity" and for social mobility to (the same) newly arrived students, and Spanish as a language of "convenience" in the modern language, lower secondary context. This chapter examines how the conflicting expectations and demands that teachers of different languages encounter can influence their teacher identity and offers insights into how to better prepare language teachers for multilingual language classrooms through language teacher education programs.

In what follows, I first describe the Norwegian context of language teaching, before briefly introducing the concept of the linguistic marketplace, followed by a discussion on the concept of teacher identity and teacher agency. Next, I describe my approach to autoethnography. Following this, I explore the impact that language ideologies influencing the three contexts of language teaching had on my teacher identity development, as I attempted to implement multilingual teaching approaches within a monolingual curriculum. Finally, I provide some concluding remarks in which I discuss the implications for modern language teacher education.

5.2 Language Teaching in Norway

Norwegian is the medium of instruction in primary and secondary education, as well as the dominant language in higher education in Norway. A recent government proposition for a new Education Act included an assertion of the status of Norwegian as the main language of instruction throughout the education system in Norway, in line with the Norwegian

Language Act's emphasis on Norwegian language as the primary national language. Nevertheless, English has a prominent position within the education system as a mandatory subject for all students from the first grade of primary schools to the tenth grade of lower secondary schools. Furthermore, students are required to study English for a minimum of one year in upper secondary schools. Most English teachers in Norway are non-native speakers of English (Calafato, 2021). Since Norwegian is a relatively "small" language, with approximately 5,500,000 speakers, it is common for students in higher education to be dependent on an extensive amount of literature written in English (and other Scandinavian languages).

Students who move to Norway without any previous knowledge of Norwegian (or another Scandinavian language) are required to learn Norwegian to follow ordinary education. To facilitate the acquisition of Norwegian and swift mainstreaming of newly arrived students, several provisions are in place. The students have the right to instruction in basic Norwegian and the so-called bilingual subject instruction and mother tongue instruction during the period of transition into the Norwegian education system. After this transition period, the students are still entitled to additional support in the Norwegian language subject. There are different models of organizing the introduction to Norwegian education, and individual municipalities can choose which model they prefer (Dewilde and Kulbrandstad, 2016). In many municipalities, the so-called introductory program is organized into separate or sheltered schools or departments before the students are transferred to their local school or an ordinary class within the school. Other municipalities prefer an immersion approach, where students are immediately included in an ordinary class, with the instructions in basic Norwegian and other provisions offered as pull-out instructions (Dewilde and Kulbrandstad, 2016).

In a lower secondary school, all students can choose to study a second modern language (formally described as a "foreign language," as opposed to English, which is only referred to as "English"). French, German, and Spanish dominate the field of second modern language teaching in Norway. However, Italian, Mandarin, and Russian are also among the 14 different languages schools across Norway offer as a second modern language (Norwegian Directorate for Education and Training, 2022). Although it is not required to study a second modern language, the students will later not qualify for university admission unless they have completed an intermediate course in a second modern language in an upper secondary school. Hence, the study of a second modern language is, in effect, a requirement to access higher education in Norway, and most students in lower secondary schools do, in fact, choose to study a second modern language (in 2022, 74% of students in lower secondary schools did so). In Norway, most modern language teachers are non-native speakers of the languages they teach (Calafato, 2021). In upper secondary, students can choose not to follow classes in a second modern language in school and instead opt to take a written exam at an intermediate level in one of the 22 languages offered (Norwegian Directorate for Education and Training, 2022). This list of languages includes many languages spoken by students with migrant backgrounds. Hence, students can fulfill the second modern language requirement for higher education through an exam in their family's heritage language (e.g. Amharic, Estonian, Filipino, Hebrew, or Tamil).

There is a clear hierarchy of languages within Norwegian education (Iversen, 2021), from the primary national language, Norwegian, and the mandatory, international language of high prestige, English, through other prestigious modern languages students can study in school, to less prestigious languages they can choose to study on their own, and then take an exam. Beyond the 22 languages offered for such exams, approximately 300 other languages spoken in Norway have no recognition within the education system (Kulbrandstad, 2020). Rather, different models for introducing newly arrived students to Norwegian education all aim for a swift mainstreaming of students into Norwegian-medium education. This hierarchy is re-enforced and re-enacted every day in the linguistic marketplace.

5.3 The Linguistic Marketplace

To analyze how my teacher identity was shaped by the conflicting expectations and demands that teachers of different languages encounter, I draw on Bourdieu's theory of the economy of symbolic exchanges (Bourdieu, 1991, p. 37). Bourdieu distinguished among three forms of capital: economic, cultural, and social. Linguistic capital lies at the core of cultural capital (Bourdieu, 1987). Bourdieu (1977, 1987) described, at length, how linguistic capital is converted through the linguistic marketplace into the material marketplace and how linguistic practice acquires an economic value (Bourdieu, 1991, p. 69). This happens when, for example, the cultural capital associated with speaking French (also linguistic capital) lands you a prestigious job in trade or diplomacy, which leads to economic capital. This commodification of language resources is a key

5 Teaching Languages in the Linguistic Marketplace

component of Bourdieu's theory of the economy of symbolic power. Bourdieu (1991) explained,

> Linguistic exchange (. . .) is also an economic exchange which is established within a particular symbolic relation of power between a producer, endowed with a certain linguistic capital, and a consumer (or a market), and which is capable of producing a certain material or symbolic profit. (p. 66)

In other instances, Bourdieu (1993) also used "game" and "field" to describe how something acquires a particular value according to specific rules. According to Bourdieu (1984, 1991), to have the opportunity for upward social mobility, one needs to demonstrate command of the linguistic practices valued in the particular market, game, or field. Bourdieu (1991) explained that specific markets operate according to their own logics. For example, the value of Norwegian language skills within Norwegian education is much higher than that in the global market of linguistic and communicative resources. This value is clearly related to the *symbolic* value of Norwegian within Norwegian society and because of the *material* value of Norwegian language skills within the material market of Norwegian society. Del Percio et al. (2017, p. 56) claimed that

> The price that a specific linguistic practice acquires in a given market depends on the capacity of the speaker to be recognized as an agent able to produce a form of speech that, within the said market, is considered the most prestigious.

Del Percio et al. (2017) indicated that the linguistic marketplace continues to operate according to particular local rules. Despite the international forces of globalization, this process has not transformed the world into a single village but rather a network of villages, with their own rules and codes (Blommaert, 2010, p. 23). Locality is, in other words, still highly relevant. Within the education system, there are numerous factors that can potentially contribute to the rise in the value of particular language resources. When a given language becomes mandatory to qualify for higher education, its value increases.

Although some researchers have criticized Bourdieu's conceptualization of the linguistic marketplace in strictly economic terms as oversimplified (e.g. Irvine, 1989), the ideological hierarchization of different language resources within a given society is widely accepted. This is a well-known process, which has been described by sociolinguists in various ways, such as a process of "linguistic differentiation" (Irvine and Gal, 2000), and the result of such a differentiation process has been described as the "hierarchy of prestige" (Liddicoat, 2013), "sociolinguistic hierarchies" (McNamara, 2019, p. 114) and, by Bourdieu himself, as a "hierarchy of languages" (Bourdieu, 1991, p. 68).

5.4 A Poststructuralist Perspective on Teacher Identity

Teacher identity "provides a framework for teachers to construct their own ideas of 'how to be', 'how to act' and 'how to understand' their work and place in society" (Sachs, 2005, p. 15). As such, teacher identity "bring[s] together the social memberships and identities one enjoys outside the teaching profession to inform one's professional practice" (Canagarajah, 2017, p. 70). The social memberships and identities we enjoy outside the teaching profession are always influenced by the language ideologies of the particular context within which the teacher operates. As this volume illustrates, there are multiple ways of conceptualizing identity (see Introduction to the volume). In what follows, I explain the conceptualization of identity used in this paper and provide a brief overview of the key research regarding language teacher identities.

Within poststructuralist thinking, the term *subjectivity* has frequently been used to emphasize social mediation in identity formation, involving discourse and power (see, for example, Foucault, 1978). Even though the reality is described through discourse, discourse also produces reality (e.g. Foucault, 1981). Thus, I concur with McNamara (2019) in his argument that "although subjectivity is powerfully experienced as a private feeling, something lying deep inside us, its origins lie outside us, in the social world and in the discourses that circulate within it" (p. 1). Our personal subjectivity or subject position is the result of the discourse that surrounds us (McNamara, 2019). McNamara (2019) defined subject positions as "possibilities for subjectivity, possibilities for being recognized as a certain kind of subject" (p. 10). Furthermore, he described how subjects are called into being whenever they are assigned a certain subject position by others. Consequently, we come to see ourselves as we are seen by others. This is why subjectivity is also the result of power, insofar as the way other people call us into being or how they assign us to particular subject positions is an exercise of power.

Also writing from a poststructuralist perspective, Botsis (2018) distinguished between *identity* and *subject position* and defined the former as "an articulation of momentary fixedness in a sea of change, that is, contextual and interactional, as opposed to 'authentic'" (p. 19). Thus, Botsis acknowledged the subjective experience of an identity while recognizing the contextual, interactional, and fluid nature of the articulated identity. Following Botsis (2018), this paper applies "identity" to describe the momentary articulation of my identity at different points in time while highlighting how this identity was in constant flux, influenced by the forces of the linguistic marketplace. In my analysis, I draw attention to how teachers' identities are governed by subject positions available within the given linguistic marketplace, for example, at a specific school. These subject positions are constructed through discourse (McNamara, 2019).

When individuals refuse to conform to the predefined subject position, they are considered eccentric or outsiders by their community and culture (Baxter, 2016). Schools are brimming with discourses regulating both students' and teachers' behaviors. Although the conceptualization of a "good student" or a "good teacher" might vary somewhat from one school to the other, the local conceptualizations of the "good teacher" are highly influenced by larger discourses in society about how a "good teacher" behaves. The degree to which individuals refuse to conform to the predefined subject position is linked to an individual's agency. Agency can be defined as "a measure of individual awareness or control over the means by which subjects are 'interpellated' or called into existence" (Baxter, 2016, p. 38). An individual's degree of agency is neither constant nor stable. Rather, Baxter (2016) indicated that individuals are positioned "in relations of power that are constantly shifting, rendering them at times powerful and at other times powerless" (p. 39). Researchers have pointed out that a clear understanding of one's teacher identity can lead to a sense of agency and empowerment (Beauchamp and Thomas, 2009).

Although researchers have confirmed that teacher identities are constantly evolving and shifting according to context (Beauchamp and Thomas, 2009; Kayi-Aydar, 2019; Song, 2016), they have also indicated that the transition from teacher education to teaching can be a particularly destabilizing time in teachers' professional identity formation (Beauchamp and Thomas, 2011). In a recent review of non-native English teacher identity research, Yuan (2019) found that what newly graduated teachers had learned through teacher education often clashed with the established school curriculum and practice they encountered once they transitioned into teaching. Thus, recently graduated teachers can experience a lack of agency and "a feeling of being on the outside of a community looking in" (Beauchamp and Thomas, 2011, p. 7). How my teacher identity developed alongside my sense of agency is a key aspect of the following description of my own transition from teacher education to teaching.

5.5 Autoethnography

Busch (2017) argued that "lived experience of language can hardly be observed from an outside perspective, [but] it can be approached through first-person accounts" (p. 52). She proposed that biographical research methods, such as autoethnography, are useful when investigating questions of "subject positions or identity constructions, language and emotion, fears and desires associated with ways of speaking or language attitudes linked to language ideologies or discourses on language" (p. 46). Hence, recent research on language teacher identity has increasingly looked at autoethnography as a methodological approach to explore the complexity of teachers' lived experiences (Sánchez-Martín, 2020; Tavares, 2022; Zacharias, 2019; Raza, 2024). Autoethnography is a reflexive research method that relies on the researcher's subjective experience, and the primary source of data is the researcher's memory (Chang, 2008). Winkler (2018) explained that it is widely accepted that participants in qualitative interviews refer to experiences based on their memory and, therefore, argued that the researcher's memory should serve as an equally valid source of data. Thus, autoethnography draws on elements from both autobiographical and ethnographic research in order to open up other ways of knowing (Winkler, 2018). By acknowledging and incorporating the subjective and emotional sides of the research project, autoethnography consequently challenges hegemonic understandings of what research should be (Ellis et al., 2011). In language teaching research, teachers' lived experience is increasingly acknowledged as an important source of pedagogical knowledge for language teachers (Canagarajah, 2020; Tavares, 2022).

Working on the current paper, I reflected on my previous experience as a language teacher in three language teaching contexts, which are described in Table 5.1. The teaching experiences included in this paper span the first three years of my teaching experience, from the autumn of 2015 to that of 2017.

To reconstruct my experiences, I proceeded to read my master's thesis and to consider various PowerPoint presentations I had saved from my time as a language teacher in secondary schools, as well as notes and worksheets I found together with my old teacher planners/calendars. In addition, I reread an article I wrote together with a colleague about an action research project we conducted in my classroom (Krulatz and Iversen, 2020). The different artifacts facilitated the reconstruction of my previous experiences as a language teacher (e.g. Chang, 2008). Thus, I could describe my experiences in the three separate language teaching settings.

5 Teaching Languages in the Linguistic Marketplace

Table 5.1 Three language teaching settings.

Time period	Teaching setting	Comments
2015–2016	Spanish (as a modern language) teacher at a lower secondary school (age 14–15), in Norway	Two lessons per week
2016–2017	Norwegian (as a second language) teacher at an introductory program for newly arrived students (age 13–16)	Nine lessons per week, same group of students as the group below
2016–2017	English (as a second language) teacher at an introductory program for newly arrived students (age 13–16), in Norway	Two lessons per week, same group of students as the group above

The descriptions were written separately to contrast my experiences from the three teaching settings. To secure the anonymity of my colleagues and students, I refrained from mentioning any names or locations. For ethical reasons, I focused the descriptions on my own teaching and development and avoided unnecessary descriptions of colleagues and students. Despite the use of the above-mentioned artifacts, the descriptions of my previous teaching experiences that follow below should be interpreted as a reflection of how I currently understand these experiences, rather than a description of what I thought at the time (e.g. Winkler, 2018). As I reconstructed my immediate experiences from the three settings, I reviewed different theories that could help articulate my experiences and contribute insights into how teachers' identities are influenced by the restrictions surrounding them. In what follows, my descriptions of my experiences from the three teaching settings are presented in light of relevant theories.

5.6 Teaching a Language of Convenience: Destabilizing Identity

When I had finished my initial teacher education in 2015 as an English, Norwegian, and Spanish teacher and commenced my master's studies in English teaching, I was identified as a professional teacher with insights into recent research and current theories about language teaching and learning. I saw language learning as an avenue for cross-cultural awareness (Byram, 2008; Kramsch, 1993) and critical thinking (Byram, 2008; García, 2009; Kramsch, 1993). Furthermore, inspired by researchers such as Cenoz (2009), Cummins (2000), and García (2009), I was convinced that a multilingual approach to language teaching could be transformative for students' learning.

As a master's student, I was offered a part-time position as a Spanish teacher for a class of 15 lower secondary students at a school located in a middle-class neighborhood in a large city in Norway, with few students with racially or linguistically minoritized backgrounds. Rather, the vast majority of students at the time belonged to the white, Norwegian-speaking majority population. All students were already studying English in school. Immersed in theories of multilingual education from my teacher education (e.g. Cenoz, 2009; Cummins, 2000; García, 2009), I passionately drew on the students' linguistic repertoires in teaching Spanish and generally used Norwegian and Spanish in alternation. Moreover, I initiated projects about social justice issues in Spain and Latin America to develop students' cross-cultural awareness and critical understanding.

Despite my enthusiasm for finally being able to enact the theories I had thus far only read about, I was confronted with the reality of what I now consider the linguistic marketplace. To this class of Norwegian teenagers, Spanish was a language nearly void of symbolic and material values (e.g. Bourdieu, 1991). Although Spanish was convenient whenever they visited Spain on holiday, the language was perceived as having very limited relevance to their daily lives in Norway. As opposed to their experience with English, the students did not listen to music in Spanish or watch any films or series in Spanish, nor did they know anyone who spoke Spanish. My impression was that most of the students took Spanish to fulfill the requirement for a second modern language in order to be admitted to higher education. In other words, the limited value of Spanish within the linguistic marketplace of Norwegian education was associated with its requirement for further education.

As researchers have indicated, the transition from teacher education can be destabilizing for newly graduated teachers, and the first teaching position is often a highly formative context (Beauchamp and Thomas, 2011). At the onset of my teaching at this school, I had constructed a teacher identity based on theories and methods acquired through my teacher education. Nevertheless, I soon experienced that my teacher identity was still vulnerable (e.g. Beauchamp and Thomas, 2011). The experiences of teaching Spanish to rather indifferent teenagers seriously impacted my teacher identity. The disconnect between the theories I had studied in university and the realities of the Spanish classroom not only led me to doubt the adequacy of the theories I had so enthusiastically embraced in teacher education, but I also started to doubt my own competence as a language teacher. As my teacher identity as a professional teacher up to date on recent research was quickly destabilized. I was simultaneously disempowered and consequently aligned myself with the subject position offered to me by the discourses of the classroom. From being an idealistic language teacher who believed in the importance of language learning for intercultural understanding and critical thinking, I transformed into a salesman of Spanish as economic capital for future exchanges (e.g. Bourdieu, 1991, 1993). The multilingual approach I had first initiated to develop intercultural understanding, metalinguistic awareness, and deeper understanding of the Spanish language seemed to be beside the students' expectations from a Spanish teacher. The students expressed a preference for working with the textbook, where they learned how to order food in a restaurant and ask for the way to the beach. Tasks aimed at developing the students' metalinguistic awareness almost seemed beyond the pale. Consequently, I complied with the classroom's subject position as a Spanish teacher. Although I remained convinced of the importance of language learning for intercultural understanding, critical thinking skills, and value for future education, I left the Spanish teacher position feeling rather unsuccessful as a language teacher and with a growing doubt about the appropriateness of multilingual approaches to language teaching.

5.7 Teaching a Language of Necessity: Disintegrating Identity

After completing my master's degree in 2016, I moved to a different Norwegian city and was hired at an introductory program for newly arrived students as an English and Norwegian language teacher. Introductory programs are, in practice, set up to facilitate the quick acquisition of Norwegian as the language of instruction and are therefore often influenced by the strong ideological conviction of monolingual approaches to language teaching (Beiler, 2020, 2021; Burner and Carlsen, 2019). The students' excessive use of English outside English classes was a prevalent concern for many teachers, as their mandate as Norwegian teachers was to ensure the students' acquisition of Norwegian and transfer to ordinary education. Moreover, the particular program where I worked had been set up to provide *intensive* Norwegian language instruction to speed up the acquisition of Norwegian, and the administration and teachers were thus expected to contribute to the rapid mainstreaming of their students into Norwegian education. The expectation was that students should acquire sufficient competence in Norwegian to follow ordinary instruction after just six months—an expectation that was rarely accomplished. Nevertheless, it was clear that in the local linguistic marketplace, all languages beyond Norwegian were devoid of value (e.g. Bourdieu, 1991).

As a newly graduated student, I was obviously humbled by the experience of entering a school staffed with highly competent teachers with qualifications specifically geared toward teaching Norwegian as a second language, as well as with long experience in the classroom. Because of my previous failed attempts at implementing a multilingual approach to language teaching, my teacher identity was heavily influenced by my awareness of my limited teaching experience. Based on my experiences from my previous teaching position, I saw myself as a teacher with a too naïve and theoretical perception of how language teaching happened and was eager to learn how it was "actually done." From my first weeks in the classroom and from discussions with colleagues, my suspicions that my studies in language teaching were out of touch with the complex and messy reality of real-life schools, where students' Norwegian skills were regularly assessed and reports were written on the individual student's progress, were generally confirmed. Initially, it seemed ridiculous to waste time on my illusory theories on multilingual education. Other tasks were more acute: Students needed to learn Norwegian quickly. In the hallways, signs reminded students to "Speak Norwegian" and in teacher meetings experienced colleagues stressed the importance for students to practice their Norwegian as often as possible.

Similar to Yuan's (2019) findings, I experienced that what I had learned through teacher education clashed with the established school curriculum and practice. This led to insecurity in my teacher identity and a subsequent sense of a lack of agency. Beauchamp and Thomas (2009) wrote that a teacher's realization of his or her identity may result in "a sense of agency, of empowerment to move ideas forward, to reach goals or even to transform the context" (p. 183). My initial experiences from the introductory program led me in the opposite direction: to keep my ideas about multilingual language teaching to myself and adapt to the curriculum and practices already established at the school. I began to restrict my own and my students' use of other languages than Norwegian in the classroom, and to practically disregard my students' linguistic resources beyond Norwegian in my teaching. I was afraid of stepping outside the predefined subject position of an efficient and effective Norwegian language teacher (e.g. Baxter, 2016).

5.8 Teaching a Language of High Prestige: Regaining Agency

At the same time that I started teaching Norwegian in the introductory program, I was also assigned to teach English. During the English lessons, the students were divided into two groups depending on whether they had studied English before or not. I was responsible for the students who had already studied some English before they arrived in Norway. During my first year of teaching in the introductory program, I made scattered attempts to implement a multilingual design to my lessons; I asked the students to translate key vocabulary to other languages they knew, asked them to explain and compare key grammatical rules in English in these languages, and encouraged students sharing the same languages to discuss texts together before we performed whole-class conversations of the text. Furthermore, I made frequent references to Norwegian vocabulary and grammar during the English lessons. Still, the boundaries among the different languages were upheld. The students were expected to produce monolingual texts and oral presentations, and I mostly taught through the medium of English during English lessons while restricting my use of English beyond the allocated English lessons.

In my second year as a teacher in the introductory program, my former English professor from teacher education reached out and invited me to collaborate on an action research project in which we were going to capitalize on my students' multilingualism in writing instruction. In this project, we combined the Norwegian and English lessons, and I taught academic writing as a cross-curricular project. Moreover, we planned to include students' previous languages in the project. Through collaboration to develop a multilingual writing project, the theories I had already dismissed seemed to regain relevance. During this process, I experienced a greater sense of agency than I had experienced so far in my teaching career. Hence, I was empowered to try to change the teaching context and identify new subject positions.

Contrary to my experience with the lower secondary Spanish students, the multilingual approach to writing instruction, after some initial reservation, was greeted with enthusiasm from the students. They soon realized that their previous writing instruction in Greek, Tagalog, or Somali was still relevant and could be applied to writing in both English and Norwegian (for more information about the project, see Krulatz and Iversen, 2020). A contributing factor to the students' acceptance of this multilingual approach to writing instruction was probably that I incorporated two languages of high value into the instruction. The students were learning both English and Norwegian simultaneously using their other languages to facilitate this process. Hence, it was hardly necessary to highlight the possible exchanges between cultural and economic capital.

As I started to voice my opinion about how we should approach language teaching in a more multilingual way, I realized that many of my colleagues were open to more multilingual approaches and, indeed, had already enacted multilingual approaches to language teaching in their own classrooms. From being identified as a theoretical teacher detached from classroom realities, I took the subject position of a professional teacher with training in recent theories of language teaching and with the ability to apply these theories in my own classroom. Through these experiences, I regained my confidence in a multilingual approach to language teaching and was eventually motivated to pursue a PhD in education at an institution with long-standing traditions in multicultural and multilingual education.

5.9 Teacher Identity in the Linguistic Marketplace

Through this chapter, I explored the early development of my teacher identity as a newly graduated language teacher of three languages. The guiding question was how different language ideologies impacted my teacher identity development as I attempted to implement multilingual teaching approaches within the three teaching settings. Through the description of my experiences from the three contexts, I illustrated how my teacher identity was influenced by the ideologies that regulated the particular linguistic marketplace of each context. Each linguistic marketplace is defined by the value that different languages acquire, and this value is defined by ideological ideas about language in a particular setting (Blommaert, 2010; Bourdieu, 1991). When speakers take up these ideologies and accept the values associated with the given languages, these ideas also shape their subjectivity and identity. Botsis (2018) argued that "experiences of language constitute subjectivities through the ideological and discursive capacity of the symbolic economy, to both regulate social relations and open up possibilities for change" (p. 10). As already mentioned, Blommaert (2010, p. 23) argued that globalization has not transformed the world into a village, but a network of villages, with their own rules and codes. By village, we can imagine different countries, cities, schools, or even specific classrooms. Though particular logics govern the interactions in any given classroom (e.g. Bourdieu, 1991), the logics by which the classroom operates are connected to those of the school, the city, the country, as well as the global network in which the classroom is located.

My experiences with teaching English, Norwegian, and Spanish illustrate how teacher identity is influenced by the logics of the particular settings (Yuan, 2019), articulated through the students' and colleagues' expectations of me as a teacher and of the ways in which I was expected to teach. Students' and colleagues' expectations contribute to forming the available subject positions—involving both who you are expected to be as a person and how you are expected to teach (e.g. Baxter, 2016; McNamara, 2019). As a recently graduated teacher with strong education in multilingual language teaching, I was ready to enact the theories I had read so much about, but when I could not identify a subject position that would allow me to teach languages in a multilingual way, I soon adapted to the ideologies regulating the linguistic marketplace in my classroom and in my school. This aligns with previous research's findings related to the volatile nature of recently graduated teachers' identities (Beauchamp and Thomas, 2011). In my case, the contrast between what I had learned in university and what I experienced as a teacher deteriorated my self-confidence and seriously limited my sense of agency.

As I moved from one setting to the other, and as the affordances and feedback I perceived changed, my teacher identity also developed (e.g. Beauchamp and Thomas, 2011; Song, 2016): from the disillusionment of teaching Spanish to uninterested teenagers and the subsequent doubt about my academic training, through the acceptance of the idea that the students' previous languages were close to irrelevant when learning Norwegian, to the regaining of confidence and belief in multilingual approaches to language teaching with the support of my previous professor. In other words, my teacher identity responded to the subject positions that I was able to perceive in the classroom. Subject positions are not simply the result of individual students' and colleagues' expectations. These expectations are, in fact, the result of the discourses governing the local linguistic marketplace of each teaching setting.

5.10 Practical Implications for Language Teacher Education

Researchers are increasingly acknowledging teachers' lived experiences as an important source of pedagogical knowledge for language teachers (Canagarajah, 2020; Ku, 2023; Tavares, 2022), and the study of such experiences should be included as part of the education of prospective language teachers. In line with my experience with the transition from teacher education to teaching, other researchers have also found that teachers' professional identities are constantly evolving and shifting according to context (Beauchamp and Thomas, 2009; Kayi-Aydar, 2019; Song, 2016). Moreover, the teacher identity of recently graduated teachers is especially vulnerable (Beauchamp and Thomas, 2011; Yuan, 2019).

Consequently, teacher educators need to better prepare prospective language teachers for the fact that the latest innovations within the field of language teaching research might not be welcomed by all teachers and students in schools. Moreover, prospective language teachers should be encouraged to think critically about the latest pedagogical trends, and to reflect about the fact that perhaps not all pedagogies are relevant and valuable in all contexts. If a particular approach does not work well with students in one class, it may well work with other students. Through their teacher education, prospective teachers should get extensive opportunities to study the lived experiences of other teachers as well as to practice what they have learned through field placements and to discuss their experiences from field placement together with peers and teacher educators on campus. Thus, prospective language teachers can develop an understanding of the contextual and situated value of different approaches to language teaching.

Most importantly, prospective teachers would benefit from instruction in how to analyze the ideologies behind the policies and practices regulating language teaching and to identify and assess the problems associated with the commodification of languages (Iversen and Mkandawire, 2021). Prospective teachers should develop an ability to critically assess how ideological beliefs about languages contribute to restricting students' learning opportunities. A clearer understanding of the ideologies at play can also prepare student teachers to stand up for what they believe in, even when there seems to be limited room for things otherwise about language teaching.

References

Baxter, J. (2016). Positioning language and identity: poststructuralist perspectives. In S. Preece (Ed.), *The Routledge Handbook of Language and Identity* (pp. 34–49). Routledge.

Beauchamp, C., & Thomas, L. (2009). Understanding teacher identity: an overview of issues in the literature and implications for teacher education. *Cambridge Journal of Education, 39*(2), 175–189. https://doi.org/10.1080/03057640902902252.

Beauchamp, C., & Thomas, L. (2011). New teachers' identity shifts at the boundary of teacher education and initial practice. *International Journal of Educational Research, 50*(1), 6–13. https://doi.org/10.1016/j.ijer.2011.04.003.

Beiler, I. R. (2020). Negotiating multilingual resources in English writing instruction for recent immigrants to Norway. *TESOL Quarterly, 54*(1), 5–29. https://doi.org/10.1002/tesq.535.

Beiler, I. R. (2021). Marked and unmarked translanguaging in accelerated, mainstream, and sheltered English classrooms. *Multilingua. 40*(1), 2021, pp. 107–138. https://doi.org/10.1515/multi-2020-0022.

5 Teaching Languages in the Linguistic Marketplace

Block, D., & Cameron, D. (Eds.) (2002). *Globalization and Language Teaching*. Routledge.

Blommaert, J. (2010). *The Sociolinguistcs of Globalization*. Cambridge University Press.

Botsis, H. (2018). *Subjectivity, Language and the Postcolonial: Beyond Bourdieu in South Africa*. Routledge.

Bourdieu, P. (1977). *Outline of a Theory of Practice*. Cambridge University Press.

Bourdieu, P. (1984). *Distinction: a Social Critique of the Judgement of Taste*. London, UK: Routledge.

Bourdieu, P. (1987). *Ce que parler veut dire: L'économie des échanges linguistiques*. Fayard.

Bourdieu, P. (1991). *Language and Symbolic Power*. Polity Press.

Bourdieu, P. (1993). *Field of Cultural Production: Essays on Art and Literature*. Polity Press.

Burner, T., & Carlsen, C. (2019). Teacher qualifications, perceptions and practices concerning multilingualism at a school for newly arrived students in Norway. *International Journal of Multilingualism*. https://doi.org/ 10.1080/14790718.2019.1631317.

Busch, B. (2017). Biographical approaches to research in multilingual settings: exploring linguistic repertoires. In M. Martin-Jones, & D. Martin (Eds.), *Researching Multilingualism: Critical and Ethnographic Perspectives* (pp. 46–59). Routledge.

Byram, M. (2008). *From Foreign Language Education to Education for Intercultural Citizenship*. Multilingual Matters.

Calafato, R. (2021). Language teacher multilingualism in Norway and Russia: identity and beliefs. *European Journal of Education, 56*(2), 344–344. https://doi.org/10.1111/ejed.12418.

Canagarajah, S. (2017). Multilingual identity in teaching multilingual writing. In G. Barkhuizen (Ed.), *Reflections on Language Teacher Identity Research* (pp. 67–73). Routledge.

Canagarajah, S. (2020). *Transnational Literacy Autobiographies as Translingual Writing*. London, UK: Routledge.

Cenoz, J. (2009). *Towards Multilingual Education: Basque Educational Research from an International Perspective*. Multilingual Matters.

Chang, H. (2008). *Autoethnography as Method*. Left Coast Press.

Cummins, J. (2000). *Language, Power and Pedagogy: Bilingual Children in the Crossfire*. Multilingual Matters.

Del Percio, A., Flubacher, M.-C., & Duchêne, A. (2017). Language and political economy. In O. García, N. Flores, & M. Spotti (Eds.), *The Oxford Handbook of Language and Society* (pp. 55–76). Oxford University Press.

Dewilde, J., & Kulbrandstad, L. A. (2016). Nyankomne barn og unge i den norske utdanningskonteksten: Historikk og tilstandsbeskrivelse. [Newly-arrived children and youth in the Norwegian education context: history and current situation]. *Nordand – nordisk tidsskrift for andrespråksforskning, 11*(2), 13–33. https://www.idunn.no/nordand.

Ellis, C., Adams, T. E., & Bochner, A. P. (2011). Autoethnography: an overview. *Historical Social Research, 36*(4), 273–290.

Foucault, M. (1978). *The History of Sexuality*. Random House.

Foucault, M. (1981). The order of discourse. In R. Young (Ed.), *Untying the Text: A Poststructuralist Reader* (pp. 29–42). Routledge.

García, O. (2009). *Bilingual Education in the 21st Century: A Global Perspective*. Wiley-Blackwell.

Irvine, J. T. (1989). When talk isn't cheap: language and political economy. *American Ethnologist, 16*(2), 248–267. https://doi.org/10.1525/ae.1989. 16.2.02a00040.

Irvine, J. T., & Gal, S. (2000). Language ideology and linguistic differentiation. In P. V. Kroskrity (Ed.), *Regimes of Language: Ideologies, Policies, and Identities* (pp. 35–83). School of American Research Press.

Iversen, J. Y. (2020). Samisk og somali i norsk skule: Ei undersøking av språkideologiar blant lærarstudentar [Sámi and Somali in Norwegian education: an + investigation of language ideologies among pre-service teachers]. *Nordand – nordisk tidsskrift for andrespråksforskning, 16*(1), 21–35. https://doi.org/10.18261/issn.2535-3381-2021-01-02.

Iversen, J. Y., & Mkandawire, S. B. (2021). Comparing language ideologies in multilingual classrooms across Norway and Zambia. *Multilingual Margins, 7*(3), 33–48.

Kayi-Aydar, H. (2019). Language teacher identity. *Language Teaching, 52*(3), 281–295. https://doi.org/10.1017/S0261444819000223.

Kramsch, C. (1993). *Context and Culture in Language Teaching*. Oxford University Press.

Krulatz, A., & Iversen, J. (2020). Building inclusive language classroom spaces through multilingual writing practices for newly-arrived students in Norway. *Scandinavian Journal of Educational Research, 64*(3), 372–388. https://doi.org/10.1080/00313831. 2018.1557741.

Ku, E. (2023). *Teachers of Multiple Languages: Identities, Beliefs and Emotions*. Multilingual Matters.

Kulbrandstad, L. A. (2020). Minoritetsspråk i Norge: Brukere og bruk [Minority languages in Norway: use and users]. In L. A. Kulbrandstad, & G. B. Steien (Eds.), *Språkreiser: Festskrift til Anne Golden på*

70-årsdagen [Language Journeys: Festschrift for Anne Golden's 70th birthday]. Novus.

Liddicoat, A. J. (2013). *Language-in-education Policies: The Discursive Construction of Intercultural Relations*. Multilingual Matters.

McNamara, T. (2019). *Language and Subjectivity*. Cambridge University Press.

Melo-Pfeifer, S., & Tavares, V. (2024). Future teachers of two languages in Germany: self-reported professional knowledge and teaching anxieties. In S. Melo-Pfeifer, & V. Tavares (Eds.), *Language Teacher Identity: Confronting Ideologies of Language, Race, and Ethnicity*. Wiley-Blackwell.

Norwegian Directorate for Education and Training. (2022). https://www.udir.no/eksamen-og-prover/eksamen/privatist/fremmedsprak-for-privatister/.

Raza, K. (2024). Issues of legitimization, authority, and acceptance: Pakistani English language teachers and their confrontation of raciolinguistic ideologies in ELT/TESOL classrooms. In S. Melo-Pfeifer, & V. Tavares (Eds.), *Language Teacher Identity: Confronting Ideologies of Language, Race, and Ethnicity*. Wiley-Blackwell.

Sachs, J. (2005). Teacher education and the development of professional identity: learning to be a teacher. In P. Denicolo, & M. Kompf (Eds.), *Connecting Policy and Practice: Challenges for Teaching and Learning in Schools and Universities* (pp. 5–21). Routledge.

Sánchez-Martín, C. (2020). Critical autoethnography in TESOL teacher education: a translingual and cultural historical activity theory perspective for transnational spaces. In O. Z. Barnawi, & A. Ahmed (Eds.), *TESOL Teacher Education in a Transnational World: Turning Challenges into Innovative Prospects* (pp. 105–118). Routledge.

Song, J. (2016). Emotions and language teacher identity: conflicts, vulnerability, and transformation. *TESOL Quarterly, 50*(3), 631–654. https://doi.org/10.1002/tesq.312.

Swearingen, A. J. (2019). Nonnative-English-speaking teacher candidates' language teacher identity development in graduate TESOL preparation programs: a review of the literature. *TESOL Journal, 10*(4), 1–15. https://doi.org/10.1002/tesj.494.

Tavares, V. (2022). Teaching two languages: navigating dual identity experiences. *Pedagogies: An International Journal*, 1–22. https://doi.org/10.1080/1554480X.2022.2065996.

Winkler, I. (2018). Doing autoethnography: facing challenges, taking choices, accepting responsibilities. *Qualitative Inquiry, 24*(4), 236–247. https://doi.org/10.1177/1077800417728956.

Yuan, R. (2019). A critical review on nonnative English teacher identity research: from 2008 to 2017. *Journal of Multilingual and Multicultural Development, 40*(6), 518–537. https://doi.org/10.1080/01434632. 2018.1533018.

Zacharias, N. T. (2019). The ghost of nativespeakerism: the case of teacher classroom introductions in transnational contexts. *TESOL Journal, 10*(4), 1–14. https://doi.org/10.1002/tesj.499.

Part 2

Emergent and Critical Perspectives on Language Teacher Education Programs

6

Cultivating the Critical: Professional Development as Ideological Development for Teachers of Racialized Bi/Multilingual Students

Kate Seltzer

ESL and Bilingual Education, Rowan University, Glassboro, New Jersey

6.1 Introduction

In this chapter, I describe a year-long professional development (PD) project that invited three teachers of English to engage with critical theories of language, namely translanguaging, and to unpack how those theories disrupt deficit-oriented perceptions of and approaches to teaching racialized bi/multilingual[1] students. I begin by providing an overview of translanguaging and other theoretical contributions that disrupt the abyssal thinking (de Santos, 2007; García et al., 2021) rooted in normative understandings of language, bilingualism, and racialized bi/multilingual students. In addition to this theoretical framing, I review scholarship that describes how PD and other forms of teacher education and preparation can take up such critical lenses in an attempt to deepen teachers' understandings not simply of "strategies" but of the ideologies that shape their own subjectivities (Daniels and Varghese, 2020) and perceived roles in the classroom.

Next, I describe the project's research design and central PD series, which took up what I have termed a critical translingual approach to teacher development (Seltzer and de los Ríos, 2018), which draws teachers' attention to critical perspectives on language and invites them to hone the personal,

---

1 I use the term racialized bi/multilingual to refer to "people who, as a result of long processes of domination and colonization, have been positioned as inferior in racial and linguistic terms" (García et al., 2021, p. 203).

Language Teacher Identity: Confronting Ideologies of Language, Race, and Ethnicity,
First Edition. Edited by Sílvia Melo-Pfeifer and Vander Tavares.
© 2024 John Wiley & Sons Ltd. Published 2024 by John Wiley & Sons Ltd.

political, and pedagogical elements of their stances (Seltzer, 2022). I then move into an exploration of three moments from the PD series when participating teachers explicitly articulated connections between the critical texts they engaged with and shifts in thinking about their own ideologies and approaches to English teaching. The chapter concludes with a discussion of the practical implications of this PD project, namely how such a theory-informed professional learning experience can situate "practicality" within the broader endeavor of disrupting pedagogical approaches and teacher subjectivities that reify deficit perceptions of racialized bi/multilingual students.

6.2 A Critical Translingual Approach to PD: Theoretical Framings

In the United States, in-service teachers (those currently serving in classroom teaching roles) receive ongoing PD, most of which is mandated and delivered at the district and school level. Despite the availability of PD that specifically addresses the education of bi/multilingual students, many districts and schools do not provide adequate training to teachers who work with these students and fail to address their biases, which are often rooted in deficit-oriented ideologies about students' languages and cultures (Penner-Williams et al., 2019). Addressing this kind of deficit-oriented thinking about bi/multilingual students, and particularly racialized bi/multilingual students (García et al., 2021), is highly important, as these beliefs impact teachers' expectations and actions in the classroom as well as students' behavior and learning (Mellom et al., 2018).

Overall, the "increasingly technocratic, top-down" nature of mandated PD "does not involve teachers in the process of examining the pressing issues they or their students face in schools, nor does it elicit teachers' professional expertise, interests or needs" (Kohli et al., 2015, p. 9). However, models of PD that Kohli et al. (2015) describe as critical professional development (CPD), which "fram[e] teachers as politically-aware individuals who have a stake in teaching and transforming society" (p. 9), hold promise for educators who wish to hone the personal, political, and pedagogical elements of their stance and approaches to working with minoritized students (Seltzer, 2022). Across Kohli et al.'s (2015) case studies of CPD across three US contexts, they demonstrate "how teachers can be engaged in alternative pedagogical methods that are equity and justice focused" (p. 9).

The alternative, critical approaches found in CPD contexts also draw teachers' attention to *themselves* and have the potential to center what

Daniels and Varghese (2020) call teachers' raciolinguicized subjectivities, or their ways of being and relationships to others that are rooted in what Flores and Rosa (2015) term raciolinguistic ideologies. Such ideologies "trace narrow boundaries around both legitimate forms of speech as well as the bodies that can 'legitimately' speak and be heard" (Daniels and Varghese, 2020, p. 57) and thus shape classroom interactions and relationships, particularly between white, monolingual-identified teachers and racialized bi/multilingual students. As such, a model of PD that is specifically geared toward these teachers must draw on critical theories of language that bring raciolinguistic ideologies to the surface and disrupt monoglossic thinking and practices.

Translanguaging (García, 2009; García and Li Wei, 2014) is one such critical theory that invites a view of language "'from the inside out' (de Santos, 2007, p. 54), putting at the center of our work the racialized bilingual students themselves as well as their languaging, that is, their everyday language interactions through which they make sense of their world...rather than their 'language' as defined, taught, and assessed in schools" (García et al., 2021, p. 205). This centering of students' everyday language practices, and that of their families and communities, recognizes that "bilingual people language with a unitary, not dual, repertoire from which they draw features that are useful for the communicative act in which they are engaged" (p. 208).

There is a large and growing body of scholarship on how translanguaging theory can shape classroom teaching and learning (see García et al., 2017; García and Kleyn, 2016; García and Li Wei, 2014, among many others). In our (García et al., 2017) discussion of what we term a translanguaging pedagogy, we write that three interrelated elements of teaching—the stance, design, and shifts—must respond to the *translanguaging corriente*, the fluid current of students' bilingualism that runs through any classroom space in which they learn. The translanguaging *stance* is shaped by this corriente in that it takes as a starting point that students' languaging emerges from a unitary repertoire and develops in dynamic, inseparable ways. To *design* instruction and assessment opportunities that leverage this corriente, teachers must enable students to draw on all of their linguistic and semiotic resources at all times to make meaning and to communicate what they know and can do. Within their designs, teachers must also make *shifts* that respond to and move with the dynamic multidirectionality of the translanguaging corriente. This means that teachers must be flexible and learn when and how to follow that corriente and connect it back to student learning. Integral to teachers' development of a translanguaging pedagogy is a willingness to question notions of "standard language," "native speakers," and language separation policies, which are, in many educational settings, what Fairclough (1989) called ideological commonsense. The critical elements of a translanguaging stance do not develop overnight, particularly for teachers whose subjectivities, and thus perceptions of their roles in the classroom, have been shaped by raciolinguistic ideologies.

For this reason, making translanguaging theory central to PD for teachers is part of what I have termed a critical translingual approach which, when applied to teacher education and development, aims to develop and hone English teachers' raciolinguistic literacies (Seltzer and de los Ríos, 2018), or their awareness of and ability to navigate and disrupt ideologies that maintain deficit perceptions of racialized bi/multilingual students. To do this, a critical translingual approach invites teachers to engage with theory through scholarly literature and popular, multimodal texts that invite inquiry into the intersections of language, power, and identity. It encourages teachers to look closely at their own understandings of language, racialized bi/multilingual students, and approaches to teaching these students. Rather than providing simple "strategies" that are often remedial in nature, this approach provides teachers with space to process these understandings and ideologies, using theory as a lens to (re)read their experiences. Lastly, this approach asks teachers to apply these critical theories on language and considerations of their own subjectivities to their pedagogy, asking, how can we create pedagogical opportunities that bring students' translanguaging and translingual sensibilities (Seltzer, 2020a) to the surface and leverage them for engaging and meaningful classroom learning? These pedagogical considerations contrast the "quick fixes" traditional PD often provides; instead, they give teachers the opportunity to bring their creativity and critical thinking to their practice in ways that can disrupt oppressive ideologies *and* create powerful learning experiences for students.

6.3 Project Design and Methods

6.3.1 Project Overview

This project piloted a critical translingual PD series with three teachers of English, all of whom identified as white and monolingual English-speaking. I planned and facilitated the series, which took place between September 2021 and June 2022 and revolved around two research questions:

1) What does participation in a critical translingual PD series reveal about English teachers' subjectivities and ideologies in relation to language?
2) How, if at all, do teachers of English translate their professional and personal learning into their pedagogical approaches?

6.3 Project Design and Methods | 109

Table 6.1 Overview of PD sessions, September 2021–June 2022.

Sessions	Topic	Essential questions
1–2 (Sept–Oct 2021)	On Language	• How does our thinking about language shape our thinking about racialized bi/multilingual students? • What can we learn about language from racialized bi/multilingual writers? • What is translanguaging and what ideologies does it disrupt?
3–5 (Nov 2021–Feb 2022)[a]	On Teaching Racialized Bi/Multilingual Students	• How do schools/classrooms perceive and treat students' translanguaging? • How can teachers take up translanguaging theory in practice? • How can we imagine a critical translanguaging stance?
6–9 (Mar–June 2022)	On Teaching Writing to Racialized Bi/Multilingual Students	• How could a critical translanguaging stance manifest in the teaching of writing? • What could a critical translingual writing process look like? • How can we cultivate students' creativity, criticality, and confidence through the writing process?

[a] There was no meeting held in January 2022.

The PD series was carried out through monthly meetings that included (1) engagement with translanguaging and related theories that draw connections between language, identity, and power, (2) reflective writing, journaling, and discussion, and (3) "actions" that invited teachers to translate their learning into their classroom practice. The sessions aimed to elicit teachers' own histories, beliefs, and ideologies regarding language, racialized bi/multilingual students, and language and literacy teaching (see Table 6.1).

6.3.2 Participants

To recruit participants, I sent an informational email to alumni of my university's ESL/bilingual certification program and English Language Arts major. The email described the criteria for participation, which included that participants must be secondary teachers of English (i.e. they teach

6 *Cultivating the Critical*

Table 6.2 Participating teacher information.

Teacher	School context	Teaching context
Chris	Public high school in a midsized suburban district with a large (~76%) Spanish-speaking Latinx student population, with ~20% labeled English Language Learners	English Language Arts teacher to majority of Spanish-speaking Latinx students
Erica	Public middle school in a small suburban district with a racially diverse student population, with ~4% labeled English Language Learners	English as a Second Language teacher to a linguistically diverse, but majority of Spanish-speaking Latinx, group of middle school students
Laura	Public K-8 charter school in a mid-Atlantic city with a large (~70%) Asian student population, with ~24% labeled English Language Learners	English Language Arts teacher to majority of Asian students from a variety of linguistic backgrounds, as well as a small number of Latinx and African American students

students approximately 11–18 years in age in English as a Second Language or English Language Arts classrooms) and must work with students labeled English Language Learners (i.e. students mandated by the state to receive English language services). Seven teachers attended an initial meeting and three opted to participate in the project (see Table 6.2).

6.3.3 Data Collection and Analysis

Over the course of the project, I collected data from a variety of sources and aligned those data to my research questions. Data included recordings and transcriptions of each PD meeting, reflective memos that I wrote after each meeting (Maxwell, 2005), and transcriptions of a semi-structured focus group interview conducted during our last meeting which utilized dialogic interviewing techniques (Way et al., 2015). This approach to interviewing, which "allows space for questioning, change, and transformation by encouraging individuals to authentically engage with others and suspend their judgments and assumptions" (p. 721), was important for a collaborative study focused on ideologies accepted as "common sense." After nine months of data collection, I coded the data following qualitative methods (Saldaña, 2015), with initial readings utilizing codes related to my previous research and theoretical framework (i.e. "raciolinguistic ideologies" and "evidence of translanguaging stance"). I then collapsed the large set of initial codes into broader thematic categories and revisited the data, high-lighting moments from the meeting and interview transcriptions that were representative of those themes or ideas. I analyzed these moments closely using elements of discourse analysis to understand how the content of teachers' talk related to their ideologies about language (Razfar and Rumenapp, 2012) and to their roles as teachers of English to racialized bi/multilingual students. This stage of analysis further clarified the themes I had put forth, as I grappled with discrepant data (Erickson, 1986) and the nuances of participants' words.

6.3.4 Researcher Positionality

Like the participants in this project, I identify as a white, English-dominant educator. I am a former secondary English Language Arts teacher to racial-ized bi/multilingual students and currently a teacher educator to teachers becoming certified in English and bilingual education. Though my mother immigrated from Italy as a child, grew up bilingual, and maintained her bilingualism and many transnational connections throughout my child-hood, I grew up in an English-dominant home within a suburban, upper middle class, majority white community. All of these factors have limited my raciolinguistic literacies, though I have made an effort to evolve them through my education, relationships, and experiences. These elements of my positionality have impacted my subjectivity, or my understanding of self as being in "constant flux and engaged in a power-laden dialectic with oth-ers and the world" (Daniels and Varghese, 2020, p. 58).

The various forces and discourses that have shaped my relationship to myself and others have also shaped my listening and perceiving practices (Flores and Rosa, 2015), which are particularly important when addressing ideology. However, if subjectivities are not static, then there exists the possi-bility of agency; new discourses, relationships, and voices (Bakhtin, 1981; Norton and Toohey, 2011) can (re)shape who we are and how we move through the world. Through the work I have done with these three teachers—and across my career as a researcher and teacher educator—I attempt to bring to the surface the ways that power-laden discourses have shaped my *own* understanding of self and others. In this way, I think of my attention to my own positionality as part of my commitment to ethical, humanizing research *alongside* participants. My role in this research is not to "teach" other white, English-dominant educators how to work with racialized bi/multilingual students; it is to collaboratively unsettle our shared biases, unlearn harmful narratives, and ideally teach against the grain (Cochran-Smith, 1991)—with critical self-awareness—in whatever contexts we find ourselves in.

6.4 Findings

In this section, I describe three moments from the PD series that illustrate how the texts and ideas that teachers engaged with sparked their own critical thinking about language, teaching, and their roles as teachers of English. In each of these moments, I show how teachers explicitly connected their engagement with critical, theory-informed texts to their (re)thinking of their choices around classroom practices, curriculum, and assessment. Rather than simply layer new "strategies" onto the foundations of their teaching, the three teachers questioned and grappled with the deeper implications of accepted pedagogical practices and approaches that are informed by mono-glossic, raciolinguistic ideologies.

6.4.1 "I Don't Want to Contribute to the Problems That I Feel Are Just, Like, Inherent in Our System"

During the first two sessions of the PD series, the teachers and I discussed texts that offered new perspectives on language. Through our engagement with a variety of multimodal texts that offered expansive thinking around language, we discussed several essential questions, including "What can we learn about language and writing from racialized bi/multilingual writers?" One such text was an article in *Teen Vogue* by the poet Julián Delgado-Lopera (2020) entitled *Spanglish Isn't a 'Wrong' Form of English—It's How Great Stories Are Told*. Though the essay does not use the word "translanguaging," its central thesis is highly aligned with critical lenses on language and its intersections with power and ideology. For example, Delgado Lopera, who was born in Colombia and writes in what they refer to as Spanglish, says that they were told by publishers "over and over again that I can't write like this, that this is not correct, that people won't understand." And yet, they write:

> The language that is tossed aside, that is erased and discarded by the publishing industry, is *my* fuel. I take my mother's accent, her *o-mai-got* and craft a character out of it. I take my tía's *I'm gonna contártelo todo when I see you later*. My primo's watcheando la T.V, printeando la homework, haciendo la londri. This incredible sazón y tumbao, this musicality and its brilliance find their way to my stories. It's the heart of my craft. ¿Y, por qué no?

In addition to describing the languaging of bi/multilingual people with creative incisiveness, Delgado Lopera details why certain language is "tossed aside, erased, and discarded." They write of "Spanglish" that "it is not perceived as legitimate in literature because it is not legible to whiteness. Period. Spanglish is unconcerned with the white gaze, it throws the white grammar book out the window and builds one for itself ... Spanglish does not look outside, it doesn't react to whiteness, but rather looks deep inside itself for the linguistic tools it already has and shapes them." The essay's powerful take on language and the importance of writing from "this in-between space, this hybridity" provided the teachers and me with much to discuss and reflect on, particularly when we thought about how English classrooms typically do not leverage the kind of translanguaging and translingual sensibilities that an author like Delgado Lopera brings to their writing.

During the session after we read Delgado Lopera's article, which occurred a month later, high school ELA teacher Chris shared how the piece had stayed in his mind and made him think critically about his pedagogical approaches. He said that some of Delgado Lopera's descriptions of their experiences in the classroom made him think of his own students, who might be going through something similar to what Delgado Lopera describes. Chris said:

> There is a student I have—I did a survey at the beginning of class, and one of the questions was like "what subject do you find difficult?" And he said, English and Spanish, I just feel like I'm not good at either. [...] And I guess that is one of the problems of being an English teacher, especially an English teacher in a school that is predominantly language minoritized students. I don't want to contribute to the problems that I feel are just, like, inherent in our system. In fact I was even thinking about, as I was reading the article, about one thing I'm doing that probably isn't a good idea, and I should probably change. Like how [Delgado Lopera] was stressed, especially with public speaking kinds of things, those are the kinds of things I'm trying to eliminate the best I can.

Chris reflects on how his use of certain classroom practices might create stress and reify students' negative self-assessments of their own language practices. After relating a student's comment about feeling like he was "not good at either" English or Spanish to Delgado Lopera's experiences, Chris states that practices as seemingly benign and commonplace as requiring students to speak in front of the class could "contribute to the problems that ... are inherent in our system." Though he does not state exactly what those problems are, he draws a line from his student's comment to his understanding of "one of the problems of being an English teacher ... in a school that is predominantly language minoritized students," alluding to the idea that English teaching frames "standard English" as the exemplar and excludes students' other ways of languaging. This exclusion and how it might contribute to students' perceptions of themselves as "languageless" (Rosa, 2016) is one that Chris seems to want to distance himself from, leading him to question, and even contemplate eliminating, certain pedagogical strategies from his practice.

6.4.2 "Who Educates the Educators?"

During the second part of the PD series, "On Teaching Racialized Bi/multilingual Students," the teachers were formally introduced to Flores and Rosa's (2015) theory of raciolinguistic ideologies. We read excerpts from their article which first introduced the concept, watched a recording of a talk given by Flores (2021) during which he discusses these ideologies, and engaged with tweets by the two authors and others that clarified the concept through clear and accessible examples. I also shared excerpts from my own research (Seltzer and de los Ríos, 2018; Seltzer, 2020a, 2020b) that showed how one ELA teacher and her students explicitly talked, read, and wrote about the intersections of language and race.

In between our November and December meetings, I asked teachers to engage in what I called, inspired by Mentor and Sealey-Ruiz (2021), "raciolinguistic digging." Such digging is aligned with calls by many anti-racist educators for individual educators to engage in critical self-reflection. As Mentor and Sealey-Ruiz write, "before we can look at the sociopolitical struggles of racism and white privilege, we first must enter into conversation with ourselves" (p. 20). To do this requires what Sealey-Ruiz calls Archeology of the Self, "a process of excavating our personal histories to activate our own racial consciousness as a precursor to theorizing about what an antiracist pedagogy means to each of us" (p. 20). This process is particularly important for white educators, who personally and professionally benefit from remaining blind to their own privileges and biases (Picower, 2021).

To get teachers talking about their "raciolinguistic digging," I posed some reflection questions, including "Can you think of any times that you, yourself, have transmitted raciolinguistic ideologies?" Erica, the middle school ESL Language teacher, shared what she said "popped up" for her as she considered this question:

> I was reflecting a lot on vocabulary acquisition. We've had some really interesting trainings at our school with strategies for teaching vocabulary. And when I was reflecting back on those through this perspective, I feel like maybe some of the approaches or strategies that we use don't necessarily take into mind—like when we're doing vocabulary

assessment, for example, it's like a very standardized form that really doesn't take into account anything other than like [makes air quotes] standard English. And I was reading back through an article that was sort of connected to this and it posed the question, who educates the educators? And that made me reflect on, like, curriculum in general and how we're deciding what we teach and how we teach it. [...] Like we talk about, I wrote down some words that often come up in meetings, students being low or what they're missing. Gaps. Behind. Below grade level. And we really don't always focus on leveraging assets.

In her reflection, Erica does not shy away from implicating herself in what she describes as her and her fellow teachers' deficit-oriented thinking around racialized bi/multilingual students and their language and literacy practices. In their own PD work with teachers, Mentor and Sealey-Ruiz (2021) might describe this kind of reflection as both "letting go of lifelong ideas and beliefs and letting in new understanding to make way for new beliefs that engage the full humanity of others" (p. 22). Here, Erica articulates and takes ownership of her own raciolinguistic ideologies that render her assessments of students' vocabulary as "behind" or "below" and begins to see them more clearly by "letting in" and taking up the theoretical perspective offered by Flores and Rosa (2015). Their theory, which draws attention away from locating "problems" in racialized bi/multilingual students' language practices and instead focuses on the biases of *listeners*, provided the teachers with an opportunity to rethink topics like vocabulary assessment and, as Erica puts it, "curriculum in general" that are formulated with respect to remediating students' supposed gaps. It also provided them with an opportunity to consider their own and their fellow teachers' listening and teaching practices that have been shaped by raciolinguistic ideologies and negatively impact their perceptions of students, keeping them from being able to "focus on leveraging assets." In connecting this work to a different article she read that posed the question, "who educates the educators?," Erica engages in big-picture thinking about how raciolinguistic ideologies and other deficit-oriented framings of racialized bi/multilingual students are institutionalized through pedagogical practices and discourses.

6.4.3 "I Have to Think and Really, Concretely, Make Sure That It Happens"

In our last meeting, I asked the teachers to reflect on their learning and how they were thinking about their future teaching through the lenses offered in the PD series. As she was talking through some of her thinking, Laura, the

116 | 6 Cultivating the Critical

seventh- and eighth-grade ELA teacher, explicitly referenced Flores's (2020) concept of students as "language architects." In a previous meeting, Laura had mentioned that she wanted to expand her use of texts in the classroom to include those by bi/multilingual authors who themselves utilize translanguaging in their writing. Because my own research has delved into this topic, I sent Laura a copy of a book chapter I wrote on using such authors as "mentors" in the ELA classroom (Seltzer, 2020b). In that chapter, I took up Flores's (2020) call for teachers to envision an approach in which

> the role of the teacher would no longer be to teach academic language as if it were a list of empirical linguistic practices that was dichotomous with the home language practices of racialized students. Instead, the teacher's role would be to recognize that the home language practices of racialized students already align with the linguistic knowledge embedded in ... state standards and to develop lessons and units that build on this existing knowledge (p. 28).

In the chapter I shared with Laura, I wrote about how the ELA teacher I worked with took up this call and used translingual mentor texts to spark conversations with students about the intersections of language, identity, and power. In response, students voiced their sophisticated understandings of these topics and wrote powerful translingual essays. The shifts in perspective that Erica found in these texts resonated with her and prompted her to think about how to take them up in her teaching.

In part of her reflection on her learning during the PD series, she used the lens of language architecture to reflect on the curriculum her school uses, the Teachers College Reading and Writing Project, led by literacy scholar Lucy Calkins. She said:

> I'm not really sure how I can do this, but thinking about students as language architects was really powerful because we use Lucy Calkins at our school and her perspective is like "all children are authors" but we've gotten pretty far from that in practicality. So kind of going back to that idea that kids are authors, they have their own writing style, and they're not writing for you or your class. That's not the purpose of class, to teach them how to write for you, but to teach them how to discover their own writing style and how they can use that in different ways. So I have to think and really concretely make sure that it happens.

Here, Laura revisits the core of the approach taken by Lucy Calkins through the writer's workshop: that all children have a powerful story to tell and that it is the teacher's job to facilitate the process of children finding their unique writerly voices. Though at her school (and, anecdotally, at many schools where I have provided teachers with PD on working with bi/multilingual students), they have "gotten pretty far" from this core idea, Laura seems to view Flores's concept of language architecture as a kind of connecting device between the ideas we discussed throughout the series and the practicalities of her daily teaching life. By "going back to the idea that kids are authors," Laura sees a way to walk the line between implementing the mandated curriculum of her school and embracing more critical, expansive thinking around teaching writing to racialized bi/multilingual students. At the end of this quote, Laura states that she has to further flesh out her ideas about the connection between the curriculum and language architecture "and really concretely make sure that it happens." Because the emphasis on practicality is felt so strongly in schools, Laura seems to communicate that a concerted effort on her part will be necessary to (re)center the more progressive elements of the curriculum and pedagogical approach.

6.5 Discussion and Implications for Language Teacher Education

The three moments from the PD series I describe demonstrate that English teachers Chris, Erica, and Laura explicitly referenced the theory and ideas we engaged with as they reconsidered, questioned, and expanded their thinking about their pedagogical approaches and roles in the classroom. This kind of critical thinking and self-reflection relates to what Ball (2009) terms generative change, or "a process of self-perpetuating change wherein a teacher's pedagogical practices are inspired and influenced by the instructional approaches and theory that he or she is exposed to in a professional development program" (p. 48). In Ball's longitudinal study of teacher preparation in the United States and South Africa, she sought to understand how, if at all, an assets-based PD program grounded in critical theory changed teachers' approaches to teaching diverse student populations. The PD course Ball facilitated took up Bakhtin's (1981) concept of ideological becoming, or the idea that,

> our engagement with the discourses of others can influence the way that we think, and it can contribute to forming what ultimately becomes internally persuasive discourses for us—thus influencing our ideologies, thoughts, beliefs, and ways of theorizing about a body of ideas, their origin, and how they operate.
>
> *(Ball, 2009, p. 49)*

It is through these shifts that teachers, especially those who do not share backgrounds with their students, evolve their practices and approaches to pedagogical problem-solving, making them stronger teachers in what Ball refers to as culturally and linguistically complex classrooms. As Chris, Erica, and Laura engaged with the discourses of others through theory, they expressed such shifts in their thinking about language and the teaching of English. When Chris reflected on the practice often referred to as "Spanglish" and how it is treated in the classroom, and when Erica connected raciolinguistic ideologies to vocabulary assessment, and when Laura took up the concept of language architecture, they were engaged in an evolution of their thinking. They were, as Ball writes, developing "internally persuasive discourses" for themselves that have the potential to counter the deficit-laden perceptions of racialized bi/multilingual students and status quo approaches to educating them in English classrooms.

The theory they engaged with also helped the teachers to critically locate themselves in the English classroom and to grapple with their positionalities as white, monolingual-identified teachers of racialized bi/multilingual students. When Chris reflected on how his pedagogical strategies might "contribute to problems ... inherent in our system" and when Erica discussed how her ways of teaching vocabulary are rooted in perceptions of students being "low" and "behind," they started to unpack their own raciolinguicized subjectivities (Daniels and Varghese, 2020), considering how their positionalities shape their interactions with others (their students, their colleagues) and their implementation of policies and practices. And when Laura discussed re-centering the more progressive elements of her school's mandated curriculum and reframing students as authors and language architects—which, she said, they had all "gotten pretty far from"— she imagined the possibility of a different way of being in the classroom. Rather than envision and implement the literacy curriculum in ways that align with her school's possibly deficit-oriented approach, Laura imagines a way to do things differently and, by extension, be a different kind of English teacher to racialized bi/multilingual students.

This study has important implications for language teacher education. It shows that when given the opportunity, teachers are interested in and up to the challenge of engaging with complex theories and ideas. This study was completely voluntary in nature; teachers received no credit or compensation for their participation. The sessions occurred in the evenings, after the teachers had taught a full day of school. The study took place during what was arguably one of the most difficult years of teaching in recent memory— the first year "fully" back in physical buildings after COVID-19 closed so many US schools. And it took place as the pandemic continued to rage, with each of us experiencing disruption, frustration, anxiety, and fatigue as a result. And yet, the teachers showed up each month and read, discussed, shared, and imagined new possibilities for themselves and for their students. These teachers are just three of *many* who are interested in more critical, progressive ways of teaching English; and yet most PD (and teacher education more broadly) continues to focus on strategies, "best practices," and quick fixes that aim to remediate students' supposed deficiencies. This study piloted a different approach to PD, one that did not take away from the importance of the everyday practicalities of teaching but broadened teachers' field of vision so that "the practical" was not all they saw. By offering teachers the time and space to engage with alternative perspectives and to reimagine their roles and approaches in the classroom, PD can help situate practicality within broader frameworks of equity and serve the highly important function of offering teachers theory-informed, research-based perspectives that would support their disruption of monoglossic, raciolinguistic ideologies that pervade English teaching.

6.6 Conclusion

This chapter has offered insights into continuing language and literacy teacher education through PD. Though it is often utilized to address perceived "problems" in students and/or to support teachers in implementing top-down policies and practices that are linked to standardized assessments, PD could be a powerful way of addressing a different problem: the overwhelmingly white, monolingual US teaching force and their lack of preparation to be critical, self-reflective, anti-racist educators of racialized bi/multilingual students. Though PD cannot "solve" institutional issues and structures that frame these students as lacking and perceive their translanguaging as an indication that they are "low" or "behind" in their language and literacy abilities, it can equip teachers with ways of critiquing and disrupting those structures. As educators unpack their own ideologies and senses of self as teachers of English, they may be better able to unpack harmful policies and practices that so often render the schooling of racialized bi/multilinguals remedial and uninspired. If teachers, with the support of administrators and other stakeholders, could apply their critical stances and shift their school cultures toward more expansive, assets-based perceptions and ways of teaching racialized bi/multilingual students, perhaps they might work toward even broader disruptions of structural inequalities in the educational system.

References

Bakhtin, M. (1981). *The Dialogic Imagination: Four Essays by MM Bakhtin* (E. Holquist, and C. Emerson, Trans.). University of Texas Press.

Ball, A. F. (2009). Toward a theory of generative change in culturally and linguistically complex classrooms. *American Educational Research Journal, 46*(1), 45–72. https://doi.org/10.3102/0002831208323277.

Cochran-Smith, M. (1991). Learning to teach against the grain. *Harvard Educational Review, 61*(3), 279–311. https://doi.org/10.17763/haer.61.3.q671413614502746.

Daniels, J. R., & Varghese, M. (2020). Troubling practice: exploring the relationship between Whiteness and practice-based teacher education in considering a raciolinguicized teacher subjectivity. *Educational Researcher, 49*(1), 56–63. https://doi.org/10.3102/0013189X19879450.

Delgado-Lopera, J. (2020, May). *Spanglish Isn't a "Wrong" Form of English—It's How Great Stories Are Told*. Teen Vogue. https://www.teenvogue.com/story/spanglish-isnt-wrong-form-of-english.

Erickson, F. (1986). Qualitative methods in research on teaching. In M. C. Wittorck (Ed.), *Handbook of Research on Teaching* (pp. 119–161). MacMillan.

Fairclough, N. (1989). *Language and Power*. Longman.

Flores, N. (2020). From academic language to language architecture: challenging raciolinguistic ideologies in research and practice. *Theory into Practice, 59*(1), 22–31. https://doi.org/10.1080/00405841.2019.1665411.

Flores, N. (2021, November 20). From academic language to language architecture: challenging raciolinguistic ideologies in language education. *Keynote, 2021 MELEd Conference*. https://www.youtube.com/watch?v=i1Y7os71Npw&t=2449s.

Flores, N., & Rosa, J. (2015). Undoing appropriateness: raciolinguistic ideologies and language diversity in education. *Harvard Educational Review, 85*(2), 149–171.

García, O. (2009). *Bilingual Education in the 21st Century: A Global Perspective*. Wiley/Blackwell.

García, O., & Kleyn, T. (Eds.) (2016). *Translanguaging with Multilingual Students: Learning from Classroom Moments*. Routledge.

García, O., & Li Wei (2014). *Translanguaging: Language, Bilingualism and Education*. Palgrave Macmillan.

García, O., Johnson, S., & Seltzer, K. (2017). *The Translanguaging Classroom: Leveraging Student Bilingualism for Learning*. Brooks.

García, O., Flores, N., Seltzer, K., Li Wei, Otheguy, R., & Rosa, J. (2021). Rejecting abyssal thinking in the language and education of racialized bilinguals: a manifesto. *Critical Inquiry in Language Studies, 18*(3), 203–228. https://doi.org/10.1080/15427587.2021.1935957.

Kohli, R., Picower, B., Martinez, A., & Ortiz, N. (2015). Critical professional development: centering the social justice needs of teachers. *International Journal of Critical Pedagogy, 6*(2), 7–24.

Maxwell, J. A. (2005). *Qualitative Research Design: An Interactive Approach.* Sage.

Mellom, P. J., Straubhaar, R., Balderas, C., Ariail, M., & Portes, P. R. (2018). "They come with nothing:" how professional development in a culturally responsive pedagogy shapes teacher attitudes towards Latino/a English language learners. *Teaching and Teacher Education, 71,* 98–107. https://doi.org/10.1016/j.tate.2017.12.013.

Mentor, M. & Sealey-Ruiz, Y. (2021). Doing the deep work of antiracist pedagogy: toward self-excavation for equitable classroom teaching. *Language Arts, 99*(1), 19–24.

Norton, B., & Toohey, K. (2011). Identity, language learning, and social change. *Language Teaching, 44*(4), 412–446.

Penner-Williams, J., Diaz, E. I., & Worthen, D. G. (2019). Sustainability of teacher growth from professional development in culturally and linguistically responsive instructional practices. *Teaching and Teacher Education, 86,* 1–13. https://doi.org/10.1016/j.tate.2019.102891.

Picower, B. (2021). *Reading, Writing, and Racism: Disrupting Whiteness in Teacher Education and in the Classroom.* Beacon Press.

Razfar, A., & Rumenapp, J. C. (2012). Language ideologies in English learner classrooms: critical reflections and the role of explicit awareness. *Language Awareness, 21*(4), 1–22. https://doi.org/10.1080/09658416.2011.616591.

Rosa, J. D. (2016). Standardization, racialization, languagelessness: raciolinguistic ideologies across communicative contexts. *Journal of Linguistic Anthropology 26*(2), 162–183.

Saldana, J. (2015). *The Coding Manual for Qualitative Researchers.* Sage.

de Santos, B. S. (2007). Beyond abyssal thinking: from global lines to ecologies of knowledges. *Review (Fernand Braudel Center), 30*(1), 45–89.

Seltzer, K. (2020a). "My English is its own rule": voicing a translingual sensibility through poetry. *Journal of Language, Identity and Education* https://doi.org/10.1080/15348458.2019.1656535.

Seltzer, K. (2020b). Translingual writers as mentors in a high school "English" classroom. In S. Lau, & S. Van Viegen (Eds.), *Plurilingual Pedagogies: Critical and Creative Endeavors for Equitable Language (in) Education,* pp.185–204. Springer.

Seltzer, K. (2022). Enacting a critical translingual approach in teacher preparation: disrupting oppressive language ideologies and fostering the personal, political, and pedagogical stances of preservice teachers of English. *TESOL Journal, 13*(2). https://doi.org/10.1002/tesj.649.

Seltzer, K., & de los Ríos, C. V. (2018). Translating theory to practice: exploring teachers' raciolinguistic literacies in secondary English classrooms. *English Education, 51*(1), 49–79.

Way, A. K., Zwier, R. K., & Tracy, S. J. (2015). Dialogic interviewing and flickers of transformation: an examination and delineation of interactional strategies that promote participant self-reflexivity. *Qualitative Inquiry, 21*(8), 720–731. https://doi.org/10.1177/1077800414566686.

7

"The Words Flowed Like a River": Taking Up Translanguaging in a Teacher Education Program

Cecilia M. Espinosa[1], Melissa L. García[1], and Alison Lehner-Quam[2]

[1] *Department of Early Childhood/Childhood, Lehman College/CUNY, New York, United States*
[2] *Education Librarian, Library Lehman College/CUNY, New York, United States*

> *"I couldn't stop writing my poem, the words flowed like a river. This is the first time I have written using Spanish and English . . ." (Dacy, a student in Cecilia's class).*

7.1 Introduction

The question of how we can create spaces within our work where multilingualism is the norm, where it is welcomed and viewed as an important resource for content, language learning, and expression of knowledge and ways of being, is a question we have started to explore at the college level. We argue that this is an important next step because engaging in this journey of transforming an educator's stance toward multilingual students from a perspective of deficit to one of strength shifts the positionality of the emergent bilingual students by viewing multilingualism as the norm. When the students' viewpoint is repositioned, the space the college educator creates is one where multilingual students are capable of enacting more fully their agency, creativity, and capacity to engage in critical thought (Li Wei, 2011). It is no longer a stance that positions them as lacking due to labels assigned by educational institutions in the past, i.e. English language learners, limited English proficiency, or as being in need to develop academic vocabulary. Instead, we concur with España and Herrera (2020) who state that

---

Language Teacher Identity: Confronting Ideologies of Language, Race, and Ethnicity,
First Edition. Edited by Sílvia Melo-Pfeifer and Vander Tavares.
© 2024 John Wiley & Sons Ltd. Published 2024 by John Wiley & Sons Ltd.

multilingual students are "sophisticated speakers and interpreters of complex language practices" (p. 8). In this chapter, we utilize the term multilingual with the aim of providing the most inclusive term that addresses anyone who speaks more than one language. We recognize that a named language is not a linguistic object of study, but an idea that is socially constructed (Heller, 2007; Jørgensen et al., 2011; Makoni and Pennycook, 2010; Otheguy et al., 2015). We adhere to the definition put forth by Otheguy et al. (2015) which describes "translanguaging as the deployment of a speaker's full linguistic repertoire without regard for watchful adherence to the socially and politically defined boundaries of named (and usually national and state) languages" (p. 283).

We are two teacher educators and an education librarian who have been collaborating for several years on projects that focus on transforming the children's literature collection the college library offers. The purpose of our collaboration has been to offer the education students experiences where they can access children's books that serve as mirrors to themselves and the diverse young readers they will be working with once they graduate. Our partnership has been enriched by our dialogue about how to best support multilingual teacher candidates to value, affirm, and sustain their languaging practices as critical tools for thinking and learning. Central to our dialogue has been the role of translanguaging in supporting teacher candidates to capitalize on their own linguistic repertoire to construct meaning more fully, while they develop the theory and pedagogy to also engage young, diverse, and multilingual learners.

The college is one of the largest Hispanic-serving institutions in the United States. A large portion of students come from diverse multilingual backgrounds. In spite of the unique diversity of languaging practices, the statement Dacy (pseudonym) made in Cecilia's class after being invited to compose a multimodal identity poem where she could integrate her entire linguistic repertoire is not an isolated statement. Often in college, unless the students are taking a foreign language class, their home language is rendered invisible, and depending on the language, it is also frequently disregarded. English is, for the most part, the sole named language of instruction at the university. Within the context of our college, it is not rare for us to hear our college students refer to their own multilingualism as a language barrier. Often due to external perspectives that view multilingualism as an obstacle, the only remedy they have experienced is a transition to English, a bias that they have internalized. Historically, the languaging practices of multilingual people have been relegated to the home. Rarely are they invited to bring their whole person into a college learning experience. In fact, they often describe this journey as one of transitioning to English, rather than a journey of sustaining their multilingualism.

We propose a perspective of strength and possibility that normalizes our students' multilingualism and views it as an asset and resource (Espinosa and Ascenzi-Moreno, 2021). We no longer accept the silencing of multilingual voices. We believe strongly that this transformative shift needs to begin within the context of our own practice. In this chapter, we describe the ways in which we have begun to integrate translanguaging and a raciolinguistic perspective (Flores and Rosa, 2015; Rosa and Flores, 2017; Zavala and Back, 2017) within our roles. We start with a description of teacher research as our methodology, and we describe the setting where our work with translanguaging takes place. Next, we present ideas about translanguaging that have informed our work in college classrooms and the campus library. Finally, each one of us describes the ways in which taking a translanguaging stance has informed and continues to characterize our work within our respective roles in the college. Our chapter ends with implications for the field with regard to addressing matters of language issues in the development of our prospective teacher identities.

7.2 Methodology

Our study is based on teacher research. This is research that is "both social and political—that is, it involves making problematic the current arrangements of schooling; the ways knowledge is constructed, evaluated, and used; and teachers' individual and collective roles in bringing about change" (Cochran-Smith and Lytle, 1999, p. 18). In other words, we elected to engage in a research study of our own practices as teacher educators and an education librarian. We are "RE-searchers" (Berthoff, 1987) who are committed to engaging in dialogue in order to interrogate our own practices and assumptions, as we strive to examine, improve, and transform our own teaching. Our aim is to make our daily practice a site of inquiry where we can work collaboratively to ensure we offer our multilingual college students rich spaces to engage with their entire linguistic repertoire and with their subjective agency (Lugones, 2003) in learning that is liberatory and centered on social justice (Cochran-Smith and Lytle, 2009). As researchers who study their own practice, we analyzed illustrative examples of our teaching practices, looking for salient themes that emerged, and then, composed our three individual stories. In order to address ethics in this chapter, we set the

126 | *7 "The Words Flowed Like a River"*

boundaries of sharing the stories only from our practice as teacher educators and an education librarian.[1]

7.2.1 The Setting

Our college is the only public senior college in a large urban setting that is part of a metropolitan city. Our student population is diverse and mainly comes from low socioeconomic circumstances; they are primarily first-generation college students, of immigrant origin, and they live at home while attending college typically in multigenerational home settings. They come from a variety of countries. This urban setting has a diverse and dynamic population of 1,435,068 residents. The top named languages are Spanish (47.1%); English (41.6%); languages from Africa (Twi, Fulani, Yoruba, Swahili, etc.) (3.6%); French (1.6%); other Indo European (0.9%); Italian (0.6%); Arabic (0.5%); Indigenous languages including K'iche', Mam, Kechwa, and Mixtec (0.5%); Chinese (0.4%); French Creole (0.4%); Tagalog (0.3%); and Urdu (0.1%) (Neighborhood Scout, 2022). The college students reflect the demographics of the neighborhoods that surround the campus, and for the most part, once teacher candidates graduate, they are hired in schools in the area.

If one was to take a walking tour around our college campus, one would find a stunningly beautiful educational setting with gothic buildings, old trees, green spaces, and art immersed in the landscape. If one focused specifically on the language ecology of the college, one would find very few spaces where named languages other than English appear. This is in spite of the rich diversity of people and their languaging practices that make up the student population. Certainly, the halls of the foreign language department have printed texts in the hallways in their specific named languages, Italian, French, Spanish, Greek, Latin, Japanese, etc., yet the print fliers and signage visible in the rest of the college are mostly in English.

While there is a scarcity of reflections on the richness of the languaging practices of the students, if one walks a few blocks outside of the college, one finds businesses with print in Vietnamese, Spanish, Bengali, Italian, Albanian, and Arabic. Throughout these neighborhoods, one can also hear people speaking or listening to the radio in languages such as Twi, Fulani, and Yoruba. In contrast to the rich diversity of languaging practices that exist within a few blocks of the college neighborhood, a visitor taking the

---

1 Dacy, the multilingual teacher candidate, whose words open this chapter provided written permission for her statement to be included.

walking tour at the college could imagine that those who attend our college speak only English. In the next section, we introduce key ideas about translanguaging that shape our work.

7.3 Translanguaging and Translanguaging in Teacher Education

Language does not exist in isolation, outside of people's experiences (Otheguy et al., 2015, 2018; Pujolar and Rojo, 2020). It matters that educators take the perspective of the multilingual person by observing the child's capacities closely as the child draws on her entire linguistic repertoire in order to interact with others and construct meaning (García and Kleyn, 2016). This stance toward language is a critical paradigm shift for teacher educators (Espinosa et al., 2020; Zavala, 2017). At the core of language is the construction of meaning (Goodman, 1996; Goodman and Goodman, 2014). To more fully construct meaning, the multilingual person draws on their entire linguistic repertoire in dynamic ways (Espinosa and Ascenzi-Moreno, 2021; García, 2020). Mignolo (2000) asserts that language is not a set of rules (phonics, grammar) to be learned, instead, he argues language is "thinking and writing between languages" (p. 226). He states that what people do when they language is attribute their own meanings to language. García and Li Wei (2014) contend that through our languaging practices we become, we create, we respond, and we learn about how to be in the world as whole people.

Language can oppress and it can also liberate, Mignolo (2000) insists. In articulating the transformative power of translanguaging, García and Li Wei (2014) remind us that what people do is they language. By this, they mean that, "Language is not a simple system of structures that is independent of human actions with others, of our being with others" (p. 8). These researchers argue that "the term *languaging* (italics original) is needed to refer to the simultaneous process of continuous becoming of ourselves and of our language practices, as we interact and make meaning in the world" (p. 8). People engage in languaging practices that are dynamic, fluid, and always evolving (García, 2009). This is a very different stance from the conceptualization of language as static and assumes language can be studied in isolation, as bits and pieces and devoid of human meaning. Additionally, García and Kleyn (2016) argue that socio-political circumstances have led to the development of language hierarchies that produce prejudice against speakers of certain varieties. These hierarchies are visible in educational sites and tend to reproduce inequities that exist in societies, thus rendering the languaging practices of particular groups as problematic and in need of remediation (García and Otheguy, 2017).

Translanguaging can be a powerful tool to radically bridge the opportunity gap. Translanguaging exists in communities as the norm (Espinosa and Ascenzi-Moreno, 2021; García et al., 2017; García and Espinosa, 2020; García and Kleifgen, 2018). In contrast in teacher education programs, even programs that offer bilingual education, the lens has been monolingual, treating each language separately (Espinosa et al., 2020). It matters that teacher candidates have opportunities to move from reading theory and research about translanguaging to concrete experiences that lead them to observe, engage with, and experience translanguaging throughout their teacher preparation program (García and Kleyn, 2016). Additionally, it matters that teacher educators take the necessary steps to ground their courses in ways that invite their students to examine complex issues of linguistic and racial oppression (Espinosa et al., 2020; Flores and Rosa, 2015; Rosa and Flores, 2017). It is essential that teacher candidates learn to "consider students' ways of knowing and their use of their entire linguistic repertoire as valid contributions to the classroom learning community" (España and Herrera, 2020, p. 21). Flores and Rosa (2015) and Zavala and Back (2017) claim that language and race cannot be separated. They contend that we need to examine the complex ways in which language ideologies produce raciolinguistic hierarchies, resulting in the racialization of linguistic otherness.

Reading researcher Rosenblatt (1995) wrote

> There is no such thing as a generic reader or a generic literacy work; there are only the potential millions of individual readers or the potential millions of individual literary works. A novel or a poem or a play remains merely ink spots on paper until a reader transforms them into a set of meaningful symbols. (p. 25)

Children's literature visionary Bishop (1990) radically noted, "when children cannot find themselves reflected in the books they read, or when the images they see are distorted, negative, or laughable, they learn a powerful lesson about how they are devalued in the society of which they are part" (para. 4). We argue that for emergent multilingual students it is not enough to see visual images of their worlds in the texts they read, they need to see reflections of themselves in the languaging practices of the characters they meet. If we are to disrupt monolingualism, we need to offer texts where translanguaging is the norm (Espinosa and Lehner-Quam, 2019), after all, Peterson and Eeds (2007) asserted that "literature is the illumination of life" (p. 18).

Researcher Li Wei (2011) asserted, "translanguaging creates a social space for the multilingual user by bringing together different dimensions of their personal history, experience, and environment, their attitude, belief, and ideology, their cognitive and physical capacity into one coordinated and meaningful performance" (p. 1223). If translanguaging affords multilingual students equitable learning opportunities, it is of critical importance that we reframe what is considered the norm and strive to normalize the multilingual practices of students (García and Kleyn, 2016). Next, we share illustrative examples (stories) of our own teaching practices within our respective roles at the college, as we strive to normalize the languaging practices of our teacher candidates. We begin with the story of Cecilia's practice within one of the courses she teaches.

7.4 Capitalizing on Our Languaging Practices: Cecilia's Story of Her Pedagogical Practices

As a faculty member teaching the class, I am keenly aware that I am a language policymaker. I can set the tone from day one and create a space to invite the students from the start of the semester to bring into the class their entire linguistic repertoire. In this section, I share the ways in which I invite teacher candidates in a graduate-level class to experience translanguaging as we think about the implications for their own practice. Although in this course, there is a requirement for the students to be bilingual, the students arrive at the course with a monoglossic ideology about language, including their own languaging practices. They have grown up keeping languages separate between home and school. If they attended a bilingual program as students when they were in elementary school, these programs followed strict language separation ideologies. Additionally, I find that most of the students come to class thinking of translanguaging as a scaffold used by teachers to remediate a situation when a student needs translation, not as a dynamic and liberating practice for multilingual people.

I begin the semester by inviting them to experience the work of well-known bilingual poets who translanguage, such as Young Poet's 2022 Laureate, Elizabeth Acevedo. As a class, we listen to Acevedo recite her poem titled *Inheritance: A Visual Poem* (Acevedo, 2022) a couple of times. We also read it in print. This is a poem about reclaiming ancestry. It is also about resisting and fighting back against anyone who has told their people to hide their natural hair. We examine it from a reader's and writer's perspective. We also study bilingual poetry written by past students. In addition, we read and discuss the essay on colorism by Alsace and St. Jean (2021) who assert that "understanding the deep-rooted history and modern-day implications, as well as how individuals and groups might begin to battle colorism, are ways in which schools, school systems, and other institutions might begin to ensure greater equity and inclusion at all levels" (p. 19).

Next, I invite the class to compose an identity poem that integrates their entire linguistic repertoire, and, at the same time, I encourage them to take a critical perspective on the world, i.e. gender, race, language, colorism, poverty, or ecology. The next week, we come prepared to share our poetry and visual images. As we share, we marvel at the translanguaging capacities each one of us has. We talk about what it meant to be invited to utilize their entire linguistic repertoire. It was during this instance that Dacy shared, "I couldn't stop writing my poem, the words flowed like a river. This is the first time I have written using Spanish and English." Similarly, to Dacy, other students recall that they too have never been invited to utilize their entire linguistic repertoire in a college classroom. We talk about what it felt like to be able to bring all of themselves into this literacy experience. They often share how it enabled them to recall particular memories that had been hidden for a while. They talk about how liberating it felt not to censor their languaging practices.

The following week I asked the class to prepare two artifacts: a written, drawn, multimodal personal language portrait and a photo essay of their school, their classroom, and its community language ecology. In the language profile assignment, they are asked to explore and reflect on their own languaging practices. The purpose is for the class to see how these languages live within their lives (Espinosa and Ascenzi-Moreno, 2021). They might start by thinking about named languages and how these exist within their lived experiences. As a result of this assignment, they discover that as multilinguals they, in fact, translanguage throughout the day. These fluid and dynamic languaging practices emerge as the norm in their language portraits. For some of the teacher candidates, this is an opportunity to consider how to reclaim and legitimize a language practice. Others talk about the ways in which Spanish draws from various indigenous languages, reminding us of our mestizaje and colonization (Quijano, 2019). For others, it affords the opportunity to illustrate how, through their interest in anime, they learned some Japanese via technology.

When students prepare and present their language ecology photo essays of the school's neighborhood, the school, and their classrooms, they are surprised by the ways in which schools create rigid separation between the language ecology of the community and the languages visible in the school. We talk about the strict isolation of languages in bilingual dual-language schools and the ways in which other languages spoken by families are often invisible (Sánchez et al., 2022). When I ask them to think about who the students in their classes are and compare them to their own findings in their photo essays, this artificial separation becomes more evident, and a dialogue emerges about what can be done in schools and classrooms in order to ensure its language ecology reflects the community's languaging practices. We discuss the powerful message schools can send about valuing the languaging practices of the children, their families, and the communities (Menken et al., 2018). These three experiences aided me in setting the tone in our college classroom that says translanguaging is a valuable practice in this learning community.

As the semester continues, translanguaging becomes more and more the norm in our classroom. We explore, for example, the work of children's book authors who translanguage. Students are also asked to keep a writer's notebook. The intention of this assignment is to invite students to write *en español en su cuaderno de escritura*. This experience also leads several teacher candidates to reclaim their Spanish, as they grow as writers and learn to become more comfortable using translanguaging to resist English monolingualism. It is without a doubt, in these moments that they can experience translanguaging's transformative power. In the next section, education librarian Alison shares the ways in which she and her colleagues in the campus library intentionally strive to normalize the languaging practices of the education students by creating a welcoming environment and multilingual collection.

7.5 Serving the Campus Community Through Multilingual Library Services and Collections: Alison's Story of Her Pedagogical Practice

Addressing multilingualism in the library requires intentionality. College libraries can support multilingualism in a number of ways, through the languages included in library collections, through discovery tools that students use to find materials in the library, through services provided by library faculty at the reference desk, and by instruction in library classrooms. Some of these library components require habits of mind and practices that are addressed at an individual or faculty level and others may require systemic change. For example, during library instruction classes librarians can employ critical information literacy approaches to explore database content and problematic search language to support a critical understanding of the socio-political aspects of the creation and distribution of knowledge (Tewell, 2018).

7 "The Words Flowed Like a River"

While not all librarians in our library are multilingual, those who are, use their linguistic repertoire to support students in multiple languages in library classrooms and at the reference desk. The library's Head of Reference is working on creating a list of frequently used library terms in multiple languages for library faculty and also plans to offer library tours in various languages. Students often seek her out at the reference desk for consultations in Spanish. The values statement on diversity and inclusion in our library's recently adopted Mission, Vision, and Values document opens with: "Fostering a library environment where all members of the Lehman community experience a remarkable sense of belonging" (Lehman College, 2021). As a way to increase awareness of diversity, the library's Diversity and Inclusion working group sponsors a library faculty and staff discussion group series. Readings and film viewings led to conversations among library faculty about ways to serve all students and supported ongoing reflection of our service and teaching practices.

The library's social justice values statement articulates that we develop "robust collections reflecting the Bronx's diverse communities" (Lehman College, 2021). Collection development requires resources. A number of collaborative research grants sought out by the authors of this chapter have improved the books for youth collection. These grants have provided opportunities to study children's and college students' interactions with multilingual books and to build a collection of books and related discovery guides. This work involved research, discovery of multilingual book authors and illustrators, sources for multilingual books, and identification of ways to find them easily in the library system. We worked together to build awareness of the collections on campus by offering workshops focused on the new collections, incorporating the collections into library instruction, writing articles for campus publications, and publishing our research.

These grants provided greater knowledge of our campus and the broader community. Our initial research grant titled *Children's Literature for Bilingual and Latino Children: Mirrors and Windows* provided us the opportunity to study young children's multimodal experiences with culturally and linguistically relevant books. Research conducted in K-2nd grade classrooms resulted in children studying and then creating their own bilingual books (Ascenzi-Moreno et al., 2022; Espinosa and Lehner-Quam, 2019).

Through this grant, the library expanded to include books in Spanish, bilingual Spanish–English books, and books with translanguaging, where characters in stories communicated utilizing their whole linguistic repertoire. Languages were the focus of the collection development process. There were relevant multilingual books already in the library and these were also highlighted in new discovery tools. To spotlight the collection the

7.5 Serving the Campus Community Through Multilingual Library Services and Collections | 133

books were shelved together in a prominent location, library displays featured new titles, and new discovery tools eventually evolved into this guide: https://libguides.lehman.edu/ChildrensBooksThemes.

Our next grant *Affirming Identities: The Power of Diversity in Children's Literature* led us to explore the diverse stories and reading experiences of teacher candidates at the college. The research design included a survey into their identities and experiences with books. Through our greater understanding of our community, we developed a collection in which teacher candidates and the children with whom they work could find themselves in a book. We also offered workshops to the entire campus around the new collections (Lehner-Quam et al., 2020).

The research led to the development of books for youth collection, where identities, such as linguistic, racial, and gender, were the focus of the collection development process. Realistic fiction books with central characters and their families who spoke multiple languages were added to the collection. Yasmin (Faruqi and Aly, 2018), whose family speaks English and Urdu, and the St. Lucian children of *The Field* (Paul and Alcántara, 2018) who communicate in St. Lucian Creole expanded the diversity of languaging practices in the library. As a result of a collection process focused on identity, the languages collected in the library expanded.

Subsequent grants included research into nonfiction, where the collection development process focused on works created by BIPOC (Black, Indigenous, and people of color) authors and illustrators have led to an expanded collection of biographies, STEM, and history titles. Our grant in progress *Exploring Contemporary Caribbean Children's and Young Adult Literature: Implications for Culturally Responsive and Sustaining Education* provides opportunities to explore story traditions and genres coming from the Caribbean. We are looking into who is speaking to children and adolescents and their experiences today with stories that come out of a rich oral tradition. Through this grant, the languages collected in the library and our knowledge of who is publishing in these languages will continue to grow. We expect to have books with translanguaging or multilingual books in the languages of the Caribbean, which are extensive and varied, including Spanish varieties, French, Haitian Creole, St. Lucian Creole, Dominica Creole, Patois, and English. We expect these new books to further reflect the identities of the students on campus.

Faculty requests for library workshops focused on these collections have expanded over the periods of these grants (Lehner-Quam, 2022) and have focused on specific class assignments, including diverse author studies, finding new multilingual books, and finding social justice books. Each of these grants has provided opportunities to learn and deepen knowledge about our community, languages, books, discovery tools, authors and illustrators, and the interactions between individuals and stories, all of which inform how we can better serve our students. The intentional collection development has provided the campus with a book collection reflective of the student body and relevant to their work in the schools. In the next section, Melissa shares how she scaffolded her observation and assessment course in ways that invite teacher candidates to reflect on their own languaging practices while considering implications for their own practice.

7.6 Child Development Reflections: Melissa's Story of Her Pedagogical Practice

In the introductory graduate course, I work with teacher candidates who are returning to college to pursue their initial state certification in early childhood education. Approximately, a quarter of the class will complete the bilingual extension. While the majority are already working in classrooms as educators, there is a shared concern about meeting graduate-level academic standards given their past educational experiences.

I intentionally plan several peer community-building activities where we share who we are. For example, our first-class teacher candidates write replies to questions: "What language(s) do you speak, read, or write in?"; "What do you hope to accomplish this semester and/or get out of the course?" As homework, they collect visual self-data on their digital literacy usage over the course of a day. Teacher candidates discuss their data by accessing a shared slide deck in class. For each of the (3) three pictures, they note what language modality (listening, speaking, reading, and/or writing) is most reflected. In many instances, multiple modalities and languages describe the photographed moment. In preparation for observing a child culminating in a descriptive child review, we discuss how a digital day might look and sound for young children. Reflecting on who we are as learners and educators is central to the coursework emphasis on learning to see children in their entirety.

Language is central to how we form our perceptions of each other and our environment. Espinosa and Bachman (2023) define *maestra* as, "an educator whose practice is deeply grounded in the community she serves" (p. 4). Thinking as a *maestra* implies an organic relationship reflected in language as a social construct existing in the spaces where people interact. Listening and speaking in multilingual ways roots one within the community. Thus, a conscious awareness of context, where *maestras* are spending time with children, facilitates the quality of shared stories evolving between the learner and their family with the *maestra*. To further explore the details that will inform how we see children, our third-class session meets in the library for a diverse children's book workshop. After a presentation on finding books in the new collections, teacher candidates select a book they will read to children.

We begin by reflecting on a favorite story from our own childhood memories. As a group, we discuss selecting a book that we remember someone reading to us, reading on our own, and/or connecting to a story we can recall hearing orally. I invite teacher candidates to recollect if the story was shared in a language other than English. This oral story category is significant. Discussion around how lullabies, nursery rhymes, and phonetic books expand the guidelines for what literacy memories teacher candidates recall as young learners themselves. UNESCO defines literacy as,

> Beyond its conventional concept as a set of reading, writing and counting skills, literacy is now understood as a means of identification, understanding, interpretation, creation, and communication in an increasingly digital, text-mediated, information-rich and fast-changing world.
>
> *(Literacy, 2021)*

Our conversation is grounded in how the story goes beyond the physical book being present within our literacy recollections. Teacher candidates reflect on "ways of being and languaging [that] are treated with dignity and are safeguarded" (Espinosa and Bachman, 2023, p. 5). Upon leaving the library with two picture books—one of their own childhood and one to read aloud to children—teacher candidates draft an early learning recollection. Emphasis on using the narrative form to present rich detail within their childhood memory works in conjunction with our course text, *Art of Awareness: How Observation Can Transform Your Teaching* by Carter and Curtis (2022). As educators, we are the audience for each other's stories. Our goal is to listen and see each peer's story as a picture within our mind's eye while we read.

Among the recollection stories shared, there are multiple languages used. The voice of caretakers: mother, grandmother, and aunt are often present. They communicate care, love, and an overall sense of seeing the whole child emerge. Through storytelling that draws on their entire linguistic repertoire, the listener/reader's perspective is broadened. The relationship between contextual setting and meaningful learning is deepened. This activity expands on how teacher candidates recall their language usage in ways that provide insight into who their caretakers were to them and how language use characterizes who they are today as educators in formation.

In our next class, we compose a double-entry journal. Returning to the books they selected in the library from their own childhood, teacher candidates select a quote to dialogue with. The CUNY NYSIEB guide (Espinosa et al., 2016) describes the double-entry journal as a tool for learners to process what they are reading. The emphasis in the double-journal entry is on a reader's constructing their own meaning of the text. Within the translanguaging scope of accessing tools for "Writing as Dialogue," the double-entry journal is highlighted for how it "invites students to utilize their entire linguistic repertoire in order to fully construct meaning" (Espinosa et al., 2016, p. 24). Centering teacher candidates in a manner that models how they will work with young learners and their families requires a range of open-ended literacy tools. As evidenced in spoken comments within the graduate classroom such as, "Oh, I didn't know we could respond in Spanish or Albanian or Fulani" the multilingual teacher candidates benefit from an explicit discussion about how we as educators and learners feel empowered to bring all aspects of who we are to our critical thinking process. Students nod or comment after the exercise on how they were "not aware" of how they could approach the writing task. As faculty, I explicitly model how processing thought in more than one language can look and sound, in response an engaged murmur grows in the classroom as writing unfolds among the teacher candidates.

A raciolinguistic perspective (Flores and Rosa, 2015; Rosa and Flores, 2017) works toward undoing historically embedded relationships between language and a BIPOC community. Further discussion and exploration of how a language is a living form of expression; therefore, dynamic representation of who we are as people is not only theorized in the graduate class but also experienced. Through classroom practices that incorporate learning tools such as self-observation and the double-entry journal, multilingual teacher candidates experience an expansive approach to learning. Within the graduate class, we reflect upon our own language experiences and how to invite young learners to draw on all of their developing skills and capitalize on their own languaging practices.

7.7 Implications and Conclusion

Teacher education has the capacity to disrupt the raciolinguistic ideology (Flores and Rosa, 2015) of large numbers of teachers, as well as develop a theory and practice informed by the transformative power of translanguaging

7.7 Implications and Conclusion | **137**

to leverage their students' entire linguistic repertoire more fully. As evident in the three interwoven stories shared, teacher educators and library faculty have the power to ensure diverse languaging practices are welcome in the college classroom. Teachers as learners benefit from forming new experiences with twenty-first-century understandings of language. It matters that these experiences begin with a focus on how children, their families, and communities language (García and Li Wei, 2014).

Translanguaging can exist as the norm in a multiplicity of campus life. Therefore, to fully develop a deep knowledge of translanguaging theory and practices, teacher candidates can participate in engagements that allow them to draw from their own lived experiences, as well as from observing, dialoguing, questioning, reflecting, and creating new spaces for translanguaging to be the norm in their daily lives. Within our own and our students' languaging practices, we must find opportunity channels where words will flow. For instance, when college and library faculty collaborate on translanguaging possibilities, monolingualism is decentered. Teacher education and college library faculty have the capacity to model a broad and inclusive learning community that supports teacher candidates' future partnerships with school librarians, such as the development of diverse children's book collections where learners can find themselves in books.

College and library faculty members are language policymakers. We create invitations for the whole person to come into our learning spaces. It is only then, that students can more freely enact their agency by capitalizing on their entire linguistic repertoire to more fully construct meaning. These three stories illustrate that change can begin with individual agency and faculty coming together to re-imagine what it means to take a perspective of strength toward the languaging practices our teacher candidates bring with them. A stance that recognizes, builds, and sustains their multilingualism requires purposeful efforts. One example of intentional next steps is continuing discussions among teacher candidates and faculty around patterns of languaging practices within our urban communities. Reflection on how we construct a language that embraces the whole person invites a collaborative consciousness among faculty co-conspirators and within the college classrooms.

Additionally, to improve language education for prospective teachers, we recommend that

- Education and library faculty need to receive professional development in translanguaging theory and pedagogy, so they can create these intentional spaces in their respective roles from a perspective of multilingualism as an asset and as dynamic.

- All prospective teachers need to be invited to engage in practices that disrupt monolingualism and the ways in which bilingualism has been traditionally taught and conceived.
- Educators disrupt the artificial barriers created between home and community languaging practices and school language practices.
- The language ecology of the educational site reflects the languaging practices of the students, faculty, and other members that make up this diverse learning community.
- A multilingual task force needs to be created at the college level in order to deepen and enhance the vision of multilingualism as the norm in college life and classrooms, particularly in schools of education.

To conclude, a raciolinguistic perspective (Flores and Rosa, 2015) creates opportunities for faculty and students at the university to critically examine and disrupt socially constructed ideologies about race and language. Explicit attention to how we use language and the invitations we create as *maestras* within a learning community honors, centers, and bridges the opportunity gap. It matters that we create learning spaces filled with possibilities for all students to thrive (Love, 2019). Finally, it is important to note that, as we engage in this journey, we need to expand our circle and invite other faculty members, departments, and programs at the college to re-imagine how they can take a perspective of strength toward their students' diverse languaging practices and thus socially constructing a new collaborative critical consciousness.

References

Acevedo, E. (2022). *Inheritance: A Visual Poem*. Quill Tree Books.

Alsace, T., & St. Jean, M. (2021, winter). Combatting colorism in bilingual and ENL education: a battle whose time has come. *NYSABE Bilingual Times*, 19–21.

Ascenzi-Moreno, L., Espinosa, C. M., & Lehner-Quam, A. (2022). Move, play, language: a translanguaged, multimodal approach to literacies with young emergent bilinguals. In S. Brown, & L. Hao (Eds.), *Multimodal Literacies in Young Emergent Bilinguals: Beyond Print-centric Practices* (pp. 117–130). Multilingual Matters.

Berthoff, A. (1987). The teacher as RE-searcher. In D. Goswami, & P. Stillman (Eds.), *Reclaiming the Classroom: Teacher Research as an Agency for Change* (pp. 28–38). Boynton/Cook.

Bishop, R. S. (1990). Mirrors, windows, and sliding glass doors. *Perspectives: Choosing and Using Books for the Classroom*. 6(3), ix–xi. Rpt. in Reading is

Fundamental, 2015. https://scenicregional.org/wp-content/ uploads/2017/08/Mirrors-Windows-and-Sliding-Glass-Doors.pdf.

Carter, D., & Curtis, M. (2022). *Art of Awareness: How Observation Can Transform Your Teaching*, second edition. Redleaf Press.

Cochran-Smith, M., & Lytle, S. (1999). The teacher research movement: a decade later. *Educational Researcher, 28*(7), 15–25.

Cochran-Smith, M., & Lytle, S. (2009). *Inquiry as Stance: Practitioner Research for the Next Generation* (Practitioner Inquiry Series). Teacher College Press.

España, C., & Herrera, L. (2020). *En comunidad: Lessons for Centering the Voices and Experiences of Bilingual Latinx Students.* Heinemann.

Espinosa, C., & Ascenzi-Moreno, L. (2021). *Rooted in Strength: Using Translanguaging to Grow Multilingual Readers and Writers.* Scholastic.

Espinosa, C., & Bachman, R. (2023). Becoming maestras, learning to attend with care. *Schools: Studies in Education*, Spring 2023.

Espinosa, C., & Lehner-Quam, A. (2019). Sustaining bilingualism: multimodal arts experiences for young readers and writers. *Language Arts, 96*(4), 265–268.

Espinosa, C., Ascenzi, L., & Vogel, S. (2016). *A Translanguaging Pedagogy for Writing: A CUNY NYSIEB Guide for Educators.* CUNY NYSIEB. https:// www.cuny-nysieb.org/wp-content/uploads/2016/05/TLG-Pedagogy-Writing-04-15-16.pdf.

Espinosa, C., Ascenzi-Moreno, L., Kleyn, T., & Sánchez, M. (2020). Transforming urban teacher education: the City University of New York. In City University of New York-New York State Initiative on Emergent Bilinguals (Ed.), *Translanguaging and Transformative Teaching for Emergent Bilingual Students: Lessons from the CUNY-NYSIEB Project* (pp. 257–260). Routledge.

Faruqi, S., & Aly, H. (2018). *Yasmin the fashionista.* Picture Window Books, a Capstone imprint.

Flores, N., & Rosa, J. (2015). Undoing appropriateness: raciolinguistic ideologies and language diversity in education. *Harvard Educational Review, 85*(2), 149–171. https://doi.org/10.17763/0017-8055.85.2.149.

García, O. (2009). *Bilingual Education in the 21st Century: A Global Perspective.* Malden, MA and Oxford: Basil/Blackwell.

García, O. (2020). Translanguaging and Latinx bilingual readers. *The Reading Teacher 73*(5), 557–562. https://doi.org/10.1002/trtr.1883.

García, O., & Espinosa, C. (2020). Bilingüismo y translanguaging. Consecuencias para la educación. En Martín-Rojo, L., & J. Pujolar Cos (coords.). *Claves para entender el multilingüismo contemporáneo* (pp. 31–61). Editorial UOC y Universidad de Zaragoza.

García, O., & Kleifgen, J. (2018). *Educating Emergent Bilinguals: Policies, Programs and Practices for English Learners*, second edition. Teachers College Press.

García, O., & Kleyn, T. (Eds.). (2016). *Translanguaging with Multilingual Students: Learning from Classroom Moments*. Routledge.

García, O., & Otheguy, R. (2017). Interrogating the language gap of young bilingual and bidialectal students. *International Multilingual Research Journal, 11*(1), 52–65. https://doi.org/10.1080/19313152.2016.1258190.

García, O., & Li Wei. (2014). *Translanguaging: Language, Bilingualism and Education*. Palgrave Macmillan.

García, O., Johnson, S., & Seltzer, K. (2017). *The Translanguaging Classroom. Leveraging Student Bilingualism for Learning*. Caslon.

Goodman, K. (1996). *On Reading*. Heinemann.

Goodman, K., & Goodman, Y. (2014). *Making Sense of Learners Making Sense of Written Language: The Selected Works of Kenneth S. Goodman and Yetta Goodman*. Routledge.

Heller, M. (ed.) (2007). *Bilingualism: A Social Approach*. Palgrave Macmillan.

Jørgensen, J. N., Karrebæk, M.S., Madsen, L. M., & Møller, J. S. (2011). Polylanguaging in superdiversity. *Diversities, 13*, 24–37.

Lehman College (2021). *Library Mission, Vision, and Values Statement*. https://lehman.edu/library/mission.php.

Lehner-Quam, A. (2022). Diversifying and transforming a public university's children's book collection: librarian and teacher education faculty collaboration on grants, research, and collection development. *Collection Management, 47*(2–3), 157–178.

Lehner-Quam, A., West, R. K., & Espinosa, C. M. (2020). Developing and teaching with a diverse children's literature collection at an urban public college: what teacher education students know and ways their knowledge can grow about diverse books. *Behavioral & Social Sciences Librarian, 36*(4), 171–208.

Li Wei (2011). Moment analysis and translanguaging space: discursive construction of identities by multilingual Chinese Youth in Britain. *Journal of Pragmatics, 43*, 1222–1235.

Literacy. (2021) March 8. UNESCO. https://www.unesco.org/en/literacy/need-know.

Love, B. L. (2019). *We Want to do More Than Survive: Abolitionist Teaching and the Pursuit of Educational Freedom*. Beacon Press.

Lugones, M. (2003). *Pilgrimages/Peregrinajes: Theorizing Coalition Against Multiple Oppressions*. Rowman & Littlefield Publishers.

Makoni, S., & Pennycook, A. (2010). *Disinventing and Reconstituting Languages*. Clevedon, UK: Multilingual Matters.

Menken, K., Rosario, V., & Guzmán-Valerio, L. A. (2018). Increasing multilingualism in schoolscapes: new scenery and language education policies. *Linguistic Landscape, 4*(2), 101–127.

Mignolo, W. (2000). *Local Histories/Global Designs, Coloniality, Subaltern Knowledges, and Border Thinking*. Princeton University Press.

Neighborhood Scout. (2022). Bronx, NY: Demographic Data. https://www.neighborhoodscout.com/ny/bronx/demographics.

Otheguy, R., García, O., & Reid, W. (2015). Clarifying translanguaging and deconstructing named languages: a perspective from linguistics. *Applied Linguistics Review, 6*(3), 281–307.

Otheguy, R., García, O., & Reid, W. (2018). A translanguaging view of the linguistic system of bilinguals. *Applied Linguistics Review, 10*(4), 625–651.

Paul, B., & Alcántara, J. (2018). *The Field*. NorthSouth Books, Inc.

Peterson, R., & Eeds, M. (2007). *Grand Conversations: Literature Groups in Action*. Scholastic.

Pujolar, C. J., Rojo, L. M. (coords). (2020). *Claves para Entender el Multilingüismo*, Editorial UOC y Universidad de Zaragoza.

Quijano, A. (2019). Colonialidad del poder, raza y capitalismo. *Debates En Sociología, 49*, 165–180. https://doi.org/10.18800/debatesensociologia.201902.01.

Rosa, J., & Flores, N. (2017). Unsettling race and language: toward a raciolinguistic perspective. *Language in Society, 46*(5), 621–647.

Rosenblatt, L. M. (1995). *Literature as Exploration*, fifth edition. The Modern Language Association of America.

Sánchez, M. Espinet, I., & Hunt, V. (2022). Student inquiry into the language practices de sus comunidades: Rompiendo fronteras in a dual language bilingual school. In M. Sanchez, & O. Garcia (Eds.), *Sin miedo: Transformative translanguaging espacios* (134–155). Multilingual Matters.

Tewell, E. C. (2018). The practice and promise of critical information literacy: academic librarians' involvement in critical library instruction. *College & Research Libraries, 79*(1), 10–34.

Zavala, V. (2017). Nuevos bilingüismos y viejas categorías en la formación inicial de docentes. *Revista Peruana de Investigación Educativa, 1*, 61–84. https://doi.org/10.34236/rpie.v9i9.58.

Zavala, V., & Back, M. (Eds.) (2017). *Racismo y lenguaje*. Pontificia Universidad Católica del Perú, Fondo Editorial.

8

Linguistic Journeys: Interrogating Linguistic Ideologies in a Teacher Preparation Setting
Ivana Espinet

City University of New York, Kingsborough Community College, New York, United States

> *I would have never imagined that the preparation (or lack thereof) that I received from my teacher education program would contribute to me reproducing the same racial and linguistic inequities I was hoping to dismantle.*
>
> April Baker-Bell (2020, p. 4)

8.1 Introduction

I teach in the Education Program at a public community college in New York City (NYC). Every semester, before the start of classes I send all my students a list of questions to help me learn about them. The last two questions are: Do you have any suggestions for me, as an educator, that could help your learning process in this course? Is there anything else about yourself that you would like to share?

Often at least one student will answer that they don't speak or write "good English" and will need help. I've also had Latinx students tell me that they don't speak English or Spanish well when they find out that I am from Argentina and that my home language is Spanish. For example, Yolanda, who moved to New York as an adult from the Dominican Republic, explained to me: "I tried to use the correct and proper way of speaking Spanish with people, but I talk fast and cut out many words in my vocabulary ...."

Language Teacher Identity: Confronting Ideologies of Language, Race, and Ethnicity,
First Edition. Edited by Sílvia Melo-Pfeifer and Vander Tavares.
© 2024 John Wiley & Sons Ltd. Published 2024 by John Wiley & Sons Ltd.

As Rosa (2019) observes referring to the stigmatization of US Latinxs' English and Spanish linguistic practices: "whereas bilingualism is generally associated with abilities in two languages (e.g., English and Spanish), it becomes redefined as linguistic deficiency altogether" (p. 127). Dominant ideologies of monoglossic standards (García, 2009; Martin et al., 2019) and "languagelessness" or views that some people are unable to use any language legitimately (Rosa, 2019) inform teachers' perceptions of bilingual students. My students have often internalized these ideologies after years of early schooling experiences in which their language practices were viewed as deficient. Most of them have had experiences in NYC schools, in "mainstream" English only classrooms and have not had an opportunity to use their linguistic repertoires fluidly. I also often hear from my students early in the semester that their goals as educators are for the children in their classes to use "proper" English or "standard" English reproducing the raciolinguistic ideologies that deemed them deficient.

April Baker-Bell (2020) points to the damage that we can do as teacher-educators, if we don't attempt to disrupt a cycle that trains teachers to continue to reproduce language ideologies that deem children's language practices as deficient. As critical teaching about the connections between language and power has been missing in teacher preparation programs until recently, this has contributed to furthering the oppression of language-minoritized populations[1] and reproducing the status quo in educational spaces (Martin et al., 2019).

In this chapter, I describe three classroom activities in the context of the course "Teaching Emergent Bilinguals" for pre-service teachers. These assignments are meant to begin a journey that requires pre-service teachers to examine the connections between language and power in their practice and in the educational contexts in which they will work. However, as educators, we know that this is just the beginning of an ongoing cycle of self-reflection and advocacy.

8.2 Developing Teachers' Stances and Leadership

Deborah Palmer (2018) highlights the urgency of supporting the development of bilingual teachers' leadership as a struggle for justice. She describes bilingual teachers'' leadership as "intricately tied to cultural and linguistic

---

1 I use the term language-minoritized population to refer to those considered bi/multilingual in two or more named languages who fall across a spectrum of bilingualism, as well as English-speaking students whose language practices are stigmatized, such as African-American, or students from Caribbean descent because they are subject to similar deficit-oriented ideologies (Seltzer and García, 2020).

identities and praxis and building broad networks of professional allies" (p. 2). This encompasses the development of professional identities as leaders and advocates. While the focus of her work is on bilingual teachers, I believe that it is essential that we strive to support the development of teacher leadership for all teachers working with emergent bilinguals and language-minoritized students in a variety of contexts. Katzenmeyer and Moller (2009) define teacher leadership as a practice that goes beyond the classroom, supporting the work of other educators as they continue to advance and examine their practices within their own classrooms. In my view, this must include collaboration with other educators in their school communities as overall educational advocacy at district, city, and national levels.

Seltzer (2022) advocates for focusing on the personal, political, and pedagogical elements of teachers' stances to enable them to take up such an approach with the students they teach. García et al. (2017) describe teachers' translanguaging stance as a positioning that recognizes that all students' linguistic and multimodal practices are critical for learning. Teachers with a translanguaging stance seek to reclaim the language practices of bilinguals and understand that it is essential to put them at the center of their educational experiences. España and Herrera (2020) propose critical bilingual literacies (CBLs) approach that offers a path for bilingual teacher preparation rooted in social justice. The CBL framework has four guiding principles: The first principle encourages educators to engage in an ongoing cycle of self-reflection on their language and identity formation, unpacking their experiences to explore their language practices. The second is to practice a pedagogy that focuses on "unlearning" notions of linguistic supremacy that uphold racialized language hierarchies, including unlearning purist ideologies of language. The third principle advocates for an analysis of the relationships between language, literacies, and power in texts, curriculum, and the world. The fourth principle is to create intentional spaces that celebrate the dynamic language practices of emergent bilingual children in schooling and engage them in translanguaging. While España and Herrera's work focused on CBL as an approach for bilingual teachers, I would argue that this framework needs to be applied to the work with all educators, not just bilingual teachers. It is also essential that we use it not only to foster the development of personal and pedagogical stances but also to examine how those are intertwined with a political stance. As Paulo Freire explained, teaching is a political act (Freire, 1970) and as such, pre-service teachers need an opportunity to reflect on and develop their personal, political, and pedagogical stances.

The course that I share in this chapter is designed with a translanguaging perspective and attempts to provide critical lenses so students can examine their language practices and ideologies and consider how these might manifest in their pedagogical practices. Translanguaging theory and pedagogy also provide a framework to resist raciolinguistic ideologies (Flores and Rosa, 2015), creating room for affirming learning experiences for emergent bilingual children.

8.3 Pre-service Teachers at a Community College

The course that I describe here is part of the Teacher Education Program at Kingsborough Community College, City University of New York, an urban public community college in NYC. The college offers two-year degrees; if students decide that they want to continue in a teacher preparation program, they have to transfer to a four-year institution to continue their studies. The overall population of the college in 2021 was 37.4% Black, 15% Asian, 17.7%, Latinx, and 29.1% White (many of whom are immigrants from Eastern European countries) (Kingsborough Community College, City University of New York, 2022). Most students work at part-time jobs and care for children/parents and come from language-minoritized populations.

Some of the students who are in the education program are paraprofessionals in schools or work in after-school settings. Most of them hope to continue to work as paraprofessionals, work in early childhood centers, or transfer to a four-year college to complete their degree in early childhood or childhood studies and become certified teachers.

Given the population of NYC, it is fair to expect that all teachers will be working in classrooms with bilingual students, whether or not they are officially classified as Multilingual Learners/English Language Learners (MLLs/ELLs).[2] In NYC, approximately 16% of students enrolled in public schools are officially identified as MLLs. However, 42% of students enrolled in NYC public schools have a home language other than English (New York City Department of Education, Division of Multilingual Learners, 2021).

---

2 The NYC Department of Education uses the term Multilingual Language Learners/ English Language Learners (MLLs/ELLs) for students who are not yet proficient in English, according to New York State's standardized assessment. In the rest of the article, I chose to use the term "emergent bilinguals" because it emphasizes students' potential to become bilingual. Using the term "emergent bilinguals" recognizes bilingualism as "a cognitive, social, and educational resource" (García and Kleifgen, 2010, p. 3). However, when referring to data from the NYC DOE, I still use the term MLLs.

In order to introduce future teachers who will work in a variety of settings with emergent bilinguals, the course explores language acquisition theories; the historical, philosophical, and pedagogical evolution of how educational institutions have approached their work with emergent bilinguals; and pedagogical strategies focusing on the role of educators in supporting emergent bilinguals learning language and literacy across content. One of the key goals is for pre-service teachers to understand teachers' roles in working toward equity for emergent bilinguals.

Throughout the course, students engage in personal reflections in connection with their own experiences growing up, as students in the community college and educators. In turn, I also share my own experiences as an emergent bilingual. During the first part of the course, the students read articles and listen to podcasts and videos on language, literacies, and power. For instance, we learned about the dynamic bilingualism (García, 2009) that is enacted through their translanguaging (García and Li Wei, 2014), raciolinguistic ideologies (Flores and Rosa, 2015), listened to Jamila Lyiscott's 3 *Ways to Speak English* (Lyiscott, 2014) and read her blog post *Your Pedagogy Might be More Aligned with Colonialism than You Realize* (Lyiscott, 2017). The second part of the semester is focused on translanguaging pedagogy and developing a translanguaging stance (Collins et al., 2019; García et al., 2017), as we turn to classroom instruction.

I collected data during two semesters in which I taught the course. The first semester I had 14 students; in the second, I had 18 students. All of the course assignments were submitted using Blackboard, an online learning platform used by the college, so they are in a digital repository. In this chapter, I focused on a "Reflection on personal language practices" assignment, "Classroom practices reviews" assignments, as well as discussion board responses to classroom readings and short videos. In addition, I often take notes after my classes, mostly to reflect on the class and to remind myself of what themes and threads I need to follow in the following meetings. I find that sometimes, there are new threads/ideas that come up during a discussion or an activity that I am not able to address or make the time to explore in depth because we are trying to accomplish a particular task, but that I want to return to at a later class. I used some of these notes as data for this chapter. The data were thematically analyzed with inductive and deductive coding, looking carefully at participants' own words. In the initial reading of the data, I drew on deductive codes from the existing literature that included translanguaging; language ideologies; personal, political, and pedagogical teacher stances; and language hierarchies. As I analyzed the data, themes emerged connected to students' understandings of the relationships between home and school language practices, school and district language policies, and translanguaging theory and praxis. Through analysis of the students' work, I illustrate the ways in which students voiced their understandings of these intersections.

As a college professor doing research in my classroom, I was aware that I brought in a particular lens and that there is an unbalanced power relationship between students and teacher. While I had obtained permission through the institutional IRB process to conduct research in my classroom before teaching the courses, I asked students for permission to analyze and use their class work after they completed the course so they would not feel obligated to agree to it. Furthermore, all of the students whose work I share in this paper had graduated from the college by the time I asked for permission, given that many of them were in their last semester when they took the class.

8.3.1 Starting Points: Examining Our Language Practices

As educators, our experiences in the world impact how we approach teaching and learning.

During the first week of the course, I ask students to write a "Reflection on personal language practices" that they share with peers. I use this first assignment as an opportunity to have students share their experiences and ideas before we engage with readings, so they can later re-examine their initial thoughts and use them as a springboard for discussions as we review new literature. This assignment provides a lens to uncover experiences with languaging that they might not have recalled before or thought about. We return to their writings later in the semester to re-read them in light of the literature and ideas that we've engaged with, inviting an inquiry into the intersections of language, power, and identity, using theory as a lens to examine our own lives, experiences, and ideologies, as well as how they were shaped.

One common thread among the students was the dissonance between home and school language practices and values, as many of them recalled feelings of inferiority and the invisibility of their language practices in their schooling experiences. They often highlighted the fractured nature of linguistic home and school practices. For example, Eduardo,[3] a Mexican-American student, described how during his early years, speaking Spanish was a source of pride and joy. As in many other immigrant families, his parents valued home language development as essential to maintain

---

3 I used pseudonyms for all the students' names to protect their privacy.

cultural identity and to facilitate intergenerational relationships (Carreira and Rodriguez, 2011; Kim, 2011; Valdés, 2021). He describes the shift that he experienced when he entered elementary school, recalling an early moment from his schooling that made him want to become invisible:

> In my community, but as well as in my family, the only language that I was surrounded by was Spanish. During my summer vacations from school, I would travel to Mexico all the time because I would go see my grandparents and with them, it's just Spanish only. I remember when I started elementary school which was when everything took a downturn in my life because I was struggling to communicate with my teachers and my classmates in English because at home even though my siblings spoke English, they would speak Spanish because of my mother. So, I was what they called an "ELL" student. At school, I will get into trouble sometimes because I didn't speak English and my teachers would tell me: "When you are in my classroom you must speak English." I would feel as if I didn't belong in that classroom environment. [sic.]

Eduardo's experience is not unique. Many other students expressed a similar feeling about being shut down and excluded because they could not perform in monolingual ways in school. They described a feeling of not belonging and the stigma that the ELL label carried for them.

Yalina, who grew up in Pakistan and is trilingual in Urdu, Punjabi, and English, wrote about feeling judged by others and inadequate, as she felt isolated from peers and teachers.

> When thinking about learning English made me realize how frustrating and challenging experience was for me. Many classmates of mine used to think I was dumb, don't know anything but they don't realize that I can write and speak very well. My intelligence and intellect was judged by my English proficiency. I was not very verbal in class and was quite shy with an awful accent and pronunciation, since my high school was not bilingual. If students cannot communicate in certain languages to share their problems, there's no way that a teacher can help. [sic]

Another common thread was the complicated relationships between families and schools as family members felt inadequate in navigating their relationships with schools. Dora began her narrative describing how her mother had emphasized learning Spanish as a means to foster linguistic identity

8.3 Pre-service Teachers at a Community College | 149

and pride in family history. However, later on, she shares a traumatic event as she was language brokering in school for her mother:

> The purpose of my mother teaching us Spanish throughout the years of my childhood was part of introducing our cultural language. The goal for us as her children was always to know about our background and culture. She would always encourage my siblings and me to speak Spanish, read Spanish, and write Spanish. My mother believed that if we kept talking Spanish, we would never forget about our background and all the struggles they left behind due to low income and lack of access to education (...) One experience I'll never forget was at the age of 12, attending middle school in my freshman year. It was the first semester of the parent-teacher conference. Usually, my older sister would be translating, but there were some inconveniences, and she couldn't make it. I remember it was our turn to speak with the professor of ELA, and I would notice my mother's face turning red and watery eyes. Still, most of all, the confusion of facial expression of not being able to say, 'I need a Spanish translator!.' She would look at me and start questioning me with these exact words and doubting me. '¡Qué está diciendo Dora! ¿Qué hiciste?.' In other words, 'What is she saying, What did you do?' I would feel insecure because I would see my classmates with parents who spoke English and Spanish. I would feel in a position that made me feel insecure around other people because they would stare or say, 'your mom needs to learn English.' [sic]

While schools in NYC offer translation services, they are often unreliable. In her reflection, Dora had shared earlier that she was used to doing language brokering for her family in other settings as many children of immigrant families do (Orellana, 2009), yet in the context of helping to translate for her mom at a parent–teacher conference in school, she felt that she and her family were judged by others.

Part of our classroom process was for students to read each other's writing, ask questions, and provide feedback on their writing. This allowed students to understand their peers' experiences and engage with them. This process provided a scaffold for everyone in the class to think about what kinds of teachers they wanted to become by recognizing each other's traumatic experiences and considering how to move forward as educators.

As they were introduced to new literature, students also started to reframe their experiences. For example, Dora shared with the class: "I didn't know that Spanglish[4] is translanguaging, I thought it was something that we did at home and not supposed to do in other places." The term "Spanglish" has often been used to stigmatize the language practices of Latinx because they do not conform to monolingual ideologies of what is seen as grammatical correctness (Flores and Rosa, 2015). Learning about translanguaging gave Dora a lens to understand her families' dynamic language practices. Having a new term to describe her language practices that were not rooted in a deficit view empowered her to validate and legitimate them and provided a platform for examining about how it might impact her approach to teaching.

Exploring their own experiences and being explicit about the emotional and political contexts of their language practices and how they are a complex part of their identities provided a platform for students to think critically about how language practices are valued differently. It also empowered them to view themselves as social actors who can challenge these hierarchies.

8.3.2 Widening the Lenses: Understanding District and School Language Policies

Teachers are often negotiating macro policies that developed outside of their context without their input (Menken and García, 2017). Researchers have found that the language policies carried out in NYC schools are largely determined by school teachers and principals (Ascenzi-Moreno et al., 2016) and that school language practices are often driven more by the ideologies of educators than by formal/official language policies (Menken and Solorza, 2015).

Unfortunately, pre-service teachers rarely receive preparation or guidance on how to understand, negotiate, and manage top-down educational policies in ways that support the education of minoritized students. It is important for pre-service teachers to understand how their work plays out in the larger context of language education policies. Their work is impacted by the decisions of what kinds of programs will be offered, the language allocations in the programs, and mandates concerning curriculum and assessment. The work of teachers in the classroom is not isolated from the larger mandates from school and district administrations. Pre-service teachers need to learn early on how to understand and navigate policy mandates that will impact their practices.

---

4 The term "Spanglish" is often used to refer to the speech of Spanish speakers in the United States. However, this term has been used "with the clear implication that it is not Spanish, connecting, sadly, to an old North American tradition of denigrating immigrants from the Spanish-speaking world" (Otheguy and Stern, 2011, p. 97).

8.3 Pre-service Teachers at a Community College | 151

In order to explore the macro-level language policies that will affect their work, I designed an activity in which they learn about the program offerings for emergent bilinguals in their districts. I began with a short presentation explaining the different programs offered in NYC DOE schools and program goals (Dual Language Bilingual Education, Transitional Bilingual Education, and English as a New Language[5]). We discussed the historical roots of bilingual education and pedagogical implications of each one of those programs. Then, I asked the students if they had experience with any of the programs when they were in school. All my students who are bilingual and grew up in NYC were in English as a New Language program; none of them had been in a bilingual program.

The NYC educational system is the largest school system in the nation with over a million students (New York City Department of Education, 2022). At the elementary and middle school level, NYC is divided into 32 school districts, each of which is divided further into school zones based on residential boundaries.[6] While most of my students have attended NYC public schools, when I ask them what school district they attended or live in currently, they generally don't know. I briefly explain how the system is organized and teach them how to find out for which residential district their home or school is zoned. The last step is for them to analyze the program offerings. In groups of three, they compared who are the students in their districts, what are the program offerings for them, and discussed whether they felt that the students were well served, considering what they had learned about each program.

Overall, district-level data reveals great disparities in the program offerings, even in districts with similar percentages of MLLs/ELLs. These disparities exist despite the fact that the New York State Education Department mandates that each school district must provide bilingual education when there are 20 or more MLLs who speak the same home language in the same grade (The Commissioner's Regulations (CR) Part 154, New York State Education Department (2014), Office of Bilingual Education and English as a New Language). However, in reality, 80% of MLLs in NYC are placed in ENL programs, in which instruction is mostly monolingual in English (New York City Department of Education, Division of Multilingual Learners, 2022).

---

5 For more information about these program offerings in New York City, see https://www.schools.nyc.gov/learning/multilingual-learners/programs-for-english-language-learners.

6 In NYC, there are also public charter school and magnet schools that are not bound to a residential zone. However, since most students in elementary and middle school attend districts schools, in this activity, we focus on those.

The students were shocked by the disparities. After reviewing the data, Eduardo commented: "I don't understand this ... my district has only 2 bilingual programs and more students than Ana's district? Hers has 25 programs!" His reaction was not unique. In looking at district offerings, they begin to understand the roots of some of the inequities that they have experienced as students.

The last step is to learn how to advocate both at the school level and in the context of the larger city school system. This includes, for example, how to reach out to politicians and community boards. They also learn about the rights of parents and students to access bilingual education so they can advise and support them in navigating the system which often can be overwhelming for families of emergent bilinguals. As Menken and García (2017) remind us, teachers can use their agency as policymakers in the classroom by shaping learning experiences for their students that honor their language practices. However, it is also essential that teachers see themselves as advocates for the macro educational policies that will affect them, their students, and their families.

8.3.3 Learning from Experienced Teachers

In order to implement a translanguaging pedagogy, pre-service teachers need to begin to develop what García et al. (2017) have called a translanguaging stance. To develop such a stance, teachers need to experience translanguaging and how it works in teaching and learning. They need to be able to see the connection between theory and practice in the context of a classroom setting. Yet, the reality is that this is not always present in the classrooms in which pre-service teachers do fieldwork. While the benefits of translanguaging practice and pedagogy has been well documented (Cenoz and Gorter, 2021; Creese and Blackledge, 2010; García-Mateus and Palmer, 2017; Espinet et al., 2018; Espinosa and Lehner-Quam, 2019; Sánchez and García, 2021), pre-service and in-service teachers often report that translanguaging has yet to be regularly accepted as a pedagogical practice in pre-Kindergarten to 12 classrooms (Martínez et al., 2015; Pontier and Tian, 2022).

As teacher educators, we need to provide the means for pre-service teachers to observe and analyze the practices of experienced teachers who implement translanguaging pedagogy. To do so, I used videos of experienced teachers so we could collectively observe and debrief. One of the videos was of a fourth-grade teacher in a bilingual Spanish classroom, Gladys Aponte (see https://www.cuny-nysieb.org/classroom-videos/ambassador/gladys/). Before viewing the lesson, my students read and listened to Gladys as she provided background on how, from the beginning of the school year, she highlighted the many ways and reasons individuals translanguage. She explained how, during read-alouds and reading lessons, the class considered why an author may have translanguaged and discussed the effects that specific translanguaging moves can have on readers. In addition, Gladys described how she regularly modeled and explained her own translanguaging and she made space for students to reflect on their fluid language practices as fourth-grade bilingual authors.

Later on, my students watched videos of a lesson focused on author's craft in which the fourth-grade class analyzed several texts they had read throughout the year, including their own writing pieces, and created a list of reasons for why authors translanguage. In the video, Gladys explained that she told her students that through the lesson, she would translanguage and she encouraged them to also translanguage freely. As they watched, students were encouraged to take notes and make connections between specific points in the lesson and what they had learned through readings or experiences in the course. After viewing the videos, each of my students wrote a journal with their observation and analysis that they later shared:

> The teacher used many helpful strategies throughout the lesson to implement in her class. To start with, she does not limit herself or students to only stick to one language, she uses both languages half and half based on class language repertoire. She knew that her students are bilingual learners. The classroom setting is done according to their needs and students' language backgrounds. She provided opportunities to work collaboratively in groups using both languages that they know and one which they are learning. [sic] (Yalina)

> Gladys was able to implement a lot of effective strategies in her lesson, the most prominent one being vocabulary inquiry across languages. Gladys is able to foster an ongoing discussion and deeper inquiry about specific vocabulary usage and is not limited by a single language. This is demonstrated when Gladys' students translanguage and are curious about how certain words have cultural ties and they are able to explore that word across two different languages. This really allows them to reach a deeper understanding. [sic] (Laura)

Connecting, theory and praxis is central to understanding how teachers reaffirm students' language practice in the context of a classroom. In their own schooling, many of my students had experienced how their home language practices were unwelcome. Observing a teacher who invites translanguaging into her classroom and leveraged her students dynamic bilingual practices for literacy learning helped them to envision what their own classrooms could look like. They were able to observe concrete strategies, such as group work, in which students used their dynamic bilingualism and vocabulary inquiry in which students leveraged their complex linguistics repertoire to make sense of how and why authors chose wording in their writing.

8.4 Conclusion

As teacher educators, we need to rethink our approach to teacher preparation; otherwise, we will continue to reinforce language hierarchies and deficit approaches to teaching emergent bilingual children and students from language-minoritized populations. It is essential to envision models for teaching pre-service teachers in which they have opportunities to confront societal raciolinguistic ideologies that might have impacted their own education and build a translanguaging stance that welcomes and supports the development of students' dynamic language practices. This is an ongoing journey that can include a three-pronged approach:

- Building a culture of reflection on our own histories as learners and educators by unpacking our journeys and language ideologies. As April Baker-Bell (2020) points out, we have a responsibility to disrupt a cycle that trains teachers to continue to reproduce language ideologies that regard students's language practices as deficient. The first place to start is by creating a space to collectively share and examine our experiences with raciolinguistic ideologies (Flores and Rosa, 2015) and monoglossic standards (García, 2009) in order to begin to develop a translanguaging stance and to "unlearn" notions of linguistic supremacy (España and Herrera, 2020).
- Opportunities to analyze macro-language policies that affect students, families, and educators. Teachers and school administrators are often expected to implement language policies that developed outside of their school context without their input (Menken and García, 2017). To support the development of pre-service teachers' professional identities as leaders and advocates (Palmer, 2018), it is imperative that they understand the language policies that will affect their work, how they are devised and implemented, and what is their impact on the lives of children and families. A critical understanding of the local language education policies at work can provide a platform to build teacher leadership as a practice that goes beyond the classroom and the school community.

- Building intentional spaces to collectively observe and analyze the practices of experienced teachers who implement a translanguaging pedagogy and celebrate the dynamic language practices of emergent bilingual children. Given that in their own schooling, pre-service teachers rarely had a chance to experience spaces in which translanguaging was welcomed or leveraged for learning, we need to provide opportunities to connect theory and praxis by observing other educators in action. Collective observation includes examining the design of a classroom community as a translanguaging space, as well as studying the instructional moves and shifts that educators make as they implement a lesson.

Focusing on these three areas, teacher preparation programs can implement pedagogical approaches that support teacher candidates in developing a clear stance as educators, leaders, and advocates. We need to nourish and grow the personal, political, and pedagogical elements of teachers' stances through self-reflective activities, analysis of the language policies within the local educational contexts, and models for fostering classroom communities that celebrate and nurture students' language practices.

References

Ascenzi-Moreno, L., Hesson, S., & Menken, K. (2016). School leadership along the trajectory from monolingual to multilingual. *Language and Education*, *30*(3), 197–218. https://doi.org/10.1080/09500782.2015.1093499.

Baker-Bell, A. (2020). *Linguistic Justice: Black Language, Literacy, Identity, and Pedagogy*. Routledge.

Carreira, M. M., & Rodriguez, R. M. (2011). Filling the void: Community Spanish language programs in Los Angeles serving to preserve the language. *Heritage Language Journal*, *8*(2), 1–16.

Cenoz, J., & Gorter, D. (2021). *Pedagogical Translanguaging*. Cambridge University Press.

Collins, B. A., Sánchez, M., & España, C. (2019). Sustaining and developing teachers' dynamic bilingualism in a re-designed bilingual teacher preparation program. *International Journal of Bilingual Education and Bilingualism*, 1–17. https://doi.org/10.1080/13670050.2019.1610354.

Creese, A., & Blackledge, A. (2010). Translanguaging in the bilingual classroom: a pedagogy for learning and teaching? *The Modern Language Journal*, *94*(1), 103–115.

España, C., & Herrera, L. Y. (2020). *En comunidad: Lessons for Centering the Voices and Experiences of Bilingual Latinx Students*. Heinemann.

Espinet, I., Collins, B., & Ebe, A. (2018). Leveraging students' translanguaging practices to strengthen the school community. In A. M. Lazar, & P. Ruggiano Schmidt (Eds.), *Schools of Promise for Multilingual Students: Transforming Literacies, Learning, and Lives* (pp. 118–133). Teachers College Press.

Espinosa, C., & Lehner-Quam, A. (2019). Sustaining bilingualism: multimodal arts experiences for young readers and writers. *Language Arts, 96*(4), 265–268.

Flores, N., & Rosa, J. (2015). Undoing appropriateness: raciolinguistic ideologies and language diversity in education. *Harvard Educational Review, 85*(2), 149–171.

Freire, P. (1970). *Pedagogy of the Oppressed.* Herder & Herder.

García, O. (2009). *Bilingual Education in the 21st Century: A Global Perspective.* Wiley/Blackwell.

García, O., & Kleifgen, J. (2010). *Educating emergent bilinguals: Policies, programs and practices for English language learners.* Teachers College Press.

García, O., & Li Wei. (2014). *Translanguaging: Language, Bilingualism and Education.* Palgrave Macmillan.

García, O., Johnson, S. I., & Seltzer, K. (2017). *The Translanguaging Classroom: Leveraging Student Bilingualism for Learning.* Caslon.

García-Mateus, S., & Palmer, D. (2017). Translanguaging pedagogies for positive identities in two-way dual language bilingual education. *Journal of Language, Identity & Education, 16*(4), 245–255.

Katzenmeyer, M., & Moller, G. (2009). *Awakening the Sleeping Giant: Helping Teachers Develop as Leaders.* Corwin Press.

Kim, J. (2011). Korean immigrant mothers' perspectives: The meanings of a Korean heritage language school for their children's American early schooling experiences. *Early Childhood Education Journal, 39*(2), 133–141. https://doi.org/10.1007/s10643-011-0453-1.

Kingsborough Community College, City University of New York (2022). *Institutional Profile.* Retrieved August 23, 2022 from https://www.kbcc.cuny.edu/irap/enrollmentdata.html.

Lyiscott, J. (2014). *3 Ways to Speak English.* TED Feb.

Lyiscott, J. (2017). *Your Pedagogy Might Be More Aligned with Colonialism Than You Realize.* Retrieved August 23 from https://medium.com/@heinemann/your-pedagogy-might-be-more-aligned-with-colonialism-than-you-realize-1ae7ac6459ff.

Martin, K. M., Aponte, G. Y., & García, O. (2019). Countering raciolinguistic ideologies: The role of translanguaging in educating bilingual children. *Cahiers Internationaux de Sociolinguistique, 16*(2), 19–41.

Martínez, R. A., Hikida, M., & Durán, L. (2015). Unpacking ideologies of linguistic purism: how dual language teachers make sense of everyday translanguaging. *International Multilingual Research Journal, 9*(1), 26–42. https://doi.org/10.1080/19313152.2014.977712.

Menken, K., & García, O. (2017). Language policy in classrooms and schools. In T. McCarty, & S. May (Eds.), *Language Policy and Political Issues in Education* (pp. 1–16). Springer.

Menken, K., & Solorza, C. (2015). Principals as linchpins in bilingual education: the need for prepared school leaders. *International Journal of Bilingual Education and Bilingualism, 18* (6), 676–697. https://doi.org/10.108 0/13670050.2014.937390.

New York City Department of Education (2022). DOE *Data at a Glance*. Retrieved September 20, 2022 from https://www.schools.nyc.gov/about-us/ reports/doe-data-at-a-glance.

New York City Department of Education, Division of Multilingual Learners. (2021). *2020–2021 English Language Learner Demographic Report*. New York: Author. Retrieved July 19, 2022 from https://infohub.nyced.org/docs/ default-source/default-document-library/sy-2020-21-ell-demographics-at-a-glance.pdf.

New York City Department of Education, Division of Multilingual Learners (2022). *2021–2022 English Language Learner Demographic Report*. New York: Author. Retrieved January, 2023 from https://infohub.nyced.org/docs/ default-source/default-document-library/sy-2021-22-ell-demographics-at-a-glance.pdf.

New York State Education Department (2014). *Chancellor's Regulations Part 154: Services for pupils with limited English proficiency*. Retrieved from http://www.nysed.gov/common/nysed/files/programs/bilingual-ed/ terms-154-1-effective-through-2014-15.pdf.

Orellana, M. (2009). *Translating Childhoods: Immigrant Youth, Language and Culture*. Rutgers University Press.

Otheguy, R., & Stern, N. (2011). On so-called Spanglish. *International Journal of Bilingualism, 15*(1), 85–100.

Palmer, D. K. (2018). *Teacher Leadership for Social Change in Bilingual and Bicultural Education*. Multilingual Matters.

Pontier, R. W., & Tian, Z. (2022). Paradigmatic tensions in translanguaging theory and practice in teacher education: introduction to the special issue. *Journal of Language, Identity & Education, 21*(3), 139–143. https://doi.org/1 0.1080/15348458.2022.2058857.

Rosa, J. (2019). *Looking Like a Language, Sounding Like a Race: Raciolinguistic Ideologies and the Learning of Latinidad*. Oxford University Press.

Sánchez, M. T., & García, O. (Eds.). (2021). *Transformative Translanguaging espacios: Latinx Students and Their Teachers Rompiendo Fronteras Sin Miedo*. Multilingual Matters.

Seltzer, K. (2022). Enacting a critical translingual approach in teacher preparation: disrupting oppressive language ideologies and fostering the personal, political, and pedagogical stances of preservice teachers of English. *TESOL Journal, 13*, e649. https://doi.org/10.1002/tesj.649.

Seltzer, K., & García, O. (2020). Broadening the view: taking up a translanguaging pedagogy with all language minoritized students. In Z. Tian, L. Aghai, P. Sayer, & J. Schissel (Eds.), *Envisioning TESOL Through a Translanguaging Lens: Global Perspectives* (pp. 23–42). Springer.

Valdés, G. (2021). Afterword: No quiero que me le vayan a hacer burla: issues to ponder and consider in the context of translanguaging. In M. T. Sánchez, & O. García (Eds.), *Transformative Translanguaging Espacios: Latinx Students and Their Teachers Rompiendo Fronteras Sin Miedo* (pp. 292–301). Multilingual Matters.

Part 3

Confronting Ideologies of Ethnicity, Language, and Accent

9

Racialization of the Japanese Language in the Narratives of Brazilian Undergraduate Students

Fabiana Cristina Ramos Patrocínio[1]
and Paula Garcia de Freitas[2]

[1] Sector of Human Sciences, Letters and Arts, Department of Education, Federal University of Paraná (UFPR), Curitiba, PR, Brazil
[2] Sector of Human Sciences, Letters and Arts, Department of Letters, Federal University of Paraná (UFPR), Curitiba, PR, Brazil

9.1 Introduction

Theories that examine the relations between race and language, such as raciolinguistics (Flores and Rosa, 2015; Kubota, 2015; Kubota and Lin, 2010; Rosa and Flores, 2017), seek to understand how social structures stigmatize and racialize individuals in their language practices. That is, how people are judged in their language practices by racial ideas. Based on these theories, this text intends to problematize the ideologies of race and language present in the narratives of Japanese language students participating in the research reported here.

According to Rosa and Flores (2017), raciolinguistics seeks to understand how categories of race and language are "co-naturalized" within historical, colonial processes and social structures (Rosa and Flores, 2017, p. 1). From this point of view, understanding raciolinguistics as a theoretical perspective allows questioning the structures that naturalize and stigmatize categories of race and language. The purpose of raciolinguistics is not only to question the social injustices generated by linguistic and racial hierarchies but also to propose new perceptions about race and language that contribute to fairer societies. According to the authors, it is crucial to understand how these social structures are determinants in the stigmatization of race and language rather than a perspective that focuses only on individual

Language Teacher Identity: Confronting Ideologies of Language, Race, and Ethnicity,
First Edition. Edited by Sílvia Melo-Pfeifer and Vander Tavares.
© 2024 John Wiley & Sons Ltd. Published 2024 by John Wiley & Sons Ltd.

language practices. Moreover, it is necessary to understand how the formation of modernity and the creation of nation-states stigmatized and racialized the modern subject. Understanding how this process institutionalized colonial hierarchies and shaped how languages and people are perceived and legitimized through raciolinguistics contributes to a transnational view of how co-naturalizations of race and language articulate within colonial and nation-state contexts. In this sense, other nation-state societies can benefit from the theories of raciolinguistics to question patterns of race, peoples, and language practices, in stigmatized and racialized contexts.

For Rosa and Flores (2017), the fact that European colonization has shaped modernity has made their perspectives turn to the "colonial distinctions between Europeanism and non-Europeanism, which extends to whiteness and non-whiteness" (Rosa and Flores, 2017, p. 2).[1] The authors suggest considering works that address the denaturalization of the exclusionary race and language categories and works that propose new visions committed to social justice. In this way, their analyses are not just content to accept that the categories of race and language are given and are, therefore, enough to classify such categories. They also set out to question and understand how the co-naturalizations of race and language were created in colonial contexts, where whiteness appears as a superstructure, and how structural racism runs through institutions and the organization of relations in the world, which are operated by the logic of whiteness.

According to Kubota and Lin (2010) however, questions about race and racism are not reduced to whites and non-whites but are more specific while demonstrating the same phenomenon in different groups of people, such as non-white people concerning aboriginal people, and the racism suffered by Asians in Canada, for example. According to Kubota (2015), it is imperative to comprehend how racism functions as a system of excluding bodies or racialized concepts, stemming not only from individual racism but also from institutional and epistemological facets. It is essential to adopt a broader perspective beyond scrutinizing racism solely at an individual level and to grasp how institutions are infiltrated by racism, perpetuating the privilege of specific groups while marginalizing others. The normalization of certain racialized notions within these spheres enables the persistence of racism and inhibits discussions regarding the consequences and effects of racialization.

---

1 Central to our raciolinguistic perspective is an analysis of the continued rearticulation of colonial distinctions between Europeanness and non-Europeanness and, by extension, whiteness and non-whiteness.

Monoglossic linguistic ideologies posit an idealized language as a norm that adjudicates the linguistic practices of specific groups, such as non-white English speakers (Flores and Rosa, 2015). These groups face linguistic practices being deemed deficient due to the racialization they experience as non-white English speakers. The authors thereby illustrate how raciolinguistic ideologies shape the perceptions of both speakers and listeners, dictating which groups of speakers are validated in their language practices while others are not. Congruently, Joseph (2004) states that linguistic and racial–linguistic ideologies associate the belonging of a language to a single people and tend to construct a racialized image of a particular language. These same authors (Flores and Rosa, 2015; Joseph, 2004; Rosa and Flores, 2017) argue that the creation of nation-states produced nationalist ideologies, racial hierarchies, and nationalist ideals that are perceived when we exclusively and monoglossically standardize the image of languages to certain peoples with certain phenotypes.

Like other languages, Japanese takes linguistic and racial ideologies that remain naturalized in its teaching, mainly when not problematized. According to Kubota and Lin (2010), learning a second language generates interactions with other cultures that often, through teaching materials or other dominant social discourses, promote racialized images of teachers, students, and people, which can be reproduced and reinforced.

9.2 Methods and objectives

Based on these theories and with this perspective, this chapter intends to propose reflections and questioning about how the Japanese language is stigmatized and racialized when not spoken by Japanese people or descendants.

The original data presented in this chapter were collected in a university extension course for undergraduate Japanese language students at the University of Paraná entitled *Among Perceptions and Reflections: A Dialogue on Language and Japanese Language Learning Experiences* as part of my Master's degree research program.

Such a course aimed to provide a space where the students, Brazilians of Japanese descent or not, could narrate their experiences with the Japanese language. This chapter presents excerpts of students' experiences during the discussions. The students' expressions that were analyzed in this text emerged from the course's proposed discussion about their perception of the native speaker and from the activity which allowed the students to freely narrate the events that marked their experiences as Japanese language

164 | 9 Racialization of the Japanese Language

learners. The following sections present analysis and reflections on the discourses of three participants, henceforth named John and Mary (non-descendants) and Tanaka (descendant), in light of the racial–linguistic theories that support the subject. This chapter intends to present how the racialization of the Japanese language affects students of Japanese descent and non-Japanese descent.

All participants were informed about the study and agreed to participate by signing an Informed Consent Form. The confidentiality of participants' identities was maintained for the use of their data in the aforementioned research. Participants were aware that they could withdraw from the study at any time.

Notably, the narratives chosen for analysis refer to a particular context of Japanese-speaking students, and there is no intention of generalization.

9.3 The Racialization of the Japanese Language

In this section, we deliberated upon the way the students perceive themselves within the Japanese teaching and learning process.

9.3.1 Perception of Non-descendants as Japanese Students

A racialized image of the Japanese language as legitimate only for Japanese descendants was perceived in the narratives of the participants, congruent with Joseph (2004). These students describe the feelings of inadequacy and not belonging to a place traditionally occupied by the Japanese. The association of the Japanese language with descent seems to generate conflicting feelings, racial hierarchies, and the impostor syndrome (Bernat, 2008).

In the excerpt below, Mary describes how she feels about teaching Japanese. She has been studying Japanese for over ten years and has gone through various Japanese language institutions and courses before entering the undergraduate course. She started learning Japanese through the influence of Japanese pop culture, such as cartoons (*anime*) and comic books (*manga*). Mary states how she used to feel inside a Japanese classroom as a non-descendant:

> And another thing that I also noticed at that time was a look of belittling from the teachers, which I can only understand because I was not of descent. That was the feeling I had. 'Oh, what are you doing here? You do not deserve to be here. You cannot be here. You do not

9.3 *The Racialization of the Japanese Language* | **165**

belong here.' The difficulties with *hiragana*[2] at that time gave me the feeling of incapacity, and I ended up giving up. Then my life went on and on. (Mary—oral account of her experience learning Japanese)

In this account, Mary describes a "look of contempt" from the Japanese language teachers, which according to her interpretation, was because she was not of Japanese descent. She racializes herself as a non-descendant, perceiving herself as not authorized and consequently delegitimized to study Japanese in the teacher's eyes, almost as if she was not worthy of being in a classroom studying Japanese. The feeling of delegitimization by the teacher, feelings of imposture, inadequacy, intellectual falseness, and inauthenticity are consistent with the impostor syndrome described by Clance and Imes (1978), which described subjects who, in spite of the feelings of falseness, are successful in their activities and achievements. Bernat (2008), while studying the self-perception of non-native language teachers, identified feelings of imposture, which included inauthenticity and inadequacy in acting as a non-native language specialist and teacher.

Similar feelings were perceived in Mary's speech when describing how she feels as a non-native Japanese language learner. Like the non-native speaking teachers in Bernat's (2008) research, the student feels that she does not deserve to occupy the place she does, raising concerns such as: "Oh, what are you doing here? You do not deserve to be here. You cannot be here. This is not your place." It is essential to point out that these voices echo in her imagination just from the teacher's gaze that, since not bearing phenotypically Japanese characteristics, was not expected in that particular teaching context. In this sense, the unsaid awakens in Mary the impostor syndrome, which associates descent with the deservingness of occupying a place traditionally belonging to the descendants. Her perception stems from a social structure that associates a body with a language, the image of a face with a culture, in which not matching these standardizing ideologies (Flores and Rosa, 2015) generates conflicting and disconcerting feelings, as seen in her speech. The result, unfortunately, was the student's withdrawal from the undergraduate course.

The Japanese language is an example of how languages are associated only with the image of single phenotypes, as stated in the studies of Joseph (2004), Rosa and Flores (2017), and Flores and Rosa (2015). Only phenotypically Asian faces are usually imagined as speakers when we refer to the Japanese language. The image of a non-Asian face as a Japanese speaker

---

2 One of the Japanese syllabaries that students learn when being literate in Japanese.

seems uncommon in the social imagination. Even today, with all the permeabilities and mobilities generated by globalization, the migrations and interconnections provided by an interconnected world, which supposedly make national borders increasingly blurred and questionable, it is not enough to undo the imagination that this language belongs to a single group of speakers, mostly based on physical traits.

Mary's discourse coincides with a story published in the Brazilian media about a young woman of no Japanese descent who seeks a Japanese language course, and the warning is that there are no vacancies. That is because she is not of Japanese descent and, therefore, there would be no reason for her to study the language, in the view of the course attendant:

> I went to register, and they asked me, 'Oh, are you a descendant?' No, I answered. Moreover, they said, 'Oh, but why do you want to study Japanese? Unfortunately, there will not be a place for you. Better to give the place to someone who will learn and use the Japanese language, not you'. I left there crying (Sayuri, 2021, online)

In the two accounts, it is possible to problematize the ideologies contained in the statements and how the reproduction of racialized images of Japanese students and speakers happens. In another similar situation, the delegitimization of foreign Japanese speakers, meaning non-Japanese descendants, can also be seen in the lecture by Kubota (2020). The author recounts an event in which a Polish reporter for the Japan Times newspaper, who is also a fluent Japanese speaker, addresses the Japanese Foreign Minister in an official interview speaking in Japanese. In this particular episode, after stating a question in fluent Japanese, the Minister answers her question in English. Surprised by the reply, the reporter asks the Minister if he thinks she is "an idiot" since the communication could have continued in the event's official language. Even though the Minister denies this was his intention, he continues treating her as a non-speaker of Japanese. Cases such as these demonstrate how people interested in the Japanese language or Japanese speakers have their language practices delegitimized for not conforming to the stereotypes of Japanese speakers. In this case, the reporter is treated as if she cannot understand Japanese even when she addresses the Minister in perfectly clear Japanese and asks for the conduction of the interview to be in that language. The Minister's attitude of not treating her as a legitimate speaker makes the reporter feel disrespected.

In a study by Inoue (2003), Japanese women's speeches were judged as "defective" by the Japanese male listener. The author shows how the social construction of the Japanese male listener by language ideologies determined how women's speech was heard and judged. Rosa and Flores (2017) take Inoue (2003) as a basis to talk about the social construction of the interlocutor, called by them *the white listener*. Such construction by hegemonic ideologies determines how these subjects hear and racialize the language practices of non-whites. Rosa and Flores (2017) draw on Inoue's theories to talk about how the white listener is socially constructed by hegemonic ideologies that determine how they hear and racialize non-white language practices. Both Inoue (2003) and Rosa and Flores (2017) focus their analysis on how another listener has been socially constructed to judge and determine the language practices of social subjects. In that context, the ideals of whiteness judged the language practices of non-whites, re-signifying Inoue's (2003, p. 2) "Japanese male listener" subject to the "white listener" subject (Rosa and Flores, 2017, p. 7). Similarly, this work draws on the same background to propose not a Japanese listener, but the subject "listener of Japanese," which would be the interlocutor, who is not necessarily native Japanese or of Japanese descent. However, it is the subject who, regardless of nationality, has been socially constructed by nationalistic ideologies of linguistic and racial purity, who judge the language practices of non-descendants and descendants through these ideals.

In the aforementioned excerpts, it becomes evident that the social construction of the "listener of Japanese" figure envisions the practice of the Japanese language as exclusive to individuals with Japanese heritage. This figure, as a distinct entity, appears to wield a determining influence in evaluating and perceiving the language behaviors of both non-descendant and descendant subjects. Similar to how a white listener racializes non-white individuals and condemns their language practices in line with whiteness ideals, the "listener of Japanese" figure seems to follow a similar pattern, racializing non-descendants and stigmatizing their language behaviors based on notions of linguistic and racial purity. Given these observations, it appears that non-descendants are appraised as inadequate speakers, and the relationships they manage to establish are tinged with subordination, as their bodies are perceived as occupying an inferior position compared to those of Japanese descent in the contexts of Japanese language instruction and learning.

Joseph (2004) elucidates how the ideologies propagated during the formation of nation-states impinge upon our perception of the world. Consequently, racialized concepts persist, delineating specific languages to particular ethnicities. The conception of linguistic and racial purity, stemming from such ideologies, presupposes the compartmentalization and hierarchical structuring of peoples and languages. Thus, attributing phenotypic attributes, geographic origin, religion, language, and traditions to define an exclusive national identity appears integral to the collective imagination.

Furthermore, the imposition of a national language as the standardized medium of communication for a populace played a pivotal role in fostering unity, delineating national boundaries, and nurturing nationalist ideals, often expressed through a romanticized pursuit of linguistic purity. As proposed by Makoni and Pennycook (2006), in contemporary times, it is imperative to transcend notions of linguistic territorialization that tether language to specific geographic confines. This perspective facilitates the acceptance that Japanese, for instance, is employed and spoken globally, transcending its native roots and being embraced by diverse communities, including non-Japanese individuals.

As expounded by Kubota and Lin (2010), the constructs of race, racialization, and racism exert influence across social, cultural, and political dimensions, giving rise to intricate power dynamics necessitating scrutiny. These dynamics, as evidenced in the aforementioned accounts, significantly shape our perceptions, sentiments, and interactions with the world. The presented reports vividly illustrate how students, in perceiving themselves (and being perceived) as non-native and non-descendant, encounter delegitimization in their roles as Japanese speakers and learners. This perception appears entwined with prevailing hegemonic ideologies, which, in turn, imbue their bodies with racialized connotations and invalidate their status as users of the Japanese language.

Conversely, ideologies that delegitimize non-Japanese descendants as proficient Japanese speakers seem to exclusively attribute Japanese language aptitude and membership to individuals of Japanese descent and their progeny. This underscores the overarching influence of these ideologies in shaping not only linguistic identity but also the contours of belonging, affirming the intricate interplay between language, heritage, and perception.

9.3.2 The Perception of Descendants as Japanese Learners

The accounts obtained from participants of Japanese descent also indicate a sense of non-belonging within the formal language learning context, as they are expected to exhibit certain behaviors and skills that do not align with their identities.

The student Tanaka, a research participant of Japanese descent, has been studying Japanese at Japanese schools from a very early age by the will of

9.3 The Racialization of the Japanese Language | 169

her parents. She later graduated from Universidade Federal do Paraná with a degree in Japanese language and participated in exchanges in Japan.

> Or in Japan when I went on exchange, right? They would look at a person with a foreign face and speak very slowly, very detailed, the person knew a lot of Japanese, but they would treat that person as if they did not know anything, right? Moreover, I, who had a Japanese face, would talk fast like that, as if I knew everything. (Tanaka—a comment made during the class discussion about the native speaker. Class Transcript)

This account exemplifies how descendants become subject to racialization and encounter stigmatization in their language practices. Descendants are evaluated as inherent speakers, even when this perception does not align with reality. These dual instances of racialization pose inherent problems, fostering racial hierarchies that perpetuate stereotypes and power dynamics. These hierarchical structures and instances of stigmatization effectively bolster the process of racialization, whether through attributing expertise based on phenotype or underestimating them as Japanese speakers due to their lack of heritage. Such dynamics seem to establish a framework of racial domination and subordination.

Kubota (2021) see race, as such, as a historical, social, and political construct discursively created to separate human beings and judge where they belong based on phenotypic characteristics. The perception of races as ontological divisions that divide people into discrete categories underpins racialization, which, in turn, can escalate into racism, favoring certain groups over others. Consequently, many scholars advocate for centering race studies around the analytical domains of racialization and racism rather than conceiving race as an ontologically determined category.

For Rosa and Flores (2017), the project of modernity constructed and naturalized the concept of race and languages as separate objects and delimited to specific groups, thus producing this difference to "racial others." For the authors, a racial–linguistic perspective

> seeks to understand the interaction of language and race within the historical production of the nation-state/colonial governmentality and how colonial distinctions within and across nation-state boundaries continue to shape contemporary linguistic and racial formations. (p. 3)

In this quote, the authors refer specifically to European colonialism and the racial and linguistic hierarchies established concerning colonized

9 Racialization of the Japanese Language

nations and non-Europeans. However, the influence of nationalistic ideals produced in forming modernity also resonated among non-European nations, such as Japan (Inoue, 2003). As stated by Okamoto (2018), this country also carries ultranationalist ideologies that place Japanese people as superior as compared to others, establishing linguistic and racial hierarchies, which have remained even among immigrants in Brazil.

Therefore, even in a non-European context, it is possible to draw on raciolinguistic theories (Flores and Rosa, 2015; Rosa and Flores, 2017) to question the linguistic and racial ideologies that run through Japanese language students' perceptions of Japanese language instruction. As addressed in the students' excerpt, issues about race (descent and non-descent) and language association only with Japanese bodies consistently appear within these narratives.

9.3.3 A Parallel Between the Effects of Racialization Among Descendants and Non-descendants

The notions of race and language as separate objects belonging to specific groups and the hierarchies established by racial–linguistic ideologies appear in this Mary's speech when talking about her experience learning Japanese. It seems that her previous experience in the Japanese language classroom was traumatic and affected her way of relating to the language and her teaching-learning process. In her words,

> And what can I take away from that? Some conclusions that I have come to over that time. One thing that I realized that I hope is not happening so much nowadays because this is something that hurts, something that hurts a lot, this segregation between descendant students and non-descendant students. For lack of a better word, I put in quotes 'this fetishization' of the difficulty of the language. So, instead of saying: 'No, you can do it, with effort, you can do it. It takes time.' No, it is impossible. You cannot do it. It is too much *kanji*.[3] It is too different; you cannot do it. Here are the teachers who, in quotes, 'hold' this knowledge instead of sharing it. That is something I have noticed a lot over the years. Furthermore, this presumption of incapacity is because you are not a descendant. So, 'I do not expect you to succeed because you are not a descendant' as if the descendants had something in their brain that we do not have as if

---

3 Japanese ideograms.

they were more capable than us. (Mary—oral account of her experience learning Japanese)

According to the student, there is a separation between students of descent and non-descent, suggesting that racialization establishes racial hierarchies placed by racial–linguistic ideologies. In her speech, there are indications of the perception that, if she were of descent, she would be perceived and treated differently, as if she would be authorized to study and learn Japanese. It is also clear from her account that teachers perceive the Japanese language as a language for descendants, who naturally learn it. For non-descendants, there is an assumption that they cannot learn Japanese, linking learning ability to descent and inability or difficulty to non-descent. The way the teachers emphasize that the Japanese language is perhaps more difficult for non-descendants makes the students uncomfortable.

The following account brings the opinion of John, another non-Japanese descent student in the class when the role of native speaker was discussed, which also expresses the discomfort generated by the association of Japanese language learning with descent:

One of the several reasons I chose to study the Japanese language was the difficulty and the fact that several people say it is difficult, especially for a non-descended Westerner. This choice is largely driven by my self-confidence, which I often question. So, I chose something that is not easy and that I enjoy, to prove to myself that it is possible and that I am capable. (John—comment made in class during the discussion about the native speaker. Class Transcript)

John has been studying Japanese for seven years and went through various institutions before entering the Japanese language course at Universidade Federal do Paraná. His speech brings another example of the stigmatization faced by non-Japanese descents as linguistically flawed in their usage of the Japanese language. Racialization of their bodies causes listeners not to see their linguistic competence. Instead, these learners are perceived as linguistically deficient, even when they fail to point out these deficiencies. Kubota (2015) also shows how Chinese students were excluded from public schools in British Columbia in the early twentieth century because they were not proficient in English when based on race.

As pointed out by Rosa and Flores (2017), the problem does not seem to be the supposed linguistic failures of these students, but rather the racialization of their bodies that do not allow the "white listeners" to perceive non-white people as competent in the English language as are native speakers. A similar process seems to happen with non-Japanese descendants in their use of the Japanese language. The lack of heritage makes them be seen as less capable of learning the language, attributing the capability of learning Japanese language only to descendants. This way, the Japanese language practiced by non-descendants is perceived illegitimately, as is seen in another excerpt from the student Mary. Her narrative shows how racialization in the classroom affects her perception of learning Japanese.

> My expectations of the course and the teacher are that I will no longer receive negative reinforcement from the teachers (such as 'you cannot do it'; 'it is too hard'), which, unfortunately, is a common place for those studying this language. And I perceive that rigor of students of Japanese descent is demanded that is not present for non-descendants as if being descendant automatically makes someone more capable of learning; I would like to one day realize that this segregation no longer exists. (Mary—oral account of his experience learning Japanese)

Once again, racialization linked to the perception of descent and non-descent seems to be strong in this student's experience. Kubota and Lin (2010) caution that, as second language practitioners, our ideas about race must be scrutinized, as they impact how we teach and understand our students. A committed and critical stance can confront explicit and implicit racism that, in one way or another, generates social injustices. Flores and Rosa (2015) highlight how racial and linguistic purity ideologies are potent constructs that ultimately determine how specific groups should behave as language users. In the case of this research, the association of the Japanese language with descent seems to mark the experience of both non-descendant and descendant students.

In the same direction as Mary's opinion, John states that he feels oppressed and judged due to his lack of heritage.

> And I can safely say that the same course is nothing compared to Japanese, compared to a Japanese language classroom, and how isolated you feel, excluded because you are different because you are not Japanese. Why are you learning this? I know many people say this, but it is cumbersome. You feel it on your shoulders all the time. It is very complicated; it is not like an English class, an English class, everybody takes an English class, it does not matter what face you have, it does not matter if you have crossed eyes, or if you do not have crossed eyes. (John—Comment made in class during the discussion about the native speaker. Class transcript)

In this excerpt, the student shows how he feels excluded for being different from what a Japanese language learner is expected to look like. The feeling of imposture, as seen in Mary's statement "Why are you learning this?," brings once again the socially constructed and shared idea that not only the Japanese language belongs only to the Japanese and their descendants but also that learning it can construct meaning only for this group. John's speech, laden with pain and feelings of exclusion, shows that, for him, studying Japanese as a non-descendant is "heavy," it is like carrying a burden all the time, the burden of non-descent. The participant even compares his experience teaching English (most likely here in Brazil) and that, according to his experience, the physical traits which designate descent are not as determinative as in a Japanese language classroom in which the phenotype is salient.

According to Flores and Rosa (2015), analyzing the power relations behind raciolinguistic ideologies is necessary to understand the non-charging of non-racialized people for their idealized language practices. In contrast, even when they adhere to idealized practices, racialized people face institutional exclusion from the hearing subject who judges these practices. The exclusion caused by racialization and raciolinguistic ideologies determines that certain groups can enjoy certain language practices while others cannot. In the same perspective, Kubota (2015) points out how institutional systems privilege some racialized groups while marginalizing others, and John's account seems to corroborate that this exclusion exists and generates suffering.

In contrast to the reports of non-descendants, which indicate that the Japanese language classroom context reinforces how "flawed" and "incapable" they are, the racialization of the Japanese body assigns qualifications linked to the descent that are disconnected from reality and creates discomfort in the racialized body, as can be seen from the following account of Tanaka:

> I always felt terrible about this Japanese being good at math, that I was never good at math, and then people would say: ah, but you are Japanese, how come? Or when I was good at something, they would say it was because I was Japanese and not because I tried hard or because of my ability, right? (Class Transcript)

In this account, we notice the discomfort generated in the participant by attributing to her identity characteristics and skills based purely on her physical traits. Racializing her that way prevents people from seeing her identity, as she states in her narrative.

Through these accounts, it is possible to deduce that the racialization of descendants and non-descendants produces stereotypes and judgments that do not necessarily correspond to the way these people try to construct meanings in the world. The student's narrative shows that Japanese people are almost always read by common sense, highlighted mainly by the phenotype, which inhabits people's imagination. In her narrative, she shows how these totalizing ideas affect her identity and the way she places herself in the world. Her framing within a notion of race with fixed ideas ignores a transracial perspective, which, according to Alim (2016), allows racialized bodies to be read and translated beyond hegemonic perspectives on language and race and on language and phenotype. Transgressive perspectives question homogeneous ideas about what is socially and culturally naturalized (Pennycook, 2007) and transracial subjects show that their linguistic practices not only create and translate new racial categories, but also highlight the fallacy of normative and hegemonic ideas of race that are in the field of biology, genetics, and ancestry (Alim, 2016).

Given the analysis of the excerpts presented throughout the course, it can be affirmed that racial and linguistic ideologies indeed exert an influence on our perception of the world, corroborating the ideas put forth by Kubota and Lin (2010). Frequently, a populace's representation seems constrained to the reduction of phenotypic and stereotypical features, a phenomenon that unfolds when particular peoples or groups of individuals are ascribed fixed, idealized, and imagined identities, along with the exclusive ownership of a language attributed to a singular group. In the educational context, these notions appear even more entrenched, reinforcing the disconnection between imagined identities and actuality.

Within this context, in the instance of the Japanese experience, a discernible division between descendants and non-descendants becomes apparent, diverging from Hall's conception of postmodern identity (Hall, 2020). Hall posits that the concept of ever-evolving hybrid and flexible identities emerges from societal influences, personal encounters, temporal markers, and engagement with alternative identities. Hence, adopting the notion of a steadfastly established identity, as seems to pervade the Japanese teaching paradigm, appears incongruous within the contours of postmodern times.

9.4 Discussion

Based on the deliberations presented in this chapter, we deduce that Japanese language students, whether of descendant or non-descendant background, exhibit raciolinguistic ideologies within their narratives.

The students' narratives showed how powerful raciolinguistic ideologies are in stigmatizing, racializing, and hierarchizing language users, both descendants and non-descendants. According to Rosa and Flores (2017), it is necessary to denaturalize standardized linguistic categories to change how certain language users are socially perceived. It is necessary to dismantle racialized hierarchies to alter the social position of specific language speakers. In the case of this research, it seeks to show the need to alter the status of Japanese language learners to a legitimate position. This change means a change in how Japanese speakers are seen and heard socially.

Nascimento (2019) states that we are born in a world in which racial and socioeconomic conditions are imposed on racialized bodies, yet it is possible, through language, to fight against socially unjust realities. Bringing to our research perspectives that question and denaturalize linguistic and racial prejudices is a way to join this struggle for social justice.

This text aligns with the desire of Rosa and Flores (2017) in that it is necessary to deconstruct the racial–linguistic ideologies, both white subjects described in their studies and the "listener of Japanese" subject in the case of this study. The reports analyzed in this article sustain that they have a substantial impact on the teaching-learning of this language on Brazilian soil. By deconstructing the ideologies of the listener, it would be possible to open possibilities for a language education that challenges racially hegemonic perspectives to make room for heteroglossia perspectives.

It is intriguing to observe how, even in Brazil, a country recognized for its ethnically diverse society influenced by European, Asian, African, and Middle Eastern heritage, linguistic racialization persists between Brazilian descendants and non-descendants. What is even more remarkable is the presence of such racialization among groups of non-descendants, solely based on their pursuits and activities. Often, foreign language students, with no cultural or phenotypical connection to the native speakers of a language, face questioning from other non-descendants about their choice to dedicate time to that specific language or activity, especially regarding ancestry. It is puzzling, for instance, that a person with no Japanese heritage would enroll in a Japanese language program, receiving inquiries not only from descendants but also from individuals with no racial or cultural ties to Japan.

From this observation, the authors' concept presented throughout the text can be extrapolated. Racialization is so deeply ingrained in society that even within a country lacking a prevalent phenotype, prejudice emerges against personal choices and activities without any connection to cultural identification on the part of the accuser. Therefore, it is not solely a perception of ownership of linguistic or cultural value by descendants toward non-descendants but also a sentiment that conveys a prohibition or a "lack of right" for someone who, for some reason, may not be considered deserving of acquiring that particular cultural or linguistic trait.

This phenomenon can be comprehended through an understanding of society's micro-hierarchies, which, even within comparable social strata, assert authority and fabricate nonexistent reasons to subjugate individuals who might diverge from their narrow worldview. Coupled with this is the cultural and socioeconomic abyss prevalent within Brazilian society, which already harbors many of the prejudices discussed in this text. Consequently, we discern a society struggling to apprehend that which deviates from common sense.

Henceforth, alongside the ongoing pursuit of ameliorating social inequalities, an antiracist pedagogy becomes increasingly imperative. This pedagogy engages in questioning ideologies that perpetuate systems of dominance and, in doing so, introduces critical examination with students concerning how didactic materials, media, the entertainment industry, audiovisual content, dominant narratives, and more, reproduce linguistic and racial stereotypes, as discussed by Kubota (2015). The author proposes a reflection on who benefits and suffers from these racial stereotypes so that it is possible to think of ways to transform these discriminations and inequalities.

As stated by Pennycook (2001), it is necessary to problematize cultural and linguistic hierarchies that perpetuate illegitimate power relations and generate social injustice. Congruently, Khubchandani (2003) argues that it is possible to better understand a diverse society if there are no cultural value scales that insist on devaluing speakers and their linguistic practices with others, allowing room for plural and inclusive linguistic perspectives.

According to Cushing (2022), no pedagogy or policy is apolitical, and so teachers need to question their own internalized and politicized linguistic ideologies because the consequence of sociolinguistic ideologies is the maintenance of social inequality. In congruence, Paulo Freire (1975) also argues that language and every pedagogy are ideological, so what needs to be questioned and analyzed is whether the ideologies that permeate teaching favor the social exclusion of a group or work so that stereotypical ideas about race and language are questioned and fought. Therefore, an anti-racist and problematizing pedagogy emerges as an essential political instrument. This pedagogy must be implemented in the pursuit of mitigating social disparities, encompassing educational, cultural, and socioeconomic domains.

9.5 Conclusion

In this chapter, we have discussed how students of Japanese language, whether descendants or non-descendants, grapple with feelings of inadequacy as they occupy spaces still idealized as belonging to specific racial and ethnic groups. The stigmatization of linguistic groups can prompt these students to perceive how their language practices are devalued within a dominant linguistic context, leading to introspection about their identities, which may not align with an imagined ideal of a speaker.

Within the realm of foreign language instruction, where strong associations between language and race persist, it becomes imperative to embrace a pedagogy that champions linguistic and racial diversity and perpetually dismantles linguistic stereotypes linked to race. This can be achieved through classroom discussions concerning how linguistic ideologies and beliefs are perpetuated in society through common knowledge, media, instructional materials, literature, and other sources. Fostering an appreciation for linguistic and cultural diversity within the classroom is another avenue to recognize that the notion of a pure language bound to a specific race is a fallacy incongruous with the global linguistic pluralism, even within the realm of the studied foreign language, such as Japanese.

This can be accomplished by incorporating narratives and experiences that celebrate linguistic and cultural diversity, while also challenging stereotypes. Another method to facilitate reflections on race, language, and linguistic bias involves bringing students' own experiences into the classroom, enabling an understanding of how they navigate the process of acquiring a foreign language. This could provide an opportunity to explore issues related to linguistic racism that can be scrutinized, while also valuing students' linguistic and cultural repertoires and their unique yet plural identities.

By creating a classroom environment that embraces diversity and challenges linguistic prejudice and racializations, the process of learning a foreign language can become a positive experience, devoid of causing distress or compromising students' identities. Beyond this, it should instill in these learners the confidence that their language practices are legitimate, while also emphasizing the need for them to engage as students and potentially as future educators in combating and questioning the ingrained racializations and linguistic biases within society and institutions. Hence, it is equally essential to invest in teacher education, ensuring that educators are equipped to navigate the issues addressed in this chapter and possess an awareness of their role in countering discourses that perpetuate racialization and racial and linguistic hierarchies.

In this endeavor, it is plausible to envision a future where institutions, and perhaps even society at large, refuse to naturalize racism in any of its manifestations.

References

Alim, H. S. (2016). Who's afraid of the transracial subject. In H. S. Alim, J. R. Rickford, & A. F. Ball (Org.). *Raciolinguistics How Language Shapes Our Ideas About Race*. New York: Oxford University Press, (pp. 33–54).

Bernat, E. (2008). Towards a pedagogy of empowerment: the case of "impostor syndrome" among pre-service no-native speaker teachers in TESOL. *ELTED, 11*.

Clance, P. R., & Imes, S. (1978). The imposter phenomenon in high achieving women: dynamics and therapeutic intervention. *Psychotherapy Theory, Research and Practice, 15*(3).

Cushing, I. (2022). Raciolinguistic (re)resistance and building alternative words. In I. Cushing (Org.). *Standards, Stigma, Surveillance Raciolinguistic Ideologies and England's Scholls*. eBook ed. Lancashire: Palgrave Macmillan.

Flores, N., & Rosa, J. (2015). Undoing appropriateness: raciolinguistic ideologies and language diversity in education. *Harvard Educational Review, 85*(2).

Freire, P. (1975). *Pedagogia do oprimido*. 2. ed. Rio de Janeiro: Paz e Terra.

Hall, S. (2020). *A identidade cultural na pós-modernidade*. 12. ed. Rio de Janeiro: Lamparina editora.

Inoue, M. (2003). The listening subject of Japanese modernity and his auditory double: citing, sighting, and siting the modern Japanese woman. *Cultural Anthropology, 18*(2).

Joseph, E. (2004). *Language and Identity: National Ethnic, Religious*. 1. ed. Hampshire: Palgrave Macmillan.

Khubchandani, L. M. (2003). Defining mother tongue education in plurilingual contexts. *Language Policy, 2*, 239–254.

Kubota, R. (2015). Race and language learning in multicultural Canada: towards critical antiracism. *Journal of Multilingual and Multicultural Development, 36*(1), 3–12.

Kubota, R. (2020). *Confronting Racism in Japanese Language Education* [Vídeo]. UBC Asian Studies. Youtube. https://www.youtube.com/watch?v=Zpu3oHaqQ-0.

Kubota, R. (2021). Critical antiracist pedagogy in ELT. *ELT Journal, 75*(3), 237–246. https://doi.org/10.1093/elt/ccab015.

Kubota, R., & Lin, A. (2010). Race, culture, and identities in second language education: introduction to research and practice. In Kubota, R., & Lin, A. (Org.). *Race, Culture, and Identities in Second Language Education*. 2. ed. (1–24). Abingdon: Routledge Taylor & Francis Group.

Makoni, S., & Pennycook, A. (2006). In S. Makoni, & A. Pennycook (Org.). *Disinventing and Reconstituting Languages*. [S.l.]: Typeset by Wordworks Ltd.

Nascimento, G. (2019). *Racismo Linguístico: Os subterrâneos da linguagem e do racismo*. Belo Horizonte: Grupo Editorial Letramento.

Okamoto, M. S. (2018). A educação ultranacionalista japonesa no pensamento dos nipo-brasileiros. *History of Education*, *22*(55), 225–243.

Pennycook, A. (2001). Introducing critical applied linguistics. *A Critical Applied Linguistics*: *A Critical Introduction*. [S.l.]: Lawrence Erlbaum Associates.

Pennycook, A. (2007) *Global Englishes and Transcultural Flows*. New York: Routledge.

Rosa, J., & Flores, N. (2017). Unsettling race and language: toward a raciolinguistic perspective. *Language in Society*, *46*(5), 621–647. https://doi.org/10.1017/S0047404517000562.

Sayuri, J. (2021). Acadêmica Brasileira Viraliza Unindo Kimono e Cabelo Afro no Japão. BBC News Brasil. https://www.bbc.com/portuguese/brasil-56639395.

10

Ethnic Accent Bullying, EFL Teaching and Learning in Mongolia

Bolormaa Shinjee[1,2] and Sender Dovchin[1]

[1] Curtin University, Australia
[2] National University of Mongolia, Mongolia

10.1 Introduction

Mongolia is a country located between the Russian Federation and the People's Republic of China. Until 1990, Mongolia was a socialist country, a satellite of the Soviet Union under communist rule (Wickhamsmith and Marzluf, 2021). During this socialist period, western cultural and linguistic elements were strictly banned by the ruling communist party. The Russian language was the most prevalent foreign language in Mongolia, taught as a compulsory subject in tertiary and higher education institutions (Cohen, 2004, 2005; Namsrai, 2004). In early 1990, with the collapse of the Soviet Union, the ruling communist authorities of Mongolia resigned without confrontation, undoubtedly marking the end of 70 years of communist rule (Ginsburg, 1995). Mongolia peacefully transformed itself from a socialist to a democratic society, and it was the beginning of a new social, political, and economic order for the newly democratic Mongolia (Dovchin, 2017). Following the advent of democracy in 1990, English has risen to prominence as the fresh entrant among foreign languages in Mongolia, solidifying its position as the most sought-after language within the Mongolian foreign language education landscape. Beginning in 1990, Mongolians have begun linking the function of English with globalization and establishing connections to the global community. In the mid of the shift from socialism to democracy, the Mongolian government initiated various language programs and strategies to position English as the primary

---

Language Teacher Identity: Confronting Ideologies of Language, Race, and Ethnicity,
First Edition. Edited by Sílvia Melo-Pfeifer and Vander Tavares.
© 2024 John Wiley & Sons Ltd. Published 2024 by John Wiley & Sons Ltd.

tool for communication, education, and commerce within Mongolia (Shinjee and Dovchin, 2023). In less than 20 years, English has become an indispensable part of Mongolian society, and its popularity changed the education system and interpersonal communication in Mongolia. With the expansion of bilateral and multilateral relations of Mongolia with other nations since 1990, based on its extended interest in today's growing technology and science, learning the English language as a foreign language has found greater importance. English has also been rapidly spreading to Mongolia through new media: websites, mobile phones, public and private television packages, sports and movie channels, and radio stations that transmit Voice of America and the BBC. Furthermore, there is a rise in the establishment of global universities where instruction is conducted exclusively in the English language (Brooke, 2005).

During the transition period from socialism to democracy, the Mongolian government started promoting multiple language programs and policies to place English as the main means of communication, education, and business in Mongolia. Commencing in 1992, the initial batch of 400 Russian language instructors underwent training to transition into English teachers at prominent institutions such as the National University of Mongolia, the University of Humanities, and the Mongolian University of Science and Technology (Cohen, 2004). The Mongolian government issued a resolution in 2008, approving the National Program of English language learning and teaching between 2009 and 2020. This resolution states that English language teaching shall be organized in accordance with the basic competencies of the mother tongue, and the main foreign language taught at all levels of education will be the English language (Ministry of Education and Science, 2021). Furthermore, the action plan on promoting the quality of English language teaching was approved by the decree of the Minister of Education and Sciences on 7 May 2021 within the framework of "Vision-2050," which is expected to be discussed by the Parliament of Mongolia in mid-2022. The objective of this action plan is to form the basis of future policies and measures for English language education in Mongolia. It will create further conditions and terms for the participation of English instruction in educational institutions, governmental and non-governmental organizations, teachers, and students in Mongolia (Ministry of Education and Science, 2021). It is required that every student must learn English for at least 7 years in public schools and 12 years in private schools. English is mandatory as an entrance exam to higher education institutions. The Ministry of Education and Science developed the National Core Curriculum for English Language Education intended for primary and secondary schools in 2015, in accordance with the Common European Framework of

Reference for Languages (CEFR) (Ministry of Education and Science, 2015). The implementation of curricula is significantly influenced by the role that teachers assume. Although the government has taken steps to enhance the standard of English language education within schools, there are concerns expressed by Mongolian English teachers in this study regarding their working conditions, including factors such as sizable class enrollments and resource deficiencies, that exert a notable influence on the quality of English as a Foreign Language (EFL) instruction in Mongolia (Marav et al., 2020). The significance of educators' pedagogical knowledge and convictions is pivotal. Consequently, the integration of reflective methods and chances for professional growth must be seamlessly integrated into teachers' continual professional journey (Choi and Lee, 2018). Teacher self-efficacy, defined as the perception of one's own teaching aptitude, substantially influences classroom dynamics. This aspect is additionally intertwined with instructors' language proficiency, which significantly affects their capacity to competently lead their classes and fulfill their role as language models for students. Several aims are associated with advancing English and enhancing English education within Mongolian policy frameworks, aligning with the objectives outlined in the National Program for Enhancing English Language Teaching Quality. These objectives encompass enhancing the training of English language instructors; ameliorating the working conditions of teachers, particularly in rural regions; establishing benchmarks for English instruction; and selecting and implementing inventive approaches to English teaching resources, textbooks, and pedagogical technologies (Fleming and Shinjee, 2022). Moreover, substantial advancements in the realm of English language education are evident through both extended and immediate initiatives and undertakings carried out by international as well as domestic entities, with the goal of renovating the Mongolian English education system (Orosoo and Jamiyansuren, 2021).

However, there is a growing difference in students' English language competencies, particularly speaking skills and pronunciation, due to their varied socioeconomic, geographical, and ethnic backgrounds in tertiary institutions where they are required to pass IELTS 6.5 score or equivalent skills (Fleming and Shinjee, 2022). Furthermore, a study conducted by Marav (2016) highlighted how disparities among Mongolian university students were intricately linked to their prior exposure to English before entering university. Based on the caliber of their prior education, several university students encountered exclusion from various educational and economic opportunities associated with their competence in the English language. The rural population in Mongolia is mostly from minority ethnic backgrounds in Mongolia. The majority ethnic group in Mongolia is

Khalkha Mongolians (95% of the population), whose official language is the Mongolian language with the *Khalkha* as the main dialect. However, there are other ethnic minority groups such as *Kazakh, Zakhchin, Durvud, Uuld, Torguud, Buryat*, and *Uriyankhai* (Davaadorj and Yanjindulam, 2020) in Mongolia, whose practice of the Mongolian language is determined by their distinctive regional and rural dialects (Davaadorj and Yanjindulam, 2020). Many students from these rural and regional areas from different ethnic backgrounds migrate to the capital city Ulaanbaatar to acquire higher education as the public and private universities are centralized in the city. Regrettably, there is a tendency for students from rural and regional areas to experience "ethnic accent bullying"—"bullying towards English as second/foreign language speakers based on their biographical English accent—the accent connected with one's sociolinguistic histories and biographies" (Dovchin, 2020b, p. 3) despite their fulfillment of the entrance English language test, which may cause unequal opportunities and power across EFL settings. They are discriminated against by their "ethnic," "regional," and "rural" English accents due to the lack of access to "standard-like" English in the classroom settings. Particularly, the dominant group or EFL teachers expect the other ethnic minority groups to speak unaccented standard English without considering their different ethnic backgrounds and if they do not speak the way they are expected then they are considered to be accented (Lippi-Green, 2011). This assumption and attitude cause disparities and unequal power within the community and EFL institutional settings based on different English accents. In Mongolia, for example, ethnic minority groups must adopt the dominant linguistic norms and policies in an institutional setting (Dovchin, 2022), and ethnic accent bullying has been recognized based on the speakers' non-standardized English accents in institutional contexts (Dovchin, 2020a), where standardized English accents are considered as an indication of affluent or urban background or highly educated person (De Klerk and Bosch, 1995).

Accordingly, there is a need for university EFL teachers to increase their critical awareness of accent discrimination among students and minimize those prejudicial behaviors in EFL classrooms. The discriminative attitude is not only among students, but it also occurs between teachers and students in both covert and overt ways.

This study, thus, aims to investigate how students from different ethnic minority groups from regional areas of Mongolia may experience "ethnic accent bullying" both from urban peers and their teachers in terms of their English accents. In so doing, we seek to increase the critical awareness of ethnic accent bullying in EFL teaching and learning contexts in Mongolia.

The chapter aims to address two main research questions:

1) In what ways and how do EFL students in Mongolia experience ethnic accent bullying?
2) What is the pedagogical implication of ethnic accent bullying for EFL teaching and learning context in Mongolia?

In so doing, we will present the concept of "ethnic accent bullying" (Dovchin, 2019; Field, 2013; Munro et al., 2006) in the next section.

10.2 Ethnic Accent Bullying

Ethnic accent bullying constitutes a facet within the broader framework of linguistic racism, denoting the act of discriminating against individuals based on their distinctive "biographical accent" (Blommaert, 2009), as well as their perceived "ethnic" or "foreign accent" (Dovchin, 2020a, 2020b). The perception of accent-focused discrimination can occur when there are other different accents to compare with (Lippi-Green, 2011) and standardized English accents are considered as an indication of affluent or urban background or highly educated person (De Klerk and Bosch, 1995). Bullying based on ethnic accents could influence how one's English proficiency is perceived, and this disparity may not result in comparable treatment to accents associated with the so-called native English varieties from the United Kingdom, Australia, the United States, and Canada. The speaker with an "ethnic accent" turns into "what he or she speaks, and speaking it transforms him or her into what is suggested by their accent" (Dovchin, 2020b, p. 4). Those different accents are judged differently by "standardness" (Sewell, 2016, p. 93), and once that "standardness" cannot be achieved due to their race, ethnical group, and nationality (Hall et al., 2010; Rosa, 2016; Sue et al., 2007). According to Creese and Kambere (2003), ethnic accents hinder one's opportunities of being successful or accepted by society and are perceived as undereducated.

There are two types of "ethnic accent bullying"—overt and covert forms of "ethnic accent bullying." Overt "ethnic accent bullying" refers to verbal and non-verbal prejudicial acts, which occur in obvious forms of mocking, laughing, teasing, undermining, attacking (De Costa, 2020), and labeling one's way of speaking (Dryden and Dovchin, 2021; Dovchin and Dryden, 2022). Lipinski and Crothers (2013), in which the intention is to distress someone for possessing ethnic accent, not the standardized accent. Those diminishing acts toward the victims of "ethnic accent bullying" injure their dignity and pride as they are offensive, disgracing, and embarrassing. The common forms of overt "ethnic accent bullying" include mocking (Chun, 2009), which involves an act of laughing at one's ethnic accent; sarcasm (Lee and Katz, 1998), and it is an act of attacking verbally using irony to convey contempt; assigning to a category inaccurately or restrictively and labeling (Sue et al., 2007).

Covert "ethnic accent bullying" refers to prejudicial acts that occur where people judge one's English accents in veiled, subtle, or hidden ways (De Costa, 2020; Dryden and Dovchin, 2021), and it is practiced through passive-aggressive and indirect acts. Covert "ethnic accent bullying" is a "symbolic violence" (Bourdieu, 1991), which refers to a form of violence practiced against marginalized (minority) groups. It is also a "social exclusion" (Field, 2013), which is an act of hindering one's participation in non-institutional and institutional interactions on purpose, leaving out the group, and excluding or ignoring one's presence based on ethnic accents or background (Hogg, 2016). The harm caused by social exclusion is far more critical than it sounds; it has a negative effect on one's thoughts and feelings, which leads to loneliness, depression, and a sense of being an outsider among peers (Khvorostianov and Remennick, 2017). Being rejected in the form of social exclusion could be the most upsetting and damaging event in people's lives (Leary, 2022).

Both covert and overt "ethnic accent bullying" are determined by different hierarchical levels raised by social inequalities (Blommaert, 2010), which can happen in institutional and non-institutional settings in any context. Overt and covert ethnic accent bullying can potentially harm one's self-confidence and develop "linguistic inferiority complexes" (Tankosić and Dovchin, 2021). A linguistic inferiority complex refers to a type of psychological distress that is amplified when one's abilities and attitudes are denigrated or rejected by other people (Kenchappanavar, 2012, p. 1). The detrimental impact of ethnic accent bullying may lead to chronic psychological and emotional distress such as a sense of non-belonging, anxiety, low self-esteem, an inferiority complex (Dovchin, 2019) and even suicidal ideations (Dovchin, 2020a, 2020b), which leads to mental health issues such as self-marginalization, loss of social belonging, social withdrawal, and self-vindication (Dovchin, 2020a, c). Speakers with ethnic accents may feel the inferiority complexes, thus aiming to "purify and refine" their "terrible," "non-standard," and "unaccepted" accents to become ideal EFL speakers (Dovchin, 2020b, p. 5). Therefore, many English speakers with ethnic accents try hard to correct their pronunciation and speak standardized English (Blommaert, 2009) to prevent themselves from becoming victims of ethnic accent bullying.

While previous studies on ethnic accent bullying have mostly focused on multicultural contexts from the Global North such as Australia (Dobinson and Mercieca, 2020; Dovchin, 2020a), the United States (Chun, 2016), Spain

(Corona and Block, 2020), and Canada (Creese and Kambere, 2003), we note, in this chapter, that it is not necessarily a phenomenon that occurs only in multicultural settings. As data in our chapter present that ethnic accent bullying can also be practiced within the linguistically homogenous contexts of the Global South due to local conflicts such as rural, regional, and ethnic minority dialects or accents. This chapter, thus, seeks to present how domestic students from minority groups in Mongolia experience ethnic accent bullying during EFL classes through two specific forms of practices, "overt" and "covert" ethnic accent bullying, and how the combination of this overall harmful experience may further cause emotional and psychological issues.

10.3 Research Methodology

This study has adopted semi-structured interviews (Copland and Creese, 2015), which examined the EFL learners' lived experiences in terms of their English accents. Five questions were asked regarding their background information, such as ethnicity, their first and second languages, and their evaluation of their English language competencies. Fifteen questions were asked regarding their language practice in institutional settings and its relation to ethnic accent bullying. However, some additional follow-up questions were asked where necessary. Each interview was conducted via the Zoom social platform and continued for up to 90 min. All the interviews were audio-recorded, conducted in the Mongolian language, and later transcribed and translated into English by the researchers.

Given the delicate nature of the research information, this part delineates the ethical issues involved and the methods employed to handle them. Before gathering data, all participants were provided with a participant information document (detailing goals, purposes, ethical matters, and researcher's contact details), a consent form, and the project brochure, distributed digitally. In the context of the online environment, the participants were obligated to manually sign the consent form, then scan the paperwork and send it back to the researcher. Taking part in the research was a matter of personal choice, and participants were informed that they had the option to abandon the research project at any point without facing any negative consequences. After gathering data, the information was encoded, and any personally identifiable details of the participants were eliminated during the analysis phase. To guarantee anonymity, all participants were assigned fictitious names. The gathered data has been maintained in strict confidentiality.

10.3.1 Data Collection and Analysis

In this chapter, we focus on three students from regional areas with different ethnic minority groups in Mongolia. The data collection process employed purposive snowball sampling (Miles et al., 2014), which entailed reaching out to potential participants via email addresses. This method facilitated the recruitment of three EFL female students from various socioeconomic and regional backgrounds from the National University of Mongolia, wherein participants were invited to partake in semi-structured interviews (see Table 10.1). The interviews were strategically designed to center around the participants' encounters with ethnic accent bullying within educational environments. Conducted in an online format, all individual interviews were recorded in audio. The interviews, ranging from 60 to 90 min in duration, were conducted exclusively in the Mongolian language. This linguistic choice was deliberate, aiming to create an environment where participants felt at ease expressing their thoughts comprehensively and candidly (Mann, 2011). However, some English words were used during the interview. The interview questions were formulated to understand what linguistic racism would look like to them in institutional settings. Interviews were conducted in the Mongolian language and were translated by the researcher.

The data from this study were transcribed into English by the researchers and analyzed through thematic analysis as "it provides core skills that will be useful for conducting many other kinds of analysis" to locate the main questions, patterns, and themes, which derived from the data collecting stages (Braun and Clarke, 2006, p. 78). The aim of conducting thematic analysis was to explore key patterns and themes and adopt these themes to label the research.

The two initial themes we discussed throughout the interviews were *ethnic accent bullying reasons* and *consequences of ethnic accent bullying*, then further investigation of patterns across the data set. This method of pattern investigation enabled us to see the shared experiences of the participants and concentrate on how these initial themes had similarities (Braun

Table 10.1 Participant information.

Participant name	Age	Gender	Ethnic group	Province
Tuya (modified name)	18	Female	Zakhchin	Khovd province
Uyanga (modified name)	19	Female	Khalkha	Uvurkhangai province
Aryana (modified name)	19	Female	Kazakh	Bayan-Ulgii province

and Clarke, 2012). The initial themes of ethnic accent bullying reasons and consequences of ethnic accent bullying that we indicated were analyzed, and two varieties of themes emerged (i) overt ethnic accent bullying and its consequences and (ii) covert accent bullying and its consequences.

Students from rural areas of Mongolia with different ethnic backgrounds find it challenging to study English at higher education institutions with other students from the city as they have fewer opportunities to learn and practice their English due to their limited resources and opportunities compared to the local students of the main ethnic group *Khalkha*. They have to adjust to the standard English norms in institutional settings. These students have experienced covert and overt linguistic racism toward their poor English skills, especially their "non-standard" English accents and mispronunciations.

10.4 Overt Ethnic Accent Bullying

This section outlines the types of overt ethnic accent bullying that English learners may face, such as being laughed at, mocked, and objectified through overt ethnic accent bullying. The first participant to share her experiences is Tuya, a student at the National University of Mongolia. Tuya is from Mankhan soum of Khovd province, which is located in a remote region of western Mongolia. Currently, she is a first-year law student who arrived in Ulaanbaatar, the capital city of Mongolia, in 2021. Her ethnic group is *"Zakhchin,"* which is a subdivision of the larger Oirat-Mongol ethnicity and there are about 29,766 *"Zakhchin"* people living in Altai, Mankhan, Must, and Uyench soums in Khovd province in Mongolia (Purevjav, 2014). The modern *"Zakhchin"* dialect is different from other Mongolian dialects in its "vibrant consonants and double vowels" (Purevjav, 2014, p. 13). During an hour-long interview, Tuya describes her experiences with overt ethnic accent bullying due to her strong *"Zakhchin"* accented English, which represents her ethnic background of *"Zakhchin,"* "There is a local accent, and our people from Khovd pronounce the letter 'H' as 'K'. For example, the word 'inherent' is pronounced 'inkerent'." As soon as Tuya pronounces the letter "H" as "K," the peers in the classroom would explicitly laugh in the classroom. Tuya further describes the incidents of overt ethnic accent bullying, where both teachers and peers laughed at her English accent in the classroom,

> English teachers in rural areas do not speak English. All lessons are taught in Mongolian. We didn't make reading or speaking at all. I was not prepared to study with students from urban areas. I failed my first English

class after entering\university. I assumed that teacher was asking for my name when the teacher asked something in English, so I introduced myself in English, and the peer students and the teacher laughed at me [my English and my accent]. I was so shocked and ashamed of myself.

Here, Tuya describes the bullying she has faced in the classroom, stating that students laughed at her accent in a noticeable and obvious way while she was responding to the teacher's questions. While Tuya accepts that she does speak with an accent that cannot be rectified in the short term, this demonstration of overt ethnic accent bullying by peers in her class deeply affects her, causing her feelings of linguistic inferiority complexes such as frustration and humiliation. As Tuya notes,

I was so shocked and ashamed of myself. After this class, I stopped volunteering and tried to avoid answering questions, or even I tried to hide from my teacher's sight. I was reading an article in class, and they asked me to stand up and read it, and when I stood up to read it, I was very nervous and sweaty, but at that time, I was afraid that I would mispronounce it, even though I didn't.

Tuya's experience shows us how overt ethnic accent bullying acts are practiced during the EFL class in a linguistically homogenous context. Because of her daily experiences of ethnic accent bullying, her willingness to learn the English language has decreased as she is afraid of speaking in English due to her low self-esteem, shamefulness, and anxiety. In fact, Tuya explains that she does not feel safe and comfortable to be in the EFL class, even though she feels like an "outsider" in the classroom.

The second participant to share her experiences is Ariyana, a representative of a minority ethnic group (Kazakh) in Mongolia, where the Kazakh language, one of the Turkic root languages, is the dominant language in Bayan-Ulgii province (Barcus and Werner, 2010; Soni, 2008). She describes how her EFL teachers discriminate against her English accent during the EFL classes for her ethnicity and accents. One of the overt ethnic accent bullying examples is when the EFL teacher got frustrated and raised her voice when she read a paragraph in English. Ariyana felt that her teacher made biased judgments as she turned "deaf" to students' other important mistakes while focusing more on her accent mistakes. As Ariyana explains some derogatory behavior toward her ethnic accent,

Sometimes my English teachers get angry and start yelling when I make mistakes during English class, where I feel thrilled to practice

> the language. When I make pronunciation mistakes, my English teachers tend to get annoyed and say, 'You mustn't pronounce it like that! You must learn how to pronounce it!'. I felt that the teachers ignored other students' mistakes but picked up my every single mistake because I am from a different ethnic group which is the minority in Mongolia. I felt really bad about it and got humiliated by it.

These types of overt ethnic accent bullying are also common (Lippi-Green, 2011) beyond the classroom contexts as they may also happen in public places. For instance, when participant 1, Tuya wanted to buy a book called "Pride and Prejudice" from the bookstore to improve her English language competency, the shop assistant could not understand her pronunciation of "Pride and Prejudice." Tuya had to write the name of the book and showed to the shop assistant. She was finally understood by the shop assistant via written forms of her English.

Overall, Tuya and Ariyana, both representatives of Mongolian ethnic minority groups from regional Mongolia, are targeted due to their ethnic minority background and accent; when the peer students and EFL teachers laugh at them, they frame their English variety as problematic for communication, questioning their legitimacy and suitability as proper English speakers (Rosa, 2016). This accent bullying toward their English repertoires in a form of laughter designed to subordinate them as incomprehensible English speakers (Piller, 2016). As a result of this bullying, these participants become "alive to [their] marginality in English and to a perpetual falling short of the imagined ideal of 'perfect' homogenous English" (Piller, 2016, p. 203). They feel excluded from the English class groups because of their ethnic-accented English, and they try to avoid group activities and classroom activities because they do not feel either confident reading out loud in English or answering the teachers' questions in front of their peers and teachers.

10.5 Covert Ethnic Accent Bullying

In this section, we present examples of covert linguistic racism as practiced through social exclusion in EFL classroom settings. Such hidden social exclusion is shown eventually to cause the internalization of negative feelings of being "inferior." Here we present how classroom exclusions and peer rejections, based on one's "ethnic-sounding" accent, can lead to a lack of support from peers, which eventually leads to long-lasting psychological trauma and inferiority complexes.

Uyanga (19), a young Mongolian woman and a student at NUM who arrived in Ulaanbaatar in 2021, was quite satisfied and confident with her English when she first arrived. However, she started having doubts about her English as soon as she started communicating with urban Mongolians. Her ethnic group is "Khalkha," the main ethnic group of Mongolia (Yagi, 2020). She has been learning English for six years at a rural public school in Taragt, Uvurkhangai province, where the distinctive regional dialect is extensively used (Dovchin, 2019a, p. 95). Despite her dominant ethnic group belonging, her English accent was bullied based on her distinctive "regional" accent. One of the most prevalent covert ethnic accent bullying examples is when Uyanga's peers in the classroom were not willing to work with her as a group for her English class because of her English accent. As Uyanga explains,

> If the teacher makes us a group, the other students are not happy when I am in one group with them, and they give me a horrible look that I'd better get out of the team. They are afraid of losing marks because of me, as we are assessed as a team. I feel comfortable being in a group with students from rural areas like me. Other students from the rural areas with heavy English accents prefer to skip the classes, or they feel vulnerable and cry after the English class.

Here, Uyanga describes a situation she encounters at times when her classmates work as a group, and she feels excluded due to her English accent. Uyanga acknowledges that this behavior is intentional because her urban background classmates are not comfortable with her English to the extent that they are afraid of getting lower marks for their performance. Essentially, Uyanga's classmates downgrade her English ability due to her accent and make her feel rejected and excluded when they are working as a group.

In a similar vein, participant 2, Ariyana describes the covert ethnic accent bullying she has encountered in the classroom when the teacher asks her to pronounce the words many times until she pronounces them correctly. Ariyana thinks that teachers focus more on fixing her accent rather than working with other students. As Ariyana explains,

> My English teachers from my high school even asked me to pronounce the word as many times as I pronounce them correctly. This was so scary for me. I have a feeling that the teachers tend to focus only on me rather than the group. I feel terrified about it, and I try hard not to make mistakes. The possible cause of these might be that

they expect much more from me because I belong to an ethnic minority group, and there is a misconception that we are good at learning foreign languages as we are bilingual.

The accent-induced discrimination adversely affects students' self-confidence, motivation, language learning abilities, and identities (Despagne, 2013; MacIntyre et al., 2009), and teachers' negative attitude toward learners' language learning process might restrict their participation in classroom activities and limit their access to learning sources (Dörnyei and Ushioda, 2009; Noels, 2001). As Ariyana acknowledges,

I prefer to practice my English speaking with native speakers of English rather than in a classroom because they do not judge how I speak and without mocking, they just simply correct my mistakes. So, I feel safer speaking to them. I am afraid of talking in English to other students during class, whereas I feel more confident talking in English outside of the classroom. But I have limited access to speaking English outside of the classroom.

This covert ethnic accent bullying at times puts these women in an awkward social situation, as their English accents are covertly viewed as "rural" and essentially, "low status" since it does not conform with urban English-accented norms in Ulaanbaatar (Cohen, 2004). Their interlocutors hear that they speak with accents and reach the decision that they are incomprehensible, thus paving the way for them not to be listened to (Piller, 2016). Essentially, urban Mongolians, upon hearing their speech and accents, make a conscious or subconscious decision whether they will participate or not, and as the research participants have experienced, will reject that participation if they are deemed incomprehensible, leaving these participants to carry the lion's share of the communicative interaction (Lippi-Green, 2011).

10.6 Conclusion

In this chapter, we aim to raise critical awareness and expand the concept of ethnic accent bullying, drawing on data examples of female students at the National University of Mongolia, who are all from different ethnic minority groups of regional or rural areas of Mongolia. All these students from ethnic and rural backgrounds who participate in EFL pedagogical settings acknowledge that they have felt different forms of overt and covert ethnic accent bullying from their peer students and their English lecturers. These students were bullied due to their "non-standardized" or "rural" English accents, which reflect their minority ethnic or regional or rural backgrounds. Our study indicates that these forms of ethnic accent bullying might influence one's psychological and emotional well-being (Dovchin, 2020b) and develop inferiority complexes such as low self-esteem (Piller, 2016), feeling of being less intelligent (Wang & Dovchin, 2022), and other psychological distresses. Thus, the participants feel ashamed about not being able to speak the way of the dominant groups or the other EFL learners. Overall, ethnic accent bullying toward a marginalized group of society is practiced, re-practiced, and maintained intentionally or unintentionally by the dominant "privileged" groups (Burr, 2006), but such bullying acts toward one's accent in EFL settings can be prevented.

Based on the findings derived from these data, a series of practical suggestions are proffered for EFL teachers in the context of mitigating ethnic accent bullying. Initially, to mitigate the risk of perpetuating discriminatory behaviors toward marginalized segments and to ensure equitable participation of all EFL learners, irrespective of their ethnic and rural origins, it is advisable for educators to foster heightened awareness regarding implicit or explicit attitudes and practices prevalent within the classroom (Canagarajah, 2017; Fox and Stallworth, 2005). By actively cultivating consciousness surrounding ethnic accent bullying within the EFL classroom, educators can engage in a proactive stance against instances of such bias targeting marginalized students. Beyond curbing such practices, this proactive endeavor promotes an equitable landscape for language engagement, while concurrently offering support to vulnerable learners navigating prejudiced contexts. The act of raising awareness constitutes an encompassing strategy that extends its influence across various educational stakeholders—encompassing EFL educators, policymakers, and students. This heightened awareness, once assimilated, facilitates the acceptance of diverse accent variations and deepens the collective comprehension of the multifaceted implications stemming from ethnic accent bullying. This heightened sensitivity warrants its due consideration within the framework of policy formulation. An essential facet of this pedagogical endeavor involves the capacity of EFL educators to discern indicators of bullying directed at susceptible students. It is acknowledged that the emotional, psychological, and cognitive dimensions inherent to marginalized EFL learners may potentially hamper their linguistic acquisition (Gkonou et al., 2020). The perpetual experience of anxiety and depression exposes these learners to persistent emotional and psychological duress, thereby impeding the optimal absorption of educational content. This distinctive aspect underscores the necessity for interventions aimed at ameliorating depressive symptoms, a factor inherently tied to these learners' academic progression. The resultant improvement in the quality of EFL learning experiences for marginalized groups is anticipated to foster a more nurturing and encouraging educational ambiance, thus enriching language proficiency and bolstering active participation within the classroom context (Tomlinson, 2011). Within the scope of their professional role, EFL educators are ideally positioned to offer comprehensive assistance to marginalized students grappling with discriminatory behaviors (Dovchin et al., 2018). This encompasses the ability to appropriately refer students to psychological counseling and therapeutic services, alongside the incorporation of interactive social content aimed at fostering an inclusive and supportive pedagogical environment.

In conclusion, it becomes incumbent upon educators to adopt an unwavering stance against the propagation of bullying practices within institutional settings. The envisioned outcome is reflective of the aspiration toward a "democratic" classroom ethos, ensuring uniform treatment for every participant (Steele et al., 2022). The methodical implementation of these outlined recommendations reflects educators' commitment to nurturing a learning environment characterized by inclusivity, equity, and mutual respect.

References

Barcus, H., & Werner, C. (2010). The Kazakhs of Western Mongolia: transnational migration from 1990–2008. *Asian Ethnicity, 11*(2), 209–228.

Blommaert, J. (2009). A market of accents. *Language Policy, 8*(3), 243–259.

Blommaert, J. (2010). *The Sociolinguistics of Globalization.* Cambridge University Press.

Bourdieu, P. (1991). *Language and Symbolic Power.* Harvard University Press.

Braun, V., & Clarke, V. (2006). Using thematic analysis in psychology. *Qualitative Research in Psychology, 3*(2), 77–101.

Braun, V., & Clarke, V. (2012). *Thematic Analysis.* American Psychological Association.

Brooke, J. (2005). For Mongolians, E Is for English, F Is for future. *The New York Times.* February 15. https://www.nytimes.com/2005/02/15/world/asia/for-mongolians-e-is-for-english-f-is-for-future.html.

Burr, V. (2006). *An Introduction to Social Constructionism.* Routledge.

Canagarajah, S. (2017). *Translingual Practices and Neoliberal Policies.* (pp. 1–66). Springer, Cham.

Choi, E., & Lee, J. (2018). EFL teachers' self-efficacy and teaching practices. *ELT Journal, 72*(2), 175–186.

Chun, E. W. (2009). Speaking like Asian immigrants: intersections of accommodation and mocking at a US high school. *Pragmatics, 19*(1), 17–38.

Chun, E. W. (2016). The meaning of Ching-Chong: language, racism, and response in new media. In H. S. Alim, J. R. Rickford, & A. F. Ball (Eds.) *Raciolinguistics: How language Shapes Our Ideas About Race* (pp. 81–96). Oxford University Press.

Cohen, R. (2004). The current status of English education in Mongolia. *Asian EFL Journal, 6*(4), 1–21.

Cohen, R. (2005). English in Mongolia. *World Englishes, 24*(2), 203–216.

Copland, F., & Creese, A. (2015). *Linguistic Ethnography: Collecting, Analysing and Presenting Data.* Sage.

Corona, V., & Block, D. (2020). Raciolinguistic micro-aggressions in the school stories of immigrant adolescents in Barcelona: a challenge to the notion of Spanish exceptionalism? *International Journal of Bilingual Education and Bilingualism, 23*(7), 778–788.

Creese, G., & Kambere, E. N. (2003). What colour is your English? *Canadian Review of Sociology/Revue canadienne de sociologie, 40*(5), 565–573.

Davaadorj, B., & Yanjindulam, V. (2020). Current trends of the study of Oirat dialect and Western Mongolian Folklore. In J. Reckel, & M. Schatz (Eds.), *Oirat and Kalmyk Identity in the 20th and 21st Century* (pp. 177–190). Universitätsdrucke Göttingen.

De Costa, P. I. (2020). Linguistic racism: its negative effects and why we need to contest it. *International Journal of Bilingual Education and Bilingualism, 23*(7), 833–837.

De Klerk, V., & Bosch, B. (1995). Linguistic stereotypes: nice accent-nice person? *International Journal of the Sociology of Language, 1995*(116), 17–38.

Despagne, C. (2013). Indigenous education in Mexico: indigenous students' voices. *Diaspora, Indigenous, and Minority Education, 7*(2), 114–129.

Dobinson, T., & Mercieca, P. (2020). Seeing things as they are, not just as we are: investigating linguistic racism on an Australian university campus. *International Journal of Bilingual Education and Bilingualism, 23*(7), 789–803.

Dörnyei, Z., & Ushioda, E. (Eds.). (2009). *Motivation, Language Identity and the L2 Self* (vol. 36). Multilingual Matters.

Dovchin, S. (2017). Uneven distribution of resources in the youth linguascapes of Mongolia. *Multilingua, 36*(2), 147–179. https://doi.org/10.1515/multi-2015-0065.

Dovchin, S., Pennycook, A., & Sultana, S. (2018). Transglossia: From translanguaging to transglossia. In Dovchin, S., Pennycook, A., & Sultana, S. (Eds.), *Popular culture, voice and linguistic diversity: Young adults on-and offline* (pp. 27–56). Springer.

Dovchin, S. (2019). Language crossing and linguistic racism: Mongolian immigrant women in Australia. *Journal of Multicultural Discourses, 14*(4), 334–351.

Dovchin, S. (2020a). Introduction to special issue: linguistic racism. *International Journal of Bilingual Education and Bilingualism, 23*(7), 773–777.

Dovchin, S. (2020b). The psychological damages of linguistic racism and international students in Australia. *International Journal of Bilingual Education and Bilingualism, 23*(7), 804–818.

Dovchin, S. (2020c). Translingual English, Facebook, and gay identities. *World Englishes, 39*(1), 54–66.

Dovchin, S. (2022). *Translingual Discrimination*. Cambridge University Press. https://doi.org/10.1017/9781009209748.

Dovchin, S., & Dryden, S. (2022). Translingual discrimination: skilled transnational migrants in the labour market of Australia. *Applied Linguistics, 43*(2), 365–388.

Dryden, S., & Dovchin, S. (2021). Accentism: English LX users of migrant background in Australia. *Journal of Multilingual and Multicultural Development*, 1–13.

Field, J. E. (2013). Relational and social aggression in the workplace. In J. Lipinski, & L. M. Crothers (Eds.), *Bullying in the Workplace* (pp. 179–191). Routledge.

Fleming, K., & Shinjee, B. (2022). English high-stakes testing and constructing the 'international' in Kazakhstan and Mongolia. *Applied Linguistics Review*. https://doi.org/10.1515/applirev-2022-0067.

Fox, S., & Stallworth, L. E. (2005). Racial/ethnic bullying: exploring links between bullying and racism in the US workplace. *Journal of Vocational Behavior, 66*(3), 438–456.

Ginsburg, T. (1995). Political reform in Mongolia: between Russia and China. *Asian Survey, 35*(5), 459–471.

Gkonou, C., Dewaele, J. M., & King, J. (Eds.). (2020). *The Emotional Rollercoaster of Language Teaching* (vol. 4). Multilingual Matters.

Hall, D. L., Matz, D. C., & Wood, W. (2010). Why don't we practice what we preach? A meta-analytic review of religious racism. *Personality and Social Psychology Review, 14*(1), 126–139.

Hogg, M. A. (2016). Social identity theory. In S. McKeown, R. Haji, & N. Ferguson (Eds.), *Understanding Peace and Conflict Through Social Identity Theory: Contemporary Global Perspectives* (pp. 3–17). Springer International Publishing.

Kenchappanavar, R. N. (2012). Relationship between inferiority complex and frustration in adolescents. *IOSR Journal of Humanities and Social Science, 2*(2), 1–5.

References | 197

Khvorostianov, N., & Remennick, L. (2017). 'By helping others, we helped ourselves': volunteering and social integration of ex-soviet immigrants in Israel. *VOLUNTAS: International Journal of Voluntary and Nonprofit Organizations*, *28*, 335–357.

Leary, M. R. (2022). Emotional responses to interpersonal rejection. *Dialogues in Clinical Neuroscience*, *17*(4), 435–441.

Lee, C. J., & Katz, A. N. (1998). The differential role of ridicule in sarcasm and irony. *Metaphor and Symbol*, *13*(1), 1–15.

Lipinski, J., & Crothers, L. M. (Eds.). (2013). *Bullying in the Workplace: Causes, Symptoms, and Remedies*. Routledge.

Lippi-Green, R. (2011). *English with an Accent: Language, Ideology, and Discrimination in the United States*. Taylor & Francis Group.

MacIntyre, P. D., MacKinnon, S. P., & Clément, R. (2009). The baby, the bathwater, and the future of language learning motivation research. In Z. Dörnyei, & E. Ushioda (Eds.), *Motivation, Language Identity and the L2 Self* (pp. 43–65). Multilingual Matters.

Mann, S. (2011). A critical review of qualitative interviews in applied linguistics. *Applied Linguistics*, *32*(1), 6–24.

Marav, D. (2016). Mongolian student' digital literacy practices: the interface between English and the Internet. *Trabalhos Em Linguistica Aplicada*, *55*(2), 293–318. https://doi.org/10.1590/010318134962176441.

Marav, D., Podorova, A., Yadamsuren, O., & Bishkhorloo, B. (2020). Teaching global English in a local context: teachers' realities in Mongolian public schools. *Asia Pacific Journal of Education*, *42*(2), 276–289. https://doi.org/10.1080/02188791.2020.1823316.

Miles, M. B., Huberman, A. M., & Saldana, J. (2014). *Qualitative Data Analysis: A Methods Sourcebook*, third edition, Sage.

Ministry of Education and Science (2015). *The National Core Curriculum*. Ulaanbaatar.

Ministry of Education and Science. (2021). *Action Plan of Improvement of Quality of English Language Teaching and Learning in Mongolia*. https://www.meds.gov.mn.

Munro, M. J., Derwing, T. M., & Sato, K. (2006). Salient accents, covert attitudes: consciousness-raising for pre-service second language teachers. *Prospect*, *21*(1), 67–79.

Namsrai, M. (2004). *English Language Curriculum Standards*. Ulaanbaatar: Mongolian Ministry of Education Culture and Science.

Noels, K. A. (2001). Learning Spanish as a second language: learners' orientations and perceptions of their teachers' communication style. *Language Learning*, *51*(1), 107–144.

Orosoo, M., & Jamiyansuren, B. (2021). Language in education planning: evaluation policy in Mongolia. *Journal of Language and Linguistic Studies, 17*(3), 1608–1614. https://doi.org/10.52462/jlls.116.

Piller, I. (2016). *Linguistic Diversity and Social Justice: An Introduction to Applied Sociolinguistics.* Oxford University Press.

Purevjav, E. (2014). Current trends in Oirat dialect studies. *Senri Ethnological Studies, 86,* 9–17.

Rosa, J. D. (2016). Standardization, racialization, languagelessness: raciolinguistic ideologies across communicative contexts. *Journal of Linguistic Anthropology, 26*(2), 162–183.

Sewell, A. (2016). *English Pronunciation Models in a Globalized World: Accent, Acceptability and Hong Kong English.* Routledge.

Shinjee, B., & Dovchin, S. (2023). Sociolinguistics in Mongolia. In M. J. Ball, R. Mesthrie, & C. Meluzzi (Eds.), *The Routledge Handbook of Sociolinguistics Around the World* (pp. 197–205). Routledge. https://doi.org/10.4324/9781003198345.

Soni, S. K. (2008). Mongolian Kazakh diaspora: study of largest ethnic minority in Mongolia. *Bimonthly Journal of Mongolian and Tibetan Current Situation (Taipei, Taiwan), 17*(3), 31–49.

Steele, C., Dovchin, S., & Oliver, R. (2022). 'Stop Measuring Black Kids with a White Stick': Translanguaging for Classroom Assessment. *RELC Journal, 53*(2), 400–415.

Sue, D. W., Capodilupo, C. M., Torino, G. C., Bucceri, J. M., Holder, A., Nadal, K. L., & Esquilin, M. (2007). Racial microaggressions in everyday life: implications for clinical practice. *American Psychologist, 62*(4), 271.

Tomlinson, B. (Ed.). (2011). *Materials Development in Language Teaching.* Cambridge University Press.

Wang, M., & Dovchin, S. (2022). "Why Should I Not Speak My Own Language (Chinese) in Public in America?": Linguistic Racism, Symbolic Violence, and Resistance. *TESOL Quarterly, 57*(4), 1139–1166. https://doi.org/10.1002/tesq.3179.

Wickhamsmith, S., & Marzluf, P.P. (Eds.). (2021). *Socialist and Post-Socialist Mongolia: Nation, Identity, and Culture* first edition Routledge. https://doi.org/10.4324/9780367350598.

Yagi, F. (2020). Systematization of Kazakh music in Mongolia: activities of theater and radio station during the Soviet era. *Asian Ethnicity, 21*(3), 413–424.

Part 4

Disrupting Raciolinguistic Ideologies

11

Englishes as a Site of Colonial Conflict: Nuances in Teacher Enactment of a Transraciolinguistic Approach

Patriann Smith[1], Crystal Dail Rose[2], and Tala M. Karkar-Esperat[3]

[1] *Department of Language, Literacy, Ed.D., Exceptional Education & Physical Education, University of South Florida, United States*
[2] *Department of Curriculum & Instruction, Tarleton State University, United States*
[3] *Department of Curriculum and Instruction, Eastern New Mexico University, United States*

Across the globe, teachers of language and literacy increasingly leverage Englishes[1] (Kachru, 1992) across their home countries and destination countries such as the United States. During this process, ideological tensions emerge based on novel expectations for the use of Englishes in and beyond literacy and language classrooms (Smith et al., 2018). Undoubtedly, such tensions arising from institutional norms in host and receiving countries influence how teachers respond to the growing population of linguistically diverse students in US schools. Yet, teacher responsiveness to linguistic diversity in the United States often foregrounds language differences while inadvertently overlooking institutional norms that reinforce racialized English language practices (Martin et al., 2019; Rosa and Flores, 2017).

---

1 **Englishes**: The term "Englishes" refers to the many different varieties of English that represent a plurality, variation, and change within the English language as a norm (Kachru, 1992). Englishes represent the interweaving of both standardized (e.g. Standard American English) and non-standardized (e.g. African-American English) forms. We use non-standardized Englishes in this paper to refer to Englishes that do not adhere to what has been determined to be a Standard English within a given context. Linguists refer to these variations as dialects, or New Englishes (Kirkpatrick and Deterding, 2011) and to their counterparts, standardized Englishes, as those that have been typically adopted for use in literacy classrooms (e.g. Standard American English).

Language Teacher Identity: Confronting Ideologies of Language, Race, and Ethnicity,
First Edition. Edited by Sílvia Melo-Pfeifer and Vander Tavares.
© 2024 John Wiley & Sons Ltd. Published 2024 by John Wiley & Sons Ltd.

11 Englishes as a Site of Colonial Conflict

In light of how coloniality frames this experience, García (2022) has recently observed:

> The national formation of what we now know as the U.S. was based on a simple colonial logistic—embrace white immigrants from other places and reject those considered non-white within their own territory: Native Americans, Mexican Americans, and enslaved African Americans.

Responding to this conundrum, this study illustrates how transnational institutional norms influenced literacy and language teachers as they contended with raciolinguistic ideologies (see Alim, 2016; Rosa and Flores, 2017) in Englishes across international contexts. The purpose of the study was to describe the sites of contestation of language ideologies based on Englishes from the cross-cultural insights and identities of former "foreign-born" literacy teachers (*i.e. currently functioning as immigrant multilingual teacher educators*). We examined how colonialism, language ideology, and World Englishes informed former literacy teachers' use of Englishes in classrooms within their countries of origin, and also how they were informed by these experiences, currently, as teacher educators in the United States (see Kachru, 1992; Thompson et al., 2011).

Our rationale for exploring this dynamic is based on an absence in the literature concerning the role of raciolinguistic ideology as steeped in (post) colonialism. Moreover, we acknowledged the need for research that explores how such ideologies intersect with the corresponding instructional practices of educators who functioned as former literacy teachers in linguistically diverse classrooms of the Majority World. Our data examined in this study locates the site for contestation of colonial conflict within these seven former teachers who, based on their various linguistic identities, had enacted literacy instruction using Englishes (i.e. standardized and non-standardized) as well as additional languages (e.g. Tagalog, Spanish, Korean, and Arabic) based on ideologies often influenced by colonialization, and which, though possibly different from their beliefs, could have been displayed in their actions. Heeding the call by Rosa and Flores (2017), we also concurrently explored the impact of the power of racialization, based on (post) colonization as a function of institutional norms, on the use of language of these former literacy teachers, as well as their ways of navigating such ideologies currently, as teacher educators. In doing so, we were aware that even while certain racialized immigrant teachers and educators are regarded as an oppressed community of professionals who often grapple with challenges surrounding English language use based on expectations within and beyond academia while receiving little support (Smith et al., 2018), they also daily leverage agentive transnational literacies (Smith et al., 2023) that allow them to disrupt normative practice and thrive.

To conduct the examinations outlined above, we drew from "cross-circle Englishes" (see Smith, 2020; see also Galloway and Rose, 2018 on Global Englishes) in conjunction with *a transraciolinguistic approach* (Smith, 2020), exploring the implicit assumption that linguistically responsive teaching can occur: (i) in the absence of teacher attention to racialized language practice and (ii) with undue attention to the influence of "foreign-born" teachers' raciolinguistic ideologies in literacy and language instruction in the United States. The lenses undergirding this study allowed us to examine how participants bridged national identities; navigated institutional and cultural linguistic biases; consolidated monoglossic and heterroglossic ideological norms in response to racialized language; and reflected metalinguistic, metaracial, and metacultural understanding. Semi-structured interviews (Seidman, 2012) conducted with participants, interviews with their students, and artifacts served as data. We used inductive and deductive analysis via constant-comparative methods to identify codes, categories, and themes (Charmaz, 2006).

As we show later, through the findings, this study responds to the call for translanguaging with Englishes (Smith, 2020; Smith and Warrican, 2021) and to the need for merging translanguaging with Global (World) Englishes (in language and literacy teaching) (García, 2022). García argues:

> ... by putting [Global English Language Teaching: GELT] and translanguaging along each other, ... [it is possible to] show the language education profession how to truly ensure that English language practices are owned by the many bilingual/multilingual communities that dream of English being part of their repertoire. For all of us to own Englishes, language education must blend a translanguaging paradigm with that of World Englishes Language Teaching, ensuring that speakers can leverage their own practices in interactions, and that others listen to them with intent and purpose that value their languaging, however different this may be.

While we do not take up translanguaging as an explicit construct in this chapter per se, we align our discussions in keeping with these calls, inviting literacy and language teachers and educators, whether they are people of color or not, and whether they teach students of color or not, to draw from their identities as they address raciolinguistic ideologies in the teaching of Englishes (Martin et al., 2019; Rosa and Flores, 2017; Smith, 2019) as well

11.1 Immigrant Multilingual Teachers Crossing Transnational Boundaries

We situate this study that addresses how institutional colonial norms influence teachers of literacy and language based on their racial identities by turning to the literature on what are often referred to by US nationals as "foreign-born" literacy and language teachers. In this selective review, we discuss prior research concerning their attitudes and beliefs as related to the use of Englishes for teaching language and literacy; tensions between teacher beliefs and practice according to the context; teacher enactment of ideologies in the classroom; and finally, former "foreign-born" literacy teacher practices in the United States.

11.1.1 Teacher Beliefs About English for Teaching Language and Literacy

Our review of teacher beliefs indicates that teachers are largely guided by ideologies that influence their practice but that there are exceptions. For instance, Assalahi (2013) sought out to discover Arab teachers' beliefs about English grammar teaching practices; the rationale behind those beliefs; whether or not self-reported practices aligned with their beliefs; and how teachers develop these beliefs. The author discovered that teachers' beliefs about grammar teaching and their teaching practices were aligned. All of the teachers reported using grammar instruction that was forms-focused; they used L1, terminologies, and corrected errors. With regard to how teachers developed beliefs, participants credited college preparation and training as the most effective sources for beliefs about grammar teaching. Similarly, Bamanger and Gashan (2014) found similar results as their teachers' beliefs aligned with practice as well. They conducted a study to explore the beliefs around teaching English reading strategies among Saudi teachers. The study also examined whether or not these beliefs influenced their practice in the classroom. After analysis, they found a consistent correlation between the beliefs of Saudi teachers concerning teaching reading strategies and how they actually teach in their classrooms. In contrast, Tavakoli and Baniasad-Azad (2017) examined Iranian high school English language teachers' perceptions, knowledge, and insights of vocabulary teaching to compare their language ideology with classroom practice in teaching vocabulary. The authors found two beliefs surrounding vocabulary instruction—participants' "real beliefs," which contain their true understanding and knowledge of teaching, and participants' "modified beliefs," which were molded with the challenges encountered (p. 1541). Teachers utilized cognitive-behavioral strategies such as translation and memorization and did not appear to utilize metacognitive or socio-affective approaches. They reflected competence with regard to their knowledge of teaching language; however, this knowledge was not evident in practice.

11.1.2 Tensions Between Teacher Beliefs and Practice Based on Context

The review of contextual factors affecting the beliefs and practices of teachers of language and literacy in the literature revealed several tensions. For instance, Jamalzadeh and Shahsavar (2015) examined contextual factors (i.e. social/institutional) and their effect on Iranian teachers' beliefs and practices in language teaching. After analysis, the authors found that teaching context does not affect teachers' beliefs and no significant difference was found between their beliefs and practice in the classroom. Alternatively, Basturkmen (2012) reported contrasting results among beliefs, context, and practice in a review of studies examining the correlation between language teachers' beliefs and classroom practices. The majority of studies reviewed revealed a limited correlation between teachers' stated beliefs and their practices. There was an indication that "context and constraints mediated the relationship between teachers' stated beliefs and practices—teachers across the case studies reported external factors making it difficult for them to put their beliefs into practice" (Basturkmen, 2012, p. 291).

In another study, Mak (2011) found similar results among Asian teachers of English. When the Western-based Communicative Language Teaching (CLT) model was implemented, tensions between beliefs about language teaching influenced their perceptions and practice. In this situation, context impacted not only beliefs but also actions. Similarly, Liu and Xu (2011) reported that context impacted beliefs and practice as well. The authors led a discussion regarding Western influences on pedagogy involving English instruction in China and concluded that Chinese English teachers are negotiable, flexible, and adaptive concerning English Language Teaching reform. Their study showed that teachers readily shifted identities to adapt depending on the context. Doğruer et al. (2010), who examined the beliefs and practices of Mediterranean university faculty, found that language-mediated context. That is, depending on the language of instruction in the department (English or Turkish), teaching styles were significantly different where beliefs about teaching English remained the same. Specifically, participants across departments agreed that foreign language aptitude is important; however, when teaching styles were examined, participants who taught in Turkish medium departments had differences in small group activities. Faculty who taught in English medium departments consistently used small group activities whereas participants in Turkish medium departments used these sometimes. Even so, the study showed that beliefs were similar regardless of the medium of instruction. Participants agreed that the language aptitude of learners was most important, followed by motivation and expectations of learners. Here, beliefs were found to be similar while teaching styles were different depending on the context and language of instruction. For the Iranian teachers whose beliefs concerning English instruction were explored by Gerami and Noordin (2013), it was found that teachers had a great deal of knowledge about English language teaching and vocabulary instruction; however, the approaches they used to teach vocabulary conflicted with their actual beliefs. The study showed also that teachers' practice did not include any metacognitive and socio-affective strategies.

11.1.3 Teacher Enactment of Ideologies About English in Teaching

Exploring ideological elements in English teaching revealed how these functioned to influence practice. For instance, Kesevan (2016) studied the language ideologies of both "native" and "non-native" Malaysian teachers. This study expanded on former studies to point out language ideologies as more than beliefs surrounding language practices. The ideologies included the mediation between language and broader social structures such as gender, nationality, and sociocultural background in addition to language practices. The study's findings are consistent with the idea that teacher ideologies and classroom practices are at times incongruent and differ based on their background experiences. In fact, according to this research, teachers may not even be aware of the reciprocity of how experiences situate ideologies and ideologies influence teaching practice. Based on this study, Kesevan concluded with a call to action, stating, "If teachers consider their own language ideologies, they could actually form awareness about their tacitly held ideologies and further be cautious if there is any gap between what they belief they are doing and what the students are receiving in actual" (p. 153). Extending the conversation about ideologies, Flórez and Basto (2017) found that Colombian teacher beliefs are molded by experience.

Prior to teaching, preservice teachers held the following common beliefs about teaching: *Teachers should always correct students, motivation is not necessary to teach; translation is not the best method in teaching English; pronunciation, grammar, and classroom management are the most difficult aspects of teaching; you should not speak in English until you can do so correctly; and memorizing lessons is most effective.* All beliefs except correction of students changed after participants gained teaching experience. This study aligns with pre-existing research that teacher experiences inform ideologies.

11.1.4 Former "Foreign-Born" Literacy Teachers in the United States

Examining former teachers of literacy and language currently functioning in the United States revealed variation in the negotiation between ideological beliefs and practices. For instance, Aneja (2016) examined four "non-native" preservice English teachers in a graduate language teacher education program at a large university in the northeastern United States. Specifically, the author explored how the teachers negotiated "non-native" speaking with regards to their own self-conceptualizations and self-positioning, as well as how they experienced dichotomized notions of "native" and "non-nativeness" (p. 577). Aneja found the participants negotiated their own identities, were positioned by others in ways that reinvented ideas of "non-nativeness" and linguistic privilege, and were purposeful in altering their communicative practices in order to either align with or deviate from the norms within the context. These acts impacted their identity negotiation and beliefs. Similarly, Steadman and Vogel (2018) examined six "non-native" preservice teachers who also reported a shift in their beliefs. All preservice teachers were in their first year of a graduate-level TESOL (Teaching English to Speakers of Other Languages) program at a major public research university in the southwestern United States. In the study, graduate coursework, teaching composition courses, and a critical examination of the role of the English language in the lives and teaching practices of the preservice teachers altered their understandings about the English language and teaching. As a result, preservice teachers engaged in critical reflection leading to identity development characterized by negotiations, shifts, and conflicts.

In contrast, Huang (2014) conducted a study with six "non-native" English speakers teaching at secondary schools in the northwestern United States. The teachers viewed themselves as "effective, multilingual speakers of English" (p. 126). Their identities as "non-native" English-speaking teachers coexisted with identities positioning their countries of origin and immigration experience. Ruecker et al. (2018) conducted a similar study with 78 participants representing 35 countries teaching in 24 different states within the United States. The participants also expressed confidence in their English and teaching abilities, with many of them generally seeing their "non-native" English-speaking status as a "non-issue." The number of years of teaching experience increased their confidence levels. Also, they believed they had more positive than negative experiences as "non-native" English speakers (see Cook, 2015 for a complication of this term); however, some respondents noted their international or English as a second language (ESL) students seemed to prefer a "native" English speaker. The majority of respondents believed their multilingual status was a positive attribute in the classroom.

Overall, as shown, the literature on "foreign-born" literacy and language teachers and on their attitudes and beliefs points to the county of origin, the context, and their own experiences as variables concerning the use of Englishes for teaching language and literacy. These orientations confirm our assumptions that the raciolinguistic ideologies of such teachers as relates to institutional norms across countries of origin and countries of destination often remain overlooked. The literature confirms the need for our focus in this study that attends to the usefulness of such insights from former literacy teachers across transnational contexts.

11.2 Raciolinguicizing World/Global Englishes in a "Post-colonial" Transnational World

This study proposes the use of World Englishes and raciolinguistics as lenses to understand sites of contestation of language ideologies based on Englishes from the cross-cultural insights of former language and literacy teachers. The study of World Englishes originally attempted to explain the spread and use of English based on the ideas of geographic and national identity of those who speak and teach it (Kachru, 1992). Three concentric circles, "inner," "outer," and "expanding," explained the ways in which Englishes are used across the globe (Kachru, 1992). With the increase in globalization, Englishes in these circles have come to extend beyond geographical and national identity such that there is overlap across circles in the ways that users leverage their Englishes (Canagarajah, 2006; Canagarajah and Said, 2011; see also Galloway and Rose, 2018 for a discussion on Global Englishes). With this overlap, the accompanying English language ideologies, that is—ways of thinking about the standardized and non-standardized

11.2 Raciolinguicizing World/Global Englishes in a "Post-colonial" Transnational World

forms of English that they use—undergo change depending on the geographical locations of individuals as well as their emerging national identities (see Smith, 2020 for a discussion on "cross-circle" Englishes).

Language ideologies can be based on standardized language which represents "a bias toward an abstract, idealized homogenous spoken language, ... imposed and maintained by dominant bloc institutions ... and drawn primarily from the spoken language of the upper middle class" (Lippi-Green, 1997, p. 64) or it may denote the opposite—ways of thinking about the often non-standardized language forms. For the former literacy teachers in this study, their feelings and beliefs about standardized (e.g. Standard American English, African-American English Vernacular Trinidadian Standard English) and non-standardized Englishes (e.g. Trinidadian English-lexicon Creole) from the identities developed in their home countries directly influenced how they used and taught English literacy in their home countries as well as how they came to make sense of these perspectives in reporting their experiences based on their current English language ideologies as current immigrant teacher educators.

Thus, these lenses allowed us to examine the former English literacy and language teachers' instructional practices and the way their beliefs influenced the institutional norms governing language choices made in their teaching of literacy. More broadly, because colonial practices heavily influenced the literacy curriculum and language education policies (Brown, 2014; Canagarajah, 2006; St. Hilaire, 2011; Thompson et al., 2011) under which some of these former literacy teachers operated, this study frames their overall experiences with Englishes and their ideologies as inextricable from the influences of colonialization, and thus, institutionalization (Rosa and Flores, 2017). In doing so, we acknowledge how raciolinguistic ideologies— ways of thinking about race and language that insist on delegitimizing racialized populations even when they attempt to approximate language use that is deemed "acceptable," "standard," or "proper"—operate as a function of colonization (see Rosa and Flores, 2017) in institutionalizing how individuals operate as interlocutors of literacy and language practice.

Specifically, we view *a transraciolinguistic approach* (Smith, 2019, 2020, 2022) as a lens through which to consider institutions as a mechanism for disrupting these ideologies (see Rosa and Flores, 2017). Transraciolinguistics refers to what is at the same time, "between," "across," and "beyond" various representations of raciolinguistics (see Smith, 2019, 2020, 2022 for detailed discussions). A transraciolinguistic approach, informed by transracialization and a raciolinguistic perspective (see Alim, 2016; Rosa and Flores, 2017), emerged from research conducted with racialized Black

Caribbean immigrant students and educators, all of whom spoke multiple Englishes (Kachru, 1992) and who were shown to simultaneously undergo shifts in thinking about how they thought about race (i.e. *metaracial*), thinking about how they thought about culture (i.e. *metacultural*) and thinking about how they thought about language (i.e. *metalinguistic*). Using the lens of a transraciolinguistic approach, we examine how institutional norms (can) function as a mechanism for *metalinguistic, metacultural*, and *metaracial* agency leveraged in the identities of teachers and educators choosing to work in literacy and language classrooms.

11.3 Methods

11.3.1 Participants

This Institutional Review Board (IRB)-approved study, which took place over a period of two years (2016–2018), was conducted at a large southwestern public university in the United States. The study included eight participants, all female: Chloe, Elena, HyeRan, Olivia, Rana, Shenella, Teya, and Tilini [pseudonyms applied]. Participants were between the ages of 30 and 55 years old and originated from Korea [HyeRan], Pakistan [Rana], Palestine [Teya], Philippines [Chloe & Elena], St. Lucia [Shenella], Ukraine [Olivia], and Vietnam [Tilini]. The former teachers had each functioned in a teaching capacity for at least 2 years at the university level and had each taught for at least 4 years in their former countries. Each participant either had a doctoral degree or was working toward completion of such. They had each learned English differently, and the context of using English was broad. For instance, English taught in the Philippines, Pakistan, Vietnam, and the English-speaking Caribbean (i.e. St. Lucia) is shaped by post-colonialism, and thus its use in these contexts was formerly referred to as the "outer circle Englishes" (Kachru, 1992). In these countries that were colonized by Britain, English played an important role in education, governance, and culture and there remains a broad range of proficiency in English use—some users are considered proficient, and others are considered to have minimal use of a variety of Englishes. The remaining participants learned English as a foreign language because their "native" languages are different. However, English is considered to be the common language to communicate with "non-native" speakers in these countries. Such uses of English were formerly identified as "expanding circle Englishes" (Kachru, 1992). Nationals of the countries were expected to use English to correspond with those in the "inner circle" (Kachru, 1992) where English is used as the first and dominant language.

11.3.2 Data Sources, Collection, Procedures

Given the volume and richness of the data and the intent to obtain an in-depth understanding from the stories of the former literacy for this study, only analyses from the questionnaires and from the individual interviews (Seidman, 2012) of participants were drawn upon. Relying on these data allowed for a holistic understanding of participants' experiences and identities based on their backgrounds as former teachers while also acknowledging their current and evolving roles and identities as individuals, scholars, and educators. Data sources involved a questionnaire containing 19 questions about the educators' background experiences in language and education in their home countries and in the United States, completed by educators prior to the interview. Interviews were based on an interview protocol of 21 questions that ranged from broad educational experiences in the home country to specific experiences with English and literacy instruction across participants' home and US contexts and classrooms. Interviews were conducted with each participant face-to-face, by phone conference, or by Zoom conference. Each interview lasted approximately one hour and totaled approximately 20 pages of 12-point font single-spaced transcripts.

11.3.3 Analysis

Following the transcription of the interviews, I (first author), identifying as a Black immigrant multilingual educator in the United States, and a former international student, facilitated initial member-checking to be sure that transcripts were representative of participants' intended meanings. Inductive analyses via open coding (Charmaz, 2006) of these data were then carefully conducted in conjunction with the third author and my then research assistant, Tala Karkar-Esperat, now Assistant Professor in the United States. Using an Excel spreadsheet, Tala and I first engaged in the iterative process of identifying codes and aligning them with excerpts and corresponding categories. As a Palestinian immigrant Arabic and English-speaking educator herself, and as an emerging scholar, Tala brought an etic (Charmaz, 2006) perspective to these analyses given her absence from the process prior to analysis. She also used the emic (Charmaz, 2006) approach because she was able to identify with the educators as a former international student at the time of the study and now as a current international literacy educator. Together with Crystal Rose (second author), who is White, a non-immigrant American, "monolingual," and was born and raised in the United States, we obtained further perspective on how to examine the data from an "outsider" perspective "looking in." We collaboratively, carefully, and iteratively engaged in the recursive examination of the data compiled in the Excel spreadsheet, returning to raw data to identify additional codes. Upon reaching saturation and agreeing upon the initial list of codes and categories, we designated codes related to participants' cross-cultural insights and conflicts.

11.4 Findings

The purpose of this study was to describe how raciolinguistic ideologies emerged as a function of institutional norms in the cross-cultural insights and identities of seven literacy educators after their migration to the United States. The study was designed to examine how colonialism influencing (raciolinguistic) language ideologies (beliefs and teaching approaches) based on evolving notions of World Englishes, informed former literacy and language teachers' use of Englishes in classrooms as well as their current responses as teacher educators. Findings that follow show how these current educators from different cultures used their prior teaching experiences, and specifically, elements of *a transraciolinguistic approach*, as mechanisms for unveiling the colonial and institutional influences of World Englishes on their language ideologies and the beliefs that shaped their practices. We now present themes and subthemes emerging from our analysis.

11.4.1 Colonially Inherited Raciolinguistic Ideologies

The colonially inherited raciolinguistic ideologies reflected in the identities of a number of the teachers in this study were illustrated in two major ways: (i) preference for standardized English in the home country and (ii) focus on basic language skills. The participants used these mechanisms as former teachers in their countries of origin, which in turn, influenced their current practice and identities as teacher educators.

11.4.1.1 Preference for Standardized English in the Home Country
Chloe and Elena originated from the Philippines, and they used English in their daily life, much like Shenella who originated from St. Lucia in the Caribbean. However, as reflected by their metalinguistic

understanding—*thinking about their thinking about language* (Smith, 2019), their formal command of the language was dependent on the context. Mirroring notions of translanguaging as the reflection of an inherent linguistic repertoire by racialized multilinguals, as espoused by García et al. (2021), Chloe shared, "We speak Taglish, Filipino English. It's like Spanglish, you mix English and Filipino." Elena explained:

> It depends where you are. If you're in the city, then it's English effectively, or functionally it's English. Even if they would say, "Oh, it's Tagalog," but schools would still use English as the main medium of instruction because they have this thinking that if you have a good command of English then you are at an advantage, and so they want kids. Parents alike would send their kids to schools who would use English as the medium of instruction ... . So they will use English with an accent.

Yet, as reflected, Elena also subtly used a metaracial understanding—*thinking about her thinking about race* (Smith, 2019)—in her observation of the ways that institutional norms privilege certain Englishes that are based on white norms (Rosa and Flores, 2017). Chloe confirmed, "We normally follow the American English pattern. It's just we don't use a lot of slang." Similarly, in Vietnam and Ukraine, Standard English was used. Tilini, who comes from Vietnam, described:

> So the English I speak and I teach at home [is] much more like British English. I don't know how—because I was living in the center. So, in the center, people only use British pronunciation ... . In Vietnam, they are very focused on grammar. And the student[s], they can write very well, but they can't communicate very well because they don't have an English-speaking environment. And the school didn't create [a] favorable condition for them to do that.

Olivia shared that English taught in Ukraine "was all about grammatical accuracy, especially in reading and writing. So, it's all about grammar drills and making sure that there were no grammar mistakes and errors." According to other participants, HyeRan from Korea, Rana from Pakistan, and Teya from Palestine, English taught in their countries as teachers were similar to that in Ukraine and in Vietnam.

As shown via metalinguistic, and sometimes, metaracial understanding, across participants former locales, institutional norms dictated that the English language in these countries was formerly identified as "expanding circle" Englishes (Kachru, 1992) where English is taught in a passive way and is mostly focused on writing and grammar. Participants' reflection on these norms based on raciolinguistic ideologies (Rosa and Flores, 2017) suggests that the institutionalization of these mechanisms individually impacted the teachers in their former locales. In doing so, institutional norms functioning based on the "white" listening subject transcended national boundaries (Smith, 2020).

11.4.1.2 Emphasis on Basic Language Skills

Participants' use of metalinguistic understanding influenced their description of the Englishes taught in their various countries of origin as focused on structure and drills and how this influenced their current approaches to Englishes as teacher educators. Learning grammar and writing was a common priority among participants. Olga stated, "It was all about grammatical accuracy." HyeRan also indicated, "I tried to use the standard grammar in my reading, writing, and speaking." Also reflecting on metalinguistic understanding, Tilini shared, "In Vietnam, the focus [is] on grammar." Similarly, but extending to simultaneously demonstrate metalinguistic, metacultural, and metaracial understanding, Rana asserted:

> Obviously, ... using high-level vocabulary [is] extremely important. I personally have not struggled with that component in my life. Maybe the reason being that I was raised bilingually. So, my parents spoke to me in both languages. So, there was a certain level of comfort but, obviously, it's the colonialized version. We were a former British colony, so India Pakistan. So, we have a very specific way of speaking in English.

Likewise, since English learning was taught didactically, some participants shared that they still felt a degree of discomfort in using the language and they needed to practice the language before they teach. Elena stated:

> The best part there is you only recite when you have something to say and you know what you're ready to say, then say. If you're not ready, then you don't say anything, right? But if you're the instructor, you're the teacher or professor, you just have to keep on talking and facilitating that learning ... . I always believe I had to practice a presentation because I'm not really confident in speaking.

Like Elena, HyeRan felt that she needed to practice using the English language: "I prepare what [I am] going to say ... I go through [the] PowerPoint, I can practice a little bit." Chloe used a different strategy. She stated, "I have to be careful about how I'm speaking now ... In order for me not to repeat myself, I guess I have to shorten my request or my questions."

Mirroring previous research from other immigrant educators in the United States (Smith, 2020), the use of metalinguistic understanding appeared to be accompanied by metaracial understanding in the discussions of certain participants but absent from others. In other words, certain participants spoke largely about their Englishes in terms of strengths and weaknesses as relates to proficiency based on institutional norms and considered practice as a continuous process for them in learning the language. This indication demonstrated their constant attention to approximating what they believed to be an ultimate "better" form of English based on what we have since come to describe as the internal "white audit"—a self-based auditory for insistently criticizing attempts at language approximation based on the "white gaze" (see Flores and Rosa, 2015).

11.4.2 Sources for Inadvertently Subscribing to Raciolinguistic Ideologies

Participants appeared to use metalinguistic understanding to point to varied sources as a basis for ideological reference in their home countries, which in turn influenced beliefs and identities about language and literacy in the United States. Immigrant educators seemed to sometimes create their language ideology from their family and community's beliefs. For instance, Shenella realized that it was important for her to speak standardized English eloquently. She indicated, "My parents did not—they prohibited us from speaking French Creole in the house. They were very adamant that English be used." Shenella found that her students in the United States who looked like her had different beliefs than what she expected. She explained:

> And so, I think a lot of it came from that expectation of, "How does a Black person speak English?" They speak it like this. But here's this Black person. She doesn't fit in [with] the people that speak Black English or the people that are Black who speak English, rather. And

she, of course, doesn't sound white. So, where does she fit? And so, their brain now has to develop a new schema to place me into that box in their minds as to where I fit, right? So, that I think was part of the conflict that they faced. Part of that could be said to be a racialized or racial and linguistic.

Immigrant educators' experiences, beliefs, and approaches assisted them in reflecting on the importance of mastering the English language. Tilini stated, "Because I work as a teacher of English, so English [is a] major—[that] play[s] [a] very important role in my life just to show me to earn a living and to communicate with people in the world." Olivia appeared to support Tilini's observations, stating, "It's just a job for and the responsibility for scholars. It's that awareness and appreciation that should be in every classroom ... It's the responsibility of every professor bringing that awareness and raising that awareness and appreciation in every classroom." Teacher immigrants' experiences with language allowed them to understand the differences in using Englishes across their various hybrid identities. For instance, Chloe said, "We love to beat around the bush, go around, and go around, and not go straight to the point ... Then coming to the States, I'm like, 'People are looking at me funny because I'm not getting to the point.'"

On a broader scope, some immigrants encountered situations that encouraged them to make users aware that their own language ideology was valid. Shenella shared:

I remember being asked, am I not from the Caribbean? I also remember being asked, isn't it just like people swinging on trees? How could they possibly speak English that well? ... I was coming from the Caribbean. We just had never placed any emphasis on the color of our skins.

Participants' use of metalinguistic understanding demonstrated that institutionally normative preferences for certain approximations of Englishes influenced how their families, communities, and ultimately, they themselves, made the decision to prioritize certain Englishes over others (Smith, 2020; Smith et al., 2018) even while attending to existing variations across these Englishes. In doing so, there were opportunities for reflecting more deeply through metalinguistic and metaracial awareness about how coloniality undergirded institutional expectations and informed the cross-racial, cross-linguistic, and cross-cultural identities.

11.4.3 Transraciolinguistics in World Englishes as Part of a "Postcolonial" Era

Certain participants appeared to reflect elements of a transraciolinguistic approach—*metalinguistic, metacultural, metaracial understanding*—as they leveraged agentive responses based on their evolving identities in response to the challenges of using Englishes based on institutional norms. HyeRan stated:

> "The biggest challenge that I faced was the use of the English language, especially speaking and listening ... When the students use any idioms, speak too fast, etc., I sometimes have difficulties in understanding what they say."

Also reflecting metalinguistic understanding in her reflection, Chloe indicated that she had similar challenges with her students. "It is difficult to understand students ... Because of the way, it's [language] being used. I mean, I know a bit of idioms and things like that but when like, 'My homie.'" Pronunciation of Englishes created difficulty in communication. Chloe asserted:

> The first-year problem when I was teaching [in the US] ... So, I would say something like, "Erika' instead of "Eureka". I didn't know how to pronounce it. So, the students would always laugh, and they would always maybe go, "Miss, that's not how you pronounce it."

Much like the two previous participants, Shenella used her metalinguistic understanding but also partially began to reflect metaracial understanding, when she observed that she encountered a similar challenge while working across different contexts:

> There were many other experiences where people couldn't understand what I was saying, while I was still having the response that other people felt I was speaking English very well. It was always these two responses that caused me to wonder, "How is it that some people are saying that I speak English so well and I write English so well and the other individuals seem to have so many problems understanding what I said?"

Shenella also recognized, using metalinguistic and metaracial understanding, that when she was teaching in K-12 schools, using formal language with the students created a barrier in communication—much like other international participants, emphasizing effective interaction in her Englishes.

I realized at that point in time that even if I was talking to African-American kids who were the same color as me, that was not as important as creating a communicative bridge between myself and them. [I realized that I didn't need to necessarily sound so formal which would prevent them from focusing on the content of what I was saying].

Despite these challenges, all participants made effective communication with their students a priority, an observation which is in keeping with the emphasis of the institutionally leveraged Global Englishes Language Teaching (GELT) as extending beyond "the old language skills of listening, speaking, reading, and writing" and focusing instead on "new" "communicative activities of reception, production, interaction, and mediation" (García, 2022). Notwithstanding, and also in line with tensions identified by García (2022), a number of participants described the use of formal language to feel accepted or to fit in, which aligned with a desire for "white" listening subject approval (Rosa and Flores, 2017) and an insistence on the internal "white audit" (see Vijay Ramjattan, 2019 for a discussion on the esthetics of listening to racialized speakers in relation to language). For instance, HyeRan's metalinguistic understanding did not appear to be accompanied by metaracial understanding even as she had successes with enhancing communication, reflecting a shift in her linguistic identities. She shared, "I feel responsible for the challenges in communication with students. To compensate [for] my non-standard English, I try to confirm my students' understanding and correct communication with them."

Some immigrant teacher educators changed the way they spoke, their pace, and their pronunciation to fit in and be accepted in the United States. Chloe shared:

> I eventually developed a little bit of an accent in the way I guess most Americans would speak. It's not very awkward anymore ... when I was teaching chemistry. So, when you're doing chemical equations you would say, 'Okay, place the equations before this and that.' I had learned that you use the word *plug-it-in.*

Drawing on her metalinguistic and metaracial awareness, Shenella shared:

> I recall trying to be sure that I was speaking standard English at all times in the class. I recall trying to speak Standard English at all times whenever I spoke to a white person. And I don't think it was a conscious decision.

11.4 Findings | 219

Elena, though, used her metalinguistic understanding to make a conscious decision regarding how she would defy institutional norms leveraged in the US space:

> When I started living here, especially when I was volunteering in the schools, I wanted to sound normal because, I mean, whether I like it or not I'm already an outsider, and I'm trying to belong. But it's more of a natural thing, I guess, and so I was using language to belong. So, I didn't want to sound weird to them, to the students and to the classroom teacher, just so that she will understand me.

Here, Elena appears to prioritize communicative effectiveness based on GELT institutional norms and, as she does this, inadvertently subscribes to raciolinguistic ideologies dictating that certain ways of using Englishes are "better." This dynamic reflects recent tensions highlighted by García (2022) regarding how racialized users of Englishes navigate communicativeness as juxtaposed against the liberation of the racialized as a basis for translanguaging. In turn, it reflects how raciolinguistic ideologies may have been directly connected to Elena's prioritization based on her language identity.

In contrast to Elena, HyeRan emphasized that it is difficult for some immigrants to sound American, equating the attempts at aligning with raciolinguistically based institutional norms for the use of Englishes as "American." Making use of metaracial and metalinguistic understanding to denounce, to a certain degree, the "white gaze" and the internal "white audit," she chooses to subscribe to the goal of effectiveness in communication. HyeRan stated:

> I tried to speak Standard English like native English speakers; however, it is not easy for me. It is also not very important for me to speak like British or American English speakers. The most important thing that I think in the use of English is appropriate communication by using correct sentence structures and grammar rather than the use of a perfect accent. I don't have high confidence in speaking English, and I am still trying to improve my English.

Extending beyond these extremes, Shenella demonstrated intentionality in how she deviated from American institutional norms and used Englishes to increase teachers' awareness of language ideologies. She shared:

> And I do make a very intentional effort to redirect people to the fact that I'm actually using a specific word and explaining it. So, if I say, *dustbin*, which is how—the word we use for *trash can* back home, and I say dustbin, and somebody says, trash can, I will say, 'Yes, can you place this in the dustbin?' And if they ask me, 'What do I mean

by dustbin?' I'll explain. And if they don't, well then, they've just learned another word for trashcan, in my opinion.

The diverse language ideologies embraced by the immigrant multilingual educators based on the complexities of their linguistic, cultural, and racial identities reflected institutional norms based on coloniality and steeped in raciolinguistics transcending their countries of origin and countries of destination in their teaching and daily lives. Their experiences and practices showed that the language ideologies influencing these institutional norms varied depending on how the former teachers deployed metalinguistic, metacultural, and metaracial understanding as they navigated multiple people and contexts, all of which were directly informed by their ever-shifting identities.

11.5 Conclusion

This study sought to describe how raciolinguistic ideologies emerged as a function of institutional norms in the cross-cultural experiences of seven literacy educators after their migration to the United States. We were interested in examining how colonialism influencing (raciolinguistic) language ideologies (beliefs and teaching approaches) based on evolving notions of World Englishes, informed former literacy and language teachers' use of Englishes in classrooms as well as their current responses as teacher educators. We were concerned about understanding more clearly, how the lived experiences of these teachers reflecting their various linguistic, cultural, and racial identities, merged, evolved, and collided. Our findings reflected that (i) institutional norms functioning based on the "white" listening subject transcended national boundaries; (ii) tensions persisting in participants' desire for "white" listening subject approval even while they reflected metalinguistic, metaracial, and metacultural understanding as reflected by their linguistic identities; (iii) grammar and writing were used as key avenues for reinforcing expectations of the "white" listening subject in non-US contexts; (iv) families and communities of color sometimes performed a function as gatekeepers of the internal "white audit" (Smith, forthcoming) beyond the United States; and (v) there was an affinity for monoglossic English ideologies based on affect (i.e., how participants felt) despite the display of metalinguistic and metaracial understanding.

Findings from this study highlight the need for removing attention solely from identities evolving in the racial multilingual individual to focusing also, and more so, on the ways in which institutional norms based on coloniality reify raciolinguistic ideologies in literacy and language practice that privilege an instantiation of certain teacher identities over others. This study also points to the role of immigrant multilingual teacher educators in clarifying these nuances that become visible via elements of a transraciolinguistic approach. Beyond this, the study responds partially to the recent call by Ofelia García (2022) to consider how notions or racialized languaging can intersect with Englishes to propel the field forward. Much like Smith (2020) observes in articulating a heuristic for considering how translanguaging might center the racialization of language, and advocates for considering race, language and migration intersectionally in the use of translanguaging with Englishes (Smith, 2020), García (2022) invites considerations that envision what it might mean to engage Global English Language Teaching (GELT) and translanguaging in concert.

From this study, we observe how the international landscape might move beyond the individual and corresponding identity shifts at the micro level to better attend to the influences of the institution on teacher linguistic identity development and evolution. Focusing on institutions may be critical, as this study suggests, given that their practices for literacy and language teaching are often steeped in raciolinguistic ideologies impacting identity as a function of coloniality (Rosa and Flores, 2017). We noticed that former literacy and language teachers, because of varying degrees of metalinguistic, metacultural, and metaracial understanding, did not often realize the impact of colonialization on their English ideologies, and in turn, their identities, until they were no longer teaching in their home countries. Much like previous research has shown (e.g. Smith et al., 2018; Smith, 2020), they also reflected discrepancies between their ideologies about standardized and non-standardized Englishes and their use of these Englishes in their literacy practice, despite owning their multilingual heritage.

It is clear from this study that teachers of literacy who migrate to the United States and other countries develop a nuanced understanding of how seemingly silenced raciolinguistic ideologies in their countries of origin become visible in the countries of destination. This recognition can equip them to identify the ways in which a transraciolinguistic approach can be fostered by teacher preparation programs to enable teachers to develop the metalinguistic, metacultural, and metaracial knowledge base required for teaching linguistically diverse (immigrant) learners. This recognition can also help to bridge gaps when enacting literacy instruction in K-12 schools by redefining standards and teaching literacy based on these standards in a way that requires both monolingual and multilingual populations to engage with the tenets of a transraciolinguistic approach.

11 Englishes as a Site of Colonial Conflict

Among the implications arising from this study are the need to

1) Extend beyond individual understandings of teacher identity at the micro level to engage with the individual–institutional connections based on racialized languaging that inform language and literacy teachers across the various locales within which they work.
2) Identify opportunities for identifying and addressing racialization of language that occurs covertly in language and literacy teachers' and educators' home countries as well as overtly in the destination countries to which they may migrate.
3) Delve deeply into the hybridities observed in the racialized languaging practices of language and literacy teacher educators and scholars by drawing from self-reports as well as observations of practice in tandem.

References

Alim, H. S. (2016). Introducing raciolinguistics. In H. S. Alim, J. R. Rickford, & A. F. Ball (Eds.), *Raciolinguistics: How Language Shapes Our Ideas About race* (pp. 1–30). Oxford University Press.

Aneja, G. A. (2016). (Non) native speakered: rethinking (non) nativeness and teacher identity in TESOL teacher education. *TESOL Quarterly*, *50*(3), 572–596.

Assalahi, H. M. (2013). Why is the grammar-translation method still alive in the Arab world? Teachers' beliefs and its implications for EFL teacher education. *Theory & Practice in Language Studies*, *3*(4), 589–598.

Bamanger, E. M., & Gashan, A. K. (2014). In-service EFL teachers' beliefs about teaching reading strategies. *English Language Teaching*, *7*(8), 14–22.

Basturkmen, H. (2012). Review of research into the correspondence between language teachers' stated beliefs and practices *System: An International Journal of Educational Technology and Applied Linguistics*, *40*(2), 282–295.

Brown, C. S. (2014). Language and literacy development in the early years: foundational skills that support emergent readers. *Language and Literacy Spectrum*, *24*, 35–49.

Canagarajah, S. (2006). Changing communicative needs, revised assessment objective: testing English as an international language. *Language Assessment Quarterly*, *3*(3), 229–242.

Canagarajah, A. S., & Said, S. B. (2011). Linguistic imperialism. In J. Simpson (Ed.), *The Routledge Handbook of Applied Linguistics* (pp. 388–400). Oxford: Routledge.

Charmaz, K. (2006). *Constructing Grounded Theory. A Practical Guide Through Qualitative Analysis*. London: Sage.

Cook, A. L. (2015). Building connections to literacy learning among English language learners: exploring the role of school counselors. *Journal of School Counseling, 13*(9), 3–43.

Doğruer, N., Meneviş, İ., & Eyyam, R. (2010). EFL teachers' beliefs on learning English and their teaching styles. *Procedia—Social and Behavioral Sciences, 3*, 83–87. https://doi.org/10.1016/j.sbspro.2010.07.015.

Flores, N., & Rosa, J. (2015). Undoing appropriateness: raciolinguistic ideologies and language diversity in education. *Harvard Educational Review, 85*(2), 149–171. https://doi.org/10.17763/0017-8055.85.2.149.

Flórez, S.s., & Basto, E. E. (2017). Identifying pre-service teachers' beliefs about teaching EFL and their potential changes. *Profile: Issues In Teachers' Professional Development, 19*(2), 167–184. https://doi.org/10.15446/profile. v19n2.59675.

Galloway, N., & Rose, H. (2018). Incorporating global Englishes into the ELT classroom. *ELT Journal, 72*(1), 3–14.

García, O. (2022). "Not a bad thing": a commentary on translanguaging among Chinese bilinguals. *Applied Linguistics Review, 13*(3), 433–437.

García, O., Flores, N., Seltzer, K., Li Wei, Otheguy, R., & Rosa, J. (2021). Rejecting abyssal thinking in the language and education of racialized bilinguals: a manifesto. *Critical Inquiry in Language Studies, 18*(3), 203–228.

Gerami, M. R., & Noordin, N. B. (2013). Teacher cognition in foreign language vocabulary teaching: a study of Iranian high school efl teachers. *Theory & Practice In Language Studies, 3*(9), 1531–1545. https://doi.org/10.4304/tpls.3.9.1531-1545.

Huang, I. (2014). Contextualizing teacher identity of non-native-English speakers in U.S. secondary ESL classrooms: a Bakhtinian perspective. *Linguistics and Education, 25*(1), 119–128.

Jamalzadeh, M., & Shahsavar, Z. (2015). The effects of contextual factors on teacher's beliefs and practices. *Procedia—Social and Behavioral Sciences, 192*, 166–171. https://doi.org/10.1016/j.sbspro.2015.06.024.

Kachru, B. B. (Ed.). (1992). *The Other Tongue: English Across Cultures*. University of Illinois Press.

Kesevan, H. V. (2016). Classroom ideologies and teaching practices of native and non-native English teachers in EFL classrooms. *International Journal of English Linguistics, 6*(5), 146. https://doi.org/10.5539/ijel.v6n5p146.

Kirkpatrick, A., & Deterding, D. (2011). World Englishes. In *The Routledge handbook of applied linguistics* (pp. 373–387). Routledge.

Lippi-Green, R. (1997). *English with an Accent: Language, Ideology, and Discrimination, in the United States*. New York: Routledge.

11 Englishes as a Site of Colonial Conflict

Liu, Y., & Xu, Y. (2011). Inclusion or exclusion?: A narrative inquiry of a language teacher's identity experience in the "new work order" of competing pedagogies. *Teaching and Teacher Education, 27*(3), 589–597. https://doi.org/10.1016/j.tate.2010.10.013.

Mak, S. H. (2011). Tensions between conflicting beliefs of an EFL teacher in teaching practice. *RELC Journal, 42*(1), 53–67. https://doi.org/10.1177/0033688210390266.

Martin, K. M., Aponte, G. Y., & García, O. (2019). Countering raciolinguistic ideologies: the role of translanguaging in educating bilingual children. *Cahiers Internationaux de Sociolinguistique, 16*(2), 19–41.

Ramjattan, V.A. (2019). *Working with an Accent: The Aesthetic Labour of International Teaching Assistants in Ontario Universities*, (Doctoral dissertation). University of Toronto, Canada.

Rosa, J., & Flores, N. (2017). Unsettling race and language: toward a raciolinguistic perspective. *Language & Society, 46*(5), 621–647. https://doi.org/10.1017/S0047404517000562.

Ruecker, T., Frazier, S., & Tseptsura, M. (2018). "Language difference can be an asset": exploring the experiences of nonnative English-speaking teachers of writing. *College Composition and Communication, 69*(4), 612–641.

Seidman, I. (2012) *Interviewing as Qualitative Research: A Guide for Researchers in Education and the Social Sciences*. Teachers College Press.

Smith, P. (2019). (Re)Positioning in the Englishes and (English) literacies of a Black immigrant youth: towards a 'transraciolinguistic' approach. *Theory into Practice, 58*(3), 292–303. https://doi.org/10.1080/00405841.2019.1599227.

Smith, P. (2020). "How does a Black person speak English?": beyond American language norms. *American Educational Research Journal, 57*(1), 106–147. https://doi.org/10.3102/0002831219850760.

Smith, P. (2022). A transraciolinguistic approach for literacy classrooms. *The Reading Teacher, 75*(5), 545–554. https://doi.org/10.1002/trtr.2073.

Smith, P. (Forthcoming). *Black Immigrant Literacies: Translanguaging Imaginaries of Innocence*. Cambridge University Press.

Smith, P., & Warrican, S. J. (2021). Migrating while multilingual and Black: beyond the '(bi)dialectal' burden. In E. Bauer, L. Sánchez, Y. Wang, & A. Vaughan (Eds.), *A Transdisciplinary Lens for Bilingual Education: Bridging Translanguaging, Sociocultural Research, Cognitive Approaches, and Student Learning*. New York, NY: Routledge. ISBN: 9781003152194.

Smith, P., Warrican, S. J., Kumi-Yeboah, A., & Richards, J. (2018). Understanding Afro-Caribbean educators' experiences with Englishes across Caribbean and U.S. contexts and classrooms: recursivity, (re) positionality, bidirectionality. *Teaching and Teacher Education, 69*, 210–222. https://doi.org/10.1016/j.tate.2017.10.009.

Smith, P., Warrican, S. J., Kumi-Yeboah, A., & Karkar-Esperat, T. (2023). Rethinking race in research on migration: transnational literacies as a tool. In E. Shizha, & E. Makwarimba (Eds.), *Immigrant Lives: Intersectionality, Transnationality, and Global Perspectives* (pp. 44–68). Oxford, England: Oxford University Press. https://doi.org/10.1093/oso/9780197687307.003.0003.

St. Hilaire, A. (2011). *Kweyol in Postcolonial Saint Lucia: Globalization, Language Planning, and National Development*. Amsterdam, PA: John Benjamins.

Steadman, K.-A., & Vogel. (2018). From college composition to ESL: negotiating professional identities, new understandings, and conflicting pedagogies. *System, 76*, 38–48.

Tavakoli, M., & Baniasad-Azad, S. (2017). Teachers' conceptions of effective teaching and their teaching practices: a mixed-method approach. *Teachers and Teaching* 23(6), 674–688. https://doi.org/10.1080/13540602.201 6.1218326.

Thompson, B. P., Warrican, S. J., & Leacock, C. J. (2011). Education for the future: shaking off the shackles of colonial times. In D. A. Dunkley (Eds.), *Readings in Caribbean History and Culture: Breaking Ground* (pp. 61–86). Plymouth, United Kingdom, Lexington.

12

The Raciolinguistic Enregisterment and Aestheticization of ELT Labor

Vijay A. Ramjattan

International Foundation Program, New College, University of Toronto, Canada

12.1 Introduction

Due to the colonial spread of the English language around the world, embodied whiteness and the notion of nativeness in English are deeply intertwined (e.g., Motha, 2014; Phillipson, 1992). That is, being a "native English speaker," an alleged expert of the language, means that one is racialized as white (Kubota and Lin, 2006; Motha, 2014; Ramjattan, 2015).[1] According to this logic, then, a "non-native English speaker" is racialized as nonwhite and thus considered to be a deficient user of the language (Kubota and Lin, 2006; Ramjattan, 2015). This racialized binary of native and non-native speaker is a prime example of what is called raciolinguistic enregisterment, a process whereby racial and linguistic categories are jointly constructed and "naturalized as discrete [and] recognizable sets" (Rosa and Flores, 2020, p. 95). Raciolinguistic enregisterment provides a grossly simplified understanding of the relationship between the English language and its users. Once again, this understanding is made possible through colonial histories of colonized populations being made to believe that emulating a native English speaker from an imperial center like the United Kingdom or

---

1 Rather than being objective linguistic categories, "native" and "nonnative English speaker" are ideological constructions produced from histories and systems of colonialism (see Motha, 2014; Phillipson, 1992). Recognizing their role in reproducing simplistic ideas about users of English, I still use both terms to emphasize how these ideological categories have material effects in the world.

Language Teacher Identity: Confronting Ideologies of Language, Race, and Ethnicity,
First Edition. Edited by Sílvia Melo-Pfeifer and Vander Tavares.
© 2024 John Wiley & Sons Ltd. Published 2024 by John Wiley & Sons Ltd.

the United States was the only means to "linguistically civilize" themselves (see Phillipson, 1992). Another noteworthy point about raciolinguistic enregisterment concerns its sensory dimensions. For Rosa (2019), a simpler way to understand this process is to consider how "individuals come to *look* like a language and *sound* like a race [emphasis mine]" (p. 7). This conception of raciolinguistic enregisterment underscores how race can be both seen and heard, thereby demonstrating the role our bodily senses play in creating race. Beyond reinforcing the idea of race as biology, this sensory construction of race upholds racist institutions and systems by making race a material property that needs to be managed (Sekimoto and Brown, 2020).

Indeed, the central issue with raciolinguistic enregisterment involves its institutional consequences (Rosa and Flores, 2020). When someone is labeled as either a native or non-native speaker of English on account of their racial categorization, for instance, this is often done to materially reward or disadvantage them. This is particularly the case in the context of English language teaching (ELT), an industry that relies on colonial histories and white supremacy to market English as an exclusive good to be purchased for socioeconomic success in the globalized economy (Gerald, 2020, 2022; Jenks, 2017). That is, if nativeness in English is a marker of expertise in the language and, furthermore, nativeness is tied to whiteness, then the ELT industry has to provide workers who physically and vocally embody whiteness for prospective student-customers. In this regard, ELT can be understood as aesthetic labor, a type of labor in which looking good for the job entails being white while sounding right means having a voice associated with the stereotypically white, English-speaking Global North (Ramjattan, 2015, 2019a). The purpose of this chapter is to explore the consequences of this aesthetic labor, which operates in conjunction with raciolinguistic enregisterment. Specifically, such labor creates racial hierarchies in the ELT job market and furthers the deskilling of the profession.

To support this argument, the chapter offers a critical review of pertinent literature on various facets of ELT labor. It is structured as follows. First, I offer an overview of the aestheticization and consequent racialization of labor to better understand aesthetic labor and its professional consequences. Focusing on ELT afterward, I detail how the demand for aesthetic labor creates less employment opportunities and material rewards for racially minoritized teachers (as well as their white counterparts in some cases). I also describe the deskilling of the profession, whereby the aesthetic traits of workers are more pertinent for professional success than technical knowledge. Throughout the chapter, I outline possible tactics to disrupt conceptions of the white native speaker as the ideal worker in ELT.

12.2 Aestheticizing and Racializing Labor

The body has always been a central component of labor. Whether it is the factories of the Industrial Revolution or the modern-day construction industry, workers have had to use and consequently put their bodies in danger in order to be given a wage (Warhurst and Nickson, 2020). Even with the increase in knowledge- and service-based industries where there is seemingly more emphasis on mental activities than physical ones, the body remains an important source of labor. For example, in the context of transnational call center work, Rajan-Rankin (2018) argues that agents need to teach their bodies to stay alert and be ready to interact with customers calling from a different time zone. Warhurst and Nickson (2020) further stress the importance of the body in the service industry by noting how workers are expected to manage the aesthetic qualities of their bodies for the sake of gaining and/or maintaining employment. This is understood as performing aesthetic labor.

Concisely defined as the work of *looking good and sounding right*, the notion of aesthetic labor concerns how employers recruit workers with a preferred array of corporeal and vocal characteristics able to be manipulated and exploited in order to please the senses of consumers (Warhurst and Nickson, 2020). Aesthetic labor is about workers physically and orally embodying the brand of the organizations for which they work and ultimately making customers have a positive perception of the service or product they offer (Warhurst and Nickson, 2020; Williams and Connell, 2010). One prominent example of this point is retail work. In the context of a clothing store, for instance, employers might hire workers who physically match the target demographic of the clothing they sell in order to show customers what the merchandise could look like on themselves (Williams and Connell, 2010). With regard to sounding right in particular, aesthetic labor is also exemplified by the vocal requirements for broadcast journalism, which outline the need for clear, fluent speech to convey important information to viewers (Powers, 2021). Rather than being neutral, objective job descriptions, it is important to recognize how looking good or sounding right in these workplace contexts is always ideological and thus has the potential to reproduce various social inequalities.

Returning to the example of broadcast journalism, the need for vocal clarity often operates on an ableist understanding of oral communication by excluding jobseekers with "speech disorders" from becoming journalists (Powers, 2021). In addition to being informed by ableism, sounding right for the job can be racialized at the same time. Take, for instance, ELT, the main type of aesthetic labor to be discussed in this chapter. ELT is a vocal type of aesthetic labor given its promotion of the native English speaker as the ideal teacher of the language, whose accent can be marketed as something for student-customers to emulate in their own learning (Harrison, 2014). However, remembering the previous discussion of the raciolinguistic enregisterment of nativeness and whiteness, sounding right for ELT is interconnected with looking good in the sense that embodying whiteness is all that is needed to be perceived as vocally competent for the job (Ramjattan, 2019a). There are certainly professional consequences associated with this raciolinguistically enregistered aesthetic labor.

First, when looking good and sounding right are deemed inherent traits of ideal workers rather than discriminatory job requirements, those who neither look good nor sound right tend to blame themselves for any employment hardships they face (Williams and Connell, 2010). Thus, whether they are denied a position or financially penalized for not having the desired aesthetic traits, these workers may perceive such circumstances as a result of some personal failing. Moreover, in industries that uphold whiteness as the aesthetic norm, racially minoritized workers may need to engage in various types of impression management to emulate whiteness and/or compensate for lacking it (e.g., Ramjattan, 2021; Wissinger, 2012). This can then result in deskilling as the emphasis of work remains on looking and sounding like a desirable worker instead of developing technical skills and knowledge. Such issues are relevant in the context of ELT given how the raciolinguistic enregisterment that occurs in the field shapes teacher identity. Rather than define themselves in terms of professional accomplishments, for instance, teachers' sense of professional identity is shaped by how well they match the figure of the white native English speaker (Nigar et al., 2023). The development of teacher identity has to grapple with how teachers look and sound because the ELT industry creates barriers or opportunities based on what teachers look and sound like. These points are all explored below.

12.3 The Consequences of Raciolinguistically Enregistered Aesthetic Labor in ELT

12.3.1 Employment Discrimination

[The employer asked,] 'Where did you do your studies?' And I replied, 'Here in Toronto.' She went, 'And anywhere else?' I replied, 'No.' She then asked, 'What language do you speak at home?' And I said, 'At home, I speak English.' She then asked, 'And your parents?' 'They speak about six or seven different languages all mixed up,'

I replied, 'But I can't speak those languages. I can only speak English.' And after that, she went, 'But when you communicate with them, how does that work?' I said, 'They have jobs in Canada. They understand English perfectly.' And then [...] she said, 'Okay, but we're really looking for a native speaker.' And I said, 'That's fine because I am a native speaker.' Just as I said that, a white woman came out with a Scottish accent. And I thought, 'Gee, she's not a native speaker [because her first language may be Gaelic or Scots] and she's working here.' So I didn't know what to take from it, but they never called me back

(Ramjattan, 2015, p. 698).

The above story comes from a self-described multiracial native English speaker named Josh (a pseudonym), who had applied for a teaching position in a private language school in Toronto, Canada. As shown in his interview with the employer of the school, Josh had a difficult time in convincing her that English is not only his dominant language but also, the only language he uses when communicating with his multilingual parents. But why was the employer adamant in discursively positioning Josh as a non-native speaker of English? Based on Josh's noticing of the white woman working at the school, it is possible that the employer was hearing his race rather than the actual sound of his voice. In other words, because Josh did not look like a native English speaker, his native speakerhood was deemed suspect. Conversely, because of her embodied whiteness, the Scottish-accented woman was seemingly more employable than Josh even though she might not have sounded entirely native. While this woman might not exactly sound right to work at the school, her corporeal whiteness possibly allows her employer to "hear past" her voice seemingly on account of her ability to pass as a native English speaker. Here, it is important to emphasize how passing is not a linguistic performance where the woman engages in language practices associated with English nativeness, but rather, the ability to correspond to an imagined image of a native English speaker (for more on the complexities of passing, see Melo-Pfeifer in this volume; Piller, 2002).

Josh's narrative provides an entry point into understanding how the demand for aesthetic labor in ELT, fueled by raciolinguistic enregisterment, perpetuates employment discrimination. If whiteness is intertwined with nativeness in English, then it becomes a technical qualification that employers can freely require from ELT jobseekers. This can be evidenced by such things as the images on recruitment websites showing white individuals as prospective teachers (Ruecker and Ives, 2015) and even job advertisements explicitly asking for native English speakers who are white (e.g., Mahboob

12.3 The Consequences of Raciolinguistically Enregistered Aesthetic Labor in ELT

and Golden, 2013). On the "more subtle" side, job application processes may require teachers to racially identify themselves. In the South Korean context, for instance, Jenks (2017) notes how most ELT employers require job applicants to submit a photograph of themselves, which then allows employers to choose teachers on the basis of their ethnoracial background. No matter their form, all of these labor practices communicate the same point: teachers who are racialized as nonwhite need not apply. It is also important to note here how this employment racism can and does intersect with sexism. For example, in the East Asian context in particular, Kobayashi (2014) notes how white *cisgender men* are often positioned as the ideal instructor due to such things as male hiring managers preferring to hire other men and the alleged sexual allure of white men (a topic to be discussed later).

Perhaps the most insidious tactic used to hire as many white (male) teachers as possible relates to immigration laws pertaining to employment. Whether it is parts of East Asia, the Middle East, or Latin America, ELT employers might tell international teachers that a work visa can only be issued to them if they have a passport from the United Kingdom or various settler colonial states such as the United States, Canada, Australia, and New Zealand, countries with large white populations that also dictate global norms with regard to English language use (Alshammari, 2021; Mackenzie, 2021; Ruecker and Ives, 2015). Even though this legal requirement does allow for racially minoritized teachers from these countries to obtain work, it is important to highlight how such a rule generally excludes teachers from majority nonwhite nations who, due to colonial histories with some of the above-mentioned countries, have an expert command of English. For example, although many Indian speakers of English would consider themselves native to the language on account of British colonialism, their variety of English is often perceived as a corrupted version of British and other Global North Englishes (e.g., Ramjattan, 2019a). Moreover, thinking about teachers like Josh, even if there are racially minoritized teachers who are legally entitled to work in regions like East Asia and the Middle East, they may have a difficult time proving that their English sounds good enough to employers who cannot hear past their race.

As Alshammari (2021) notes, fighting against this hiring discrimination is challenging since those with institutional power are the ones who uphold simplistic categorizations of linguistically qualified and unqualified teachers. However, external pressure may help facilitate change. For example, large international ELT organizations such as TESOL (Teaching English to Speakers of Other Languages) must engage in activist work that publicly calls out schools for their racist (and sexist) hiring practices and subsequently engages in public pedagogy highlighting how demands for nativeness in

English reinforces white supremacy (Gerald, 2022; Ramjattan, 2015; Ruecker and Ives, 2015). This work should be coupled with changes to employment laws, which not only recognize nativeness as a discriminatory job qualification but also do not tie employment eligibility to nationality. In terms of changes to hiring practices within organizations, one-on-one interviews could be replaced with panel interviews so that different interviewers can calibrate their assessments of an applicant and question each other in the event that one interviewer relies on raciolinguistic enregisterment to judge the suitability of a candidate. Such a change has the potential to place more emphasis on technical qualifications instead of aesthetic ones.

12.3.2 Lower Wages

Even though racially minoritized individuals may face perceptual and institutional barriers to securing teaching positions, this is not to say that they fail to become teachers altogether. However, even when they do secure employment, they can still be disadvantaged by the demand for raciolinguistically enregistered aesthetic labor. This is primarily seen by the financial penalties for not embodying the right racial aesthetic.

For example, in their study of Filipino teachers working in English-medium private schools in Thailand, Perez-Amurao and Sunanta (2020) detailed that since these teachers do not look or sound white, which are deemed important professional traits for Thai customers, school administrators could justify paying them lower wages. Indeed, whereas a white native English speaker from the United Kingdom or Canada can make around 35,000 baht (Thai currency) a month at a typical private school, their Filipino counterpart makes 15,000–25,000 (Perez-Amurao and Sunanta, 2020). Such pay disparity can further be explained by the presentation of Filipino teachers as "cheaper options" for customers, who cannot afford the tuition for schools that mostly hire white native-English-speaking instructors (Perez-Amurao and Sunanta, 2020). This is an example of schools profiting from what Panaligan and Curran (2022) call "discounted nativeness," which describes how employers recognize the English proficiency of Filipino teachers due to being former US colonial subjects yet are able to mistreat these teachers because of this colonial history. Panaligan and Curran (2022) explore this point in the context of the online ELT gig economy, where employers might rely on the "American-sounding" pronunciation of Filipino teachers to convince customers that they are conversing with a native speaker of US English (especially in audio-based companies) while paying them a lower wage because they are not perceived as true native English speakers.

12.3 The Consequences of Raciolinguistically Enregistered Aesthetic Labor in ELT 233

What is important to note about the example of Filipino teachers is that when aesthetic laborers can only partially fulfill the sensory requirements of their work, their wages can be lowered. That is, if a Filipino teacher can only sound right and not look good for ELT, then employers can justify not properly compensating them for their labor. What is also noteworthy about this issue is that it can apply to only looking good as well. For instance, referring to the ELT industry in Chinese cities such as Beijing and Xi'an, Lan (2022) explains how the rising costs of recruiting foreign teachers who are white native English speakers with proper credentials have made Chinese recruitment agencies and schools rely on white non-native speakers from Europe and Latin America as more cost-effective alternatives. In fact, while these teachers can be paid a lower salary than their native-English-speaking counterparts, their corporeal whiteness allows schools to charge heightened tuition fees for customers desperate to be taught by a "genuine" native speaker of English.

Given that both white and nonwhite teachers can be given lesser pay due to the demand for aesthetic labor, it is worthwhile for all ELT professionals to fight together for greater material compensation for their labor. Although certainly uncomfortable and possibly culturally inappropriate in certain workplace settings, sharing the amount of one's salary with colleagues may shame employers into paying every employee equally no matter their ethnoracial background. Moreover, the fact that employers can work around having employees who do not physically and/or vocally match the white native English speaker should give workers the confidence to demand these employers to move away from using bodily aesthetics in their labor practices. While such activities may require union organizing, which could be difficult due to the precarious nature of most ELT work (e.g., Lan, 2022; Panaligan and Curran, 2022), Perez-Amurao and Sunanta (2020) also call for national governments to work together in ensuring labor protections for migrant ELT professionals, which can include ensuring that they are adequately paid for their pedagogical labor.

12.3.3 Just Whiteness for Sale

Beyond denying employment and lowering wages, another significant problem with the use of raciolinguistically enregistered aesthetic labor in ELT is its deskilling of the profession. That is, if looking and sounding white is all that is needed to be considered a competent teacher, this neglects the importance of having formal teaching qualifications and experience. This is certainly seen in job postings stating how recruiters have no qualms about hiring teachers with a lack of formal credentials as long as they are native

English speakers from stereotypically white countries in the Global North (e.g., Lan, 2022; Ruecker and Ives, 2015). Furthermore, it is evidenced by teachers simply offering their aesthetic whiteness as a classroom experience for students. Indeed, many white native-English-speaking teachers may complain about essentially being used as "living props" to entice students to learn English rather than directly teaching them the language (Breckenridge and Erling, 2011; Lan, 2022). With regard to the experiences of white western teachers working for the Japan Exchange and Teaching (JET) Program, for example, Breckenridge and Erling (2011) explain how local Japanese teachers do not necessarily share the role of instructor with these white teachers, but instead, use them as models to highlight the exotic foreignness associated with using English. As one of their participants summarized, "So, I'm sort of—look at the white girl—that's my role" (Breckenridge and Erling, 2011, p. 92). And as one local teacher commented, "We like to have a foreigner in the class, just so we can see you and hear you speak" (Breckenridge and Erling, 2011, pp. 92–93). Such low professional expectations likely demotivate white teachers from showcasing any real pedagogical skills, but also signal the potential disposability and replaceability of white bodies as anyone who looks and sounds white can easily take over the position of another (Lan, 2022).

When thinking about white teachers being presented as exotified commodities for visual and aural consumption, this exotification can carry sexual connotations as well. In fact, when thinking about aesthetic labor in such places as restaurants where women servers might need to wear sexually provocative clothing to attract the heterosexual male gaze, it is important to recognize that an effective way to please the bodily senses of (potential) customers is conjuring up sexualized fantasies of the service being offered (Warhurst and Nickson, 2020). With ELT in particular, Appleby (2013) explores this point in a study about white Australian cisgender men working in Japanese private conversation schools. Taking note of Japanese women's perceptions of white western men as being "more chivalrous, romantic, and sophisticated than Japanese men" (Kubota, 2011, p. 481), Appleby (2013) details how schools actively pair white male teachers with Japanese female students in order to connect English language learning to exotic fantasy and romance. That is, if one learns English from an alluring white man, then this could increase the likelihood of finding a white romantic partner through the use of English. But once again, by relying on the heterosexual masculinity of certain white native English speakers instead of actual training and teaching experience to attract customers, Japanese conversation schools deskill these speakers and position them as replaceable commodities.

12.3 The Consequences of Raciolinguistically Enregistered Aesthetic Labor in ELT

How can white native-English-speaking teachers be perceived as professionally valuable beyond their somatic whiteness? Although the examples provided in this section suggest larger institutional changes to certain English language programs, perhaps one answer is to redefine the relationship between foreign and local teachers. As Breckenridge and Erling (2011) argue with regard to JET, there should be a formal collaboration between both parties in terms of team teaching, which would allow foreign teachers to not only showcase their existing pedagogical skills but also develop new ones. Furthermore, because such teaching situations provide excellent opportunities for intercultural learning, team teaching can consist of developing critical language awareness among students, where they can question nativeness as a racialized learning goal and possibly find ways to individually challenge the commodification of whiteness in the ELT industry (Breckenridge and Erling, 2011; Kubota, 2011). These are admittedly small steps to change, but they should at least inspire larger and longer-lasting change.

12.3.4 Erasure of Expertise and Compensatory Identity Work

Whereas aesthetic labor may allow white teachers to do very little in the classroom and still be perceived as having some pedagogical value, their nonwhite counterparts might struggle to be deemed an ELT professional in the first place. Indeed, for racially minoritized teachers, aesthetic labor facilitates the erasure of their professional expertise, even when they may be exceptional instructors. This point is echoed by Amin (1997), who states that when students believe only white people to be native English speakers and use the language in a "correct" manner, racially minoritized teachers are not able to successfully negotiate a professional identity while teaching.

In a small study exploring the everyday interactions between racially minoritized instructors and international students in Toronto, I came to appreciate this issue by noting how the linguistic knowledge of the former group was often distrusted by the latter (Ramjattan, 2019b). For one of the participants named Maria (a pseudonym), an ethnoracially Japanese teacher originally from Brazil, her physical appearance was used by her students as a marker of her allegedly deficient knowledge of English grammar, which is exemplified here:

> [I was teaching the] present perfect and if you could use [it] with 'today' or not. I told my students that you could, depending on the time of the day you were using it. One student actually checked with another teacher who was actually a nonnative teacher as well. She

was ... white, blonde-haired, and blue-eyed. She told the student that you can never use 'today' with the present perfect. So the student actually went further and searched it, and he came back to me like two days later and said, 'You know what. You were right.' It was actually quite interesting (p. 382).

Even though the student did eventually come to accept her explanation about the present perfect, Maria's story highlights how expert grammatical knowledge seemingly has a racial look. Maria and her colleague both identify as non-native speakers of English and are thus deemed to be less competent in the language than their native counterparts. However, as evidenced by the student seeking out her advice, the corporeal whiteness of Maria's colleague made her knowledge of the present perfect somehow superior to that of Maria. Through relying on this raciolinguistic enregisterment to seek help, the student perceptually deskilled Maria.

Because teachers like Maria often face constant challenges to their knowledge of the English language, they typically engage in various types of compensatory identity work to communicate to students that they are professionally qualified in spite of not being white native English speakers. Using Maria as an example again, she consciously chooses what to wear to prevent student skepticism about her professional knowledge and background:

On the first day of class, I will not wear something casual. I will not come to school wearing like overalls and boots because some students might ask you more questions [about your personal background]. So I tend to dress somehow more formally

(Ramjattan, 2019b, p. 384).

By wearing more formal attire and thereby signaling that she is a mature teacher with a lot of professional experience, Maria attempts to present herself as someone who can help students learn English despite not looking or sounding like an ideal teacher of the language. Beyond individual choice, it is important to note that compensatory identity work can also be organizationally prescribed. Returning to Perez-Amurao and Sunanta's (2020) study about Filipino teachers working in Thai schools, for instance, the bodies of these teachers are monitored and regulated by management in order to compensate for their marginalized positioning in the Thai ELT industry. Specifically, because the majority of the Filipino teaching workforce in Thailand consists of women, many teachers are subject to stereotypically feminine job requirements such as wearing makeup and watching their body weight in order to make themselves beautiful and thus aesthetically appeal to students who may have wanted white instructors (Perez-Amurao and Sunanta, 2020). Whether it is institutional policies or individual decisions, the compensatory identity work needed to be performed by racially minoritized teachers makes their labor superficial. That is, instead of dedicating time and effort to deepen their knowledge of grammar or learning innovative teaching methodologies, for example, these teachers have to remain focused on their looks all because they do not conform to white aesthetic norms upheld in their respective workplaces.

Although their pedagogy may be threatened by having to compensate for their lack of the right racial aesthetic for work, it is precisely through pedagogy that racially minoritized teachers can challenge racist perceptions of themselves (Ramjattan, 2019b). Just one of many examples, Charles' (2019) narrative inquiry of Black American ELT professionals in South Korean secondary schools highlights how teachers can strive to change student opinions of different ethnoracial groups through their daily teaching. Indeed, in order to counteract various anti-Black stereotypes prevalent in the South Korean context, the teachers in Charles' (2019) study sought to be ambassadors of Black US culture in the classroom by doing such things as using course materials on Black history and openly questioning students' stereotypical views of Black people in a respectful manner. Of course, doing such work should not be the sole responsibility of Black or racially minoritized teachers. All ELT professionals must make it a pedagogical habit.

12.4 Concluding Thoughts

This chapter has explored the negative impact of the raciolinguistic enregisterment and aestheticization of ELT labor. When nativeness (and hence pedagogical expertise) in English is intertwined with somatic whiteness, the labor of ELT professionals becomes a matter of emphasizing one's whiteness or compensating for it when one lacks it. As detailed above, this aesthetic labor, like aesthetic labor in general, creates labor-market and labor-process inequalities (Ramjattan, 2019a; Warhurst and Nickson, 2020). In addition to denying racially minoritized teachers employment or higher salaries on account of not being white native English speakers, the use of aesthetic labor in ELT positions them as failed workers who must engage in impression management to satisfy student-customers. What is vital to emphasize here is that raciolinguistically enregistered aesthetic labor disadvantages white instructors as well. While teachers who can pass as native

English speakers because of their corporeal whiteness might be given lower wages since they only pass as native, those who are native can become deskilled aesthetic "props" in the classroom. In the end, aesthetic labor is not a fringe issue affecting a minority of teachers, but rather a fundamental problem of the ELT industry.

When it comes to anti-racist remedies to this issue of aesthetic labor, several suggestions have been made in various parts of this chapter ranging from legal reforms and union organizing to reconfigurations in teaching arrangements and developing critical pedagogies. Underlying all of these tactics should be an understanding that if race and racism are sensorily reproduced, then anti-racism must attend to the racist inclinations of our bodily senses (Sekimoto and Brown, 2020). That is, if whiteness is seen and heard to be genuinely superior to nonwhiteness with regard to expertise in ELT, critical interventions are needed to disrupt this racist perception and its material effects. In terms of something like employment law, this means acknowledging how workplace racism can take visual and aural forms. Regarding pedagogy as another example, teachers can fight against notions of racially minoritized English speakers being unintelligible by actively using course materials showcasing a range of accented Englishes, thereby showing students that it is possible to understand speech that is not white-coded.

While such strategies for change come to take shape, it is also necessary to further understand the complexities of aesthetic labor in ELT and its reliance on raciolinguistic enregisterment. In fact, there are several questions that future research should explore in order to foster more equitable ELT workplaces. To begin, although all teachers racialized as nonwhite can be perceived as pedagogically lacking when compared to a white native English speaker, how might the demand for aesthetic labor affect an instructor of one ethnoracial background differently from another? Moreover, while aesthetic labor in ELT is mostly about the intersection of race and language, it was seen how other social markers such as gender and sexuality also constitute salient job criteria (Appleby, 2013; Perez-Amurao and Sunanta, 2020). Therefore, how might other intersecting types of social differentiation like class and age simultaneously inform the specifications of aesthetic labor? Finally, how might school context shape the performance of this labor? That is, does aesthetic labor operate in the same way in both publicly funded and privatized educational institutions? In a neoliberal globalized economy where individuals need to envision themselves as sets of skills to be deployed as labor (Urciuoli, 2008), such research questions can point out the ludicrousness of relying on bodily aesthetics to determine who is (not) a good worker.

References

Alshammari, A. (2021). Job advertisements for English teachers in the Saudi Arabian context: discourses of discrimination and inequity. *TESOL Journal, 12*(2), 1–13. https://doi.org/10.1002/tesj.542.

Amin, N. (1997). Race and the identity of the nonnative ESL teacher. *TESOL Quarterly, 31*(3), 580–583. https://www.jstor.org/stable/3587841.

Appleby, R. (2013). Desire in translation: white masculinity and TESOL. *TESOL Quarterly, 47*(1), 122–147. https://doi.org/10.1002/tesq.51.

Breckenridge, Y., & Erling, E. J. (2011). The native speaker English teacher and the politics of globalization in Japan. In P. Seargeant (Ed.), *English in Japan in the Era of Globalization* (pp. 80–100). Palgrave Macmillan.

Charles, Q. D. (2019). Black teachers of English in South Korea: constructing identities as a native English speaker and English language teaching professional. *TESOL Journal, 10*(4), 1–16. https://doi.org/10.1002/tesj.478.

Gerald, J. P. B. (2020). Worth the risk: towards decentring whiteness in English language teaching. *BC TEAL Journal, 5*(1), 44–54. https://doi.org/10.14288/bctj.v5il.345.

Gerald, J. P. B. (2022). *Antisocial Language Teaching: English and the Pervasive Pathology of Whiteness*. Multilingual Matters.

Harrison, G. (2014). Accent and 'othering' in the workplace. In J. M. Levis & A. Moyer (Eds.), *Social Dynamics in Second Language Accent* (pp. 255–272). Walter de Gruyter.

Jenks, C. J. (2017). *Race and Ethnicity in English Language Teaching: Korea in Focus*. Multilingual Matters.

Kobayashi, Y. (2014). Gender gap in the EFL classroom in East Asia. *Applied Linguistics, 35*(2), 219–223. https://doi.org/10.1093/applin/amu008.

Kubota, R. (2011). Learning a foreign language as leisure and consumption: enjoyment, desire, and the business of *eikaiwa*. *International Journal of Bilingual Education and Bilingualism, 14*(4), 473–488. https://doi.org/10.1080/13670050.2011.573069.

Kubota, R., & Lin, A. (2006). Race and TESOL: introduction to concepts and theories. *TESOL Quarterly, 40*(3), 471–493. https://doi.org/10.2307/40264540.

Lan, S. (2022). Between privileges and precariousness: remaking whiteness in China's teaching English as a second language industry. *American Anthropologist, 124*(1), 118–129. https://doi.org/10.1111/aman.13657.

Mackenzie, L. (2021). Discriminatory job advertisements for English language teachers in Colombia: an analysis of recruitment biases. *TESOL Journal, 12*(1), 1–21. https://doi.org/10.1002/tesj.535.

Mahboob, A., & Golden, R. (2013). Looking for native speakers of English: discrimination in English language teaching job advertisements. *Voices in Asia Journal, 1*(1), 72–81. https://payungsakk.wixsite.com/viawebsite/volume-1.

Motha, S. (2014). *Race, Empire, and English Language Teaching: Creating Responsible and Ethical Anti-racist Practice.* Teachers College Press.

Nigar, N., Kostogriz, A., Gurney, L., & Janfada, M. (2023). 'No one would give me that job in Australia': when professional identities intersect with how teachers look, speak, and where they come from. *Discourse: Studies in the Cultural Politics of Education.* Advance online publication. https://doi.org/10.1080/01596306.2023.2239182.

Panaligan, J. H., & Curran, N. M. (2022). "We are cheaper, so they hire us": discounted nativeness in online English teaching. *Journal of Sociolinguistics, 26*(2), 246–264. https://doi.org/10.1111/josl.12543.

Perez-Amurao, A. L., & Sunanta, S. (2020). They are 'Asians just like us': Filipino teachers, colonial aesthetics and English language education in Thailand *Sojourn: Journal of Social Issues in Southeast Asia, 35*(1), 108–137. https://doi.org/10.1355/sj35-1d.

Phillipson, R. (1992). *Linguistic Imperialism.* Oxford University Press.

Piller, I. (2002). Passing for a native speaker: identity and success in second language learning. *Journal of Sociolinguistics, 6*(2), 179–208.

Powers, E. (2021). Seeking "skilled, poised, fluent" verbal communicators: aesthetic labor and signaling in journalism job advertisements. *Newspaper Research Journal, 42*(1), 12–28. https://doi.org/10.1177/0739532921989884.

Rajan-Rankin, S. (2018). Invisible bodies and disembodied voices? Identity work, the body and embodiment in transnational service work. *Gender, Work & Organization, 25*(1), 9–23. https://doi.org/10.1111/gwao.12198.

Ramjattan, V. A. (2015). Lacking the right aesthetic: everyday employment discrimination in Toronto private language schools. *Equality, Diversity and Inclusion, 34*(8), 692–704. https://doi.org/10.1108/EDI-03-2015-0018.

Ramjattan, V. A. (2019a). Raciolinguistics and the aesthetic labourer. *Journal of Industrial Relations, 61*(5), 726–738. https://doi.org/10.1177/0022185618792990.

Ramjattan, V. A. (2019b). Racist nativist microaggressions and the professional resistance of racialized English language teachers in Toronto. *Race Ethnicity and Education, 22*(3), 374–390. https://doi.org/10.1080/13613324.201 7.1377171.

Ramjattan, V. A. (2021). The transracial aesthetic labour of an international teaching assistant. *Equality, Diversity and Inclusion, 40*(8), 973–985. https://doi.org/10.1108/EDI-12-2020-0365.

Rosa, J. (2019). *Looking Like a Language, Sounding Like a Race: Raciolinguistic Ideologies and the Learning of Latinidad.* Oxford University Press.

Rosa, J., & Flores, N. (2020). Reimagining race and language: from raciolinguistic ideologies to a raciolinguistic perspective. In H. S. Alim, A. Reyes, & P. V. Kroskrity (Eds.), *The Oxford Handbook of Language and Race* (pp. 90–107). Oxford University Press.

Ruecker, T., & Ives, L. (2015). White native English speakers needed: the rhetorical construction of privilege in online teacher recruitment spaces. *TESOL Quarterly, 49*(4), 733–756. https://doi.org/10.1002/tesq.195.

Sekimoto, S., & Brown, C. (2020). *Race and the Senses: The Felt Politics of Racial Embodiment.* Routledge.

Urciuoli, B. (2008). Skills and selves in the new workplace. *American Ethnologist, 35*(2), 211–228. https://doi.org/10.1111/j.1548-1425.2008.00031.x.

Warhurst, C., & Nickson, D. (2020). *Aesthetic Labour.* Sage.

Williams, C. L., & Connell, C. (2010). "Looking good and sounding right": aesthetic labor and social inequality in the retail industry. *Work and Occupations, 37*(3), 349–377. https://doi.org/10.1177/0730888410373744.

Wissinger, E. (2012). Managing the semiotics of skin tone: race and aesthetic labor in the fashion modeling industry. *Economic and Industrial Democracy, 33*(1), 125–143. https://doi.org/10.1177/0143831X11427591.

13

Issues of Legitimization, Authority, and Acceptance: Pakistani English Language Teachers and Their Confrontation of Raciolinguistic Ideologies in ELT/TESOL Classrooms

Kashif Raza

Werklund School of Education, University of Calgary, Calgary, AB, Canada

13.1 Introduction

Since the introduction of raciolinguistics as a lens (Alim et al., 2016; Flores and Rosa, 2015; Rosa and Flores, 2017) to study the ideologies through which English language teachers or Teachers of English to Speakers of Other Languages (TESOLers) are racialized, researchers have explored how these ideologies impact language teacher employment (Jee and Li, 2021; also Ramjattan, 2024), teacher identity (Duran and Saenkhum, 2022), teacher relationships with students and colleagues (Chen et al., 2021), and the field of language teaching in general (Kubota and Lin, 2006; Raza et al., 2021b; Smith, 2024). Duran and Saenkhum (2022), for instance, have pointed to the ways native–non-native speaker dichotomy shapes the latter's identity as less qualified teachers of English. Through duoethnography, the authors explored their own positioning as Non-Native English-Speaking Teachers (NNESTs) at an American university and how a preference for Native English-Speaking Teachers (NESTs) is still prevalent in the field of English Language Teaching (ELT)/TESOL. Raza et al. (2021b) have also identified discrimination toward NNESTs and leaders who struggle to earn legitimization and authenticity at their workplaces in Qatar because of their non-native status as well as the hierarchical discrimination toward TESOL as a less respected field in academia. Additionally, Dovchin and Dryden (2022) found *translingual name discrimination* and *translingual English discrimination* against transnational migrants in Australia. The former is a situation "where the transnational migrants' job applications are instantly

---

Language Teacher Identity: Confronting Ideologies of Language, Race, and Ethnicity,
First Edition. Edited by Sílvia Melo-Pfeifer and Vander Tavares.
© 2024 John Wiley & Sons Ltd. Published 2024 by John Wiley & Sons Ltd.

disqualified, often on the basis of the flimsiest of evidence—that is: one's 'birth name'" (p. 370). The latter restricts employment opportunities for translingual workers because of their English language proficiency. Similarly, Chen et al. (2021) studied the *symbolic violence of English* and the ways NEST–NNEST dichotomy shapes NNESTs' experiences of victimization, marginalization, and inferiority. They noted: "The strong colonial desire for learning 'authentic' English from native speakers (i.e., speak their accents, know their culture) in the TESOL field is assigning symbolic power to the type of English generally spoken by NESTs" (pp. 276–277). Last but not least, Raza and Eslami (n.d.) discussed raciolinguistic experiences of an NNEST and a leader at a branch campus of an American University in the Middle East. Reporting epistemological (legitimation of knowledge) and systematic (within institutional structures and practices) racism through an ethnographical narrative, the authors explained how issues of ethnicity, non-nativeness, color, and gender shape English language teachers' and administrators' identity and position and thus become the basis of confrontation between colleagues and administration, questioning decision-making ability of NNEST, and shaping racist practices and experiences.

Despite continuous work on confronting raciolinguistic practices and policies (e.g. this volume; Kubota and Lin, 2006; Raza et al., 2021b; TESOL International Association, 2006, 2020), issues of legitimization, authenticity, and acceptance continue to emerge for NNESTs. Since these experiences impact language teachers' work, they require continuous investigation of how these issues emerge, the factors that shape them, and what steps are or can be taken by the stakeholders such as teachers, administrators, or policymakers to address them. In order to contribute to this line of scholarship, this chapter is an attempt to unpack the raciolinguistic ideologies about Pakistani English language teachers, the expression of these ideologies in educational settings, and the initiatives taken by another Pakistani foreign language teacher (myself) at a higher education institute in Qatar to confront them. The chapter is based upon a conversation that took place between an English language learner (ELL) and her instructor (myself), the raciolinguistic ideologies that characterized the conversation, and how it became the basis of language awareness activities during the language course to confront ideologies of language, race, and ethnicity. The ELL was upset with her daughter's Pakistani teacher's English accent and the potential impact this accent may have on the student's daughter's English accent. As a case study of an English language teacher and her identity construction as an NNEST in an English as an international language (EIL) context, the chapter discusses how raciolinguistic ideologies shape EIL learners' perceptions about NNESTs and the impact these may have for language

244 | *13 Issues of Legitimization, Authority, and Acceptance*

teachers teaching English in an EIL setting. Additionally, the chapter also shares experiences of confronting such ideologies through lessons, tasks, and discussions that are informed by *English as a lingua franca (ELF)-aware teaching and learning, two-way multilingual turn in TESOL*, and *research on ELT* in the context where this conversation took place. The examples presented in this chapter may assist NNESTs, researchers, teacher educators, and policymakers in confronting dichotomous ideologies of language, race, and ethnicity in different contexts where issues of raciolinguistics are experienced by EIL instructors.

13.2 The Anecdotal Narrative and Raciolinguistic Ideologies

This incident took place in a higher education setting at a Gulf university in the Middle East during the Fall 2021 semester when I was teaching an English communication course to undergraduate female students. An Arabic-speaking EIL student, Noor (a pseudonym), reached out to me as her English language teacher after an English for Academic Purposes (EAP) class, a course focused on critical and practical reading and writing skills, with a concern that her daughter (4 years old) may develop a Pakistani English accent from her kindergarten teacher and, disapproving this variety of accent, she wanted to do something about it. Her daughter's kindergarten teacher was a Pakistani female educator with a Pakistani English accent that differentiated her syllable stress and voiced and voiceless consonants (e.g. |c/k|, |v/w|, |p| and other similar sounds) from that of an NEST and was thus characterized as an NNEST by Noor. Interestingly, Noor knew that her own English language instructor (I) that she raised the issue with was a Pakistani NNEST; however, she did not have any concerns about her instructor's accent because, as Noor added, her instructor sounded *different* and *clearer* from her daughter's Pakistani teacher and more like an NEST with an American accent.

As an English language teacher, I was educated in Pakistan and the United States, have a mixed accent and identify myself as an NNEST. Being aware of the dichotomy of NEST–NNEST and how it may impact the latter's work as English language teachers, I categorized Noor's concern as an incident of raciolinguistic ideology through which "ethnoracial identities are styled, performed and constructed through minute features of language (variations in phonological and morphosyntactic features, for example)" (Alim, 2016, p. 5) and NNESTs are exposed to *translingual English discrimination* that recognizes native English as the only legitimate variety (Dovchin

13.2 The Anecdotal Narrative and Raciolinguistic Ideologies | 245

Table 13.1 Overview of language awareness-based activities and lessons.

1.	English as a lingua franca (ELF)-aware teaching and learning	English as a *contact language* for enhanced *intercultural communication* between different English language speakers with a special focus on Pakistani English/accent
2.	Two-way multilingual turn in TESOL	Incorporation of students' and teachers' linguistic diversity to demonstrate the ability of multi/trans-linguals to adjust and/or switch between different languages and accents
3.	Research on English language teaching in the Gulf	Research findings indicate the preference for clarity rather than accent as a characteristic of teacher effectiveness

and Dryden, 2022; also Shinjee and Dovchin, 2023). Through these processes, Noor was portraying the identity of her daughter's Pakistani teacher as an NNEST, disapproving her Pakistani English accent as an illegitimate, unauthentic, and unacceptable variety of English, and prioritizing English accent over other qualities and capital that characterize an effective and caring kindergarten teacher (Hamre et al., 2013). In order to unsettle such raciolinguistic ideologies, I decided to create *language awareness-based activities and lessons* for all the students (including Noor) that were informed by the literature on antiracial pedagogies (Raza and Eslami, n.d.; Alim et al., 2016; Kubota and Lin, 2006; Motha, 2006) and focused on three themes (see Table 13.1). However, I did not associate any evaluation with these activities and tasks because the course outline did not allow additional assessments.

Being a reflective teacher, I kept a teaching journal (from 15 August 2021 to 18 November 2021) and recorded the activities and tasks (Raza, 2018). I also noted the literature (e.g. Alim et al., 2016) that informed the development of these activities, the ways students responded to these interventions (i.e. field notes), and how these exercises contributed to antiracist education in ELT/TESOL. Using an inductive approach during data analysis, I searched for patterns based on observation (Duff, 2008) and found three interconnected themes that dominated my lessons: ELF-aware teaching and learning, two-way multilingual turn in TESOL, and research on ELT. Aligning with the focus of this volume (i.e. confronting ideologies of language, race, and ethnicity), the next section discusses how these language awareness-based activities and tasks unsettled Noor's and other EFL learners' native-speakerism and raciolinguistic ideologies and invited them to rethink the status of English from an ELF perspective. They also stretched language learning beyond English to other languages through a two-way

246 | *13 Issues of Legitimization, Authority, and Acceptance*

multilingual approach and clarified students' values based upon empirical evidence on ELT in their context. These examples may be employed in other ELT/TESOL contexts in confronting dichotomous ideologies of language, race, and ethnicity.

13.3 English as a Lingua Franca-Aware Teaching and Learning

Despite the fact that the language program and the EAP course did not focus on English pronunciation, I realized that some students believed in native-speakerism and idealized native English accent, especially American English or British English. I was aware of native-speakerism ideologies in ELT/TESOL and how the idealization of native accent disadvantages NNESTs (e.g. Jee and Li, 2021; Kubota and Lin, 2006; Raza et al., 2021b), fosters confrontation between students and NNESTs, and creates a dichotomy of NEST–NNEST in the field of language teaching (Chen et al., 2021; Motha, 2006). In order to unsettle native-speakerism ideologies, I drew upon *ELF-aware teaching and learning approach* (Jenkins, 2012; Sifakis and Bayyurt, 2018) to invite learners to rethink their ideologies of English language and its use in Qatar. According to Sifakis and Bayyurt (2018)

> ELF-aware teaching [i]s the process of engaging with ELF research and developing one's own understanding of the way in which it can be integrated in one's classroom context, through a continuous process of critical reflection, design, implementation and evaluation of instructional activities that reflect and localize one's interpretation of the ELF construct. (p. 459)

Keeping in mind the sociolinguistic context (i.e. Qatar as an EIL setting with many varieties of English and other languages brought by immigrant workers), I designed *metalinguistic tasks and activities* that were covered along with other curricular tasks but invited learners to reflect upon ELF and its importance for EIL contexts (Sifakis and Bayyurt, 2018). These *metalinguistic tasks and activities* intended to achieve three objectives: (i) problematizing students' understanding of English as a language in teaching, learning, and use with a particular focus on the differences between EIL, English as a foreign language (EFL), and ELF; (ii) inviting students to observe how English is used in diverse contexts by paying particular attention to the differences in accents and pronunciations, and how it is used in Qatar; and (iii) emphasizing ELF in the course during tasks and assessments.

To initiate discussion on the English language and its varieties, students were provided with the following definitions of EIL, EFL, and ELF from Jennifer Jenkin's work on the changing forms and uses of English globally:

- *English as an International Language (EIL)*: In the case of English as an International Language, most of the meaningful interaction occurs between NNSs [Non-Native Speakers] rather than between an NS [Native Speaker] and an NNS. Learners are present and future members of an international community consisting largely of NNSs like themselves . . ., and entitled, through their contact with each other with the L2 [second language], to transform their linguistic world rather than merely to confirm to the NS version presented to them [Emphasis added] (Jenkins, 2006, p. 45).
- *English as a Foreign Language (EFL)*: EFL belongs to the modern foreign languages paradigm, according to which the learning of English is no different from the learning of any other foreign language, with the goal of learning being to approximate the native speaker of the language as closely as possible [Emphasis added] (Jenkins, 2011, p. 929).
- *English as a Lingua Franca (ELF)*: English as a Lingua Franca . . . refers, in a nutshell, to the world's most extensive contemporary use of English, in essence, English when it is used as a contact language between people from different first languages (including native English speakers) [Emphasis added] (Jenkins, 2013, p. 2).

Following this was a discussion on what each of these varieties of English meant for the students and for ELT/TESOL as a field. Through teacher-led questions, students were invited to think about how and why each variety is used and taught in diverse contexts, the type of variety that is practiced in Qatar, and the variety that should be taught in their context by English language teachers. In addition to sharing their views during in-class discussions, students reported their group findings and personal views via online reflective journals. Student responses from both activities showed that they found ELF as the most relevant variety in their context. Since a major section of Qatar's socio-demography consists of foreign workers from countries that are categorized as native English speaking like America, England, and Canada as well as non-native English speaking such as India, Pakistan, Philippines, and Nepal, referring to Jenkins (2013) definition of ELF, students found English as *a contact language* between different speakers in Qatar and agreed that this is the variety that should be emphasized in teaching and learning.

Students also acknowledged that differences within ELF spoken in Qatar and other EIL contexts are natural because of the linguistic diversity that

248 | 13 *Issues of Legitimization, Authority, and Acceptance*

characterizes contemporary populations in many countries with immigrants, and that "while speakers should speak with clarity and fluency, listeners should also put an effort into becoming skillful at understanding different accents," (stated Safia [a pseudonym], a student in my EAP course). To emphasize on the latter (listeners' ability to understand different accents), I purposefully played instructional videos of NNESTs, especially Pakistani English language teachers, to explain grammar, writing, and other relevant topics, and sometimes invited students to copy these accents. Similarly, they were reminded that the Program Learning Outcomes and Course Objectives did not focus on pronunciation or accent development but on clarity and fluency. To further highlight support for ELF development, tasks and rubrics, specifically for the speaking component of the course, were explained with an emphasis on the clarity and fluency of speech. This allowed students to listen to different accents, appreciate the diversity between ELF speakers, celebrate their own accents, and thus unsettle native-speakerism ideologies in language learning. These experiences reveal that the students were able to rethink their ideologies of English language and its speakers and were viewing both from an ELF perspective where intercultural communication between different English language speakers (natives and non-natives) is of significance and importance (Jenkins, 2013; Sifakis and Bayyurt, 2018).

13.4 Two-way Multilingual Turn in TESOL

After realizing that the students were able to rethink their ideologies of language, race, and accent, I decided to take the discussion further to introduce students to the movement of multilingualism in ELT/TESOL (Raza et al., 2021a) that argues for utilizing students' entire linguistic repertoire for English language learning. While this movement and most of the work impressed by it in the field of ELT/TESOL have mainly focused on integrating and employing local and first languages of learners to develop English language, scholars like Melo-Pfeifer (2021) have observed that if English continues to remain the endpoint in foreign language curricula, such movements may require a reorientation to benefit fully from *the multilingual turn*. To develop plurilingual practices that promote language learning beyond English, Melo-Pfeifer argued for reversing the acronym TESOL to TOLSE (Teaching Other Language to Speakers of English) to conceptualize "pluralistic approaches to learning and teaching as methods that allow teachers and students to capitalize on plurilingual repertoires and effectively benefit from the multilingual turn, going beyond the mere positive appraisal of linguistic diversity in the classroom" (p. 247).

Advancing this line of argument of diversifying multilingual approaches to ELT/TESOL to stretch language education beyond English, I argue that one way to contribute to such calls is by incorporating not only students' but also language teachers' linguistic repertoire in language classrooms (Raza et al., 2023). Since the multilingual turn continues to remain unidirectional with ELLs and their linguistic repertoire as the only way to design multilingual teaching practices, the incorporation of language teachers' linguistic diversity may open new doors for celebrating, promoting, and strengthening plurilingual pedagogies. Proposing this approach as a *two-way multilingual turn in TESOL*, I believe that such a practice will have three objectives: (i) encourage ELLs as well as language teachers to feel proud of their first/local/prior languages and capitalize on the entire plurilingual repertoire in language classrooms (Melo-Pfeifer, 2021); (ii) provide strong exemplars for ELLs to see how multilinguals (e.g. educators) utilize their linguistic diversity in communication and shuttle between different languages for successful meaning-making (Canagarajah, 2018); and (iii) confront monolingual ideologies of English language teaching and learning collectively by inviting students and teachers to utilize their *multilingualisms*.

Following this two-way multilingual approach, I developed upon my previous work on adapting teaching strategies to ELLs' needs (e.g. Raza, 2018, 2020) and utilized Aronin's (2021) *dominant language constellation* (DLC) approach to draw a map of the languages spoken by the students and myself (see Figure 13.1). According to Aronin (2021), the DLC "is a set of a person's most expedient languages, functioning as an entire unit and enabling an individual to meet all their needs in a multilingual environment" (p. 289). Since the purpose was to confront raciolinguistic ideologies

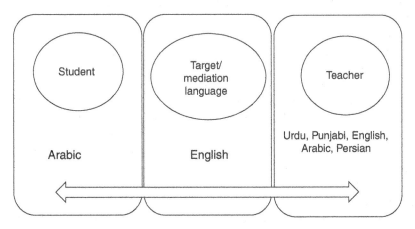

Figure 13.1 A DLC language map for two-way multilingual TESOL in practice.

toward NNESTs and invite students to rethink how they construct foreign language teachers' identities mainly through their ability to speak English with a particular accent (the so-called native English accent), I decided to highlight foreign language teachers' linguistic capital in the form of plurilingual repertoire and translingual practices (Canagarajah, 2018). Using myself as a case of a multilingual Pakistani NNEST, I discussed my knowledge of Urdu, Punjabi, Arabic, Persian, and English and how I am able to switch between different languages during communication. Similarly, I emphasized that because of my multilingual and translingual abilities, I am able to adjust my English pronunciation of different words (e.g. names of people, food, and places) based upon the language speaker I am speaking with. For example, since I speak Urdu and some Arabic, the similarity of alphabets (see Table 13.2) and the borrowing of words from Arabic to Urdu allow me to adjust my pronunciation when speaking to Arabic speakers in English. Through these examples, I showcased my English-plus linguistic capital that constitutes my multilingual identity and translingual practices of shuttling between different languages (Canagarajah, 2018) and accents as a foreign language teacher. Although I am a Pakistani NNEST, students were reminded that the other languages that embody my multilingual reality and cultural capital should not be ignored when constructing my identity as an English language teacher in a/n ELT/TESOL classroom (Chen et al., 2021).

The *two-way multilingual turn approach* in Figure 13.1 also allowed me to stretch the course objectives from a monolingual practice of keeping English as the only outcome of multilingual TESOL classrooms to creating plurilingual pedagogies where English is "a resource or basis of transfer in language learning, being attributed with mediation and remediation functions" (Melo-Pfeifer, 2021, p. 250). The central placement of English in Figure 13.1 shows how it was a target language as well as a connecting language between the students' and the teacher's linguistic repertoires. I discuss this approach and the activities developed upon it in detail in Raza et al. (2023). One of those activities involved learning about and capitalizing on shared linguistic resources of Arabic-speaking ELLs and Pakistani English language teachers and how they can be utilized for learning English and learning other languages through English. Table 13.2, for instance, introduced students to Urdu alphabets and their similarities and differences with Arabic. Although many students were surprised to see how similar Urdu was to Arabic, some showed interest in trying to read and understand the text in Urdu language. Thus, they were provided with a section of an Urdu poem by a renowned sub-continental Urdu poet Allama Muhammad Iqbal (see Table 13.2). Students were invited to read

Table 13.2 Linguistic similarities between Arabic and Urdu.

Arabic Alphabets—28	ا ب ت ث ج ح خ د ذ ر ز س ش ص ض ط ظ ع غ ف ق ك ل م ن ه و ي
Urdu Alphabets—38	ا ب پ ت ٹ ث ج چ ح خ د ڈ ذ ر ز ژ س ش ص ض ط ظ ع غ ف ق ک گ ل م ن و ہ ء ی ے
Urdu poem of Sub-continental poet Allam Muhammad Iqbal	علامہ محمد اقبال جواب شکوہ

دل سے جو بات نکلتی ہے اثر رکھتی ہے   پر نہیں 'طاقت پرواز مگر رکھتی ہے

قدسی الاصل ہے 'رفعت پہ نظر رکھتی ہے   خاک سے اٹھتی ہے 'گردوں پہ گزر رکھتی ہے

عشق تھا فتنہ گرو سرکش و چالاک مرا

آسماں چیر گیا نالہ بیباک مرا

پیر گردوں نے کہا سن کے کہیں ہے کوئی   بولے سیارے 'سر عرش بریں ہے کوئی

چاند کہتا تھا 'نہیں 'اہل زمیں ہے کوئی   کہکشاں کہتی تھی 'پوشیدہ یہیں ہے کوئی

کچھ جو سمجھا میرے شکوے کو تو رضواں سمجھا

مجھے جنت سے نکالا جو انسان سمجھا

تھی فرشتوں کو بھی حیرت کہ یہ آزاد ہے کیا   عرش والوں پہ بھی کھلتا نہیں یہ راز ہے کیا

تا سر عرش بھی انساں کی تگ و تاز ہے کیا   آ گئی خاک کی چٹکی کو بھی پرواز ہے کیا؟

غافل آداب سے سکان زمیں کیسے ہیں

شوخ و گستاخ یہ پستی کے مکین کیسے ہیں

اس قدر شوق کہ اللہ سے بھی برہم ہے   تھا جو مسجود ملائک یہ وہی آدم ہے

علم کیف ہے 'دانائے رموز کم ہے   باں 'مگر عجز کے اسرار سے نامحرم ہے

ناز ہے طاقت گفتار پہ انسانوں کو

بات کرنے کا سلیقہ نہیں نادانوں کو

آئی آواز غم انگیز ہے افسانہ تیرا   اشک بیتاب سے لبریز ہے پیمانہ تیرا

آسمان گیر ہوا نعرہ مستانہ تیرا   کس قدر شوخ زبان ہے دل دیوانہ تیرا

شکر شکوے کو کیا حسن ادا سے تو نے

ہم سخن کر دیا بندوں کو خدا سے تو نے

and understand the text while paying attention to the language for semantic and syntactic comparison and contrast of Urdu and Arabic languages. For instance, we discussed how some words such as طاقت and طاقة (meaning power or energy) and انسان and انسان (meaning human) that may sound and somewhat write differently actually mean the same thing in both languages. Similarly, we also talked about loanwords like دل (heart), خدا (God/Allah), and سخن/گفتار (speech/talk) that are borrowed from Farsi (Persian) into Urdu and make the latter a diverse and rich language. Students also tried to pronounce these words in Urdu and showed interest in continuing to learn Urdu and its similarities with Arabic. This was continued during English vocabulary lessons where we would often look for the meanings of the target words in Arabic and Urdu, thus capitalizing on the plurilingual repertoires of the students and the teacher through a *two-way multilingual pedagogy* (Raza et al., 2023).

The adoption of a *two-way multilingual approach* (Raza et al., 2023) resulted in pushing language learning practices beyond English and creating space for the recognition, utilization, and development of other languages like Arabic, Urdu, and Farsi. Similarly, it increased students' awareness of the linguistic diversity that characterizes foreign language teachers such as Pakistani NNESTs, their translingual ability to shuttle between different languages and accents (Canagarajah, 2018), and their shared linguistic capitals that can be utilized as a resource for learning foreign languages like English. A re-orientation of the status of English through *ELF-awareness activities* (Sifakis and Bayyurt, 2018) and language learning as a continuous process (Melo-Pfeifer, 2021) resulted in the plurilingual identity construction of Pakistani NNESTs who were now seen more as multilingual foreign language teachers than merely English language teachers with deficit accent.

13.5 Research on English Language Teaching in the Gulf

Research on ELT in the Gulf and my own work on teacher effectiveness in this context (e.g. Raza and Coombe, 2021) have pointed to the characteristics that constitute effective TESOL teachers but also how the words/terms used as *characteristics* are understood by the students. For instance, in Raza and Coombe (2021), we investigated students' and teachers' views about six given items related to TESOL teachers that may affect student academic performance: gender, English accent, teaching method, rapport with students, nationality, and age. While the study reported the qualities that are valued the most (teaching methodology and rapport with the students), the moderate (English accent), and the least (nationality, gender, and age), it also problematized how the terms used in the study (e.g. accent, nationality) were understood and perceived by the students. Our curiosity toward this understanding was raised by the observation that while students regarded *accent* among the most valued qualities and *nationality* as a moderate characteristic during the quantitative stage, their elaboration of the survey results during focus group discussions did not approve of the quantitative findings. We concluded that

> The meanings attached with the terms used in the survey, which were probably based upon participants' previous experiences, led them to choose differing answers. For example, participants' higher preference for English accent of the instructor, gender, and nationality in the quantitative stage was in fact linked to the clarity of speech, fluency and teaching style of the instructor.
>
> *(Raza and Coombe, 2021, p. 156)*

After discussing the findings from Raza and Coombe (2021), I invited students to reflect upon their understanding and use of the terms like *accent*, *fluency*, *clarity*, and *intelligibility*. We also discussed how these terms are viewed in the field of ELT/TESOL, the negativity associated with the term *accent*, especially when it is used under the influence of native-speakerism ideologies, and their implications for NESTs, NNESTs, and ELLs (Raza and Eslami, n.d.; Chen et al., 2021; Dovchin and Dryden, 2022; Jee and Li, 2021). Similarly, referring to the program and/or course learning outcomes about speaking skills development and assessment, students were reminded that there is a focus on communicative competence that constitutes *intelligibility*, *comprehensibility*, *coherence*, *fluency*, and *relevance*. They were also reminded that they are not expected to develop or demonstrate a particular accent as part of the speaking tasks completion or otherwise because they are in an EIL context where ELF proficiency should be the target.

13.6 Conclusion and Implications for Confronting Raciolinguistic Ideologies

The continuous occurrence of raciolinguistic experiences for NNESTs is an indication that further work is required to confront ideologies of language, race, and ethnicity in ELT/EIL/TESOL classrooms to create a shared teaching and learning space for different language groups, ethnicities, and races. This chapter (and the entire volume) is an invitation for language teachers, teacher educators, policymakers, and the field of language education as a whole to brainstorm and devise critical approaches that defy native-speakerism ideologies and decrease the NEST–NNEST divide. This will require identifying raciolinguistic ideologies in everyday interactions, designing strategies to confront these ideologies, and then sharing experiences with others for a collective response.

This chapter is an attempt to highlight how particular ways or angles of seeing foreign language teachers (e.g. their ability or lack of it to speak like native English speakers) emerge as a form of raciolinguistic ideologies for another NNEST and the initiatives taken to encounter these ideologies through language awareness activities and tasks. The three strategies discussed in the chapter, ELF-aware teaching and learning, two-way multilingual turn in TESOL, and research on ELT in the Gulf (or in other contexts), are examples of how raciolinguistic ideologies can be confronted in the context of Qatar and other similar settings. Addressing the issues of legitimacy, authenticity, and acceptance of English language teachers, these strategies clarify ELLs' ideologies of English as a language and its status/role in today's multilingual classrooms, invite them to recognize and value the linguistic and cultural diversity that characterizes multilingual NNESTs, and benefit from the shared linguistic resources brought by the students and the instructors. Similarly, these strategies call language teachers to rethink language classrooms from a two-way multilingual angle where English works as a resource, language education goes beyond English language learning, and ELLs' and language teachers' linguistic repertoires are utilized for plurilingual pedagogical approaches.

References

Alim, H. S. (2016). Introducing raciolinguistics: racing language and languaging race in hyperracial times. In H. S. Alim, J. R. Rickford, & A. F. Ball (Eds.), *Raciolinguistics: How Language Shapes Our Ideas About Race* (pp. 1–32). Oxford University Press.

Alim, H. S., Rickford, J. R., & Ball, A. F. (Eds.). (2016). *Raciolinguistics: How Language Shapes Our Ideas About Race*. Oxford University Press.

Aronin, L. (2021). Dominant language constellations: teaching and learning languages in a multilingual world. In K. Raza, C. Coombe, & D. Reynolds (Eds.), *Policy Development in TESOL and Multilingualism: Past, Present and the Way Forward* (pp. 287–300). Springer.

Canagarajah, S. (2018). Translingual practice as spatial repertoires: expanding the paradigm beyond structuralist orientations. *Applied Linguistics*, *39*(1), 31–54. https://doi.org/10.1093/applin/amx041.

Chen, Q., Lin, A. M. Y., & Huang, C. F. (2021). A Bourdieusian and postcolonial perspective on collaboration between NESTs and NNESTs. In K. Raza, C. Coombe, & D. Reynolds (Eds.), *Policy Development in TESOL and Multilingualism: Past, Present and the Way Forward* (pp. 271–285). Springer.

Dovchin, S., & Dryden, S. (2022). Translingual discrimination: skilled transnational migrants in the labour market of Australia. *Applied Linguistics*, *43*(2), 365–388. https://doi.org/10.1093/applin/amab041.

Duff, P. (2008). *Case Study Research in Applied Linguistics*. Routledge.

Duran, C. S., & Saenkhum, T. (2022). "Because she's not a native speaker of English, she doesn't have the knowledge": positioning NNES scholars in U.S. higher education. *Race, Ethnicity and Education*. https://doi.org/10.1080/13613324.2022.2088722.

Flores, N., & Rosa, J. (2015). Undoing appropriateness: raciolinguistic ideologies and language diversity in education. *Harvard Educational Review*, *85*(2), 149–171. https://doi.org/10.17763/0017-8055.85.2.149.

Hamre, B. K., Pianta, R. C., Downer, J. T., DeCoster, J., Mashburn, A. J., Jones, S. M., Brown, J. L., Cappella, E., Atkins, M., Rivers, S. E., Brackett, M., & Hamagami, A. (2013). Teaching through interactions: testing a developmental framework of teacher effectiveness in over 4000 classrooms. *The Elementary School Journal*, *113*(4), 461–487.

Jee, Y., & Li, G. (2021). The ideologies of English as a foreign language (EFL) educational policies in Korea: the case of teacher recruitment and teacher education. In K. Raza, C. Coombe, & D. Reynolds (Eds.), *Policy Development in TESOL and Multilingualism: Past, Present and the Way Forward* (pp. 119–133). Springer.

Jenkins, J. (2006). The spread of EIL: a testing time for testers. *ELT Journal*, *60*(1), 42–50.

Jenkins, J. (2011). Accommodating (to) ELF in the international university. *Journal of Pragmatics*, *43*(4), 926–936. https://doi.org/10.1016/j.pragma.2010.05.011.

Jenkins, J. (2012). English as a lingua franca from the classroom to classroom. *ELT Journal*, *66*, 486–496. https://doi.org/10.1093/elt/ccs040.

Jenkins, J. (2013). *English as a Lingua Franca in the International University: The Politics of Academic English Language Policy*. Routledge.

Kubota, R., & Lin, A. (2006). Race and TESOL: introduction to concepts and theories. *TESOL Quarterly*, *40*(3), 471–493. https://doi.org/10.2307/40264540.

Melo-Pfeifer, S. (2021). From TESOL to TOLSE: plurilingual repertoires at the heart of language learning and teaching. In K. Raza, C. Coombe, & D. Reynolds (Eds.), *Policy Development in TESOL and Multilingualism: Past, Present and the Way Forward* (pp. 245–256). Springer.

Motha, S. (2006). Decolonizing ESOL: negotiating linguistic power in U.S. public school classrooms. *Critical Inquiry in Language Studies, 3*(2&3), 75–100. https://doi.org/10.1080/15427587.2006.9650841.

Ramjattan, V. A. (2024). The raciolinguistics enregisterment and aestheticization of ELT labour. In S. Melo-Pfeifer, & V. Tavares (Eds.), *Foreign Language Teacher Identity: Confronting Ideologies of Language, Race, and Ethnicity.* Routledge.

Raza, K. (2018). Adapting teaching strategies to Arab student needs in an EFL classroom. *Journal of Ethnic and Cultural Studies, 5*(1), 16–26. https://doi.org/10.29333/ejecs/93.

Raza, K. (2020). Differentiated instruction in English language teaching: insights into the implementation of Raza's teaching adaptation model in Canadian ESL classrooms. *TESL Ontario Contact Magazine, 46*(2), 41–50.

Raza, K., & Coombe, C. (2021). What makes an effective TESOL teacher in the Gulf? An empirical exploration of faculty-student perceptions for context-specific teacher preparation. *Journal of Ethnic and Cultural Studies, 8*(1), 143–162. https://doi.org/10.29333/ejecs/538.

Raza, K., & Eslami, Z. (n.d.). Racism in TESOL leadership: a narrative inquiry of a non-native English-speaking leader (NNESL) exposing epistemological and institutional racism. *TESOL Journal.*

Raza, K., Coombe, C., & Reynolds, D. (Eds.). (2021a). *Policy Development in TESOL and Multilingualism: Past, Present and the Way Forward.* Springer.

Raza, K., Manasreh, M., King, M., & Eslami, Z. (2021b). Context-specific leadership in English language program administration: what can we learn from the autoethnographies of leaders? *International Journal of Leadership in Education.* https://doi.org/10.1080/13603124.2021.1944672.

Raza, K., Reynolds, D., & Coombe, C. (2023). Multilingual TESOL in practice in higher education: insights from EFL classrooms at a Gulf University. In K. Raza, D. Reynolds, & C. Coombe (Eds.), *Handbook of Multilingual TESOL in Practice* (pp. 5–22). Springer.

Rosa, J., & Flores, N. (2017). Unsettling race and language: toward a raciolinguistic perspective. *Language in Society, 46,* 621–647. https://doi.org/10.1017/S0047404517000562.

Shinjee, B., & Dovchin, S. (2023). Raising awareness of ethnic accent bullying in EFL teaching in Mongolia. In S. Melo-Pfeifer, & V. Tavares (Eds.), *Foreign Language Teacher Identity: Confronting Ideologies of Language, Race, and Ethnicity* Routledge.

Sifakis, N., & Bayyurt, Y. (2018). ELF-aware teaching, learning and teacher development. In J. Jenkins, W. Baker, & M. Dewey (Eds.), *The Routledge Handbook of English as a Lingua Franca* (pp. 456–467). Routledge.

Smith, P. (2024). Nuances in teacher enactment of a transraciolinguistic approach. In S. Melo-Pfeifer, & V. Tavares (Eds.), *Foreign Language Teacher Identity: Confronting Ideologies of Language, Race, and Ethnicity* Routledge.

TESOL International Association. (2006). *TESOL Statement on Racial Injustice and Inequality.* Retrieved from: https://www.tesol.org/docs/default-source/advocacy/position-statement-against-nnest-discrimination-march-2006.pdf?sfvrsn=6ff103dc_2.

TESOL International Association. (2020). *TESOL Statement on Racial Injustice and Inequality.* Retrieved from: https://www.tesol.org/docs/default-source/advocacy/tesol-statement-on-racial-injustice-final.pdf?sfvrsn=6699fadc_0.

14

Language Student-Teachers of a Racialized Background: The Transracial Construction of the Competent Language Teacher

Sílvia Melo-Pfeifer

Department of Languages and Aesthetic Disciplines Education, Faculty of Education, University of Hamburg, Germany

14.1 Introduction

The professional development of language teachers has been analyzed mainly in terms of being a native or a non-native speaker of the target language (Braine, 2010; Martínez Agudo, 2017; Medgyes, 1994). More recent research has examined the emotional and professional development of teachers of two languages (see chapters by Ku, Iversen, Melo-Pfeifer and Tavares, in this volume; Tavares, in this volume; also, Tavares, 2022a), and the multilingual development and ideologies of language (student) teachers (Ellis, 2016; Melo-Pfeifer and Chik, 2022). In these lines of inquiry, themes such as language and teaching anxiety, pedagogical advantages and challenges, professional knowledge, development and identity, or acceptance by other teachers and students are common trends (Yin Ling et al., 2015; Melo-Pfeifer and Chik, 2022; Melo-Pfeifer and Tavares, in this volume).

While this body of literature is useful for understanding particular aspects of language teacher identities, less is known about the intersection of issues related to native or non-native speakers' profiles, plurilingual identity, and plurilingual professional profiles (as in the case of teachers of two languages), with the racialized background of many language teachers. Some aspects of minority teacher identity have been covered, without a particular connection to specific school subjects, notably regarding aspects of interactional and institutional(ized) racism and discrimination,

Language Teacher Identity: Confronting Ideologies of Language, Race, and Ethnicity, First Edition. Edited by Sílvia Melo-Pfeifer and Vander Tavares.
© 2024 John Wiley & Sons Ltd. Published 2024 by John Wiley & Sons Ltd.

relationship with other school actors (teachers, parents, and students), enhanced teacher agency and resilience, and need for a change in teacher education programs and recruitment practices, to name but a few (Bräu et al., 2013; Georgi et al., 2011; Lengyel and Rosen, 2015; Rosen and Lengyel, 2023). Other studies reflect on the heuristic value and adequacy of categories such as "migrant background" when researching teacher identity, because of its unintended stigmatizing and othering effects (Rosen and Jacob, 2022).

In the field of language education, Crump has called for an understanding and critique of "the propagation of whiteness as a norm associated with native English speakers" (Crump, 2014, p. 1542), and Ramjattan (2019) analyzed racist nativist microaggressions experienced by racialized English language teachers in Toronto as well as professional resistance strategies to counter them (see also Ramjattan and Raza, in this volume).

In this contribution, I assume that a differentiated look at racialized teachers is indeed needed when it comes to language teachers, especially those teaching English, because of the ideologies underlying this particular domain (for example, native-speakerism and authenticity in language learning of additional languages). I therefore explore language teachers' professional identity, emphasizing from a raciolinguistic perspective (Flores and Rosa, 2015) how pre-service plurilingual teachers with a racialized background in Germany narratively reconstruct their coping strategies regarding their racialized hyper-visibility in initial teacher education scenarios. In this study, I analyze how different biographical elements in the construction of pre-service teachers' professional identity (including multilingualism, name, clothing, self- and hetero-identification with gender, religion, and ethnic origin) intersect with prevalent ideologies in language education such as native-speakerism, the monolingual norm, authenticity, and the non-marked white/western norm (from both the listener and the speaker). In reclaiming a professional voice in the making, the student-teachers participating in this study highlight their belonging or assignment to a migrant and ethic group, which we could designate as a racialized visible and/or audible minority following the distinction "subject-as-seen" and "subject-as-heard" (Crump, 2014). Under "visible minority," I include individuals that, because of their phenotype or supposed culturally and ethnically marked external appearance (clothing, hairstyle, etc.), are assumed as belonging to a group which is not identified as the majority.

The "audible minority" is constituted by individuals who would visibly be able to pass for a member of the majority group, as long as they do not mention their name or speak in a foreign-marked and/or non-standard way (with what is perceived as an accent or speaking a lower-prestige variety). While the visible minority can speak in a way that is constructed as accent-free and comply with other expectations of the majority group (in terms of onomastics, for example), they still have to deal with potential issues of racism and ethnocentrism; the audible minority is noticeable by the way they sound. Cumulatively, individuals can be perceived as belonging to both visible and audible minority groups, if they look and sound different to the eyes and ears of the individuals of the majority group. Conversely, individuals with the so-called migrant background may also pass for members of the majority group, whether in terms of appearance, language use, or other features: in this case, such individuals are not considered having a *racialized* background and are not part of the empirical study. Following this rationale, the research questions guiding this exploratory study are as follows:

- RQ1. How does being racialized intersect with specific language teaching ideologies in the professional lives of future language teachers?
- RQ2. Which specific strategies of transracial performance are developed and used by future language teachers during their professional development path? With which aims?

After presenting the participants and the methodological design of the study, I will focus on two biographical, problem-centered interviews (collected between October 2019 and February 2020), reconstructing the experiences of student-teachers belonging to visible and audible minorities. I will focus on how they cope with the fear of being underestimated as speakers and language teachers. To achieve this aim, I will engage in the reconstruction of their everyday racialized experiences, which are not limited to their multilingualism but extend to their names, appearance, clothing, and ability (or not) to abide by (or even transgress) the supposed non-marked white listener and speaker norms (associated with the native speaker). I will use a discourse analysis of self-reported instances of transracial and multilingual performances (following Alim, 2016) during their professionalizing path, to demonstrate that student-teacher transracial experiences result from the interconnection of raciolinguistic and language teaching ideologies. Since this is an exploratory study, I will not present the theoretical background (see the introduction to this volume) and instead move immediately to the empirical study and some of its highlights. My intention is, following a discourse analysis, to scrutinize the selected excerpts of interviews to see which theoretical aspects might be called on to interpret the data. From this perspective, this study can be said to follow a grounded theory approach.

14.2 Empirical study

14.2.1 Participants and methodology of the larger study

The interviews forming the corpus for this study were selected from a larger study about professional identity and professional development of student-teachers of additional languages with a racialized background. In total, 11 interviews with students at one German University were carried out, between 2019 and 2020. Ten semi-guided interviews were held in German and one in French, after participants were informed about the research and gave consent. The interviews were carried out by a white female student born and raised in Germany, peer of the participants. I wanted to avoid hierarchies between the participants and the researcher and allow students to express themselves more freely about their lived experiences in academia. The same student then transcribed and anonymized the interviews. The aim of the larger study was to analyze students' coping strategies with having racialized traits ascribed to their personalities, bodies, and professional competences.

For the production of Table 14.1, two aspects were considered in order to meet ethical expectations (such as anonymity and avoiding misrepresenting the participants). First, to maintain the anonymity of the participants, I avoided attributing names or pseudonyms that could misrepresent participants' self-identification, and decided instead on using numbers connected to the order of the interviews. Second, to avoid imposing categories on the participants, I used their own words to refer to their national and ethnic origins. Thus, in the column "self-reported elements of ethnic identification," I listed the elements that the participants themselves identified as deviations from those they think are associated with the majority context (the *default* in the German context). In cases of information that could lead to the identification of the individuals involved (because of their uniqueness at the university or in the reported school subjects), I changed the data with more vague descriptions (for example, "African country" instead of naming the country).

Some of the elements thematized by students in their ethnic self-identification could be anticipated, as the students are part of what I called "visible minorities" (such as wearing a veil, having an African or Asian phenotype). However, some participants referred to themselves in inverted terms, such as not looking like a Spanish or a French teacher (in the first case because of being blond; in the second case, because of wearing a veil), or not looking German and not speaking German perfectly (meaning

Table 14.1 Summary of self-reported characteristics of the 11 participants.

Code	Self-reported origin	School subjects	Self-reported elements of ethnic identification
Student 1	Parents from an Arabic country, born in Germany	French and Biology	Dari and Farsi as mother tongues; wears a veil
Student 2	Parents from an Arabic country, born in Germany	English and Spanish	Dari as mother tongue; skin color, hair, and name said to appear Spanish
Student 3	African country	French and German	One of the official languages of the country of origin as mother tongue, Black African phenotype
Student 4	Country of a former country of the Soviet Republic	French and English	Speaks a Romance language as mother tongue; name, hairstyle associated with French women
Student 5	Born in Germany, from German mother and father from an African country	German and Spanish	Skin color, hair said to appear Latin American
Student 6	Familia from an Asiatic country, born in the United States, migrated to the United Kingdom as a child	English and Spanish	Speaks a Koreanic language as a mother tongue, Asiatic phenotype, German not perfect
Student 7	Born in Germany, from German mother and a father from an Arabic country	German and Spanish	(Spanish) appearance, Spanish family name (by marriage)
Student 8	Parents from Turkey, born in Germany	French and English	Turkish mother tongue, name, appearance
Student 9	Parents from an Arabic country, born in Germany	English and Spanish	Appearance and name referred to as an index of otherness
Student 10	Country of the former Soviet Republic	French and Math	Name, accent from the mother tongue when speaking German; students say she appears German
Student 11	Parents from Poland, born in Germany	English and Spanish	Polish name, emphasizes that she has German papers, German and Polish as mother tongues, does not look like a Spanish speaker

having an accent when speaking the majority language). While the accent is only mentioned by participants who are first-generation migrants (born outside Germany), most of the students referred to the name as a clue of belonging to an audible minority (sometimes overlapping with traits of a visible minority). So, the name remains one marker of identifying and being identified as a minority, even when linguistic competences in the majority language and phenotype make the participants pass as "standard" German (Student 11).

In terms of professional identity, student-teachers display different attitudes toward their appearances: while some are happy to display their heritage in the classroom and report being proud of showing their students that minority teachers are eager learners of a variety of languages (and, as a matter of fact, most of the participants will teach two languages), others denote pride in being able to pass for native, namely when coupling "looking" and "sounding" like a native speaker of the target language. Students 2 and 4 reported that their appearance was not important as pre-service English teachers, because of the global status of English and "everybody can look like an English teacher," implying there would be a more significant need to identify for teachers of other languages, such as Spanish or French. The empirical analysis in this paper focuses on two of the students who reported the ability to pass for native and positive feelings toward it: Student 2 and Student 5.

14.2.2 The Comparative Case Study: Student-teachers 2 and 5

The analysis carried out in this study could be considered a comparison of cases. From this perspective, I consider this study to be a comparative case study, a case being defined as "an instance, incident, or unit of something and can be anything—a person, an organization, an event, a decision, an action, a location like a neighborhood, or a nation-state" (Schwandt and Gates, 2018, p. 341). I compare two cases/persons—Student 2 and Student 5—to understand their lived experiences, thus adopting an interpretative orientation. As reported in the previous section, those students, with Arabic and African-German backgrounds, respectively, exploit their ability to pass for a native speaker of the target language (in both cases, Spanish). Student 2 might be considered part of the audible minority (because of her name) and Student 5 could be considered part of the visible minority, because of her African phenotype. In both cases, students refer to their hair as an indication of ethnic identity. Student 2 refers to her hair as "dark hair," implying that the non-marked affiliation would be "blond, light hair," and Student 5 reports being confronted with questions such as "Is your hair real?" and "Can I touch it?"

Students' ability to pass for Spanish native speakers manifests itself in daily transracial performances, which they spontaneously describe to the peer interviewer. While other participants in the study also referred to different indices of ethic affiliation or assignment (Table 14.1), the two students selected for this comparative analysis specifically reported transracial practices connected to language learning ideologies. Under "transracial practices," following Alim (2016), I understand fluid practices of crossover that recreate a relationship to a race or ethnicity, challenging established hierarchies. As Alim puts it, transracialization is connected to translation and transgression of "racially ambiguous" people and can happen both across contexts and in the same interactional situation (Alim, 2016, pp. 34–35). According to the same author, "the transracial subject [is] one who knowingly and fluidly crosses borders while resisting the imposition of racial categories—calling into question the very existence of the oft-heard question: *What are you really?*" (Alim, 2016, p. 36). In this paper, I will not analyze all reported instances of participants' transracial practices but instead focus on transracial practices in educational contexts, in the exercise of their professional functions and the development of their language teacher identities.

In order to compare Student 2 and 5's transracial performances, either consciously developed or induced by the regard and/or the hearing of others in the university or school context, I selected significant moments of student-teachers' narratives where they describe when, how, why, and/or the effects of their transracial practices. Because they are so prominent in student-teachers' interviews, these moments could be called critical incidents, in the sense that they triggered a reflective work with a potentially transformative impact on their teacher identities. I will follow an openly interpretative critical discourse analysis approach to those excerpts (Chun, 2020; Willing, 2014), uncovering raciolinguistic ideologies present in language teacher education and highlighting participants' awareness of and agency during transracialization processes. Such an approach allows me to take participants' subjectivities and positions into account, from a contextualized and historicized perspective, through their use of verbal, non-verbal, and para-verbal means (the conventions for transcription were adapted from Mayring (2016) to convey detailed para-verbal and also non-verbal information).

14.3 Findings

14.3.1 Student 2: "Oh Man, You Can See It So Clearly!?"

Student 2, as presented in Table 14.1, is a pre-service teacher of English and Spanish born in Germany with parents from an Arabic country. In terms of multilingual repertoire, she explains that her family only spoke a heritage language at home, but she learnt German when she went to kindergarten. Her first additional language was English at school, followed by Spanish. When confronted with the question "Are you [nationality]?," that she seems to avoid, she reports feeling insecure and surprised: "Oh man, you can see it so clearly!?" and "I actually take that negatively." She goes on to reflect that the visibility of her minority teacher status might be due to the fact that she has dark hair and skin.

Student 2 was doing an internship at a secondary school in Hamburg at the time of the interview, supervised by an older white in-service mentor (another female teacher). In Excerpt 14.1, she reports being seen as a native speaker of Spanish and being de/re-racialized by her mentor, while at the same time fearing being unmasked by her students:

In Excerpt 14.1, the participant clearly signals that her main wish, as a future teacher, is to match the still perceived default of linguistic competence: the idealized native speaker. Passing for a native gives this participant a sense of personal achievement even if this implies suspending other elements of her identity (she repeats the words "actually,"

Excerpt 14.1

In the first internship, <there> was a positive, so for me, I felt that subjectively as positive ((laughs)), um, my tutor actually asked me, after we taught, whether I had (..) mh, Spanish roots, um, because of the pronunciation and the appearance, and (..)<there> was- I actually felt, uh, praised in that situation, because I thought that was, uh, very nice praise or of course I would like to have, uh, mother tongue- (...) so, there- I would like to master the language like ne, like a native speaker. Um, so, that was a positive experience that also stuck.

(...)

<Mmh, negative examples could be> that pupils might (..) not (.) perceive me as not competent in the language, because they think, (# 2 sec.) mh, I (.) can't speak so many languages, or, "You're not Spanish at all, so you can't teach Spanish", because pupils usually think a bit (.) simple.

14 Language Student-Teachers of a Racialized Background

emphasizing surprise and emotion, and "praise"). In this, it seems that passing for a native of Spanish is incorporated into her linguistic and professional wishes and goals and thus can also be seen as elements of the participant's (envisioned) identity as a teacher. What also makes the experience so important to Student 2 is that passing for a native was an act taking place during and after a lesson assisted by her mentor at school ("after we taught"), being directly related to a potential assessment situation (even if informal) of her professional competence. Also of note, Spanish roots are questioned not only for the ability to speak Spanish well but also for reasons of appearance: "my tutor actually asked me, after we taught, whether I had (..) mh, Spanish roots, um, because of the pronunciation and the appearance." The experience of passing as a native speaker is multilayered and lived as a "positive experience that also stuck," which attests to its intensity and lasting influence on the student-teacher.

In the second part of the account in Excerpt 14.1, Student 2 seems to convey the idea that students will see her as a more competent teacher if she is thought to be a native speaker instead of a multilingual teacher ("because they think, (# 2 sec.) mh, I (.) can't speak so many languages"). In this case, the default native speaker crosses another category: the monolingual one! Since she is reporting a hypothetical negative situation, a maximalist ideology of what it means to master a language is transferred to language students, through a fictive direct speech ("You're not Spanish at all, so you can't teach Spanish"), which combines native-speakerism, otherization, non-belonging, and the monolingual mindset.

Student 2 also reported several stay-abroad experiences in Spain, a country she identifies with. In that country, she had the professional experience of teaching German, while at the same time developing her Spanish skills. In Excerpt 14.2, she reflects the expectations of her Spanish students on what a German teacher looks like. She reveals her inability to pass for a German speaker, even if that is the language she feels most confident with.

In Student 2's account of students' perceptions, the German speaker is not supposed to look like her. Through permanent questioning of her "Germanness" (particularly in "that's a German?"), she is constructed as an illegitimate speaker and an illegitimate teacher ("who is supposed to teach"), despite being the so-called native speaker. The assumptions about her linguistic and teaching competences seem to surface even before she starts talking, being exclusively based on her appearance. This is clearly an aspect missing in some studies about being or not being able to pass for a native of a language, i.e. the assumptions produced by

14.3 Findings | 267

Excerpt 14.2

Um, mostly a bit surprised, actually. <Ähm>, especially now in Spain I have also done internships and there I took on another role, because I was introduced as a German, (. . .) <ähm>, who was supposed to teach German or at least support it. And every time I came in, the reaction was predominantly (..) "And where is the German?" (I. smiles) Because (.) I just don't look particularly German, and that's why it was always "I thought a German was coming". And then first to explain, "Yes, I am German, but my parents . . .". I had to explain again and again, which is why they are usually surprised, either because they think I'm Spanish, in Spanish classes, because they ask themselves, "Oops, that's a German? I don't really understand that." And in English, as I said, you don't associate it <so> with outward appearances, I would say.

---

raciolinguistic ideologies which are based on non-verbal signs. In this case, the participant seems to be unable to pass for a native of one of her mother tongues (i.e. German), despite being able to do so when teaching Spanish. Contrary to her silent (and consenting) reaction when passing for a native speaker of Spanish (in Excerpt 14.1), she repeatedly engages in justifications and explanations when she is unable to pass for a German native: "I had to explain again and again." So, while she is proud of passing for a native speaker of the so-called foreign language, she seems upset when one of her national identity/ies and nativeness are challenged, as if, ironically, she was just posing as the native speaker she really is.

The participant claims that passing for a native is more relevant when she is teaching Spanish. To her, and to the contrary, English is associated with globalization and transnationalism and therefore much less with a particular racial identity, as she explains in Excerpt 14.3.

This excerpt contrasts participants' representations about the pluricentricity of English and Spanish. While she recognizes that Spanish is "automatically" (and erroneously) linked to one country, she also concedes that English is deterritorialized and therefore detached from representations about the visual appearance of its speakers. Interestingly, the two appearance traits named previously to justify why she is incapable of ceasing to be who she is, someone with [Arab and/or Southern] roots (which includes dark hair and dark complexion), are now named to explain why she identifies and accepts to be identified with Spanish.

> **Excerpt 14.3**
>
> And I also find that with <English> mmh (…) when you say Spanish, you automatically associate it with a country, and English for me is m- now so global that you (.) can't really associate it with any country anymore, that is, there is also no specific appearance, or (.) you can't even categorize it like that (.), "You look English", that's why that (..) for me would actually also be fr- so questions would come up for me: "Oh really, why then?" (…) Whereas with Spanish it was clear to me, "Ah okay, I know, because of my dark hair, and because of my dark complexion."

14.3.2 Student 5: "It Could Have Been That I Am Cuban or Something"

Student 5 is a pre-service teacher of German and Spanish, born from a mixed couple and referring to German as a mother tongue. She reports that despite her father being multilingual in many different African languages, she grew up monolingually, because "he was a bit afraid of several languages and afraid to educate me bilingually, and that's why I only grew up speaking German."

Student 5's interview is dominated by two thematic strands: her experiences abroad in Latin America (particularly in the Dominican Republic) and her experiences in Germany being regarded as a member of an ethnic minority (mainly because of her hair). She frequently complains about the way random people in the street ask if they can touch her hair, which is long, dark, and densely curled. She frequently refers to Latin America as a context where she feels non-marked, in comparison to Germany, where is frequently attributed a Caribbean identity (Excerpt 14.4). Not looking like a German is something she hears both in Germany and in other countries: "You don't seem at all like a German," she was told in a trip to a different country.

> **Excerpt 14.4**
>
> Well, it's true that when I've been in the Dominican Republic or in general, when I speak Spanish or something, many people tend to think that I'm, I don't know, maybe Colombian or somewhere in the Caribbean region, and (.) since my roots come from West Africa, it's very far away, so to speak.

One element she thematizes as a sign of professional competence is the ability to tame her hair, because she wants to look professional. She sees it as important to give a first good impression as a minority teacher, which is why she tries to adapt: "maybe you shouldn't go to school on the first day with your curls so completely (. . .) open. Um, that's one thing I would do to look more professional. No, simply because when you're new at a school, <but> where I just think, <yes>, you just have to (.) have a look, but that's so (..) so, I don't know, *black hair culture* is (.) such a huge thing," she also says. Because she perceives her hair as a sign of a marked body in the school context, Student 5 thus involves herself in voluntary non-verbal acts of "converse racialization" (Mena and García, 2020), i.e. the erasure of indexical clues that could associate her with non-normative aspects of her professionality (following the same authors). As also suggested by Piller (2002), the previous quotation indicates that passing, in this case for a professional teacher, is (even more) important during a first contact in a new context. In a new school, the participant doesn't immediately want to pass as a member of the black culture, by adopting a certain hairstyle. This example shows how issues attached to *passing* and *not passing for* are strongly interconnected and can relate to context in complex and non-linear ways.

Additionally, she reports being regularly reracialized by others, for the fact that she speaks Spanish and has a dark complexion (Excerpt 14.4). Her racialization tends to be connected to Latin America, the region where she accomplished two stays abroad, one in the Dominican Republic and another in Mexico. She adds that she is not surprised about this attribution of race, as she developed a Central American accent: she even tends to support that attribution herself in order to improve her professional prospects, "because you often have native speakers as teachers." She reports experiences of teaching German in Mexico, where she did not feel subject to racialization processes despite not looking like a German.

In Excerpt 14.5, the participant expresses her doubts about the need to inform others of her origins, to make sure she was not falsely passing by someone she was not in fact ("they could think that I am- I come from somewhere in the Caribbean"). She decided not to act because she was accepted as a trainee for both languages, without being questioned about her origins or challenged in her bilingual expertise. This experience in Mexico strongly contrasts with other experiences in Hamburg, as a teacher of German as a Second Language (for refugee newcomer students, Excerpt 14.6) and as a teacher of Spanish as a curricular language (Excerpt 14.7).

In Excerpt 14.6, after being asked about her origins, she employs her African roots as a strategy to establish a connection with a Somalian student, despite knowing the limitations of such a connection: very different linguistic

Excerpt 14.5

Okay. <Ähm> (. . .) so the relationship to the pupils was always (.) very good. The last internship I had, so to speak, was quite interesting. It was an internship abroad, but it was at a German school abroad, a German school in Mexico. And what I found very interesting was that the students saw me completely directly as a German and Spanish teacher. And I also asked myself if there was somehow, I don't know, if I had to <say> something about it, if I had to say something about my origins, because I also thought that maybe they could think that I am- I come from somewhere in the Caribbean. But that wasn't the case at all. It was really interesting that um (. . .) I was introduced as a trainee in German or a trainee in Spanish and then that was just completely accepted.

Excerpt 14.6

What I noticed when I taught German, um, as a part-time job for refugees, so to speak, <there> was <totally> such a big thing that they were look-ing for a, such a connection and so, that is, that is so, are such projects where you can just somehow work together, for all kinds of students who somehow (.) have a bit of pedagogical experience, or a bit of German(..) experience..) experience, and of course there are also many homogeneous students who are simply completely German-German, and in my case I noticed that <the> pupils who were in my group, so to speak, approached me directly and said "Where are you from?", simply because they were looking for a connection, so to speak. And then the ones from Somalia kind of said, "Oh, cool, I'm from Africa too." And "How many languages do you speak?" And they were completely surprised that I only speak German, because they speak six languages themselves, or German was their sixth/seventh language and so on. And that was- but I found that very positive, because you could establish such a direct connection with the pupils and it was, so to speak, yes, very practical for me somehow that I was not (..) completely German, because then it was so (. . .) yes, you have a closeness to the pupils and they also know that you (. . .) yes, still have such a different understanding. Of course, I didn't grow up in [African Country] and only came here at the age of 16/18 like them, I have lived here all my life, but nevertheless (. . .) I recognize a small connection.

> **Excerpt 14.7**
>
> Yes, exactly, in any case through the visible characteristics, which is also understandable, because you often have native speakers as teachers. And therefore, um, exactly, that- it could also be that I- it could have been that I am Cuban or something.
>
> (…)
>
> <Ähm> here in German schools (…) I found it (.) quite normal, because I also just (.) um, that was before my stay in Mexico and um, I had such a slight (.) Dominican or Cuban accent, which is why I can also uh, completely understand it, and probably would have also asked.

repertoires ("I only speak German, (. . .) they speak six languages themselves"), different biographies and connections to German and Germany ("Of course, I didn't grow up in [African Country] and only came here at the age of 16/18 like them, I have lived here all my life"). Interestingly, as already with the case of the Caribbean identity, identities are discussed in very homogeneous ways: "I am from Africa too." This shows that a very diverse population, traits, languages, accents, etc. can be amalgamated to create a sense of undifferentiation, unity, and sameness, in the name of "a small connection," completely based on the need to feel accepted professionally.

In Excerpt 14.7, Student 5 excuses her audience for asking about her Latin origins ("which is also understandable," "probably would have also asked"), thus acknowledging the ambiguity of her own racial and ethnic status. This ambiguity most easily manifests as the impossibility to easily classify her in terms of appearance and accent.

In this excerpt, Student 5 clearly asserts that it is normal to take her for a native speaker of Spanish because of the frequency with which native teachers are present in the school. Identifying and being identified as a native speaker is thus a way to feel recognized as a teacher. She refers to the possibility to pass for Cuban, Dominican, and even Mexican (as in Excerpt 14.5), which she finds "quite normal" because of her appearance and accent.

14.4 Discussion

14.4.1 The Interplay of Raciolinguistic and Language Teaching Ideologies: Passing or Posing as a Native-speaker Teacher?

The two participants analyzed in this study give us differentiated accounts of what it feels like to be and pass as a native, that is as a legitimate speaker and teacher of a target language. In the first interview analyzed above,

Student 2 reveals how she is constructed as a native speaker of her target language (Spanish) in both her home country Germany and Spain, but not of her mother tongue German when teaching abroad. She is proud in the first case, but feels the need to explain herself in the second, to regain legitimacy. She doesn't think it is as important to (visually) pass for a native in English because of its *lingua franca* status and consequent deterritorialization. In the second interview, Student 5 is also able to pass for a native of Spanish (in her case, from Latin America). She has her German native speaker identity legitimated both by her colleagues and students in Mexico and her refugee students in Germany, who do not challenge her Germanness despite her appearance (beyond the question "where are you from?," she is not further constructed as illegitimate; see Zhu and Li Wei, 2016 on how this question frames talk as nationality and ethnicity).

Nevertheless, passing for a native speaker and competent teacher of the target language (which can refer either to the teacher's mother tongue or to an additional language) is an important accomplishment for both participants. They adopt discursive and performative strategies to sound and/or look more competent and to fit what they perceive to be the default: an idealized native teacher, which is accepted without hesitation by teachers and students. From the interpretation of their interviews, I came to perceive that they feel competing demands from their institutions: to achieve such an idealized status, both students would need to speak and look like native speakers of two differently racialized languages.

In this sense, participants made clear that a native speaker of a language should not just sound like one but also look like one (Rosa, 2019). The ability to pass as a visual and audible native seems to be perceived as the ultimate form of linguistic and professional attainment. Thus, one of the participants' professional goals, even if not always clearly stated, is framed in terms of raciolinguistic ideologies: to become a good language teacher, achieving near-native competence (equated with competing institutional demands: either with not having an accent or, conversely, developing a specific accent such as the Caribbean one), while also ideally looking like a native. Both goals (sounding and looking like native speakers) are entangled in the "neutral" accent and other constructs are based on the bias of the white listener (Tavares, 2022b). Equally, participants' investment in their own language learning and their agency in studying and teaching abroad is thus also permeated by raciolinguistic ideologies of how a native speaker of European and Latin American Spanish looks like.

The interconnection between teaching competence and raciolinguistic ideologies does not affect all the eleven students in the same way. For example, Student 11, a future Spanish teacher whose parents are Polish and who can visually pass for a German, stated that "I don't look like that, but I have experienced all that (. . .), then you don't feel so insecure." It is therefore interesting to see how ideologies of race, perceptions of linguistic and socio-cultural competence, and professional competence meet to frame student-teachers' ways of coping with being racialized, deracialized, and re-racialized (see the next section for a tentative distinction of these concepts) to improve their prospects of becoming a "good" language teacher.

Both Student 2 and Student 5 feel pride in their ability to pass for a native speaker. In this sense, performing transracial identities may be considered a conscious act of professional identity construction, which is not only performed through linguistic means (displaying a good com-mand of the target language, such as the rolled R for Spanish which both participants mention in excepts not included in this chapter) but also through the acceptance of assigned (trans)racial identities associated with nativeness. Passing, Piller (2002) reminds us, "is an act, something they [informants in her study] do, a performance that may be put on or sus-tained for a limited period only" (p. 191). In addition to being dependent on the speaker's own capacity to hold a role, passing is also dependent on external factors such as context or audience. Indeed, as is apparent from the discussed excerpts of both interviews, passing is a performance that requires spectators: the two student-teachers refer to the observers (mentors, teachers, and students) as those who can assess the credibility of their performance. Furthermore, how the performance is assessed is, in both narratives, dependent on the context. When talking about Germany, Mexico, and Spain, students tend to relativize the racialized experiences they went through. Germany is described as a country where otherness is normalized, Mexico is reported as being very diverse and therefore toler-ant toward difference, and Spain is constructed as having little contact with others and then reacting with curiosity toward different physical appearances. Contrary to these descriptions, however, it was in Germany that students report having troubles with assuming their hair or their Arabic origin, which leads me to question the extent to which otherness in the school contexts may really be normalized.

Based on this study, I propose a distinction between "passing for a native" and "posing as a native." In the first case, the native status is attributed and/ or assumed by the audience (mentor, other teachers, students). In the second case, which can be connected to the first, participants consciously accept or feel entitled to play the native status, not challenging or complexifying the audiences' assumptions. To put it short, in both cases, the audience play a crucial role. I claim that these strategies are part of a transracial construc-tion of the competent (modern) language teacher and are a strategy of defense in the construction of professional identity against established (racialized) hierarchies at school.

14.4.2 The Transracial Construction of the Competent Language Teacher

In the field of language teacher education (of a curricular language), the analysis of the corpus shows both a "racialization of linguistic competence" (Flores and Rosa, 2022) and a racialization of the teaching competence. Flores and Rosa (2015, 2022) denounce the postcolonial struggles in the racialization of linguistic competences and the attribution of decreased linguistic competences when associated with a minority. Interestingly, and differently from the report of those authors, Student 5 reclaims an identification to what is perceived as a Latin American body as this is associated with a native speaker of particular varieties of Spanish, which are valued as a form of cultural capital in Germany (instead of despised, as seems to be the case in the United States). Student 5 plays out the fantasy and rarely challenges it, because of the symbolic power she achieves as a language teacher of Spanish in Germany. Thus, Student 5 subverts what Flores and Rosa call "the reproduction of racialized linguistic deficiency" (Flores and Rosa, 2022, p. 12), embracing instead a racialized high linguistic fluency associated with a visible minority status. This example highlights the need to argue for nuanced perspectives when interpreting raciolinguistic ideologies associated with competences, as they may not apply equally across contexts and professional groups.

Despite the productive validity of the term "transracial practices" and "transracial subjects" to describe the performances and daily experiences of the two student-teachers, I consider it important to distinguish between three processes that are intertwined in the transracial linguistic experiences of my informants (based on Alim, 2016):

- Racialization of linguistic repertoires and practices—this process refers to the attribution of characteristics to languages and speakers, based on verbal and/or non-verbal clues. Student 2 is identified as a Spanish native speaker because she doesn't display an accent and looks like she could be Spanish; Student 5 is identified as a Spanish native speaker of the Caribbean space because she looks *Latina* and has a Caribbean accent when speaking European Spanish.
- Deracialization of linguistic repertoires and practices—this process refers to the annulment, erasure, or bleaching of racial and ethnic traits, associated with some languages (such as English, for Student 2) or speakers. Student 2 is deracialized as an Arabic minority teacher because her origin is not thematized by the school colleagues. Student 5 engages in non-verbal converse racialization, to be perceived as a more competent language teacher.

- Reracialization of linguistic repertoires and practices—this process refers to the continuous (cumulative or alternative) attribution of ethnic characteristics to languages and speakers, in the same interactional context or across contexts and situations. Student 2 sees that students perceive her either as a native Spanish teacher or as a non-legitimate German Speaker, and, through her successive explanations, as a minority teacher with parents from an Arabic country. Student 5 sees her identity as being associated with specific and amalgamated origins (from Cuban, Mexican, Dominican to African, Latina, and Caribbean origins, in different orders of magnitude and scales).

These three processes are involved in both passing for and posing as a native speaker of a target language, as they can be other- or self-initiated, be further negotiated and thematized or not. Following this distinction, I could extend the domains covered by "racialization of linguistic competence" (Flores and Rosa, 2022) and the "racialization of teaching competence" previously evoked to embrace the de- and re-racialization of linguistic repertoires and practices and of teaching competence. This distinction, I hope, will be productive when analyzing the transracialized lives of student-teachers of additional languages beyond pre-service teaching programs and throughout their lifetime as teachers, helping to describe the continuous and dynamic interplay of everyday racialized experiences.

As put forward by Crump (2014), fixed identity categories "are powerful in shaping (allowing and constricting) an individual's possibilities for becoming" (p. 209). Indeed, in this study, several categories of participants' racialized identities are perceived and discursively constructed as solid and fixed despite the fact that participants are able to navigate across them. These fixed categories (such as "Caribbean") enhance participants' prospects of becoming and being accepted as language teachers. As Crump reminds us, individuals ratify and/or challenge both fixed and fluid identities: "although we can theoretically deconstruct the existence of fixed notions of identity, they nevertheless make up a very real and material part of the identity possibilities that individuals are negotiating" (Crump, 2014, p. 208).

From this perspective, passing for and posing as a native speaker are not necessarily related to the intention of deceit or produce harm to the audience (Piller, 2002). Instead, these strategies are used as a protection in a hierarchical situation in which racialized minority student-teachers are entering the profession, sometimes still being evaluated by mentors as capable professional or not: passing for a native and the ability to pose as one are thus self-inflicted identities to buttress their own linguistic and professional abilities.

14.5 Conclusion

In this contribution, I have aimed to show the intersection of racialized spaces and discourses of language (teacher) education, the racialized discursive positioning of student-teachers, and their investment in engaging in different experiences of teaching and learning abroad. I analyzed the transracial performances of early female student-teachers aiming at identifying with native speakers of the target language (in both cases, the target language was Spanish). In their personal accounts of transracial performances, the ability to pass for a native speaker can be capitalized in front of students, teachers, and mentors, suggesting that these three groups are susceptible to the same native-speakerism ideologies associated with the language teacher. The analysis uncovered raciolinguistic ideologies attached to the ideal teacher of the target language: not just sound like a native speaker but look like one too.

This study had two research questions. Regarding the first, "How does being racialized intersect with specific language teaching ideologies in the professional lives of future language teachers?," I showed that student-teachers developed the desire to visually and audibly pass for and/or pose as a native speaker, considered the ideal default in the school context. They feel proud when they do so and usually insecure when they do not. In other words, actually being a native speaker is not enough to be considered one, which again allows us to problematize the native/non-native divide in language teacher identity research (see also De Costa, 2015). In terms of agency, the participants make use of their racial ambiguity to cross different racial and linguistic affiliations (imposed or assumed). This interplay of raciolinguistic ideologies and racialization of language teachers led participants to (re)construct their professional identities at the crossroads of ideologies attached to the competent language teacher and competing (often implicit) institutional demands.

In terms of the second research question, "Which specific strategies of transracial performance are developed and used by future language teachers during their professional development path? With which aims?," I can name the taming of hair, the development of specific accents to be able to claim particular speaker identities, accepting or not ascribed racialized linguistic identities, and the thematization (or lack of thematization) of origins. Other students, in the broader research project from which the two interviews analyzed here are taken further mention hairstyles, clothing, and even adopting a Spanish family name (see Table 14.1). Additionally, and this can be a perspective for further studies, I can hypothesize that student-teachers may have chosen different scenarios for their studies and teaching abroad according to what they perceive as a population phenotypically compatible with their own traits and where they could more easily merge.

A note of caution should be added to the tale arising from this study: by embracing and not contesting the attribution of a different ethnic identity in order to identify as a native speaker of the target language could potentially contribute to further minoritize minority teachers within the school context. Indeed, embracing the native-speaker hierarchization for the target language means affirming the superiority of the native teacher over the non-native teacher, or more broadly of the majority teacher over the minority one. By accepting the identity attribution imposed on them, the two teachers whose experiences were analyzed in this study do not contribute to challenging and subverting the established hierarchical order and to asserting themselves as teachers in their own right. In a way, by not challenging hierarchical identity attributions and silencing their selves, they place themselves in a precarious situation of imitating the other, rather than exerting agency in affirming their individuality. In other words, they accept the category "race and ethnicity" as a social product rather than a social process within which they could exercise some power through their everyday interactions (Alim et al., 2020). A perspective for further research could be to analyze how minority teachers with a racialized identity cope with the tensions and competitions between different identities (assigned and/or espoused) and between professional and individual traits.

Finally, I acknowledge that probably not only and not all racialized student-teachers of modern languages seek and are proud of passing for a native speaker of the target language. Other possible topics for further research emerging from this exploratory study (among others) would be comparing strategies to pass for or pose as a native speaker by racialized and non-racialized student-teachers, and comparing verbal, para-verbal, and non-verbal strategies of passing for and posing as a native speaker developed by individuals of those two groups.

References

Alim, S. (2016). Who's afraid of the transracial subject? In H. S. Alim, J. Rickford, & A. Ball (Eds.), *Raciolinguistics* (pp. 33–50). Oxford University Press.

Alim, S., Reys, A., & Kroskrity, P. (2020). The field of language and race: a linguistic anthropological approach to race, racism, and racialization. In S. Alim, A. Reys, & P. Kroskrity (Eds.), *The Oxford Handbook of Language and Race* (pp. 1–21). Oxford.

14 Language Student-Teachers of a Racialized Background

Braine, G. (2010). *Non-native Speaker English Teachers: Research, Pedagogy, and Professional Growth.* Routledge.

Bräu, K., Georgi, V.; Karakaşoğlu, Y., & Rotter, C. (Eds.) (2013). *Lehrerinnen und Lehrer mit Migrationshintergrund.* Waxmann.

Chun, C. (2020). Issues in critical discourse studies. In J. McKinley, & H. Rose (Eds.), *The Routledge Handbook of Research Methods in Applied Linguistics* (pp. 199–210). Routledge.

Crump, A. (2014). Introducing LangCrit: critical language and race theory. *Critical Inquiry in Language Studies, 11*(3), 207–224. https://doi.org/10.1080/15427587.2014.936243.

De Costa, P. (2015). Tracing reflexivity through a narrative and identity lens. In Y. Cheung, S. Said, & K. Park (Eds.), *Advances and Current Trends in Language Teacher Identity Research* (pp. 135–147). Routledge.

Ellis, E. (2016). *The Plurilingual TESOL Teacher. The Hidden Languaged Lives of TESOL Teachers and Why They Matter.* De Gruyter.

Flores, N., & Rosa, J. (2015). Undoing appropriateness: raciolinguistic ideologies and language diversity in education. *Harvard Education Review, 85*(2), 149–171. https://doi.org/10.17763/0017-8055.85.2.149.

Flores, N., & Rosa, J. (2022). Undoing competence: coloniality, homogeneity, and the overrepresentation of whiteness in applied linguistics. *Language Learning.* https://doi.org/10.1111/lang.12528.

Georgi, V., Ackermann, L., & Karakaş, N. (2011). *Vielfalt im Lehrerzimmer.* Waxmann.

Iversen, J. (2024). Teaching Languages in the Linguistic Marketplace: Exploring the Impact of Policies and Ideologies on My Teacher Identity Development. In S. Melo-Pfeifer, & V. Tavares (Eds.), *Language Teacher Identity: Confronting Ideologies of Language, Race and Ethnicity* (pp. 82–102). Oxford, UK: Wiley-Blackwell.

Ku, E. (2024). Exploring Identities and Emotions of a Teacher of Multiple Languages: An Arts-based Narrative Inquiry Using Clay Work. In S. Melo-Pfeifer, & V. Tavares (Eds.), *Language Teacher Identity: Confronting Ideologies of Language, Race and Ethnicity* (pp. 45–62). Wiley-Blackwell.

Lengyel, D., & Rosen, L. (2015). Diversity in the staff room—ethnic minority student teachers' perspectives on the recruitment of minority teachers. *Tertium Comparationis, 21*(2), 161–184.

Martínez Agudo, J. (Ed.) (2017). *Native and Non-native Teachers in English Language Classrooms.* Professional Challenges and Teacher Education. De Gruyter.

Mayring, P. (2016). *Einführung in die qualitative Sozialforschung.* Belz.

Medgyes, P. (1994). *The Non-native Teacher.* MacMillan Educational.

Melo-Pfeifer, S., & Chik, A. (2022). Multimodal linguistic biographies of prospective foreign language teachers in Germany. *International Journal of Multilingualism, 19*(4), 499–522. https://doi.org/10.1080/14790718. 2020.1753748.

Melo-Pfeifer, S., & Tavares, V. (2024). Future Teachers of Two Languages in Germany: Self-reported Professional Knowledge and Teaching Anxieties. In S. Melo-Pfeifer, & V. Tavares (Eds.), *Language Teacher Identity: Confronting Ideologies of Language, Race, and Ethnicity* (pp. 23–44). Wiley-Blackwell.

Mena, M., & García, O. (2020). 'Converse racialization' and 'un/marking' language: the making of a bilingual university in a neoliberal world. *Language in Society, 50*, 343–364. https://doi.org/10.1017/ S0047404520000330.

Piller, I. (2002). Passing for a native speaker: identity and success in second language learning. *Journal of Sociolinguistics, 6*(2), 179–206.

Ramjattan, V. (2019). Racist nativist microaggressions and the professional resistance of racialized English language teachers in Toronto. *Race Ethnicity and Education, 2*(3), 374–390. https://doi.org/10.1080/13613324. 2017.1377171.

Ramjattan, Vijay A. (2024). The Raciolinguistic Enregisterment and Aestheticization of ELT Labor. In S. Melo-Pfeifer, & V. Tavares (eds.), *Language Teacher Identity: Confronting Ideologies of Language, Race, and Ethnicity* (pp. 226–241). Wiley-Blackwell.

Raza, Kashif (2024). Issues of Legitimization, Authority, and Acceptance: Pakistani English Language Teachers and Their Confrontation of Raciolinguistic Ideologies in ELT/TESOL Classrooms. In S. Melo-Pfeifer, & V. Tavares (eds.), *Language Teacher Identity: Confronting Ideologies of Language, Race, and Ethnicity* (pp. 242–257). Wiley-Blackwell.

Rosa, J. (2019). *Looking Like a Language, Sounding Like a Race. Raciolinguistic Ideologies and the Learning of Latinidad*. Oxford: Oxford University Press.

Rosen, L., & Jacob, M. (2022). Diversity in the teachers' lounge in Germany—casting doubt on the statistical category of 'migration background'. *European Educational Research Journal, 21*(2), 312–329.

Rosen, L., & Lengyel, D. (2023). Research on minority teachers in Germany: developments, focal points and current trends from the perspective of intercultural education. In M. Gutman, W. Zayusi, M. Beck, & Z. Bekerman (Eds), *To Be a Minority Teacher in a Foreign Culture—Empirical Evidence from an International Perspective*. Springer Nature.

Schwandt, T. A., & Gates, E. F. (2018). Case study methodology. In N. K. Denzin & Y. S. Lincoln (Eds.), *The SAGE Handbook of Qualitative Research* (pp. 341–358). Sage.

Tavares, V. (2022a). Teaching two languages: navigating dual identity experiences. *Pedagogies: An International Journal*, 1–22. https://doi.org/10.1080/1554480X.2022.2065996.

Tavares, V. (2022b). Neoliberalism, native-speakerism and the displacement of international students' languages and cultures. *Journal of Multilingual and Multicultural Development*. https://doi.org/10.1080/01434632.2022.2084547.

Tavares, V. (2024). Emotional Geographies of Teaching Two Languages: Power, Agency, and Identity. In S. Melo-Pfeifer, & V. Tavares (Eds.), *Language Teacher Identity: Confronting Ideologies of Language, Race, and Ethnicity* (pp. 63–80). Wiley-Blackwell.

Willing, C. (2014). Discourses and discourse analysis. In U. Flick (Ed.), *The SAGE Handbook of Qualitative Data Analysis* (pp. 340–353). Sage.

Yin Ling, C., Y., Said, S., & Park, K. (2015) (Eds.). *Advances and Current Trends in Language Teacher Identity Research*. Routledge.

Zhu, H., & Li Wei (2016). "Where are you really from?": nationality and Ethnicity Talk (NET) in everyday interactions. In H. Zhu, & C. Kramsch (Eds.), *Symbolic Power and Conversational Inequality in Intercultural Communication, a Special Issue of Applied Linguistics Review*, 7(4), 449–470. https://doi.org/10.1515/applirev-2016-0020.

Postface

Rahat Zaidi

Werklund School of Education, University of Calgary, Canada

My story of languages involves a complex constellation of cognitive and social experiences embedded in cultural contexts. At a young age, I developed what is now referred to as *translanguaging* where I navigated Urdu (my first language), Farsi and English depending upon who I was speaking to, and learned French as an adult. I was schooled in Iran for a number of years where I was raised trilingually and attended a Farsi-speaking school. As a teenager, I was raised in Pakistan where I began to develop a clear sense of the multiple identities that were now a mark of who I was becoming. I was a student in classrooms where we read a great deal of literature handed down as a legacy of the British Empire and which served to reinforce the cultural background of my English language use (Zaidi, 2022). I am the product of three generations of migration across the subcontinent, North America, and Europe, and this trajectory is marked by relocation and displacement. As a result, language became a passion and opened the door to an exploration that led me to the Western world, receiving my PhD in Paris.

Through these experiences and my research, and with having studied and worked in several different countries, I have encountered first-hand the diverse and constant transnational movement of people that has resulted in education systems being transformed racially, culturally, religiously, and linguistically. The dynamics within Sílvia and Vander's book resonate strongly with me, because they describe the challenges faced by many multilingual and migrant educators, especially within the field of language learning.

Current research has made us very cognizant of the challenges faced by both non-English educators and students who live and work in a

Language Teacher Identity: Confronting Ideologies of Language, Race, and Ethnicity, First Edition. Edited by Sílvia Melo-Pfeifer and Vander Tavares.
© 2024 John Wiley & Sons Ltd. Published 2024 by John Wiley & Sons Ltd.

predominantly White, English mainstream culture. This "superdiversity" characterized by Li (2018a), Vertovec (2007), and Zaidi (2022) has been a strong component of my scholarship as I witness the intersection of learners, resources, objects, and, of course, educators. Colonial hierarchies continue to exist in many schools today, where "whiteness is constructed as the dominant norm" (Tajrobehkar, 2023, p. 668). Sílvia and Vander's book has mirrored my own journey of desiring to speak to the urgent necessity for research that documents and comprehends experiences of racialization. Today, the increased interest in transformative interventions mentioned in their book helps educators become more aware of how they can learn to foster an environment of equity, inclusivity, and empowerment. By centering the voices and agency of plurilingual educators (and students), the book's arguments reflect the growing reality of how we need to continue the journey toward a more just and inclusive educational landscape.

Throughout this book, Sílvia and Vander helped entrench my own feelings toward this topic, as they take a meticulous look at addressing the issues resulting from this intersection of language, teacher identity, and education. We are at a crucial time where educators, like their students, are finding themselves embroiled in opportunities and challenges that have everything to do with their identities, literacies, and resources. In addition, the contents of the book underscore what is compelling researchers to postulate around the critical relationships between language, identity, education, and social justice (Hawkins and Mori, 2018; Li, 2018a).

Educators who speak two (or more) languages and are teaching in languages that are not their own have historically been confronted with identity-related experiences and emotional dynamics. Looking toward the future, this is an ever-increasing reality that is mirrored in the dynamics of today's (and tomorrow's) schools. It is critical that schools recognize the local and translocal realities of students, educators, and communities, all of which can further inform the transformative potential these have. I am encouraged by educators who are teaching, using their second and third languages, while they learn to adopt multiple semiotic strategies so as to reposition themselves in unexpected new sites that help situate their identities. This is a constant challenge for them, as they employ a type of *transcultural repositioning* (Honeyford, 2014), or *translanguaging*, as Sílvia and Vander refer to it. This general transformative pedagogy is reflected as a means to legitimize both students' and pre- and in-service educators' linguistic repertoires (Prada, 2019).

At a young age, I also developed translanguaging as I navigated Urdu, Farsi, and English. And later on French, depending to whom I was speaking. In this sense, there is hope for future educators who must be prepared to illuminate responsive pedagogical practices in multilingual classrooms by also making space for learners' inventive and flexible cultural and linguistic practices. This also holds true for teacher education programs as they welcome migrant educators who can learn to advocate for both the student and the educator to hold up their perspectives as they rise to the challenge.

This volume encourages educators to demonstrate what they (and their students) can achieve through the power of transforming the traditional notions of native speaker and bi/multilingualism and the re-examination of their practice in the classroom. This also implies the necessity for individual agencies and faculty to come together to re-imagine what it denotes to acknowledge the strengths and capabilities that pre- and in-service multilingual educators bring with them.

I am personally struck by how Sílvia and Vander describe language teachers' educational experience and identity construction as being minoritized and affected by various factors including ethnicity, language, accent, and the pedagogical practices of educators. Research continues to critique ideologies that perpetuate standardized perceptions of culture, language, and idealized speakers, as well as the discourse that centers around homogeneity, hierarchies, and unequal power relations. It is time for change.

I look forward to the time when teacher training programs will emphasize these precepts as they work to develop theoretical and pedagogical understandings of themselves as a new breed of educator. It is time to leverage their sociocultural and linguistic strengths and be permitted to engage deeply with these educators' own identity and ideology. The authors invited by Sílvia and Vander encourage a narrative of strength and possibility that behooves pre- and in-service educators to normalize their (and their students') bi/multilingualism and view it as an asset and a resource, rather than engaging with it from a deficit position. The authors' narrative will hopefully compel us to see and understand how varying aspects of educators' plurilingual identities, raciolinguistic ideologies, and agency (both teacher and student) can work together to disrupt racism, prejudice, and build better classroom environments overall.

As a society, we have moved beyond an era of multilingualism, and the mere act of being able to communicate in several different languages is no longer sufficient. As Sílvia and Vander emphasize, and I concur, today's classrooms are increasingly being led by educators who are interweaving multiple languages and language varieties with multiple ownerships and boundaries between languages that have become much more fluid. This is crucial to all language teachers' linguistic and cultural identity. Together, today's multilingual educators can become allies in co-creating more inclusive, linguistically equitable learning spaces as they engage in disrupting the monolingual norm and destabilizing linguistic privilege.

This volume gives me encouragement and hope for a future where multilingual teachers become active agents who navigate and negotiate their identities and experiences within a complex and entangled educational environment. Highlighting this racial and linguistic entanglement helps us understand how education systems need to evolve and improve (Zaidi et al., 2023). I appreciate how this book systematically addresses this by acknowledging the intersecting ideologies of race, ethnicity, and language, particularly within the context of teacher identity and education. By delving into the unique perspectives of these educators, who have so much to offer the educational system, we can gain a deeper understanding and awareness of how racialization and inequality impact their educational journeys.

The next step is for stakeholders to lead us into developing future-forward pedagogical strategies that help educators who possess a culturally and linguistically diverse background develop their potential as professionals, not only for themselves but also for their students. This implies an agenda that allows for ongoing professional development and deep investigation into how teacher education programs can adjust and improve to accomodate this new wave of educators.

References

Hawkins, M. R., Mori, J. (2018). Considering 'Trans-' perspectives in language theories and practices. *Applied Linguistics*, *39*(1), 1–8.

Honeyford, M. A. (2014). From aquí and allá: symbolic convergence in the multimodal literacy practices of adolescent immigrant students. *Journal of Literacy Research*, *46*(2), 194–233.

Li Wei. (2018a). Linguistic (super) diversity, post-multilingualism and translanguaging moments. In A. Creese & A. Blackledge (eds) *The Routledge Handbook of Language and Superdiversity* (pp. 16–29). New York: Routledge.

Prada, J. (2019). Exploring the role of translanguaging in linguistic ideological and attitudinal reconfigurations in the Spanish classroom for heritage speakers. *Classroom Discourse*, *10*(3–4), 306–322.

Tajrobehkar, B. (2023). Orientalism and linguicism: how language marks Iranian-Canadians as a Racial 'other', *International Journal of Qualitative Studies in Education*, *36*(4), 655–671, DOI: https://doi.org/10.1080/09518398.2021.1885069

Vertovec, S. (2007). Super-diversity and its implications. *Ethnic and Racial Studies*, *29*(6), 1024–1054.

Zaidi, R. (2022). A reflection on generational diaspora & resulting linguistic acclimatization. In G. Prasad, N. Auger & E. Le Pichon Vorstman (Eds.) *Multilingualism & Education: Researchers Pathways & Perspectives* (pp. 290–297). Cambridge University Press. doi: https://doi.org/10.1017/9781009037075.035.

Zaidi, R., B. Umit, & E. Moreau (Eds). (2023). *Transcultural Pedagogies for Multilingual Classrooms: Responding to Changing Realities in Theory & Practice*. New York, NY: Multilingual Matters.

Index

a

accent   180, 183, 188, 274
accidental teacher   59
additional language   63
aestheticization   226
agency (subjective agency)   125
agency (teacher)   73, 88, 277
appearance   266, 269, 272
apprentices of observation   24–25
archeology of the Self   114
arts-based narrative inquiry   45,
     47, 60
audible minority   259
auto-ethnography   17, 64,
     68–71, 89–90

b

bilingual
   books' creation   132
   poetry   129
biographical research
     methods   89
BIPOC (Black, Indigenous, and
     people of color)   133, 136
body   171
bullying   180, 184–186, 189

c

career transition   59, 91
children   143
clay work   47, 60
colonial languages/language of
     colonization   5, 71
colonization   130
commodification of languages   83, 85
competence   275
critical information literacy   131
critical professional
     development   106
critical translingual
     approach   105, 108
cultural capital   85

d

depression   193
dialogic interviewing
     techniques   110
discrimination   258
dominant language constellation   249
double-entry journal   136
DrawingOut   47
dress code   236
dynamic language practices   154

Language Teacher Identity: Confronting Ideologies of Language, Race, and Ethnicity,
First Edition. Edited by Sílvia Melo-Pfeifer and Vander Tavares.
© 2024 John Wiley & Sons Ltd. Published 2024 by John Wiley & Sons Ltd.

e

emergent bilingual/multilingual
students 123, 127
emotional
geographies 64, 66, 76
work 67
employment discrimination 229–233
English as a lingua franca 247
ethnic identity 60, 243, 271

f

flexible bilingualism 26
foreign language 3
foreign language (teaching)
anxiety 27–29

g

general pedagogical–psychological
knowledge 24, 32, 89
generative change 117
good teacher 88

h

hierarchy of languages 85

i

identity 6, 72, 87
identity poem 130
ideological commonsense 108
immigrant
family 147
teachers 204
intelligibility 253
intentionality 131, 137
intersectionality 6, 9, 16

l

language 4, 5, 127
architecture 116
ecology 126

hierarchies 127
ideologies 64, 142, 206, 220
learning anxiety 27, 28
portrait 130
teacher identity 4, 6
languageless 114
languaging practices 126, 130,
133, 137, 169
Latinx 142
leadership 143
legitimacy 266
linguistic
capital 85–87
differentiation 87
diversity 247
marketplace 82, 85
purism 64
L2 teachers of a transnational
background 65

m

maestra 134, 138
memory 69, 89
mestizaje 130
metaracial awareness 218, 221
monolingualism 3, 64, 266, 268, 283
moral distance 66
multilingual 124
books 132
person 127
students 123
teacher candidates 136
teaching approaches 95
turn 4, 248
multimodal translanguaging 49
multiple identities 58

n

named language 124, 130
narrative inquiry 47

Index | 287

native-speakerism 3, 8, 64, 219, 226, 276–277
nonlinear career trajectories 59

p

passing for a native speaker 9, 272
performance of emotions 75, 77
phenotypes 165, 175
photo essays (language ecology) 130
physical distance 67
plurilingualism 63
plurilingual
  pedagogies 63
  teachers 24, 65, 282
power relations 67
prejudice 175
pre-service teachers of
  two languages 30
professional
  development 106, 119
  distance 66–67
  identity 259, 263

r

racial purity 167
racialization 161, 164, 202, 273–274
racialized bi/multilingual
  students 106
raciolinguicized subjectivities 118
raciolinguistic
  digging 114
  enregisterment 227
  hierarchies 129, 264
  ideologies/perspective 7, 107, 125, 136, 138, 202, 209, 242, 244, 249, 272
racism 162
realistic fiction books 133
researcher positionality 111

s

self-efficacy 182
self-observation 136
sense of self 65
social
  justice 126, 132
  turn 26
Spanish 142–143
standard English 212–214
stereotypes 236
stigma 174
subject position 87–88, 96
subjectivity 87
subject-specific didactic
  knowledge 24, 32
subject-specific knowledge 24, 32
symbolic power 86

t

teacher 5
  anxiety 24, 33
  candidates 128, 138
  education (implications for) 96, 117–119
  identity 87–88
  as a language policymaker 129
  lived experience 89, 96
  professional competencies and
    knowledge 24, 32
  of a racialized background 64
  raciolinguicized
    subjectivities 107
  research 125
  of two languages 4, 7, 23, 45, 46–47, 77
teaching
  anxiety 28
  expertise 235
  journals 69, 245

translanguaging   4, 107, 124, 127,
    137, 146, 150, 250, 281
  corriente   107
  stance   107, 125
translation   205
transnationalism   208, 267
transracialization   258, 274
transraciolinguitic approaches   201,
    209, 212

V
visual methods   31

W
ways of knowing   89
whiteness   229, 234, 272